*I dedicate this book to my grand mother Marilyn
who rescued me out of the Middle East.*

Theodore Shoebat

Cover Design: Graphics by Sher

For information, please email the author at walid@shoebat.com

ISBN: 978-0-9825679-0-6

PREFACE

Today, the anti-God camp would pick on God as a nasty tyrant being angered by man's noble efforts. Since man failed in Shinar at the Tower of Babel, he never ceased attempting to make the world one. Evil continued to create other systems to complete this mission, so Shinar was again manifested in the form of Islamic Jihad conquests and then Nazism centuries later. Both systems had a similar goal of uniting the world under one leader.

What we attempt to show here is that while the world thinks unity is good, every attempt to unify the world ended with tyranny; divided seems better. Had the world been one when 'Hitler' rose to power, how would a United States have been able to align with other nations to crush him? The call for world unity is simplistic. While we are not anti-unity since unity can either be good or evil, we are vehemently against unity under an imperfect man.

We must be vigilant, never forgetting that mediocre minds are no match for professional deception. The untrained mind cannot see tyranny coming. What we will show here is that history repeats itself. It would be of great interest to examine the cult of Shinar and the deity they worshipped at the tower and how this cult manifested itself in most of the tyrannies we have witnessed in history. The conclusion of this research is to show that there are only two religious sources; *The Bible by Yahweh or Shinar by all others*. Tyrannies all start off with the call to make the world one through uniting all tribes under one banner – one world without nationalism or tribal allegiance.

We examine many progressive thinkers – Malthus, Darwin, Richard Dawkins, Rousseau and uncover their goals.

The war between Progressives and Bible believers is at a stage where each American must stand up and make the case that the United States and its Constitution must be preserved.

"*Weak if we were and foolish,*

not thus we failed, not thus;

When that black Baal blocked the heavens

he had no hymns from us...

This is a tale of those old fears,

even of those emptied hells,

And none but you shall understand

the true thing that it tells –

Of what colossal gods of shame

could cow men and yet crash,

Of what huge devils hid the stars,

yet fell at a pistol flash."

– G.K. Chesterton

⤳ INTRODUCTION ⬳

You might ask, "So why the title 'For God or For Tyranny?' Must everyone belong to one side or the other? Why can't we be 'For No God and For No Tyranny?'"

But if we take the premise 'For No God' we must first ask ourselves which god we are denouncing. You could be anti-Yahweh, anti-Allah, anti-Shiva or anti-all gods. You might still insist that you are "For No god and for No tyranny" because you've had enough with religion.

If this is your preference, then this book is for you. The whole crux of our research in which we examine with ample evidence nations that introduced certain gods and others that eliminated the Biblical God and others that promoted no any-god altogether. It is really a fascinating study and the results are shocking.

You might counter: "All gods are tyranny. Your title leaves me with only two choices – For God who is tyranny or for tyranny"?

All right, then let us open the dialogue for everyone to examine the most popular gods. But where can we assemble for such a dialogue? The Church? You might object that this would be the narrow Christian view that their God Yahweh is the only true God. The Mosque? Muslims already insist that Allah is the only God. In fact the Muslim creed says, "There is no god but Allah."

So where do we discuss God? Schools?

Since schools and universities claim to be for dialogue, debate and research you would think that this is probably the best place to dialogue over God. The fact is that schools are the least of places that allow dialogues about God. We would have a better chance discussing God in a pub than in a school. In fact, more schools today are allowing more programs to promote His non-existence.

You might counter that: "God is not scientific and school subjects are. God is a philosophical issue."

Then why do they teach philosophy in schools? Philosophy is not scientific; it's simply an attempt to explain our existence, knowledge, truth, law, justice and the moral values that influenced the world. Why should we then study Socrates and not Jesus?

Spiritism is even part of the philosophy being taught in universities. Not only do Bible believers object to this as unscientific since it is stemming from Hinduism and its belief in reincarnation; philosophers are making it a science. Spiritism is Pseudoscience, which is a methodology, belief, or practice that is claimed to be scientific, or that is made to appear to be scientific, but which does not adhere to an appropriate scientific methodology and lacks supporting evidence or plausibility, or otherwise lacks scientific status. Pseudoscience is any subject that appears superficially to be scientific, or whose proponents state that it is scientific, but which nevertheless contravenes the testability requirement or substantially deviates from other fundamental aspects of the scientific method. Spiritist philosophical inquiry is concerned with the study of moral aspects in the context of an eternal life in spiritual evolution through reincarnation, a process its adherents hold to as revealed by Spirits. Sympathetic research on Spiritism by scientists can be found in the works of Sir William Crookes, Ernesto Bozzano, The Society for Psychical Research, William James, the Nobel Prize for Physiology or Medicine winner Charles Richet, Professor Ian Stevenson's group at University of Virginia, and Professor G. Schwartz at University of Arizona. The main characteristic of Spiritism is its emphasis on the study and investigation of the Spiritist Doctrine in its triple aspects, 'scientific', philosophical and moral.

In the 19th century, Spiritualism spawned an important offshoot, the synthetic religion Theosophy, which has had a heavy influence on 20th century pseudoscience and pseudo scientists, from Edgar Cayce to Charles Berlitz, from George Adamski to Erich Von Daniken. Even more important, Spiritualism, as it faded in the early 20th century, gave birth to all the familiar folderol about "psychics," and "psychic phenomena," including extrasensory perception, telepathy, psycho kinesis, psychic detectives, and psychic "supermen."

If spiritual matters that stem from ancient Hinduism are all suddenly declared 'scientific' by anti-Bible philosophers, why then exclude ancient writers like Ezekiel, Isaiah, Joel, Moses, Abraham and others in Scripture? These wrote fascinating predictions into the future. Why should we study Psychology 101 but not have Futurology 101?

A critical question needs to be asked. Why are they blocking only this narrow avenue – the Bible – while opening the floodgates of every spiritual avenue that is contrary to the Bible? Wouldn't this undermine the Constitution and critical thinking?

You might argue, "if we start studying about God, we will have a war in schools".

We rarely had wars discussing God in schools. These wars have nothing to do with the different gods people worship, but simply the issue of teaching the Biblical God – all the other religions or any derivatives thereof are welcome.

Who then started this war over God? The American Constitution declares that: "We hold these truths to be self-evident, that all men are created equal, that they are endowed by their Creator with certain unalienable Rights, that among these are Life, Liberty and the pursuit of Happiness." The authors of the Constitution believed in God the Creator. Why then do we see the struggle on all levels brewing between pro-God conservatives and anti-God-liberal-progressives? We have a struggle regarding everything from prayer in school, abortion on demand, God, guns, the Ten Commandments in courts and an array of issues in all facets of life from government to education and media.

We will always have struggles within. No matter what, we will always have wars. We have a war on drugs, a war on homelessness, war on pollution, war on racism and a war on God.

We also have a war of labels that we see daily in the media. We tend to lump individuals into atheists, progressives, liberals, anarchists, socialists, communists, libertarians, conservatives, neo-conservatives, liberal Christians, Christian Fundamentalists, Christian Zionists and the list goes on and on.

In fact I am guilty of doing this very thing. I started this book by creating two camps – For God or For Tyranny. You might label me as divisive. If you feel this way then you are also labeling. Everyone applies labels.

I also get a litany of labels myself. No matter what camp or side I attend – everyone applies labels – and if labeling is a sin, we are indeed all sinners.

You might say, "What if I support no side at all? I can be neutral."

No matter your choice, you are either sheep or shepherd, liberal or conservative – you will be led and you will deal with the consequences. Active or inactive, you will end up participating. You follow tax laws, traffic laws, and regulations. You will end up following whichever regulation set by whichever administration be it liberal or conservative, pro-God or not. And just in case you are anti-war, let me remind you, there is always a war. If it were not a world war, it would be a cold war. If it is not a cold war, it might be a political war, a social war, or even a racial war. No matter what label you choose for yourself, you will always suffer being a casualty of one of these wars.

The war of labels also includes name calling in which we fling sticky-labels of xenophobia, bigotry, racism and an array of inflammatory accusations against anyone who attempts to critique a specific religion, despite the critique of religion being allowed by our Constitution. I am to open debate over religion; everyone should be entitled to critique religion – any religion.

This work is not about highlighting racial differences. It is about examining issues of a philosophical, political, ideological and spiritual nature. Our intent is not to misrepresent any label within these categories since it would be difficult to tailor a perfect-fit of anyone's personal ideology. However, what we are doing here is to show the sources from some of the greatest thinkers, philosophers and ideologists that influenced mankind throughout the centuries to expose in some detail their works that influenced humanity; their faith in God or godlessness, views on the world; to unite it or not, God; remove

Him or not, religion; the consequences of religion or irreligiousness, religions; are they all equal?

But with all honesty, I had a real difficult time writing this book since reviewing every term and attempt to fit it within everyone's frame of political correctness, since we will disagree on the usage of labels. I concluded beyond doubt that the saying "you cannot please everyone" stands true.

In fact it is impossible to fully please anyone.

Now that I put it in an absolute way, you might object, "There are no absolutes."

Well, are you absolutely sure?

No one likes to be labeled. Today we have the label "Islamophobia" which is so new and popular that my spell-check on my Word program cannot identify it. This label is like twitter – new, hot and beating all the other phobia labels combined. Today you rarely hear the terms Christian-phobia, Mormon-phobia, Jehovah Witnesses-Phobia and Buddhist Phobia.

In this work, I will not address the 'phobia' family of labels. I honestly think it's a boring topic since that's all I see on TV these days; issues over racism, homosexuality, war of the sexes…frankly I am very tired of TV.

But if I must make a disclaimer it is this; throughout this book we use labels. When we use labels like progressives, leftists or liberals, we at times are pointing to the puritan type diehards. At times you might read a statement and not see it appropriate to be pigeonholed, especially since you do not fit the specific description. While you aspire liberal views does not mean you agree with everything a diehard liberal believes in. You could adhere to certain portions of liberal views. I have met many with a mix between liberal and conservative. I have relatives who consider themselves liberal and tend to vote like a liberal democrat yet support the NRA. We also address Bible believers and use this label heavily. These would be the diehard Christians within all sects from Evangelical to Catholic or believing Jews within all sects – all who consider the Bible the Word of God. We will refrain from discussing differences within this category since this is not the subject matter of this book. We also use the label "Christian liberals"; these would be anyone proclaiming the Christian faith, yet believe in liberal values such as allowing homosexual pastors to take the pulpit and permitting gay marriage.

All in all, the idea of this work is to show that what you consider yourself to be might not be what you truly want. You could even apply to yourself the label 'spiritual' and think that the specific spiritual path you are taking is a constructive thing, yet by the time you study this material you might rethink your spirituality. Is our goal to change minds? Absolutely, that is our goal. It is the reason anyone writes regardless of profession of faith or creed; even a mathematician intends to change your mind that one plus one is not the same as one times one. We do have absolutes, fact and truth – relativism can lead to error – not all points of view are equally valid. An ex-drug addict who writes to fight drug abuse intends to help children shun the evil substance away because Crack-Cocaine leads to evil. One cannot say that since a drug-addict identifies the drug as being good for him, that his 'truth' must be true. Truth is not in the eye of the beholder. Our intent is to examine the source of our values on all sides, be it liberal progressive or Biblical conservative. While we realize that all of us have certain biases, we did our best to be historically accurate.

TRYING TO PLEASE EVERYONE

Today, critiquing religion – especially Islam – is becoming increasingly more difficult. We are deluged daily with accusations of Islamophobia because critiquing Islam can alienate secular Muslims. In order to cement the necessary alliance with "traditional" Muslims, Dinesh D'Souza, a leftist writer warned: "the right must take three critical steps. First, stop attacking Islam. Conservatives have to cease blaming Islam for the behavior of the radical Muslims. Recently the right has produced a spate of Islamophobic tracts with titles like Islam Unveiled, Sword of the Prophet, and The Myth of Islamic Tolerance. There is probably no better way to repel traditional Muslims, and push them into the radical camp, than to attack their religion and their prophet."[1] He offers no prescription for how his "traditional Muslims" can repel the appeal to violence upon which jihadists everywhere base the teachings of "their religion and their prophet."

But is critiquing any faith a phobia? Certain Jewish writers critique the New Testament and do not believe in Christian dogma. This would not constitute phobia but an attempt to defend their flock from going to the other side. I know of a Toviah Singer who runs a program called Jews for Judaism. While Toviah protects adherents to remain in the Jewish faith, Christians would not label him as phobic. Writers that address fundamental Islam can never be 'phobic' since phobia constitutes unnecessary fear. If one has a phobia of heights or tunnels, would they be 'phobic' if they face head on such fears? Phobias arise from a combination of external events and internal predispositions that create unnecessary fears of a subject or situation. How could someone who fears the rise of Islamic fundamentalism be 'phobic', especially if such persons are confronting such a subject head on? Would someone phobic of heights write a manual on air gliding and take tours that involved jumping off mountaintops? Could a Muslim that exposes certain Crusader actions be Christian phobic? Hardly.

Philosopher Piers Benn suggests that people who fear the rise of Islamophobia foster an environment "not intellectually or morally healthy", to the point that what he calls "Islamophobia-phobia" can undermine "critical scrutiny of Islam as somehow impolite, or ignorant of the religion's true nature."

Benn has a valid point. The notable Islamophobic acts that are recorded hardly constitute any phobia; desecrating a Muslim gravesite or vandalism of mosques is racism not phobia. Yet the core of notable acts of Islamophobia has been applied to everyone exposing Islamic fundamentalism and the jihadist ideology from financial terrorism to mass murder. Could it be possible that such usage of labels as Benn suggests be Islamophobia-phobia?

Using the term 'phobia' to apply to racism, prejudice and discrimination is fallacious. Tovia Singer can never be 'phobic' of Christians since he invites so many of them on his radio program. Dennis

Prager, another radio talk show host who is himself Jewish also welcomes Christian guests. Both Singer and Prager are Bible believers and while they differ on matters of theology with Christians, they find the Old Testament Bible to be a common ground for both faiths. Both realize that neither side can fully please the other so they unite in their efforts to fight tyrannies.

None of us can please everyone.

Even when I began to write this study, I began typing a sentence "mankind does good and evil," then, in order to see how others viewed my phrase I came to a fork ahead since many progressives like Richard Dawkins and Peter Singer would object to using the word 'mankind' as inadequate since we progressed to learn more through evolutionary science that we are human-animals since according to such view we all belong to the animal family.

Dawkins is in the labeling business. To please progressive liberals, then I should write my sentence to say, "The human animal does good and evil"?

Hmmm? Do animals do evil? What evil does my German shepherd do? My dog likes to kill rodents that come to our yard. Could my dog have 'rat phobia'? Do I need to take my dog to Cezar Millan the Dog Whisperer for treatment?

What does Dawkins mean by "human animal"? If we are all animals, should we walk naked as animals do? Should we mate out in the open? Are we to mate with animals as Peter Singer suggests?

What about eating animals? Wouldn't it be immoral to kill and eat our animal-brethren? And if it is ok to eat animals do we eat human-animals? This alone would cause a war since many human-animals will defend themselves to prevent from being eaten by other human-animals. Gun stores will even become busier than ever for both the hunters and the hunted. I had thought you would want gun control.

Some indigenous tribes in the Amazon do this already. You might be shocked to find out that humanity went that route on all continents. We have well documented what is behind cannibalism. Modern cannibals like Armin Meiwis or Jeffrey Dahmer disturb us.

Why? We live in a Christian culture whereas cannibalism was an accepted norm in many cultures in ancient times.

As if the issue of gay marriage wasn't sufficient, will we eventually have to deal with marriage between human-animals and regular animals? Some might even argue that this would definitely help us in our population explosion. Would Dawkins and Singer prefer to live in the Amazon naked?

Perhaps you might think that would be "going too far".

Who then would be qualified to set up these moral standards? Science never has all the answers. Which god sets up such standards – we have a swap meet of tyrannical gods. We are then left with "we will be either for God who is tyranny or for tyranny?"

Perhaps we can make the discussion simpler and remove God from all aspects of our lives. Why not switch the word 'God' on everything and put 'Man'? Our coins would say "In Man We Trust" and we would sing "Man bless America" or perhaps even, "The Human-Animal bless America".

Some might argue that switching names from 'God' to 'Man' or even "The Human Animal" should be no big deal! God after all does not exist; we cannot see Him and human animals do exist since we see man. So if we rename God to Man, why should it matter? Perhaps this is change we can believe in – we are all gods – the super animal. Let us take 'God' out of the equation. Perhaps we should even remove the Ten Commandments from every building. Why not sue schools that teach the Declaration of Independence with "God" all over it? Why not go further and sue the Normandy American Cemetery Memorial and remove all crosses of our valiant soldiers who died to protect the Constitution? How far do we go with this? After all, matters of faith are of a spiritual nature. They are hardly scientific. Spiritual matters cannot be proven under the scientific lens.

Such arguments assume that science is the standard we follow for everything, including the issues that we do not know about. Even science at times has no answers regarding scientific matters. At times we observe science yet we cannot explain what we are observing. Dawkins argues that science is advancing and will give us answers to issues we do not know. Dawkins' declaration is of a prophetic nature and nothing more. Some scientists predicted forty years ago that they would eradicate all disease. Today the pharmaceutical industry cannot keep up with the ever-changing microbes. New resistant strains of old diseases are springing up. That means that patients are suffering and dying from illnesses that science predicted forty years ago would be wiped off the face of the earth. The scientists were wrong. Before science catches up with the microbes many more people will die.

Man using science fails in all his attempts to successfully predict the future, and today he wants to shelf God as an icon of antiquity.

This would remind me of totem blocks and since science tops everything, the top block would have the word 'science', the other under it would say 'philosophy', another under that one would say 'law', another under "law" would say 'morality' and another at the bottom would say 'God'.

A child comes along and pulls the bottom block. Then the whole thing collapses. As this child grows and understands physics, he becomes aware of the nature of things. He still does not fully comprehend gravity but can recognize it. Even when he grows and completes his PhD in physics he still cannot fully comprehend the cosmos, how they interact or how they relate to issues of life. Science does not have all the answers. Spiritual matters are not scientific and explaining them is like answering, "sugar" when children ask, "what is sex?"

No one can even fully comprehend how we are made male and female or what factor existed to determine the cycle of life continuing through a relationship between the two. At times the only thing we can recognize is the end result – we love but we cannot fully comprehend love, even as we marry and procreate. The dynamo is set despite our will since we all have urges that compel us to multiply.

At times we think that we can intervene in this cycle so we offer scientific methods to stop pregnancy thinking that we can pursue joy without the responsibility of rearing children. Perhaps we can even pay for sexual pleasure without love or commitment. Any interjection into this cycle seems to bring only more misery. Prostitutes seem more depressed and inclined to resort to drugs as their pimps gladly sell their bodies for money. Neighborhoods are destroyed. Moral decay creeps in and misery results.

It seems that we go through such cycles only to conclude that there is a difference between love and pleasure. Yet we cannot fully comprehend love.

What then is love? Is it the love of money, self, the earth?

What about sacrificial love? You might ask, "Why should I sacrifice anything anyway? I could get hurt." What about a fireman who might go out of his way to save you? Wouldn't that be love? And what about loving the ones that do not agree with us? What is the ultimate love? Who has ever expressed it? How far can we love? What are the limits for love? Who sets the standards for what love really is?

Even death cannot fully be explained. If something as simple as a light bulb, interjecting into its source of energy removes the light. We know that the energy simply returns to its source. Yet, we still cannot fully explain death – what happens to the dynamo of life? What source does it go back to? What happens to this dynamo?

Our body somehow runs on its own like an automatic watch; yet even an automatic watch must have someone moving it every now and then to keep it charged and going. No battery lasts forever – all must be recharged by an external source. Nothing is in motion on its own – life is what sets everything that moves.

"Sure", you might say, "but why should I believe in something I cannot see"?

You already believe in many things you cannot see that we can always detect. We cannot see electromagnetic waves but we can detect them. Evidence for any case does not necessarily mean that we have answers for every single bit of data – but having ample facts to conclude it beyond a shadow of doubt. Court cases do not get resolved by having every piece of evidence. We require enough evidence or even a single piece of evidence if it is strong enough.

Perhaps we can examine what we can fathom. Not to try to fully comprehend how they function, but perhaps we can examine what the results would be if we interject into the issues of certain things.

You might counter with, "I am still not convinced. Everything could have been set in motion through the Big Bang".

Even if we both believe in the Big Bang, life is not only about the cosmos – what about moral values or understanding spiritual matters? We have many religious sources. Does the Bible hold the answer? The Qur'ân? The Bhagavad-Gita? The Book of Mormon? How about no book at all? We only have a handful of choices.

What about creating a new religion and not even calling it religion? We can create a new philosophy altogether. We can call it "The New Man" or "The Overcoming Man." We can perhaps rewrite history and transform our nation from a Christian one into a nation based on the ideology of man. Will we be better off? Will it work? Or will it be like the child who did not understand gravity and pulled the base block? Perhaps you can write your own Ten Commandments. Perhaps everyone can write his or her own Ten Commandments. What if someone wants a hundred commandments? Then we decide that everyone can follow their own commandments and that they are not bound to anyone else's.

What sort of a foundation will the world be without the Bible? After all, why use an old writ from thousands of years ago. Should we not modernize? We advance don't we? Perhaps all religious books are outmoded. Perhaps it is time to set up a new moral code.

Bible believers of course would argue that they tried many times and all failed – every single one of them failed – 'the Bible' with its 'Ten Commandments' are the answer.

While it is true that mankind advances in his knowledge of scientific matters it is also true that mankind's moral character never advanced.

Bible believers would say – mankind without God never advanced in his moral character.

Progressives would counter – mankind with God never advanced at all in his moral character either.

Or how about – mankind's moral character has always advanced without any God.

Bible believers would argue that without God mankind always experiences moral decay. Perhaps mankind advanced in his moral accomplishment most when nations began to use Biblical morals.

But where did the Ten Commandments come from? Charlton Heston? Moses? God? What if we removed, "Honor your father and your mother" every place it is found? What if we kept nine commandments and only removed 'Thou shall not bear false witness' from our courtrooms and justice system? This alone would demolish our legal system completely. Can any courtroom operate if we reverse this rule?

Others argue that moral values are embedded in all of us – we all know when we do 'good' and we all know when we do evil. Why not keep the Ten Commandments as a human invention thought by some to be from God?

Well, this whole issue could be relative. Who after all is qualified to set up the standards of what is 'good' and what is 'evil'?

Why do we do good and evil?

Who or what embedded a sense of right and wrong within our conscience?

Does Darwin's 'reciprocal altruism' explain why we do good and evil? Perhaps we concluded certain moral values through trial and error.

Have we? If so, why do we seem to repeat the same experiments? Every time we think that we have overcome and desire to strive to be supermen we simply degrade others who are not interested in becoming supermen. We begin to think that they are less worthy than us.

Experience and history prove that every time we accuse others of being vermin, we ourselves end up acting like vermin.

Nazis treated Jews as vermin and Nazis became the vermin. We treated fetuses as leeches and we became the leeches. We murder collectively and dump human beings like sewage. No animal behaves in such a way. Why then should we be elevated to the top of the food chain? Our propensity to do evil is immense with immense consequences.

Yet whenever we attempt to elevate ourselves we end up doing the reverse. It is as if we must remain on a certain level and that like gravity, what goes up in pride must come down hard.

Every time we think we've reached our 'supermanhood' we actually are being degraded to 'animalhood', or even worse, for animals do not do what we do; they have no abortions and generally do not declare war on other animals. They kill almost entirely out of necessity.

Bible believers would argue that Evil is the process of us governing others without allowing God to govern us. We all can make choices – we can either believe that God exists or He simply is nowhere to be found. But the moral law stands, which we shall prove here – that if we remove God, the government will become God.

The government, not the individual will become the temple of worship and thus we will live in tyranny. Man can never become a god so to compensate; evil men must attempt to elevate a collective tyranny into a god.

Either God becomes king or a tyrant becomes king.

All systems that exchange all facets of Biblical ethics and displays of God seem to be loaded with spirituality. What we will see here is that progressives have no problem with spirituality, since the struggle is over issues that are spiritual. The goal is simply the end of Christianity and the advent of man focusing on himself as the absolute creator of good or more accurately, evil in the name of good.

You might argue that, "Good is in the eye of the beholder. Who can justify what is good? What is 'good' after all? Who has the right to set the laws between what is good and what is evil?"

We each have to find a moral standard. We will examine different moral standards and the choice in the end will be yours. Both of us at least should believe that forcing anyone to believe in a certain ideology is appalling.

In my view mankind does good and evil – when we collectively do good, we usually know it, but when we do evil, it is usually done in the name of good.

You heard me right – evil is always done in the name of good.

Yet, since evil masquerades as good – how then can man prove beyond a shadow of doubt, that his path to spiritual enlightenment in conjunction with his morals are indeed good?

Perhaps you might argue that, "Tyrannies can be in the eye of the beholder. Everyone sees tyrannies. Liberals would argue that Christian Fundamentalists are tyrannical. You always hear about the Zionist Lobby and the Christian 'Right' getting their tentacles into the American government."

Professor Richard Dawkins, a leading evolutionary biologist, was quoted by the British Guardian newspaper as saying, "When you think about how fantastically successful the Jewish lobby has been, though, in fact, they are less numerous I am told – religious Jews anyway – than atheists and (yet they) more or less monopolize American foreign policy as far as many people can see. So if atheists could achieve a small fraction of that influence, the world would be a better place."

Conservative Bible believers argue that liberal-progressives are simulating what the world already experienced in Communist Russia which ended up becoming tyrannical, with everyone pointing a finger at the other side.

Isn't that divisive? Wouldn't it be better to solve our differences through dialogue?

Tyrannies usually end through forced dialogue – Japan surrendered and so did Nazi Germany. Others dissolved from within after much decay and failure. It is thereby crucial to see the difference between nations that overcame tyranny and others that continue living under it. Read on.

CONFESSION – THE MISSING LINK

Let me start off by saying that our continent, before Christianity came to it, had Aztecs with an ideology that sacrificed human lives. In other continents, we have seen Communism, Nazism and before them – the French Revolution; all did such evils in the name of man ending up destroying multitudes. How could such evils gain control of entire societies?

Evil is always gold-plated acting in disguise. Only a master goldsmith with a trained inner soul is able to detect beneath the surface to rebuff a forgery. The challenge for each individual, while keeping in mind that evil can be difficult to recognize, is to search throughout history and examine some of our downfalls to see when man was able to penetrate the surface of what he thought was superior, to later recognize the consequences of his actions and only then confess that at the core of his principles was indeed something very appalling.

TO CONFESS OR TO NEVER CONFESS

Yet when it comes to all scenarios of evil in which we come to a dead end after all mayhem has been done and it seems that we at times never learn since we repeat the same experiments. And when we come to a dead end, we only have two choices when it comes to all matters of evil – confession or excuse.

Evidence shows that the United States of America, despite much criticism of its Judeo-Christian values, has far exceeded any other nation when it comes to the desirability for immigration and refuge from all non-Judeo-Christian nations. A glimpse into the findings of Religious Freedom in the World 2007 showed that countries with a Christian background were ranked highest for level of religious freedom observed. The four countries given the highest religious freedom ratings are Hungary, Ireland, Estonia, and the United States.

On the other hand, countries run by atheist governments such as communist China, Vietnam, and North Korea were ranked in the bottom two tiers. Officially, atheist countries were joined at the bottom of the religious freedom pole by countries with an Islamic background such as Pakistan, the Palestinian areas, Iran, Iraq, Saudi Arabia, Sudan and Turkmenistan. "In general, either extreme religious or extreme secular states together comprise most of the world's religiously restricted parties," commented Paul Marshall, general editor of Religious Freedom in the World 2007, during a press conference.[2]

What then makes Judeo-Christian based countries the envy of would-be immigrants? If it is a better standard of living, what then was the cause of such standards? If it is our freedom, where did such freedom come from? If it came from our Constitution, who and what made this Constitution so great? What is the difference between Judeo-Christian ethics and all others and what are the consequences of abandoning these ethics?

While Judeo-Christian societies were not immune from committing evil; the difference between Judeo-Christian nations and all others is the element of confession. There are only two choices when confronting our own evils – confession or excuse.

Germany confessed the Holocaust while Turkey, instead of confessing the Armenian genocide, seems to still be making excuses. And while it is illegal to deny the Holocaust in Germany, today it is illegal in Turkey to speak of the Armenian genocide. Socialist countries are no different.

The difference between nations that succeed in their 'pursuit of happiness' and others that don't is the element of confession. Turks today still immigrate to Germany and Germans have little desire to immigrate to Turkey. Without confession such nations are poised to repeat the same evils – and the cycle of evil continues.

Why then do Germans confess and Turks live in denial?

The answer is simple – confession is part and parcel of only Judeo-Christian ethics. We have confession booths, priests and pastors. In our court system, confessions can reduce punishment in the form of plea bargains. Alcoholics Anonymous and drug rehabilitation are entities and concepts that make confession part of the cure. We are always encouraged to take care of our wrong doings and believe in giving others a second chance. We also forgive. We had a war with Japan and once Japan surrendered we had economic trade and put aside the past.

In Judaism confession is done communally in plural. Jews confess that, "We have sinned."

We conducted trials of Nazi war criminals at Nuremberg as well as trials following war, dictatorship, and genocide in Yugoslavia, East Germany, Greece and Argentina. Saddam Hussein's trial was enforced due to American intervention. Even then, most Sunni Iraqis would still side with Saddam since he is Sunni. The Christian world did not divide between Protestant and Catholic during the Nazi trials.

Why does the Muslim world lack the element of confession? Where are the trials for all the massacres committed in the Muslim world? Where are the confessions? There are hardly any books regarding the genocide committed by Muslims for the millions of massacred Christians, Jews, Buddhists and others? On the contrary, the Islamic culture takes pride in such history.

Before invading Poland, Adolph Hitler scoffed, "Who, after all, speaks today of the annihilation of the Armenians." Earlier, Hitler had warned, "We intend to introduce a great resettlement policy...Think of the Biblical deportations, the massacres of the middle Ages and remember the extermination of the Armenians."[3]

Vahakn N. Dadrian, Director, Genocide Research Project explains: "Any effort at documenting the Armenian genocide must confront the 'Turkish denial syndrome.' That syndrome has now grown into what I have described as 'an industry of denial.' In fact, genocide denial is so prevalent that it is now becoming a field of study in its own right."[4] He adds, "Denial does not require any proof, only an assertion and a call for the "reassessment" of history; the burden is on someone else to 'disprove' the assertion. Second, genocide denial may be ignored when it is practiced by those who have no credibility and no external audience; it is another matter when genocide denial is practiced by the government of a powerful country and has as its target the governments of other powerful and influential countries, with whom that government is linked by bonds of political and military alliance."[5]

Yet till today, from the massacre of the Jews in Arabia to the Armenian genocide the excuses are typical. Editor-in-Chief of the Encyclopedia of Genocide; Executive Director of the Institute on the Holocaust and Genocide, Israel Charny, in his manual Templates for Gross Denial of a Known Genocide where he developed the 12 tactics of Turkish denial of the Armenian genocide:

1. Question and minimize the statistics.

This is one of the biggest distractions to the main issue itself. By claiming that the numbers are exaggerated or inflated, and that only a few hundred thousand were killed, not over a million, they try to completely sidetrack the entire issue. As if a few hundred thousand would not have been genocide as well.

2. Attack the motivations of the truth-tellers.

The claim that Armenians cannot be trusted because they may want reparations is like saying no victim should ever be heard, because they are biased in their pursuit of justice.

3. Claim that the deaths were inadvertent.

As a result of famine, migration, or disease, not because of willful murder. Also mention that Turks/Muslims died too at that time – without mentioning that they died on the battlefield, not at the hands of their very own government.

4. Emphasize the strangeness of the victims.

The victims were infidels (Christians), a fifth column, and not "good" Ottoman Turks.

5. Rationalize the deaths as the result of tribal conflict, coming to the victims out of the inevitability of their history of relationships.

Check. Armenians and Turks could not share that land anymore since some Armenians might prefer independence to being second-class citizens.

6. Blame "out of control" forces for committing the killings.

They often blame the very Kurds they later struggled to keep down.

7. Avoid antagonizing the genocidists, who might walk out of "the peace process." Turkey refuses to even open diplomatic relations with Armenia because it talks about the Armenian Genocide.

8. Justify denial in favor of current economic interests.

Undoubtedly Turkey's number one weapon in denying the Armenian Genocide is the constant threats to the west the military contracts worth billions will be canceled have worked wonders in legislatures considering the issue. In fact, the debate over whether to officially recognize the genocide in the west is clearly not about

For God or For Tyranny

whether it happened or not – since it very clearly did – but on just what economic/diplomatic repercussions Turkey has threatened or might retaliate with if they do recognize a 90 year old truth.

9. Claim that the victims are receiving good treatment, while baldly denying the charges of genocide outright.

Show how a few thousand Armenians were not killed in Istanbul as evidence that 2.5 million were not killed/driven out in Anatolia.

10. Claim that what is going on doesn't fit the definition of genocide. The European Union, the Secretary General of the United Nations and even Amnesty International still avoid calling the crimes in Darfur by their proper name. There are three reasons for such reluctance:

A. Another misconception is the "all or none" concept of genocide. The all-or-none school considers killings to be genocide only if their intent is to destroy a national, ethnic, racial, or religious group "in whole." Their model is the Holocaust. They ignore the "in part" in the definition in the Genocide Convention, which they often haven't read.

B. Since the 1990's, a new obstacle to calling genocide by its proper name has been the distinction between genocide and "ethnic cleansing," a term originally invented as a euphemism for genocide in the Balkans. Genocide and "ethnic cleansing" are sometimes portrayed as mutually exclusive crimes, but they are not. Prof. Schabas, for example, says that the intent of "ethnic cleansing" is expulsion of a group, whereas the intent of "genocide" is its destruction, in whole or in part. He illustrates with a simplistic distinction: in "ethnic cleansing," borders are left open and a group is driven out; in "genocide," borders are closed and a group is killed.

C. Claim that the "intent" of the perpetrator is merely "ethnic cleansing" not "genocide," which requires the specific intent to destroy, in whole or in part, a national, ethnic, racial or religious group. The U.N. Commission of Experts report of 2005 took this way out. It confused motive with intent. (Ironically, the U.N. Commission report even included a paragraph saying motive and intent should not be confused, an exhortation the Commission promptly violated, itself.) Even if the motive of a perpetrator is to drive a group off its land ("ethnic cleansing"), killing members of the group and other acts enumerated in the Genocide Convention may still have the specific intent to destroy the group, in whole or in part. That's genocide.

11. Blame the victims.

Perhaps the most insulting tactic of all, saying that actually it was the Armenians who were massacring and wiping out Turks.

12. Say that peace and reconciliation are more important than blaming people for genocide.

This is often heard from Turks, American government officials and others who have clearly never been victims of genocide. Much like telling a man whose mother was raped and murdered by the next-door neighbor that it is more important to get along with your neighbors, this will never be accepted by Armenians who deserve and need an apology and reparations. They need an apology from Turkey now not only for the genocide, but for the nearly century long denial and mis-education campaign that took place, the continued mistreatment of Armenians in Turkey, the blockade of Armenia since the early 1990s and the post-genocidal war taking even more Armenian land.

You might ask "what about the crusades?"

The west never stopped confessing its sins and condemning itself to the point of disregard for any good the crusaders ever did.

There are ways to distinguish between that which shines true and that which glitters with falsehood. Especially in today's culture where relativistic thinking and moral equivalency seems to prevail, thereby causing past errors to be repeated. We can conduct litmus tests in order to review our history and Constitution to compare with others and see what, where and which of the systems we have had that offered mankind a long tested method; to discover the end results and see if they have contributed to life, liberty and the pursuit of happiness.

We need a litmus test, especially since evil never willingly reveals itself as such. It usually masks itself with different faces or comes repackaged, disguised as causes that supposedly serve humanity. We then need to examine history and compare in order to see what changes we made to our formula; we know that evil always ends yielding the same results while never realizing the mistakes inherent in following it until we end up with great destruction of life. Unfortunately, when mankind has acted on his own, the same mistakes are always repeated.

So what do tyrannies have in common?

What is astonishing is that tyrannies have so many things in common, some of which sound good and in fact are becoming hip, cool and common in our time.

SECTION ONE

SHINAR
AND THE ATTEMPTS TO REVIVE IT

For God or For Tyranny

↔ Chapter 1 ↔

One World – A Very Old Idea

Mankind gathers in Shinar: "And it came to pass, as they journeyed from the east, that they found a plain in the land of Shinar [Babylon]; and they dwelt there…And the whole earth was of one language, and of one speech." Reading this account in Genesis 11 today would cause many to ask, "What could be wrong with man's plight to unite? Nothing could be better than having a one-world and one language." They even collectively used all their resources, took all they had, mortar and tar (petroleum): "And they said one to another, Come, let us make brick, and burn them thoroughly. And they had brick for stone, and pitch (tar) had they for mortar." They wanted to build a united one world, make a name for themselves and through their own way mankind can reach up to heaven: "And they said, Come, let us build us a city and a tower, whose top [may reach] unto heaven; and let us make us a name, lest we be scattered abroad upon the face of the whole earth."

Make "us" a name? Shinar wanted to focus on man not God. Today, the anti-God camp would pick on God as a nasty tyrant being angered with man's noble efforts. To Bible believers this was done for a good reason; mankind according to God needed restraint: "now nothing will be restrained from them, which they have imagined to do." They had set up their own laws and abandoned God. They argue that had God not intervened, mankind would be on a collision course with destruction, like a vehicle without controls.

"Mankind needs restraint" confesses the Bible followers. Progressives argue that God seems to act contrary to today's logic, "…let us go down, and there confound their language, that they may not understand one another's speech. So the LORD scattered them abroad from thence upon the face of all the earth…" Why would God scatter mankind? How could this be a loving God?

From the beginning, it seems that God's logic collides with that of man. Could a united world under a single language be awful? Are we better off united or divided up with borders and languages?

Other religious systems seem to make more sense. Islam calls for world unity without borders or tribal divisions, calling on everyone to worship God and follow a One World government prescribed by Islamic Sharî'ah law. Bible believers tend to reject that notion with many claiming that Islam is satanic. Since the evil in man failed in Shinar at the Tower of Babel, he never ceased attempting to rule the world. Evil, they argue, continued to create other systems to complete this mission, so Shinar became Nazism and centuries before it, Islamic Jihad conquests. Both systems had a similar goal to unite the world under one leader. In Islam it was Muhammad and in Nazism it was Hitler; one language for a world of Nazis (German) and Muslims claim that none can enter paradise unless they worship Allah through the Arabic language with the exclusive aim of spreading Islam. Adam, whose existence is not put into question by the proponents of this dogma, spoke Arabic as did his son Cain.[6] Bible believers argue that while the world thinks that unity is good, every attempt to unify the world ended up with tyranny – divided seems better. Had the world been under one government with 'Hitler' as its ruler, how would it have been possible for a country like the United States to align with other nations to crush Hitler? We should not think in simplistic ways.

Bible believers are not anti-unity. Unity can either be good or evil. The question is unity under whom – an imperfect man? The Bible calls on God's followers to "be as wise as serpents", we need to ask; could the serpent be disguising himself as god and desires to reverse what happened in Shinar when God confused their tongue and made many languages? Muslims are offended when Bible believers equate Islamic Jihad with Satanism and Nazism.

But we must be vigilant, keeping in mind that mediocre minds are no match for professional deception. The untrained mind cannot see tyranny coming; even good can at times be seen as evil. We think at times that a people's revolution is always a good thing.

The Communist Revolution started as a good thing and removed the Czars only to give birth to a form of tyranny that began to spread communism worldwide, hoping to control the world. Nazism began to occupy all of its surroundings. Iran's Islamic Revolution against the Shah of Iran gave birth to another tyranny that is spreading throughout all Muslim societies seeking to unite the world under a single banner – Islam To The World. Can we ignore these issues?

THE GOD OF SHINAR

You might wonder as to why I bring such an archaic story as Shinar? Well, archaic stories repeat and since history repeats itself it would be of great interest to examine the cult of Shinar and the deity they worshipped at the tower.

To answer who was the god of Shinar we need to examine ancient Babylonian archeology. In the Enuma Elish, the Babylonian creation story, we find one of the most ancient writings dedicated to Bel-Marduk the patron deity of Babylon, which we shall examine shortly. Critics of the Bible say that the Enuma Elish is a parallel to the creation myth in the Genesis account. For centuries, Moses had been believed to be the author of Genesis until Wellhausen's hypothesis was thus received by traditionally minded Jews and Christians as an attack on one of their central beliefs. But in the first half of the 20th century the science of Biblical archaeology, developed by William F. Albright and his followers, combined with the new methods of Biblical scholarship known as source criticism and tradition history, developed by Hermann Gunkel, Robert Alter and Martin Noth, seemed to demonstrate that the stories of Genesis or at least, the stories of the Patriarchs; the early part of Genesis – from the Creation to the Tower of Babel – which were already regarded as legendary by mainstream scholarship were based in genuinely ancient oral tradition grounded in the material culture of the 2nd millennium BC. Thus by the middle of the 20th century it seemed that archaeology and scholarship had reconciled Wellhausen with a modified version of authorship by Moses.

This consensus was challenged in the 1970s by the publication of two books, Thomas L. Thompson's *"The Historicity of the Patriarchal Narratives"* (1974), and John Van Seters's *"Abraham in History and Tradition"* (1975), both of which pointed out that the archaeological evidence connecting the author of Genesis to the 2nd millennium BC could equally well apply to the 1st millennium, and that oral traditions were not nearly so easily recoverable as Gunkel and others had said. A third influential work, R. N. Whybray's "The Making of the Pentateuch" (1987), analyzed the assumptions underlying Wellhausen's work and found them illogical and unconvincing.[7]

Bible believers have always argued that the Babylonian theology has always been the source of counterfeit religion contending that Enuma Elish findings was not a parallel of the Biblical account regarding Shinar but evidence of what the Bible already exposed regarding Ur and Shinar which Yahweh commanded Abraham to come out of.

In the Enuma Elish[8] Apsu and Tiamat (the water goddess) are the original father and mother gods. They give birth to a series of gods. When the gods become too noisy, they take counsel, and Apsu decides to destroy the gods. However, another god, Ea, knows his plot. Using a spell, Ea gets Apsu asleep and kills him. Ea and his consort Damkina give birth to Marduk, the patron god of Babylon who later established the constellations and the phases of the moon.[9]

In the Atrahasis Epic[10] the subordinate gods complain because of the heavy toil assigned by the principal god, Enlil. Because of this problem, the council of gods proposes that Beletili/Mami, the birth-goddess, should make man to "bear the toil of the gods" (I.191). She says that she needs the help of another god, Enki, who then undertakes to make purifying baths for the first, seventh, and fifteenth day of the month (I.206). Weila, a god with personality, is slaughtered, so that "all the gods may be cleansed in a dipping" (I.209). From Weila's flesh and blood Nintu mixes "clay," on which the gods spit (I.234). The account also mentions "spirit" (I.230), apparently derived from the slain god, which becomes an aspect of man, who is the product of the clay.[11]

To connect the creation of man from a god goes contrary to Biblical theology. Gordon Wenham concludes, "It [Genesis 1] is not merely a demythologization of oriental creations myths, whether Babylonian or Egyptian; rather it is a polemical repudiation of such myths."[12] Wenham summarizes the force of the contrasts in Genesis: "[If Genesis 1–11 presents] the nature of the true God as one, omnipotent, omniscient, and good, as opposed to the fallible capricious, weak deities who populated the rest of the ancient world; if further it is concerned to show that humanity is central in the divine plan, not an afterthought; if finally it wants to show that man's plight is the product of his own disobedience and indeed is bound to worsen without divine intervention, Gen 1-11 is setting out a picture of the world that is at odds both with the polytheistic optimism of ancient Mesopotamia and the humanistic secularism of the modern world. Genesis is thus a fundamental challenge to the ideologies of civilized men and women, past and present, who like to suppose their own efforts will ultimately suffice to save them. Gen 1-11 declares that mankind is without hope if individuals are without God. Human society will disintegrate where divine law is not respected and divine mercy not implored. Yet Genesis, so pessimistic about mankind without God, is fundamentally optimistic, precisely because God created men and women in his own image and disclosed his ideal for humanity at the beginning of time. And through Noah's obedience and sacrifice mankind's future was secured. And in the promise to the patriarchs, the ultimate fulfillment of the creator's ideals for humanity is guaranteed. These then are the overriding concerns of Genesis. It is important to bear them in mind when studying its details. Though historical and scientific questions may be uppermost in our minds as we approach the text, it is doubtful whether they were in the writer's mind, and we should therefore be cautious about looking for answers to questions he was not concerned with. Genesis is primarily about God's character and his purposes for a sinful mankind. Let us beware of allowing our interests to divert us from the central thrust of the book, so that we miss what the LORD, our creator and redeemer, is saying to us. From a purely literary point of view, it does not look as if Genesis 1 directly uses or interacts with one specific polytheistic story. Rather, it interacts with the broader polytheistic atmosphere that all the pagan stories embody. By teaching strict monotheism it repudiates the entire atmosphere of the ancient Near East".[13]

The Biblical account is a denouncement of the Emuna Elish and not a parallel of it. The Emuna Elish has more similarities with the paganism of the region that connects to the moon: "O thou Moon-god (Nannaru), who hast established our splendor, What benefit have we conferred upon thee? Come; let us make a shrine, whose name shall be renowned… They made the ziggurat [to reach] the celestial Ocean; unto Marduk, Enlil, Ea [shrines] they appointed. It (i.e., the ziggurat) stood before them majestically: at the bottom and [at the top] they observed its two horns… He (i.e., Marduk) made the gods his fathers to take their seats… [saying]: This Babylon shall be your abode. No mighty one [shall destroy] his house, the great gods shall dwell therein."[14] We even have Nebuchadnezzar who wrote on a tower built in Babylon for the purpose of bringing man to heaven: "the shrine of Merodach [Bel-Marduk], with statues and marbles I embellished as the stars of heaven. The fanes of Babylon I built, I adorned. Of the house, the foundation of the heaven and earth, I reared the summit with blocks of noble lapis lazuli."[15] Such accounts in fact are evidence to what have been already pronounced in the Bible regarding man's own creation story denouncing them as myth.

WHO IS THIS BA'AL?

The parallels between Enuma Elish and Genesis 11:1-9 are eye opening. Marduk wishes to build a tower "whose name shall be renowned" and to "make us a name". So who is this Bel-Marduk? Baal is Bel; they are one and the same. Marduk was later known as Bel, a name derived from the Semitic word Baal, or 'lord.' Bel had all the attributes of Marduk, and his status and cult were much the same. Bel, however, gradually came to be thought of as the god of order and destiny. Greek writings reference Bel as this Babylonian deity[16] also from the Dictionary Of Ancient Deities: "Marduk is the same as Bel of the Babylonian and Assyrian religion."[17]

When it comes to deities, there are many. Yet when you examine each attribute of each of these deities they are eerily similar. In reality there are only two deities – Yahweh versus His adversary – all the others. While these 'others' have different names, their attributes and even names always point to the Biblical character defined in the Bible as the Luminous One – Bel or Ba'al is referred to in the Bible as this character in several references.

ARE ALL RELIGIONS EQUAL?

The way Bible believers see it; there are two religious sources; the Bible by Yahweh or Shinar by all others. They find no other sources of spirituality besides these two.

While critics of the Bible would argue that no one has seen this 'Luminous One', he is defined in the Bible as an angel of light. Many claimed to have seen the "most beautiful of all angels." The critics should not only take their arguments over this issue with believers in the Bible. Muhammad encountered someone with this very description and so did Joseph Smith whom Christians consider a cult leader. While no one can manifest this being, many progressive elites believe in angels, worship nature, earth and Cosmos as living things. These would rarely go after cults but would always attack the Bible demanding evidence. Christians wonder why their devil becomes the Bible as the real devil lurks in disguise, even claiming to believe in the Bible, or a lost Bible to simply direct the mediocre minds to look into other sources like Islam.

There is much evidence that the idol of Bel was renamed as Allah who was hailed as the supreme god of Islam and corresponds to the Babylonian god of Baal. Historian Snorri Bergson sheds light on the origin of Allah: "The Quraysh adopted Allah as

Baal, and added the goddesses to his cult the same way as Baal had three daughters in the Fertile Crescent. They venerated him and his three female companions in his new House, the Ka'ba at Mecca."[18] Stephen Langdon confirms: "Allat was a Babylonian, or earth and moon goddess. Her consort Allah was simply the god who impregnates the earth."[19]

Others argue that if Allah was indeed introduced by Muhammad the founder of Islam, why then did the Arabs know of him long before Muhammad when Allah was only one out of many gods and goddesses in Arabia; Allat is simply the feminine name for Allah.

Muslims counter this argument since the Qur'ân denounced moon worship (Q 41:37) and that Muhammad abolished the Ba'al worship in Arabia.

While Bible believers recognize that Muslims deny any astral connection or worship, they contend that bowing several times a day towards an asteroid The Black Stone and claim it to be symbolic, they question that paying homage to it is a redemptive act since "it come to life to testify of all who touched it". From the Islamic perspective, the Black Stone will "have eyes and ears and will become alive."[20] Who can deny the paramount influences of the moon in Muslims' lives? In Islam, the moon is considered the holiest astronomical object and the guiding light for all Islamic rituals and festivals. Contradictions and conflicts are very common with the dates of Eids and Ramadan. It is a chronic problem with the moon at its nucleus. A Crescent moon and star is the symbolic sign in the national flags of most Muslim countries, and it is present over the Mosques, in the Muslim graveyard.

Allah, the Moon-God was the god of the local Quaraysh, Muhammad's own tribe well before he introduced Islam to lead his people out of their polytheism. Muhammad was a strict Unitarian who simply made Allah childless. The prophet was dual-minded to first proclaim Allah's daughters Allat, Al-Uzzah and Al-Manat as intercessors between the Arabs and Allah.[21] Later he claimed that Satan inspired this theology.

THE CRESCENT

In Judges 8:21, the word used for crescent is saharon, which literally means crescent moon. It comes from the root of sahar (Luminous) as in Isaiah 14 Hilal ben Sahar. Hilal, or heylal, is Hebrew for "Luminous" or "morning star/crescent moon," which is the very symbol of Islam.

From time immemorial we see the worship of gods that were symbolized by the image of the crescent moon. In the Bronze Age, the East, from Anatolia to Sumer and Egypt we had moon gods[22]: Arma, the Hittite Moon God, Artimes, the Greek Moon-Goddess, Coyolxauhqui the Aztec Moon Goddess, Diana the Roman Moon-Goddess, Ix Chel the Mayan Moon God, Khons the Egyptian Moon God, Mawu the African Moon God, Men the Moon God of Asia Minor (Turkey), Luna the Greek Moon Goddess, Sin the Sumerian Moon God, Suma the Hindu Moon-God, Tsuki-Yomi the Japanese Moon-God, Yarikh the Ugarit Moon God and Heng-O the Chinese Moon-Goddess.[23]

Bel or Baal simply means "lord" and is also a title of reverence to the Babylonian moon-god that Abraham left behind for Yahweh. In Asia Minor they worshiped a war deity called Men. Gyges of Lydia was the first to be called a tyrant acquires a particular significance[24] since the ancient sources are supported by the fact that there seems to be no doubt about the Phrygian or Lydian origin of the word turannos. The name of the Phrygian Moon-god Men is often followed by the epithet turannos in Greek inscriptions of Attica and Phrygia, and the name of some divinities is followed by the epithet .bd turan in Etruscan inscriptions. From Herodotos (I.14) one gathers that the Herakleid kings supplanted by Gyges had the title of tyrannos.[25]

Several Biblical scholars have argued that Gyges is behind the figure of Gog, ruler of Magog, who is mentioned by Ezekiel and in the Book of Revelation.

From Gyges to Bel, it comes as no surprise then that Jesus referred to Satan as Beelzebub or Ba'al Thubab (Arabic) in Matthew 12:24-27.

The Hastings Encyclopedia of Religion and Ethics confirms that the Arab name Allah correlates to Bel.[26] Gideon was named as "Jerub-Ba'al", the one who contends with Ba'al the moon god. Gideon was a type of the warring Messiah because he fights Ba'al. Likewise Christ, the ultimate Jerub-Ba'al (contender of Ba'al) will fight Ba'al in the flesh, and bruise his head, completing what was promised in Genesis 3:15 which we handle in the last chapter completing the circle on tyranny, how it began and how it ends.

Dr. Arthur Jeffrey, professor of Islamic and Middle East Studies at Columbia University and one of the world's foremost scholars on Islam, wrote that the name, "Allah" and its feminine form "Allat," were well known in pre-Islamic Arabia and were found in inscriptions uncovered in North Africa. According to Jeffrey, Allah, "is a proper name applicable only to their peculiar god." He adds, "Allah is a pre-Islamic name corresponding to the Babylonian god known as Bel."[27] "Bel simply means 'lord' and this is a title of reverence to the moon-god Sin"[28] Isaiah gives us a powerful picture of what Bel will do at the end of the age: "I have sworn by myself, the word is gone out of my mouth in righteousness, and shall not return, That unto me every knee shall bow, every tongue shall swear." (Isaiah 45:23-46:1) This verse is later echoed in the New Testament: "every knee shall bow, every tongue shall confess...that Jesus Christ is Lord." (Philemon 2:8-10) A few verses later, Isaiah also tells of one being in particular who is among them: "Bel bows down, Nebo stoops; Their idols were on the beasts and on the cattle." (Isaiah 46:1) This is none other than the image of the crescent-moon which the beasts wore on their necks: "Their idols were on the beasts and on the cattle", the very symbol that Gideon removed – the crescent moon (Judges 8:21). While Dawkins predicts that we will all bow to evolutionary science, the Biblical God predicts that every man, even Bel will bow down before God.

→ Chapter 2 ←

For Individualism or For Collectivism

*U*nity under freedom is the process of uniting individuals that disagree, while Tyranny is the process of forcing everyone to agree
– in unison.

THE BODY POLITIC

There has always been a Shinarian tug with the Biblical proclamation attempting to unite the peoples under a single mindset
fighting against individuality and free will. This tug manifested itself
in a spiritual struggle between the two camps; individualism and collectivism.

Take the father of Modern Liberalism Jean-Jacques Rousseau, the
17th century philosopher. In his book *The Social Contract* was the
major influence for the French Revolution – a revolt that led to the
death of tens of thousands of French Christians who disagreed with
their version of unity.

Rousseau, long before Karl Marx, called for unity, communalism,
socialism and collectivism. He denounced private property and individualism. He aspired to build the 'body politic'; "At once, in place of
the individual personality of each contracting party, this act of association creates a moral and collective body, composed of as many
members as the assembly contains votes, and receiving from this act
its unity, its common identity, its life and its will. This public person,
so formed by the union of all other persons formerly took the name
of city, and now takes that of Republic or body politic; it is called by
its members State when passive, Sovereign when active, and Power
when compared with others like itself. Those who are associated in
it take collectively the name of people, and severally are called citizens, as sharing in the sovereign power, and subjects, as being under
the laws of the State."[29] Under Rousseau there is no individuality or
private property: "EACH member of the community gives himself to

it, at the moment of its foundation, just as he is, with all the resources at his command, including the goods he possesses. This act does not make possession, in changing hands, change its nature, and become property in the hands of the Sovereign; [...] For the State, in relation to its members, is master of all their goods by the social contract, which, within the State, is the basis of all rights; but, in relation to other powers, it is so only by the right of the first occupier, which it holds from its members."[30]

Islam also desires to make the world one through uniting all tribes under its banner – one world without nationalism or tribal allegiance – the Islamic Ummah (community of Muslims). "The believers Ummah, in their love, mutual kindness, and close ties, are like one body; when any part complains, the whole body responds to it with wakefulness and fever..." "The faithful are like one man: if his eyes suffer, his whole body suffers."[31]

Islam's God created all of mankind as "tribes and peoples that they may mutually know each other."[32] In order to succeed Islam aspired for a single nation, a living organism. The problem with all such unities is dissidents that can never conform. These were labeled as "monkeys" (Q 2:62) and "pigs" (Q 5:60).

Hitler also conceived of Germany as a "living organism" consisting of German people as "cells" bound together to form the Gleichschaltung, a Nazi term for the process by which the Nazi regime successively established a system of totalitarian control over the individual, and tight coordination over all aspects of society and commerce.

Historian Richard J. Evans offered the term "forcible-coordination" in his most recent work on Nazi Germany. One goal of this policy was to eradicate individualism by forcing everybody to adhere to a specific doctrine and way of thinking and to control as many aspects of life as possible using an invasive police force. Jews were a 'bacteria' and a 'virus' – source of a "disease within the body politic" whose continued presence within Germany would lead to the nation's demise.[33]

Hitler wanted Germany to become a Volksgemeinschaft (people's community). Hitler made it plain, that he wished Germany "to forget social origin, class, profession, fortune, education, capital and everything that separates men, in order to reach that which binds them together."[34]

Reich youth leader Baldur von Schirach speaking to a huge crowd of Hitler Youth at Nuremberg said, "...here stands a young generation, a generation which knows no classes and no castes." All institutions needed to work together for the Nazi cause. Those that did so willingly were given wide latitude by the state. "Islands of separateness" – be they business, churches, or people – were worn down over time.[35]

As it is within Islam, the theme of universalism is a call of all Muslims worldwide: "The principle upon which Islam is based is the universality of all intelligent kind. Unfortunately, the western concept gives precedence to nationalism over universalism. Here lies the main conflict. So long as nationalism shall remain dominant, the ills of humanity can only multiply. We have seen that nationalistic societies tend to divide and sub-divide into endless minorities. As a result, racial friction, exploitation of the weaker sections of society and manipulation by the informed continues to plague the region. Whereas, universal fraternity can wipe off all these evils at one stroke if genuinely implemented. The intelligentsia of Islam in particular and in general of the west need to join hands to give a lead to the nations of the world and warn them, if necessary, even in crude format that 'we are all one' just as this planet is one and the universe is one. The scholars all over the world must show solidarity in promotion of this concept so that the bloody conflict of war after war and dominance of one nation by another may end swiftly and humanity step into a new orbit of progress, prosperity and peace."[36]

In a more resolute form, under Jihad in Islam by the respected Muslim scholar Sayyeed Abul A'la Al-Almaududi: "Islam is a revolutionary faith that comes to destroy any government made by man. Islam doesn't look for a nation to be in a better condition than another nation. Islam doesn't care about the land or who owns the land. The goal of Islam is to rule the entire world and submit all of mankind to the faith of Islam. Any nation or power that gets in the way of that goal, Islam will fight and destroy. In order to fulfill that goal, Islam can use every power available every way it can be used to bring worldwide revolution. This is Jihad."[37] Abdullah al-Araby in his book *The Islamization of America* cites a very frightening letter from one Catholic Archbishop to the Pope as he describes his speech during an interfaith dialogue. An excerpt from his letter recounts that during the meeting, an authoritative Muslim figure stood up and spoke very calmly and assuredly, "Thanks to your democratic laws, we will invade you, thanks to our religious laws, we will dominate you."[38]

THE GODFATHER

Rousseau, the Godfather of Modern Liberalism advocated Islam's founder Muhammad as a great role model for shaping a society. He believed that Christianity prevented a state from becoming one and that the Islamic Ummah was a great concept. Bible believers see this unity as an attempt to undo what happened in Shinar. Rousseau condemns Christian resistance of world unity: "It was in these circumstances that Jesus came to set up on earth a spiritual kingdom, which, by separating the theological from the political system, made the State no longer one, and brought about the internal divisions which have never ceased to trouble Christian peoples."[39] "As the new idea of a kingdom of the other world could never have occurred to pagans, they always looked on the Christians as really rebels, who, while feigning to submit, were only waiting for the chance to make themselves independent and their masters, and to usurp by guile the authority they pretended in their weakness to respect. This was the cause of the persecutions."[40]

When one examines all non-Biblical 'superior' ideologies, it seems that all unite against an 'inferior' Christianity while the latter stands to defend itself from 'all'. Take Darwin's half-cousin and anthropologist, Francis Galton, who founded an ideology of human engineering called Eugenics. After reading Darwin's Origin of Species, Galton became familiar with Darwin's work whereby the mechanisms of natural selection were potentially thwarted by human civilization. He reasoned that, since many human societies sought to protect the underprivileged and weak, those societies were at odds with the natural selection that was responsible for the extinction of the inferior. Galton believed that only by changing these social policies, could society be saved from a "reversion towards mediocrity," a phrase that he first coined in statistics, but later changed to the now common "regression towards the mean."[41] In 1904 he clarified his definition of eugenics as "the science, which deals with all influences that improve the inborn qualities of a race; also with those that develop them to the utmost advantage."[42] Galton wished to create a Utopia where the entire world would be a place of people with superior perfect genes. Galton wrote in his unpublished novel *Kantsaywhere* about a utopia based on eugenic laws, filled with perfect breeders where "they think much more of the race than of the individual."[43] Darwin was not simply interested in scientific research on the origin of man. He also wished for totalitarianism. He believed that in order for society to evolve, the state needed to take action by cleansing the world of people natural selection chose as weak: "We must therefore bear the undoubtedly bad effects of the weak surviving and propagating their kind; but there appears to be at least one check in steady action, namely that the weaker and inferior members of society do not marry so freely as the sound; and this check might be indefinitely increased by the weak in body or mind refraining from marriage, though this is more to be hoped for than expected."[44]

Bible believers contend that evolution caused negative results since the Bible commanded us to "be fruitful and multiply." They see a need to expose Charles Darwin's work actually basing his theory on Malthus's work on population control. Malthus was a 19th century cleric and professor of political economy, who believed that a population time bomb threatened the existence of the human race.

He viewed social problems such as poverty, deprivation and hunger as evidence of this "population crisis." According to George Grant, Malthus condemned charities and other forms of benevolence, because he believed they only exacerbated the problems. His answer was to restrict the population growth of certain groups of people.

His theories about population growth and economic stability became the basis for national and international social policy. Grant quotes from Malthus' *magnum opus*, An Essay on the Principle of Population, published in six editions from 1798 to 1826: "All children born, beyond what would be required to keep up the population to a desired level, must necessarily perish, unless room is made for them by the deaths of grown persons. We should facilitate, instead of foolishly and vainly endeavoring to impede, the operations of nature in producing this mortality."[45]

Malthus' disciples believed if Western civilization was to survive, the physically unfit, the materially poor, the spiritually diseased, the racially inferior, and the mentally incompetent had to be suppressed and isolated – or even, perhaps, eliminated. His disciples felt the subtler and more "scientific" approaches of education, contraception, sterilization and abortion were more "practical and acceptable ways" to ease the pressures of the alleged overpopulation.[46] Another solution for population growth-control by Malthus was for the poor and working classes to stop, or postpone, their multiplying activities by marrying late in life and abstaining from sex until then. He believed certain 'positive checks' would help prevent excessive population growth. These included war, famine, infanticide, diseases and homosexuality.[47]

Darwin wrote in his autobiography how Thomas Malthus influenced the theory – or should we say philosophy of evolution: "In October 1838, that is, fifteen months after I had begun my systematic inquiry, I happened to read for amusement Malthus on Population, and being well prepared to appreciate the struggle for existence which everywhere goes on from long-continued observation of the habits of animals and plants, it at once struck me that under these circumstances favorable variations would tend to be preserved, and unfavorable ones to be destroyed. The results of this would be the formation of a new species...Here, then I had at last got a theory by which to work."[48]

The co-founder for the philosophy of evolution was Alfred Russel Wallace. He too, looked to Malthus's population control agenda as an influence: "...the most important book I read was Malthus' *Principle Of Population*...It was the first work I had yet read treating any of the problems of philosophical biology, and its main principles remained with me as a permanent possession, and twenty years later gave me the sought-after clue to the effective agent in the evolution of organic species."[49]

Darwin wanted a "new species" of humans to come forth and in order for this to happen, certain people needed to be destroyed by the state. Under Darwinism, all people are but mere objects for the nation.

Another system and probably one of the most predominant anti-individualist ideologies that the left is pushing today is multiculturalism. Despite what the leftists claim, multiculturalism is a collectivist idea for it expects each person to agree with the perceptions, thoughts and judgments of his group in order for his own perceptions, thoughts, and judgments to be legitimate. Multiculturalists believe that a person's thoughts are either the collectively constructed thoughts of his racial, ethnic, or sexual group or are the thoughts foisted upon him by the dominant white male worldview.[50]

While many accuse Christianity of uniting to conspire to take over America's government, it was Christ who commanded never to unite with Rome, but unite under Rome, then through grass roots effort work on transforming its citizens.

→ Chapter 3 ←

To be Fruitful or to Not Multiply

Progressive view of Bible believers: "The Israelis are supported and egged on in their expansionism and intransigence by the "Armageddon Lobby," thirty million "Christian Zionists" who believe Israel must expand to its Biblical borders in order to bring on Armageddon and the return of Jesus Christ.

Bible believers view: The Battle of Armageddon is but the climax of a 6,000 year program by Satan to keep God's people from being saved. As the adversary, whose self-seeking caused him to be cast out of heaven, Satan declared his purpose to overthrow God and take over His universal government.

Reality is that Both Bible believers and progressives believe in prophets that warn of a coming doomsday; leftists are doomsdayers who believe in coming catastrophes – except the ones foretold in the Bible. They always follow alarmists and prophets and then denounce Christians for believing in Armageddon. Their daily mantra is the usual – save the world from a pending apocalypse – population explosion and global warming; their prophecies are self-fulfilling with one caveat – the outcome is always the opposite of what they predict.

A recent New York Times story wails that if the world's population isn't curtailed soon, the globe will start to look as poor and crowded as Calcutta. Ted Turner says mankind is breeding like "a plague of locusts" and urges couples all over the world to limit themselves to one child per family. The organization *Zero Population Growth* laments that the population of the U.S. is about twice the size it should be in order to protect the environment.[51]

William Vogt, author of a best-selling environmental diatribe called Road to Survival, who in 1948 described tropical diseases like sleeping sickness as "advantages" because they helped curb population growth and scolded the medical profession for believing it "continues to have a duty to keep alive as many people"[52]

At the World Bank, Robert McNamara discouraged financing of health care "unless it was very strictly related to population control, because usually health facilities contributed to the decline of the death rate, and thereby to the population explosion."[53]

Paul R. Ehrlich in his doomsday book *Population Explosion* predicted hundreds of millions of deaths from famine in the 1980s, today these false predictions never materialized due to the Green Revolution – hybrid grains, new fertilizers – has vastly increased harvests.

According to American correspondents who have recently visited China, a nation that once knew famine as a recurring torment now boasts rich crops. To be sure, the green revolution is not totally victorious, and there are many political obstacles between the agronomist and the hungry child. Nevertheless, it is estimated that the world's farmers can theoretically feed a population 40 times as large as today's.[54] The world food production grows exponentially at a rate much higher than the population growth, in both developed and developing countries, partially due to the efforts of Norman Borlaug's "Green Revolution" of the 1960s, and the food per capita level is the highest in history. On the other hand, population growth rates significantly slowed down, especially in the developed world.[55] Famine has not been eliminated, but its root cause is political instability, not global food shortage.[56]

In *The Population Bomb*, Ehrlich predicted in the "1970s the world will undergo famines – hundreds of millions of people are going to starve to death in spite of any crash programs embarked upon now."[57] What happened to the famines *The Bomb* predicted? Today no serious mind would deny that the last four decades were a period of abundant food for all. Ehrlich gave scenarios of a coming apocalypse that he later retracted – The Population Bomb was a dud, always has been and always will be and if we may predict the cry of such false prophets will never end till Kingdom Come!

Still, the prophets of population doomsday are warning us that "We are adding another New York City every month, a Mexico every year, and almost another India every decade," writes environmental author Bill McKibben. "New Limits to Growth Revive Malthusian Fears," warned the Wall Street Journal. "Philippines Population Climbs; Food Problems Loom," Reuters offered. The online magazine Slate summed it up neatly with a recent headline: Global Swarming. And in an accompanying piece on this page Paul and Anne Ehrlich return to the barricades citing the twin perils of overconsumption and over-population.[58] Yet, we are nowhere near running out of room on the planet. If every one of the 6 billion of us resided in Texas, there would be room enough for every family of four to have a house and an 1/8th of an acre of land – and the rest of the globe would be vacant. True, if population growth continues, soon some of these people would have to spill over the border into Oklahoma.[59]

One of the fathers of population control in the West, Thomas Malthus published six editions of his famous treatise, An Essay on the Principle of Population (1798-1826). In his Malthusian Catastrophe he warned of overpopulation leading to depleted resources and mass starvation: "there will be 7 billion people standing in line for their rations in the year 2000."[60]

And here we are today in 2009 – nothing happened.

Speaker of the House Nancy Pelosi being faithful to the population explosion dogma and to prevent a coming apocalypse says that birth control will help the economy. Pelosi ignores one major factor in the growth of any economy – economies cannot grow unless population grows.

Just altering one command in the Bible "be fruitful and multiply" (Genesis 1:28) and reverse it to "population control" as leftist Pelosi suggests, and the result is a demographic winter, which threatens us with catastrophic consequences – both economic and social.

Sure, the self-fulfilled prophecies do happen, but with reverse consequences. Population control does not enhance our way of life but diminishes it. Today, most major economists' evidence shows that more people have generated more prosperity and higher standards of living. Falling fertility rates and aging populations ultimately endanger civilization.

Philip Longman, a demographer and author of "The Empty Cradle: How Falling Birthrates Threaten World Prosperity," observes: "The on-going global decline in human birthrates is the single most powerful force affecting the fate of nations and the future of society in the 21st century."[61]

Economist Robert J. Samuelson wrote in a June 15, 2005 column in The Washington Post: "It's hard to be a great power if your population is shriveling." Samuelson warned, "Europe as we know it is going out of business... Western Europe's population grows dramatically grayer, projects the U.S. Census Bureau. Now about one-sixth of the population is 65 and older. By 2030, that could be one-fourth and by 2050, almost one-third."

In a documentary titled "Demographic Winter" in which social scientists were interviewed – a group not known for religiosity or conservatism – including demographer Phillip Longman, Patrick Fagan, psychologist and former U.S. Deputy Assistant Secretary of Health and Human Services Harry S. Dent, president of the H.S. Dent Foundation; and Nobel Laureate Gary S. Becker, Ph.D., It is an impressive list, but still, why should anyone fret about declining population? Without a doubt, warns Demographic Winter, it may portend economic decline and the death of the West. Rendering demographic-based economic forecasting, Harry S. Dent tells us that when the enormous baby-boom generation moves beyond its peak spending years – which end at age 48 – its reduced spending will cause an economic contraction, one the smaller generation following it will not be able to forestall. We will then follow in the footsteps of Japan, which had no baby boom, grayed before us, and experienced an economic meltdown in the 1990s (which Dent predicted). During this period, the Nikkei stock exchange lost 80 percent of its value, real estate depreciated with it, and Japan has wallowed in continual recession ever since. Of course, a major non-demographic factor falling outside the scope of this film – Japan's stifling corporate socialism – was also at play. Nevertheless, the film makes a compelling case that aging populations have a huge negative impact on the economy, whether in Japan or elsewhere. The birth index rose sharply from 1950 through 1957 and began to plateau from 1958 through 1961. This group was the third wave of baby boomers, the majority of whom are now moving into their mid-forties. As this huge wave of consumers moves towards age 47 to 48, the age at which family spending peaks over the coming decade they will continue the consumption patterns that will sustain the high rates of economic growth Americans have enjoyed in the past. Though such individuals do not spend at their peak–that still occurs around age 47 today and moving towards age 48 by the top of this boom–spending grows at its fastest rate over a person's lifetime during the family formation years.[62] From 1961, the end of the baby boom and 47 years, we come to 2008 – the world experienced an economic slowdown and the stock market declined.

In our own country, our baby boomers will begin crossing the threshold into retirement in 2010. Yet that is just the tip of our demographic winter iceberg. As the old increase in number relative to the young, there will be fewer workers to drive the economy and fund Social Security and Medicare. As a result, the latter may be taxed more heavily and in turn, work less and have even fewer children, creating a vicious circle.

Also, most innovators are between 30 and 44 years of age; thus, innovation will decrease commensurate with the decline of that group. Moreover, with the reduction in overall consumer spending, companies will have less incentive to fund innovation. Gary S. Becker sums up the effects well by paraphrasing Adam Smith, a pioneer of political economy: "Depressions are associated with decreasing population."

History both before and after his time instructs us that Adam Smith was correct. So who were the culprits in this coming disaster? Or even better, were Malthus and others, pioneers in their theories? Were they exploring trends that indeed threatened humanity?

Think again.

The idea of population explosion is not new at all, in fact very ancient, even as ancient as the theory of Evolution. A number of ancient writers have reflected on the issue of population explosion. Confucius (551-478 BC) was perhaps the oldest known in history and other Chinese writers cautioned that: "excessive growth may reduce output per worker, repress levels of living for the masses and engender strife". Confucius also observed that: "mortality increases when food supply is insufficient; that permanent marriage makes for high infantile mortality rates, that war checks population growth."[63]

In ancient Greece, Plato (427-347 BC) and Aristotle (384-322 BC) discussed the best population size for Greek city states and concluded that cities should be small enough for efficient administration and direct citizen participation in public affairs, but at the same time needed to be large enough to defend themselves against hostile neighboring city states. In order to maintain a desired population size, the philosophers advised that procreation, and if necessary immigration should be encouraged if the population size was too small, and emigration to colonies would be encouraged should the population become too big.[64]

Like Confucius, Aristotle concluded that a large increase in population would bring "certain poverty on the citizenry and poverty is the cause of sedition and evil". To halt rapid population increase, Aristotle advocated the use of abortion and the exposition of newborns.[65]

So what are proponents of the population explosion really interested in? Matthew Connelly of Columbia University and the author of Fatal Misconception: The Struggle To Control World Population, reveals how organizations, institutions, governments and the United Nations manipulated and coerced families, evaded political accountability and violated basic human rights to achieve their population-reduction agenda: "coercive methods, such as the 'one child policy' in some regions, have been tried in China, particularly since the reforms of 1979."[66]

The difficulties with this "solution" are of several kinds. First, if freedom is valued at all, the lack of freedom associated with this approach must be seen to be a social loss in itself. Women's groups throughout the world have persuasively emphasized the importance of reproductive freedom. The loss of freedom is often dismissed on the grounds that because of cultural differences, authoritarian policies that would not be tolerated in the West are acceptable to Asians. While we often hear references to 'despotic' Oriental traditions, such arguments are no more convincing than a claim that compulsion in the West is justified by the traditions of the Spanish Inquisition or of the Nazi concentration camps.

Frequent references are also made to the emphasis on discipline in the "Confucian tradition"; but that is not the only tradition in the "East," nor is it easy to assess the implications of that tradition for modern Asia (even if we were able to show that discipline is more important for Confucius than it is for, say, Plato or Saint Augustine).[67]

Besides control over human freedom, the issue is to enforce different moral values. The same apocalyptic adherents from the United Nations and liberal media that continually repeat the mantra that satisfaction comes from careers, romance, living for the moment, cohabitation, sexual satisfaction and using contraceptives. The days of *Bonanza*, *Little House On The Prairie* and *The Brady Bunch* are over.

Had shrinking the population been a solution to this imaginative problem why do many western nations depend on mass immigration? But mass immigration changes the national character of the western host country. Immigrants tend to have a lower education level than natives. Many never learn the language of their new home or identify with its history and heritage. Instead of being French-Algerian, they remain Algerian. By and large, those inhabitants of Germany, Belgium and France who are having large families are immigrants from the Third World – mostly Muslims.

Europe once was called Christendom. The call that Europeans of the future will heed won't be church bells, but the muezzin's call to prayer from the neighborhood mosque. Even now, there are more mosques than churches in southern France. But such statistical facts could be tagged as Islamophobia.

The population controllers at the United Nations and inside the U.S. environmental movement regarded 'mother nature' as pure and fragile and man's footprint on the Earth as the despoiler of this natural state. The other side points to this as worshiping the created, not the Creator and they are in many cases hostile toward economic development and human progress. They celebrate the planting of a new tree as magnificent progress, but abhor the planting of another fetus in a woman's womb as anti-progress.[68] You choose life you get life – including descendants. You choose death – in the form of population control, contraception, abortion, homosexuality, secularism, consumerism, unthinking environmentalism, selfishness and a live-for-the-moment ethic – and you get death, including no descendants.[69]

In conclusion, *Modern Liberalism contradicts every positive term it uses; progressiveness is hardly modern, its unity is discord, its order is disorder, its love is the hatred of prosperity, its strife for justice for the under dog is enslavement, its prosperity is poverty, its humility is the humiliation of others and it's void of confession – it offers carrots on the tips of swords and always attempts to spread its tentacles everywhere injecting tyranny, the end result of which is the destruction of human lives. Neither is 'Modern Liberalism' modern, for it has nothing to do with liberty and stems from failed ancient systems founded by tyrants that plague the annals of history. Liberals apply terms that rarely mean what they say – spreading the wealth is not the process of creating opportunity for the poor but simply robbing the rich to give to the lazy. 'Fighting sickness' through institutionalized medicine slowly kills the sick as he waits in long lines while the disease remains. They advocate the creation of Palestine, which in reality is the destruction of the state of Israel. They love lunatics they promote as philosophers and excuse terrorism as a social cause. They advocate 'earth' and promote the killing of the unborn. They equate humans with animals while advocating killing the former and saving the latter. They apply destruction to everyone and everything so long it's not them, for if they believe in what they advocate they would commit suicide through hunger – they twist everything by applying complicated terminology which never means what they try to describe – in fact it usually means quite the opposite – 'what's mine, is mine and what's yours is mine'.*

Collectivists focus on community and society while seeking to give priority to group goals over individual goals. Today we have Obama's "spread the wealth" socialism focusing on the necessity for the poor and disenfranchised to unite. Leftist President Jimmy Carter supported the 1979 Iranian revolution by releasing Ayatollah Khomeini's cohorts from jail, he "pulled the rug out from under the Shah," who liberated women in Iran by offering them education.[70] Carter turned a blind eye allowing the spark of an Islamic Revolution to set the stage and today we see the spread of Islamism worldwide. Carter openly supports dialogue with Hamas while he is always ready and available to condemn Israel.

For God or For Tyranny

→ Chapter 4 ←

Revolutions or Revulsion

With progressives either 'all religions are equally true' or 'religion is the opiate for the masses'. Both clichés contradict each other, yet progressives spotlight their denunciations only on the Bible.

One would think we would have a struggle between atheists and all religion. The truth is far from it. Why do progressives always speak positively about Islam and negatively about the Bible? Could it be true that they have so much in common?

As we shall see and like Jean-Jacques Rousseau even Hitler's aspirations complimented Islam: "The Germanic peoples would have become heirs to that religion. Such a creed was perfectly suited to the Germanic temperament. Hitler said that the conquering Arabs, because of their racial inferiority, would in the long run have been unable to contend with the harsher climate and conditions of the country. They could not have kept down the more vigorous natives, so that ultimately not Arabs but Islamized Germans could have stood at the head of this Mohammedan Empire."[71]

Hitler also hated Christianity since it "was incapable of uniting the Germans, and that only an entirely new world theory was capable of doing so."[72] Like Hitler, the French philosopher Rousseau hated Christianity since it fails to unite the world and he loved Islam: "Mahomet [Muhammad] held very sane views, and linked his political system well together; and, as long as the form of his government continued under the caliphs who succeeded him, that government was indeed one, and so far good. But the Arabs, having grown prosperous, lettered, civilized, slack and cowardly, were conquered by barbarians: the division between the two powers began again; and, although it is less apparent among the Mahometans than among the Christians, it none the less exists, especially in the sect of Ali, and there are States, such as Persia, where it is continually making itself felt."[73] French revolutionaries, influenced by Rousseau, wanted the end of Christianity and caused a holocaust of French Christians. Like Sharī'ah demands the death of dissidents, Rousseau maintained that anybody who believes in a faith which is contrary to the needs or beliefs of the state should be put to death. When Rousseau set his eyes on Christianity he saw "nothing more contrary to the social spirit" which oozed downwards to the slime of humanity. Compare that perspective with that of Hitler, who said: "I'll make these damned parsons feel the power of the state in a way they would have never believed possible... This filthy reptile raises its head whenever there is a sign of weakness in the State, and therefore it must be stamped on. We have no sort of use for a fairy story invented by the Jews."[74] Rousseau also believed that the state's army would be awful if the soldiers were Christian since "they know better how to die than how to conquer". He lamented further, "Imagine your Christian republic face to face with Sparta or Rome: the pious Christians will be beaten, crushed and destroyed, before they know where they are, or will owe their safety only to the contempt their enemy will conceive for them. [...] Christianity preaches only servitude and dependence. Its spirit is so favorable to tyranny that it always profits by such a régime. True Christians are made to be slaves, and they know it and do not much mind: this short life counts for too little in their eyes. I shall be told that Christian troops are excellent. I deny it. Show me an instance. For my part, I know of no Christian troops."[75]

Was Rousseau, the founder of Modern Liberalism, anti- religion? Was religion in his view the source of all the evil we have? Hardly: "Now, it matters very much to the community that each citizen should have a religion. That will make him love his duty; but the dogmas of that religion concern the State and its members only so far as they have reference to morality and to the duties, which he who profess them is, bound to do to others. [...] There is therefore a purely civil profession of faith of which the Sovereign should fix the articles, not exactly as religious dogmas, but as social sentiments without which a man cannot be a good citizen or a faithful subject. While it can compel no one to believe them, it can banish from the State whoever does not believe them – it can banish him, not for impiety, but as an anti-social being, incapable of truly loving the laws and justice, and of sacrificing, at need, his life to his duty. If anyone, after publicly recognizing these dogmas, behaves as if he does not believe them, let him be punished by death: he has committed the worst of all crimes, that of lying before the law."[76]

In 1920 Hitler proclaimed his official manifesto for the Nazi party. It imitates Rousseau in that it demands "freedom for all religious faiths in the state, insofar as they do not endanger its existence or offend the moral and ethical sense of the Germanic race. The party as such represents the point of view of a positive Christianity without binding itself to any one particular confession. It fights against the Jewish materialist spirit within and without, and is convinced that a lasting recovery of our folk can only come about from within on the principle: common good before individual good."[77] Hitler's manifesto mimics Rousseau. It demanded that no "individual shall do any work that offends against the interest of the community to the benefit of all." It also enjoined: "that ruthless war be waged against those who work to the injury of the common welfare. Traitors, usurers, profiteers, etc., are to be punished with death, regardless of creed or race."[78]

Hitler believed that Christianity was contrary to the Reich and he wished that Islam would become the official religion of Germany: "You see, it's been our misfortune to have the wrong religion. Why didn't we have the religion of the Japanese, who regard sacrifice for the Fatherland as the highest good? The Mohammedan religion too would have been much more compatible to us than Christianity. Why did it have to be Christianity with its meekness and flabbiness?"[79]

THE NERONIAN SYNDROME

The log is always in someone else's eye. According to Muslim apologists, "it was Christians that orchestrated Nazism and the beheadings during the French Revolution." Islam forgets that Muslims butchered the Qurayza Jews in Arabia and blamed the Jews for it. Today, Muslims kill Jewish civilians in suicide bombings while blaming their victims. Nothing has changed. *A typical Neronian psychosis is one which accuses Christians of burning Rome when Nero was the culprit. Neronians have a sadistic trait of accusing others of the crimes they themselves are guilty of committing. It is the victim that must be blamed for the victimization.*

To date, there was no element of confession by Muslim historians or scholars regarding the Qurayza massacre. However, much more disturbing is the concluding narrator comment by Karen Armstrong and M. Cherif Bassiouni. Armstrong, brimming with her infamous apologetic zeal, has the temerity to claim: "…(the massacre) cannot be seen as anti-Semitism…Muhammad had nothing against the Jewish people…or the Jewish religion. The Koran continues to tell Muslims to honor the People of the Book." In sharp contrast, a serious, respected scholar of anti-Semitism, Professor Robert Wistrich, summarizes the overall Qur'ânic image of the Jews as follows: "…there are some notably harsh passages in which Muhammad brands the Jews as enemies of Islam and depicts them as possessing a malevolent, rebellious spirit. There are also verses that speak of their justified abasement and poverty, of the Jews being '…laden with God's anger…' for their disobedience. They had to be humiliated '…because they had disbelieved the signs of God and slain the prophets unrightfully.' (Sura 2:61/58). According to another verse (Sura 5:78/82), '…the unbelievers of the Children of Israel…' were cursed by both David and Jesus. The penalty for disbelief in God's signs and in the miracles performed by the prophets was to be transformed into apes and swine…(Sura 5:60/65)…The oral tradition (hadith) goes much further and claims that the Jews, in accordance with their perfidious nature, deliberately caused Muhammad's painful, protracted death from poisoning. Furthermore, malevolent, conspiratorial Jews are to blame for the sectarian strife in early Islam, for heresies and deviations that undermined or endangered the unity of the umma (the Muslim nations)…"[80]

Within the whispered history of the French revolution we find atrocities that match those of the Taliban or what the Aztecs did to their victims when sacrificing them to the sun god. The French Revolution was more Islamic than it was Christian. The French historian and probably one of the greatest historians of his time, Alexis de Tocqueville, wrote on the French revolution: "strange religion has, like Islam, overrun the whole world with its apostles, militants, and martyrs."[81] According to Tocqueville the French Revolution was nothing more than a heathen religious movement. It was a revolt that "was not merely a change in the French social system but nothing short of a regeneration of the whole human race. It created an atmosphere of missionary fervor and assumed all the aspects of a religious revival... It would perhaps be truer to say that it developed into a species of religion, if a singularly imperfect one, since it was without God, without a ritual or promise of a future life."[82]

People who witnessed what Nazism did to Germany said similar things. In 1938, R.H. Lockhart stated in his book, *"Guns or Butter?"* Frenchmen were writing home from Nazi Germany that, "everything is moving toward a supreme conflict between the Christian world and the new Islam [Nazism]."[83]

Under this new cult, Islamic-style terrorism infected France. A disciple of Rousseau was far-left revolutionary Maximilien Robespierre or as his followers called him, "The Incorruptible." When he took over France with his reign of terror he summarized his movement quite simply in his famous Republic of Virtue: "If the strength of popular government in peacetime is virtue, the strength of popular government in revolution is both virtue and terror; terror without virtue is disastrous, virtue without terror is powerless. Terror is nothing but prompt, severe, and inflexible justice; it is thus an emanation of virtue; it is less a particular principle than a consequence of the general principle of democracy applied to the most urgent needs of the fatherland. It is said that terror is the strength of despotic government. [...] Subdue the enemies of liberty through terror and you will be right as founders of the Republic. The government of revolution is the despotism of liberty against tyranny."[84] Robespierre may have just as well pulled his instructions right out of Islam's Qur'ân: "I am with you: give firmness to the believers, I will instill terror into the hearts of the unbelievers, Smite ye above their necks and smite all their finger tips of them."[85]

In the city of Nantes, the sadistic revolutionary commander Jean-Baptiste Carrier disposed of Christian Vendéean prisoners-of-war in a horrifically efficient form of Islamic style mass execution. In the Noyades there was mass drowning when naked men, women, and children were tied together in specially constructed boats, towed out to the middle of the river Loire and then sunk. Historians believe that around 170,000 Vendéeans were killed, around 5,000 in the Noyades. When it was over, French General Francois Joseph Westermann penned a letter to the Committee of Public Safety stating: "There is no more Vendée... According to the orders that you gave me, I crushed the children under the feet of the horses, massacred the women who, at least for these, will not give birth to any more brigands. I do not have a prisoner to reproach me. I have exterminated all."[86]

More recently, French politician Philippe de Villiers, in opposing Turkish admission into the EU, visited Armenia and compared the massacre of the Christian Armenians by the Turks to the massacre of the Christian Vendéeans by the French revolutionaries. Villiers furthermore explained why the mass execution of the Vendéeans took place: "Why did it take place? Because a people was chosen to be liquidated on account of their religious faith. Today we demand a law officially declaring it as a genocide; we demand a statement from the president; and recognition by the United Nations."[87] He also said: "It's the rare case of a people rising up for religious reasons. They did not rebel because they were hungry, but because their priests were being killed."[88]

The bloody events of the Christian Vendée were long absent from French history books because of the evil light they shed on the Revolutionaries. However, they were well known in the Soviet bloc. Lenin himself had studied the war there and drew inspiration for his policies.[89]

It was as if the same evil spirit that possessed the French rebels was the same that took hold of the Muslims during the Armenian Massacre. And while westerners came to the realization of the evils perpetrated in Europe, Muslims lack the element of confession.

Historian Serge Trifkovic described the massacre by Muslims of the Greek city of Smyrna: "sporadic killings of Christians, mostly Armenians, started as soon as the Turks overran it on September 9, 1922. Within days, they escalated to mass slaughter. It did not 'get out of hand,' however, in the sense of an uncontrolled chaos perpetrated by an un-commanded military rabble. The Turkish military authorities deliberately escalated it. The Greek Orthodox Bishop Chrysostomos remained with his flock. 'It is the tradition of the Greek Church and the duty of the priest to stay with his congregation,' he replied to those begging him to flee. The Muslim mob fell upon him, uprooted his eyes and, as he was bleeding, dragged him by his beard through the streets of the Turkish quarter, beating and kicking him. Every now and then, when he had the strength to do so, he would raise his right hand and blessed his persecutors. A Turk got so furious at this gesture that he cut off his hand with his sword. He fell to the ground, and was hacked to pieces by the angry mob. The carnage culminated in the burning of Smyrna, which started on September 13 when the Turks put the Armenian quarter to torch and the conflagration engulfed the city. The remaining inhabitants were trapped at the seafront, from which there was no escaping the flames on one side, or Turkish bayonets on the other. This was the end of Christianity in Asia Minor, whose history goes back to events recorded in the New Testament itself."[90]

A missionary eyewitness to the atrocity laments: "the slaughter of the Armenians was a joy to the Turks, a massacre was heralded by the blowing of trumpets and concluded by a procession. Accompanied by the prayers of the mullahs and muezzins, who from the minarets implored the blessings of Allah, the slaughter was accomplished in admirable order according to a well arranged plan. The crowd, supplied with arms by the authorities, joined most amicably with the soldiers and the Kurdish Hamidieh on these festive occasions. The Turkish women stimulated their heroes by raising a gutteral shriek of their war cry, the Zilghit, and deafening the hopeless despair of their victims by singing their nuptial songs. A kind of wild cannibal humour seized the crowd...the savage crew did not even spare the children."[91]

Analogous to the French revolution, the crowd that watched the public executions jeered and abused those who were about to die. They rejoiced at the severed heads, adulated the leaders temporarily in power, and cursed them after they fell.[92]

Armenian Women and children were raped, the bellies of pregnant women were slashed, and men were decapitated and put on display for entertainment. Survivors were viciously dragged across Deir ez-Zor (the Syrian Desert) without food or water, at the mercy of murderous Turkish generals. By the end of the genocide, more than 1.5 million Armenians were massacred and lost.[93]

An account of one survivor, Khanum Palootzian, recalls what she witnessed: "Pregnant women were eviscerated, their stomachs cut open with swords and their babies ripped out, thrown against the rocks. These I saw with my own eyes."[94]

The violence in the Turkish massacres of the Armenians resembles the violence done to Americans by the Native Indians. In 1868, representative from Minnesota and delegate from the Territory of Montana, James M. Cavanaugh explained: "In Minnesota the almost living babe has been torn from its mother's womb; and I have seen the child, with its young heart palpitating, nailed to the windowsill. I have seen women who were scalped, disfigured, outraged. In Denver, Colorado Territory, I have seen women and children brought in scalped. Scalped why? Simply because the Indian was 'upon the warpath,' to satisfy the devilish and barbarous propensities. [...] The Indian will make a treaty in the fall, and in the spring he is again 'upon the warpath.' The torch, the scalping-knife, plunder, and desolation follow wherever the Indian goes."

Similar brutality engrossed the French revolution during the massacres of 1792; historian Stanley Loomis writes in *The Terror*: "On the morning of the third, the prison of La Force was entered and here took place the murder of the Princesse de Lamballe... The frenzy of the crazed and drunken murderers appears to have reached its highest pitch at La Force."[95] If there is any comfort for human beings as they read through the myriad of horrors and the slaughter of the innocent, perhaps it is that we might compare the slaughter of humans to sheep since sheep do not care if they are skinned after they are slaughtered. Loomis further describes the revolution's carnage: "Cannibalism, disembowelment and acts of indescribable ferocity took place here...The Princess...refused to swear her hatred of the King and Queen and was duly handed over to the mob. She was dispatched with a pike thrust, her still beating heart was ripped from her body and devoured, her legs and arms were severed from her body and shot through a cannon. The horrors that were then perpetrated on her disemboweled torso are indescribable. It has been loosely assumed that most of the other victims were, like herself, aristocrats – an assumption that for some curious reason is often supposed to mitigate these crimes."[96]

Events like these shatter the myth of class warfare which permeates leftist circles regarding the struggle between the peasants and bourgeoisie: "Very few victims were, in fact, of the former nobility – less than thirty out of the fifteen hundred who were killed."[97]

Not all events in history are equal but most of them start out the same. They are energized through class warfare and the downtrodden versus the evil aristocracy. They burn with complaint against the evil wealthy and end up setting churches ablaze. How many progressives today speak of the Mexican communist government that wanted a holocaust of all the Christians in Mexico?

Many priests were martyred while celebrating mass, either by being shot or beheaded. In a last affirmation of their faith, the Cristeros (followers of Christ) would shout, "Viva Cristo Rey!" (Long Live Christ the King) before they died. Padre Miguel Agustin Pro was one of the best known of the martyred priests. Mexican president Calles took advantage of the opportunity to execute a priest publicly in an attempt to discourage other priests from participating in politics. He ordered Pro be shot at the police station and invited reporters to the execution. Padre Pro carried a small crucifix and his rosary and held his arms out forming a cross as he was shot. Pope John Paul II beatified him on September 25, 1988.

Another martyr, San Pedro de Jesus Maldonado Lucero served as the people's spiritual mentor in Chihuahua, Mexico also suffered a tortuous fate. Soldiers in Santa Isabel, Chihuahua, arrested him and beat him to death for defying government bans on hidden religious celebrations. Maldonado's murderers used rifle butts to bash in his head and dislodge an eye from its socket. Patrick Cross writes that by 1929, some 25,000 priests in approximately 12,000 parishes could no longer minister to the spiritual needs of Mexican Catholics, who were over 10 million strong.[98]

As the overwhelming evidence indicates, systems that exchange all facets of Christian ethics and displays of God seem to be loaded with spirituality. The goal is simply the end of Christianity to advent a new era focusing on self as the absolute creator of everything good. Yet nothing that is introduced as 'new' is new at all – simply the same old recipes repackaged with the same disastrous results – misery and loss of life.

If Christianity is the source of all evil as many liberals of today claim, that 'religion' is the source of all sorts of our troubles, why is it that when these advocates get their way, they never get rid of religion? Instead, they merely replace Christianity with an ideology filled with religious tones and spiritual practices complete with rituals, methods and religious behavior. And when they complain that Christianity is too controlling, they then desire to expand their new theology and make it universal.

During the French Revolution we had the Cult of Reason that worshiped the Goddess of Reason founded by Jacques Hébert and Pierre Gaspard Chaumette. Its Goddess was mounted in churches. The Church of Notre-Dame-de-Paris became a Temple of Reason.[99] Robespierre eventually killed Hébert and other Cult of Reason members thus causing the cult to go underground. Robespierre then initiated his Cult of The Supreme Being to be practiced by all citizens of the world: "He created the universe to proclaim His power. [...] The Author of Nature has bound all mortals by a boundless chain of love and happiness. Perish the tyrants who have dared to break it! Republican Frenchmen, it is yours to purify the earth, which they have soiled, and to recall to it the justice that they have banished! Liberty and virtue together came from the breast of Divinity. Neither can abide with mankind without the other."[100] In Robespierre's eyes there were only "two parties in France: the people and its enemies. We must exterminate those miserable villains who are eternally conspiring against the rights of man... [We] must exterminate all our enemies."[101]

True unity respects critical thinking. Evil unites everyone to agree in unison with a 'You are with us or you're doomed' paradigm. This creed is no different from Allah's demand: "And those who disbelieve are allies to one another, [and] if you do not do so, there will be Fitnah (strife) and oppression on earth, and a great mischief and corruption."[102] Those "Who disbelieve" in Islam are always linked to the ones doing "mischief". And just to understand what Islam prescribes for anyone who does "mischief", Allah declared: "The punishment of those who wage war against Allah and His Messenger, and strive with might and main for mischief through the land is: execution, or crucifixion, or the cutting off of hands and feet from opposite sides..."[103] Muhammad reiterates his master's command: "If the Muslim world gives a pledge to two chiefs, the second one must be killed."[104] It was this command that caused strife and great mischief in Muslim lands. Shortly after Muhammad's death, the Muslim world suffered one of its greatest civil wars in what is called Hurub-Al-Riddeh (Wars of Defectors) and later the Shi'a and Sunni divide.

Progressives, who accuse the Bible of promoting tyranny, since everyone should obey God, should be careful what they ask for. Tyrannies go beyond promoting a dogma. They impose dogma by literally eliminating all others. In Islam the world is broken into two – Dar al-Islam (House of Islam) and Dar al-Harb (House of War) – Submit, convert or die was the call of Islam throughout the ages from Muhammad to the Ottoman Turks.

Whether Hitler or Muhammad, the call is similar. In a 1933 speech to the German army and marine commanders, Hitler said that he could not allow "the expression of any principles that stand opposed to the goal. Whoever doesn't convert must be subdued."[105] Conformity is the call of all such ideologies. Robespierre even planned on making all French wear a uniform. He also planned to raze all church steeples as "undemocratic."[106] If the government abandons God, the government becomes "the people" which in turn become "God", with omniscience and omnipresence. Robespierre made it quite clear that "The people is always worth more than individuals...The people is sublime, but individuals are weak."[107] Whether it was the French Revolution or Mexican communism, these were not Christian Revolutions. They were cults that harbored a special hatred of Christianity.

Paganism is the absence of Christianity whose rebels tried their best to wipe out any trace of Christianity in France, including the removal of all iconography, crosses and church bells from all places of worship. Such things were replaced with facades approved by the institution of revolutionary and civic cults. The enactment of a law took place on October 21, 1793 making all nonjuring priests and all persons who harbored them liable to death on sight.[108] The Muslim Turks as well wanted to ruin any relics of Christianity. As recently as 1974 Turkey invaded Cyprus and just as the Romans renamed Israel to Palestine in order to erase the memory of the Jewish State, the Turks have renamed all the cities and towns in Cyprus. Those who view the history of Muslim Turks as ancient may want to take another look.

Who today speaks of the occupation of Cyprus by Turkey? While United States President Barack Hussein Obama spoke in Turkey, he was silent on their occupation of Cyprus and kept his promise to Islam while denouncing Israel's supposed occupation of Palestine. In Turkey while speaking for Americans, he said that, "We do not consider ourselves a Christian nation or a Jewish nation or a Muslim nation; we consider ourselves a nation of citizens who are bound by ideals and a set of values." In June of 2006 Obama spoke similar lines: "Whatever we once were, we are no longer a Christian nation – at least, not just. We are also a Jewish nation, a Muslim nation, a Buddhist nation, and a Hindu nation, and a nation of nonbelievers." While our founding fathers did establish a Christian nation, they chose to respect all religions living under its laws which was not all that dissimilar from ancient Israel: "And you are to love the stranger, for you yourselves were strangers in Egypt." (Deuteronomy 10:19)

An old-style liberal Oriana Fallaci found it amazing that Enlightenment liberals could defend so enthusiastically the gross illiberal tendencies of militant Muslims and puzzled over how such seemingly different groups could end up on the same side in debates. It's not all that surprising when one considers their shared rejection of reason properly understood and the common enemy that rouses them – a lingering Christianity in the West.

Is he 'Christian', 'Muslim', or 'Liberal'? Obama was questioned by many who were labeled xenophobic for asking. Why did liberals condemn such dialogue? Obama was raised Muslim. Instead of Obama promoting Christ's "I am The way, The Truth and The Life" he promotes the notion that "All people of faith – Christians, Jews, Muslims, Animists, everyone – know the same God."

Obama simply reiterates what he learned as a Muslim: "Surely those who believe, and those who are Jews, and the Christians, and the Sabians, whoever believes in Allah and the Last day and does good, they shall have their reward from their Lord, and there is no fear for them, nor shall they grieve." (Qur'ân 2:62)

This is in no way reconciliation between all faiths. In Islam, Allah created all religions in their original state to be the same – Muslim. Islam according to the best of Muslim scholars is a universal religion that affirms other past religions prior to their corruption. Islam came to reveal the true essence of all lost faiths.

A Muslim scholar writing for the Oxford Islamic Studies sums up Islam's relation to other religions: "al-islâm teaching in the generic sense is the core and the essence of all religions of the prophets and the messengers. Ibn Taymîyah states: Because the origin of religion, that is al-islâm, is one, even though its Sharî'ah varies, the Prophet Muhammad says in valid hadiths, "Our religion and the religion of the prophets is one," and "All the prophets are paternal brothers, [even though] their mothers are different," and "The nearest of all the people to Jesus, the son of Mary, is me." Islam never offered religious plurality: "Given the principles above, it can be argued that the

Qur'ân essentially teaches the concept of religious plurality. To be sure, this does not necessarily mean an affirmation of the truth of all religions in their actual practices (in this respect, many of the actual religious practices of the Muslims are not correct because they basically contradict the teachings of the Qur'ân...)"[109]

President Obama, instead of demanding any confession from the "Muslim World" insists on wiping out American Christian heritage. He even goes much further by diminishing a thing he claims to believe in, saying the descendants of that heritage need to learn Islam: "I think that the United States and the West generally, we have to educate ourselves more effectively on Islam. And one of the points I want to make is, is that if you actually took the number of Muslims Americans, we'd be one of the largest Muslim countries in the world. And so there's got to be a better dialogue and a better understanding between the two peoples."[110]

Is Obama – who claims conversion to Christianity – defending Christian interests or doing Islam's bidding? As he spoke in Turkey, he demonstrated a leftist tendency by making no mention of Turkey's destruction of concrete evidence of the Christian and Greek history in the region of Cyprus under Turkey's occupation.

Turkey's occupation of Cyprus included vandalism by the Muslim Turks and desecration so methodical and so widespread that it amounted to institutionalized obliteration of everything sacred to Christianity. In some instances, an entire graveyard of 50 or more tombs had been reduced to pieces or rubble no larger than a matchbox. The chapel of Ayios Demetrios at Ardhana became empty but for the remains of the altar plinth, and that was fouled with human excrement. At Syngrasis, the broken crucifix was drenched in urine... At Lefkoniko, an armless Christ on a smashed crucifix overlooked the interior of Gaidhouras Church. Tombs were gaped open as far the eye can see. Crosses bearing the pictures of those buried beneath had been flattened and destroyed.[111]

In Mexico, much similar actions were taking place by the anti-clerical government based on the Mexican revolution in which the revolutionaries wrote the New Mexican Constitution commonly known as the Mexican 1917 Constitution. Article 3 of the 1917 constitution called for secular education in the schools; Article 5 outlawed monastic orders; Article 24 forbade public worship outside the confines of churches; and Article 27 placed restrictions on the right of religious organizations to hold property.

Most unbearable to Catholics was Article 130, which deprived clergy members of basic rights and made them in effect second-class citizens. Priests and nuns were denied the right to wear clerical attire, to vote, to criticize government officials or to comment on public affairs in religious periodicals.[112]

The Catholic Church did not want to retaliate violently against the government, so from 1919 to 1926, they obeyed the laws. However, in 1926, President Calles introduced legislation which fined priests $250 for wearing religious vestments and imprisoned them for five years for criticizing the government.

The Catholics eventually grew tired of living under such laws and retaliated, calling themselves the "Cristeros" or "followers of Christ." The Cristeros were willing to become martyrs for their freedom of religion. Jean Meyers, a French expert on this revolution wrote about the Cristeros attending field masses, dressed in sandals and white garments and armed with machetes. They knew that soldiers could attack them with machine guns at any time but they were willing to fight to preserve The Cross from having to be hidden due to the Mexican communists.

It's a war on Christianity. The American Civil Liberties Union has urged the Supreme Court to uphold a federal appeals court ruling that public schools be constitutionally barred from linking patriotism and piety by reciting the phrase "under God" as part of the Pledge of Allegiance.[113]

The founding fathers did not want the exclusion of Christianity from public institutions but to give a priority to a single sect within the faith. In Commentaries on the Constitution of the United States Supreme Court Justice, Joseph Story (appointed by James Madison) explained America's Christian heritage: "Probably at the time of the adoption of the Constitution, and of the First Amendment to it...the general if not the universal sentiment in America was, that Christianity ought to receive encouragement from the state so far as was not incompatible with the private religious rights of conscience and the freedom of religious worship. An attempt to level all religions, and to make it a matter of state policy to hold all in utter indifference, would have created universal disapprobation, if not universal indignation... The real object of the amendment was not to countenance, much less to advance, Mahometanism, or Judaism, or infidelity, by prostrating Christianity; but exclude all rivalry among Christian sects, and to prevent any national ecclesiastical establishment which should give to a hierarchy the exclusive patronage of the national government." (2 Vol. 2:593-595).

✦ Chapter 5 ✦

To Honor or Not to Honor – Thy Father and Thy Mother

W hen an opponent declares, 'I will not come over to your side.' I calmly say, 'Your child belongs to us already...What are you? You will pass on. Your descendants, however, now stand in the new camp. In a short time they will know nothing else but this new community. (Adolf Hitler)

For evil to triumph it must break all Ten Commandments. Tyrannies start at the level when humans are most vulnerable – the youth. This is done in order to change the minds of a single generation, usually the youth, then the rest eventually ends up as regretted or unregretted history, depending of course on the element of confession.

If we can find a method to recognize the faces of evil, perhaps the litmus test is to compare their edicts with the Ten Commandments. If we are to honor father and mother, then evil in the name of 'common good' commands us to dishonor them, even to the point of turning them in for execution.

Robespierre and his gang focused much on the family. The French revolutionaries began to create a pure society that functioned fully under their collectivist ideas without any influence from a church or parents, for these might create problems for Robespierre's plans since these minds needed to absorb a new ideology so as "to get hold of children at the moment when they are receptive to decisive impressions if we are to make them into men worthy of the Republic."[114]

To the French rebels, parents did not have a right to raise their children but "the fatherland alone has the right to raise its children."[115] One of the leading rebels Georges Danton, paralleled Robespierre's statements when he lamented, "My son doesn't belong to me, he belongs to the Republic."[116] Danton also wanted to enforce that children "belong to the Republic before they belong to their parents."[117] One French nonconformist Jean-Baptiste Leclerc proclaimed that the purpose of education is to "rescue the hearts of children from the counter-revolutionary influences of their parents."[118]

With the same mindset as Robespierre, Hitler declared: "When an opponent declares, 'I will not come over to your side.' I calmly say, 'Your child belongs to us already...What are you? You will pass on. Your descendants, however, now stand in the new camp. In a short time they will know nothing else but this new community.'"[119] It was with this ideal on the family that Hitler "sent girls to the BDM [League of German Girls] and 'Aryan' boys to The Hitler Youth...contrary to rhetoric praising the 'strong family,' [they divided up German society] to weaken family bonding and enhance total loyalty to the Führer."[120]

Nazi propaganda promoted rebelliousness toward parents and elders on television commercials and movies. In one film a Nazi teenager aggressively lectures a group of adults: "Hasn't our nation been made to feel inferior enough?" A young lady gets up and smiles at him – while one of the adult men vociferates him: "Outrageous! How dare you, whippersnapper! This is a private meeting. What gives you the right to come here and protest?" To which the Nazi teen calmly responds: "Youth gives me the right!"

Islam carries the same rebellion against parents. A former Muslim terrorist confesses: "We always visualized Abu Obeida, son of Garah, described by the Prophet Mohammed to be the nation's leader, killing his father when the latter refused to join Islam; Mosaab, son of Omair, who never listened to his mother's begging and left her to die because she rejected Islam; Abu Bakr, who told his father he would kill him if he did not join Islam. All these pictures made us crueler toward our families and our friends if they refused our version of Islam [...] it was painful to shout at my mother and father, and to swear at my brothers and sisters, threatening to kill them, but my only motive was to obey Allah and the Prophet."[121]

Yasser Arafat the head of the P.L.O terror organization, echoing Hitler, said in a speech that, "if anyone is growing weary let him stay home and send me his children."

Marxism held the same scorn for the traditional family. Friedrich Engels, Karl Marx's friend and co-author for their famous Communist

Manifesto, wrote in his 1884 book, *The Origin of the Family, Private Property and the State* for "the reintroduction of the whole female sex into the public industries," for the collective care and rearing of children, and for "the full freedom of marriage," meaning easy and unilateral divorce.[122]

Shortly after the Bolsheviks took power in Russia in November 1917, the Council of Peoples Commissars implemented this "no fault" scheme. Writing a few years later for the journal Komunistka, Alexandra Kollontai updated Engel's argument. Notably, she blamed the frailty of the family in the early 20th Century on capitalism: "There was a time when the isolated, firmly-knit family, based on a church wedding, was equally necessary to all its members...But over the last hundred years this customary family structure has been falling apart in all the countries where capitalism is dominant."[123]

More forcefully, she emphasized that traditional marriage and family everywhere were headed toward the historical scrapheap as casualties of social-economic evolution: "There is no escaping the fact: the old type of family has had its day. The family is withering away not because it is being forcibly destroyed by the state, but because the family is ceasing to be a necessity. The state does not need the family, because the domestic economy is no longer profitable...The members of the family do not need the family either, because the task of bringing up the children which was formerly theirs is passing more and more into the hands of the collective."[124]

Some parents, "narrow and petty," failed to see the course of history, and were "only interested in their own offspring." There was no room in Communist society for this "proprietary attitude."

As Kollontai wrote: "The worker-mother must learn not to differentiate between yours and mine; she must remember that there are only our children, the children of Russia's communist workers." Accordingly, children must be raised by "qualified educators" so that "the child can grow up a conscious communist who recognizes the need for solidarity, comradeship, mutual help and loyalty to the collective." She continued: In place of the individual and egoistic family, a great universal family of workers will develop, in which all the workers, men and women, will above all be comrades.[125]

When Woodrow Wilson was president of Princeton University he told an audience, "Our problem is not merely to help the students to adjust themselves to world life…[but] to make them as unlike their fathers as we can."[126]

→ Chapter 6 ←

For God or For Lunatics

Bible believers see tyrannies as rebellions renamed as Revolution, which is usually inspired by educated lunatics they call philosophers and even prophets. Such prophets can declare a rock as God, the universe and state, Fuhrer, whatever, so long as this lord is not the Biblical God – everyone ends up worshiping someone or something.

Some western philosophers such as Georg Wilhelm Friedrich Hegel and Friedrich Nietzsche are considered by the left to be two of the greatest icons and brightest open-minded philosophers, being admired by Carl Jung and Sigmund Freud. Even these were never immune from eastern ideologies.

Take Hegel and Nietzsche who promoted the Islamic Ummah philosophy along with its fanatical Jihad which includes the promise of paradise for Muslim martyrs, even ridding the public of private possession.

Such philosophers seem to compliment everything, so long as it denies the Bible and promotes revolution of any kind. Take Hegel who described Islam as, "the Revolution of the East, which destroyed all particularity and dependence, and perfectly cleared up and purified the soul and disposition; making the abstract One [Allah] the absolute object of attention and devotion, and to the same extent, pure subjective consciousness the Knowledge of this One [Allah] alone the only aim of reality."[127]

Hegel, an occultist philosopher who wished for world unity said Islam was a religion in which "all national and caste distinctions vanish; no particular race, political claim of birth or possession is regarded only man as a believer. To adore the One [Allah], to believe in him, to fast to remove the sense of specialty and consequent separation from the Infinite, arising from corporeal limitation and to give alms that is, to get rid of particular private possession these are the essence of Mahometan injunctions; but the highest merit is to die for the Faith. He who perishes for it in battle, is sure of Paradise."[128]

Hegel's vision was equal to that of Muhammad's Ummah philosophy and Hitler's gleichschaltung. Hegel was a collectivist to the bone and believed that the state has the "supreme right against the individual, whose supreme duty is to be a member of the state."[129]

Even the closest of family members in the Ummah are dispensable. Muslims must give allegiance and pledge Bi-Abi anta wa-ummi – "I would sacrifice for thee my father and my mother."[130] This is no hyperbole. It stems from the inception of Islam. The Islamic Foundation in the UK even offers Muslims the examples of Abu Ubaida Amer bin Al-Jarrah during the Battle of Badr when he killed his own father, an obstacle for Islam's advance. Abu Bakr Siddiq, Muhammad's father-in-law and first Caliph nearly killed his son and Umar ibn Al-Khattab, the second Caliph killed his uncle.[131] This, of course, is in history books today written with much pride for school children and Islamic websites, a command from the representative of Allah on earth, and honor killing of an immediate family member still takes place by his command.

Islam's anti-family ideology is not just seen in Muslim males. In the Muslim women's magazine Al-Khansa it reads: "The blood of our husbands and the body parts of our children are our sacrificial offering."[132] Dead husbands and children become nothing more than sacrifices for Allah.

Just like Muhammad who wanted to suppress individuality and fought to have the whole planet unified under one Ummah, Hegel wanted a one-world society where all people revolved around the state: "In considering freedom, the starting-point must be not individuality, the single self-consciousness, but only the essence of self-consciousness; for whether man knows it or not, this essence is externally realized as a self-subsistent power in which single individuals are only moments. The march of God in the world, that is what the state is."[133] Hegel's books have always been popular amongst the left even till this day.

Worship of the state is also an aspect of Islam. Just like Hegel saw the state as a god, Allah becomes the head of state in Islamic society. On May 27, 1999 Rafsanjani, one of the ruling Mullahs of Iran said: "If the Islamic nature and fundamental pillar of the state and the velayat-e faqih (Shiite version of khalifa) are undermined, nothing would be left around." The same day, Khatami, the so called 'reformist' and president of the Islamic Republic said in the city of Qom: "Society's parting with religion and the clergy is the beginning of our fall." Khatami in July 5, 1998 said: "velayat-e faqih is the axis and pillar of the state," and, "velayat-e faqih is the raison d'être of our state. As such, opposing it...is to oppose the fundamentals and pillar of the state...No state would tolerate assaults on its principles and pillars," he said.[134]

One Islamic site explains: "In Western democracy, the people are sovereign; in Islam sovereignty is vested in Allah and the people are His caliphs or representatives. The laws given by Allah through His Prophet (Sharî'ah) are to be regarded as constitutional principles that should not be violated..."[135]

Another Islamic site explains: "The highest organization in society is the state. Islam has given to the world the practical form and ideals of statehood. Therefore, the question of how religion should inspire, inform and discipline life is naturally related to the question of how it should be related to the highest organization of society (i.e. the state)."[136] Sayyed Qutb, the father of the Muslim Brotherhood of Egypt and the inspiration to Osama Bin Laden and Islamists worldwide, echoed Hegel when he wrote in his book *Millestones*, "that true social justice can come to a society only after all affairs have been submitted to the laws of God..."[137]

Hypocritically, while the left accuses Bible believers of transforming America into a theocracy, actually accuse such believers of doing what their great thinkers and Islamist fans seek. Progressives want the state to become the spiritual basis of everyone's lives, introducing philosophies, secular holidays, an evolutionist agenda, Islamic holidays, and an assortment of earth glorification to include initiatives such as Earth Day. This only serves to chip away at America's Christian heritage through historic revisionism making the founding fathers progressives who would support gay marriage, abortion, removing the Ten Commandments out of court rooms and prayer out of schools.

Richard Dawkins claims in his book *The God Delusion* that, "the genie of religious fanaticism is rampant in present-day America, and the founding fathers would have been horrified...the founders most certainly were secularists who believed in keeping religion out of politics, and that is enough to place them firmly on the side of those who object, for example, to ostentatious displays of the Ten Commandments in government-owned public places." (p. 41-42)

Why is it that the ACLU wants to get rid of "under God" in our Pledge of Allegiance and wants to prohibit Nativity scenes in public but at the same time wanted to end the Bush administration's domestic spying program, claiming eavesdropping on potential terrorists is illegal and unconstitutional?

The ACLU names as plaintiffs, New York University scholar Barnett Rubin,[138] atheist writer Christopher Hitchens, Tara McKelvey, an editor at The American Prospect, the National Association of Criminal Defense Lawyers, Greenpeace and the Council on American-Islamic relations.[139] And while they claim to be fighters for the Constitution, stating in their lawsuit: "By seriously compromising the free speech and privacy rights of the plaintiffs and others, the program violates the First and Fourth Amendments of the United States Constitution." In reality, they want to change it into something the founders never wanted – a document used only for the purpose of stopping Christian freedom and letting philosophies and pagan faiths such as evolution, Islam, earth worship and others to have freedoms and to overstep their boundaries.

Bible believers accuse leftists of fighting to give potential terrorists constitutional rights. They see them as majoring on the minors and minoring on the majors. To the left, closing down Guantanamo or helping some terrorists made to believe they are drowning is more important than America's national security.

Idolatry is committed, not merely by setting up false gods, but also by setting up false devils. This can be done by making men afraid of tobacco or global warming when they should be afraid of declaring themselves as God.[140]

→ Chapter 7 ←

For One Nation Under God or *For The World Under Tyranny*

L eftism is no new phenomenon. The chameleons of Shinar have rapidly extrudable tongues with a synonymous ability to change color. The original fascists were really on the left and liberals from Woodrow Wilson to Franklin Roosevelt to Hillary Clinton have advocated policies and principles remarkably similar to those of Hitler's National Socialism and Mussolini's Fascism.[141]

Several parallels can be extracted. Take the 28th U.S. president Woodrow Wilson. He believed that the state was the natural, organic, and spiritual expression of the people themselves. From the outset he believed that the government and people should have an organic bond that reflected the "true spirit" of the people, or what the Germans called the Volksgeist,[142] and what the Muslims call the Ummah.

Woodrow Wilson viewed the community as a living organism:

"Government is not a machine, but a living thing," wrote Wilson in his Congressional Government. "It falls not under the [Newtonian] theory of the universe, but under the [Darwinian] theory of organic life."[143] Wilson summed it up when he said that this "living Constitution" "must be Darwinian in structure and in practice. Society is a living organism and must obey the laws of Life...it must develop." Hence "all that progressives ask or desire is permission – in an era when 'development,' 'evolution,' is the scientific word – to interpret the Constitution according to the Darwinian principle."[144]

Wilson wanted to destroy individual rights, giving full power to the state. He mocked the 4th of July and our founders' Declaration of Independence stating that "a lot of nonsense has been talked about the inalienable rights of the individual and a great deal that was mere vague sentiment and pleasing speculation has been put forward as fundamental principle."[145] Wilson envisioned a utopia formed like a human body with each organ and cell working together as one for the common cause. Society "is accountable to Darwin, not to

Newton. It is modified by its environment, necessitated by its tasks, shaped to its functions by the sheer pressure of life. No living thing can have its organs offset against each other as checks, and live. On the contrary, its life is dependent upon their quick cooperation, their ready response to the commands of instinct or intelligence, their amicable community of purpose. Government is not a body of blind forces; it is a body of men, with highly differentiated functions, no doubt, in our modern day of specialization, but with a common task and purpose. Their cooperation is indispensable, their warfare fatal. There can be no successful government without leadership or without the intimate, almost instinctive, coordination of the organs of life and action… This is not theory, but fact, and displays its force as fact, whatever theories may be thrown across its track. Living political constitutions must be Darwinian in structure and in practice."[146]

Bible believers see Darwinism as having an ideological goal – to believe that God did not create us – that random processes formed man. This destroys the idea of absolute morality. Since we are mere products of nature and not God then we are no different than the maggots in the carcass. Morality thus becomes relative and not absolute. They see progressives steadily moving away from a Constitution based on law, toward a Constitution based on relativism[147] or a "living Constitution." This philosophy was pegged as *positivism*. Its basic tenants declared that since man evolved, his laws must evolve as well.

Under positivism, judges were to guide both the evolution of law and the Constitution. Consequently, the views of the Founding Fathers were disregarded as hampering the evolution of society. Every philosophy of law had to be the latest and greatest or else it was discarded.

An early subscriber to positivism was Oliver Wendell Holmes, Jr. who was appointed to the Supreme Court in 1902. During his three decades on the Court he argued extensively that decisions should be based upon the "felt necessities of the time" and "prevalent moral and political theories" instead of natural law and its absolute standards. Holmes claimed that, "The justification of a law for us cannot be found in the fact that our fathers always have followed it. It must be found in some help which the law brings toward reaching a social end."[148] Social evolution, relativistic thinking, and the new "positivistic" view of law were not only making serious inroads among Supreme Court justices, but in academia as well. John Dewey, signer of the 1933 *Humanist Manifesto I*, wrote in 1927: "The belief in political fixity, of the sanctity of some form of state consecrated by the efforts of our fathers and hallowed by tradition, is one of the stumbling-blocks in the way of orderly and directed change."[149]

Benjamin Cardozo, appointed to the Supreme Court in 1932, claimed, "If there is any law which is back of the sovereignty of the state, and superior thereto, it is not law in such a sense as to concern the judge or lawyer, however much it concerns the statesman or the moralist."

Charles Evans Hughes, the Supreme Court's Chief Justice from 1930 to 1941, held a similar view: "We are under a Constitution, but the Constitution is what the judges say it is."[150]

Conservatives see positivism as running amuck of the Constitution since the decisive words of the Constitution and the Declaration of Independence are now read not based on what the Founders' envisioned for America but what progressive activists interpreted.

Leftist revisionism of the Founding Fathers is out in the open with the likes of Justice Oliver Wendell Holmes who argued that the Constitution "must be considered in the light of our whole experience and not merely in that of what was said a hundred years ago."[151]

Conservatives argue that the Founding Fathers did not write the things they wrote with a base of inexperience but from centuries of *experience*. In no way would the Constitution support a *Gleichschaltung*; we are separate individuals and not a collective single body where dissidents are pointed out and dealt with.

Imagine if American students today are given a quiz titled, 'Who Taught This?': that the "true leader" uses the masses like "tools." that the masses "must get their ideas very absolutely put, and are much readier to receive a half truth which they can promptly understand than a whole truth which has too many sides to be seen all at once...Men are as clay in the hands of the consummate leader."[152] Who taught this? A – Muhammad B – Woodrow Wilson or C – Hitler?

It would be shocking that while C or even A would probably be the common choice, B is the correct answer. The exact quote came from Woodrow Wilson in his 1890 essay, *Leaders of Men*. Yet political correctness today would eliminate 'A' being a choice, lest the instructor get accused of having Islamophobia.

There are common denominators that tyrannies use; Wilson envisioned a leader for his utopia that parallels Muhammad and Hitler in which all people would accomplish every one of his commands. It would not be an exaggeration to state that the progressive elites and their wish for world unity is inline with the Islamic view of Umma and in fact complemented it – literally.

Many leftist philosophers saw Islamic civilization and its ideology as a model for the world. Take Friedrich Nietzsche's *The Antichrist* where he writes: "If Islam despises Christianity, it has a thousand-fold right to do so: Islam at least assumes that it is dealing with men…Christianity destroyed for us the whole harvest of ancient civilization, and later it also destroyed for us the whole harvest of Mohammedan civilization."[153]

Another progressive elite, H.G. Wells, a utopist who envisioned a collectivist world, considered Muhammad to be one of the "first Utopists" and a visionary who "instead of embodying the dense prejudices of Arab ignorance, opened his eyes upon an intellectual horizon already nearly as wide as the world."[154] Wells accepted Darwin's goal in that it "destroyed the dogma of the Fall upon which the whole intellectual fabric of Christianity rests. For without a Fall there is no redemption, and the whole theory and meaning of the Pauline system is vain."[155] Wells' revulsion for the Bible's story of mankind's fall complements the Qur'ân in which man's fall is absent. Allah rejects God's atonement and accepts the *shaheed's*. Wells abhorred Christianity and treasured Islam – they both shared similar worldviews.

Islam is an ideology for radical change in the likes of George Bernard Shaw who declared in his *Maxims For Revolutionists* that property "is theft."[156] Shaw was a strong proponent of eugenics and envisioned a one-world utopia under eugenic laws writing that there was "no reasonable excuse for refusing to face the fact that nothing but a eugenic religion can save our civilization"[157]

Even the legendary singer John Lennon and his wife Yoko Ono described their "Nutopia" – similar to that of Muhammad and Hegel – where "Citizenship of the country can be obtained by declaration of your awareness of Nutopia. Nutopia has no land, no boundaries and no passports, only people. Nutopia has no laws other than cosmic. All people of Nutopia are ambassadors of the country."[158]

The hippie movement of Lennon's time wasn't much different from many of the cults formed in Germany in the 19th century such as the "Kosmische Runde" or "Cosmic Circle" which was heavily influenced by the poems of self-proclaimed messiah Stefan George who believed that he "was sent by the mahatmas [Hindu priests]"[159] and whose poetry emphasized self-sacrifice and power. The Cosmic Circle envisioned a volkisch state – similar to Muhammad's utopia in which enthusiastic followers would submit themselves wholly, and without question, to the unconquerable will of a charismatic leader, one who was believed to be in possession of mysterious, even quasi-divine, powers. A few of its main tenets were equal to that of National Socialism: fuehrer worship, vague economic socialism, and the supernatural and unconscious force of the Volk collectivity.[160] It was not the church that influenced the Nazi youth but poetic lunatics, the same type of occultists that influenced much of the hippie youth in the 1960s in which they wished to usher in the Age of Aquarius where a "Universal Friendship will be ushered in, and all of humanity will be able to unite in one Brotherhood."[161]

While the hippies were enjoying their revolution, the Iranian revolutionaries were reinstating the Islamic constitution: "[to] prepare the way towards a united single world community…and to the continuation of the progressive struggle for the rescue of deprived and oppressed nations throughout the world."[162]

Iran is no anomaly; the entire Muslim world has inner struggles striving for a world under Islam. The fascist and cultic Islamic intellect, Adnan Oktar, has been pushing for a "Turkish Islamic-Union" which will have Muslims "unite at once" and "coalesce around a single leader." "If Muslims are united, if there is one leader at the head of this union, this disorder and corruption can easily come to an end. In that event, if any harm befalls a hair on the head of Muslims anywhere in the world the matter will be stopped at once, because all Muslims will act together."[163]

The Turkish-Islamic Union is not calling to unite only the Islamic world but the entire earth under Islam. All of those who join the union "will attain enlightenment."[164] This Mahdi messianic figure is an aspiration of Muslims, both Sunni and Shi'a.

President Mahmoud Ahmadinejad came to New York City and prayed before the United Nations General Assembly in September of 2005 about the coming emergence of the Mahdi: "O mighty Lord, I pray to you to hasten the emergence of your last repository, the promised one, that perfect and pure human being, the one that will fill this world with justice and peace." The Mahdi is referred to as: "the perfect human being who is heir to all prophets and pious men." The Mahdi is heir to all prophets? According to Islam, Muhammad is the final prophet and the perfect man. What Ahmadinejad was saying is that the Mahdi of Islam is essentially the reincarnation of Muhammad. According to Islamic prophecy, the Mahdi is the first of the major signs heralding the "Last-Days." This is confirmed by Ibn Katheer, the renowned Muslim scholar from the eighth century who stated that, "After the lesser signs of the Hour appear and increase, mankind will have reached a stage of great suffering. Then the awaited Mahdi will appear; He is the first of the greater clear, signs of the Hour."[165]

In 1976, the Muslim World League (Rabitah al-'Alam Al-Islami) issued a fatwa which declared that belief in a coming Mahdi is universal for all Muslims: "The Memorizers and scholars of Hadith have verified that there are reliable and acceptable reports among the Hadiths on the Mahdi; the majority of them are narrated through numerous authorities. There is no doubt that their status is unbroken and the reports sound. And the belief in the appearance of the Mahdi is obligatory…none denies it except those who are ignorant of the Sunnah and innovators in doctrine."[166]

While tradition varies between Sunni and Shi'a regarding Mahdi's appearance onto the world stage, the core belief in his coming is not a sectarian issue. It is accepted by the majority of Muslims worldwide. Even in the United States, prominent and so-called "moderate" Muslim leader Sheikh Muhammad Hisham Kabbani, chairman of the Islamic Supreme Council of America has stated that, "The coming of the Mahdi is an established doctrine for both Sunni and Shi'a Muslims, and indeed for all humanity."[167]

According to Islamic tradition, the Mahdi doesn't merely emerge as some vague great religious leader; he will return to reinstate the office of the Caliphate. Islam directs its followers: "If you see him, go and give him your allegiance, even if you have to crawl over ice, because he is the Vice-regent (Khalifa) of Allah, the Mahdi."[168] "For he will pave the way for, and establish the government of, the family [or community] of Mohammed…Every believer will be obligated to support him."[169]

The thirst for a leader to unite the world is quite strong in the present-day Islamic world as it was in Germany before the Third Reich. By and large, the Germans wanted order, believed in obedience, and longed for one man, a leader, a Fuehrer, who would lead the nation out of misery and above the world. Just as the cultist Oktar today is seeking a leader and even calls himself "the Hodja" (Muslim Messiah) to lead the Muslim world, the cultist poet, Stephan Georg, who declared himself to be the messiah for a new kingdom ruled by intellectual elites, wrote a poem in 1907 expressing the national longing for a Fuehrer which would lead Germany by "The Deed…Perhaps he who sat for years among you murderers slept in your cells: will rise up and do the deed."[170]

→ Chapter 8 ←

They Love Tyrants

W*hen looking into the essence of leftism, we see a group that calls its opponents bigots and racists; it says we are xenophobic, homophobic, Islamophobic, etc. They say we started the slave trade, massacred Native Americans, and hate the poor. Using quintessential projection techniques, the left almost entirely and completely accuses its opposition of its own sins.*

Perhaps a quiz can help explain, a game of who said that society needs to rid itself from: "invalids, its idiots and madmen, its drunkards and men of vicious mind, its cruel and furtive souls, its stupid people, too stupid to be of use to the community, its lumpish, unteachable, and unimaginative people".[171]

Who said this? A – Michael Savage, B – Jerry Falwell or C – H.G Wells? The results might be surprising.

The answer is famous progressive socialist, novelist, journalist, sociologist, and historian, H.G. Wells, a champion for socialism, birth control, the "little guy" and eugenics. He also hated Christianity, predicting, "Protestant Christianity would slowly decay, and many of those who abandoned Protestantism would turn to pseudoscientific cults, such as spiritualism, Eastern religions, witchcraft and devil worship."[172]

Christians argue that Christianity is what pleaded to save the 'little guy', for Jesus saved the prostitute and condemned the Pharisee. *Who, then, is truly religious? Is it the humble Christian or is it the Liberal Pharisee who wants nothing but the elimination of the weak?*

If the elimination of all religion should begin with Christianity why should we then turn to the cults? These too are religions followed by leftists. Wells wrote books describing his vision of a world utopia where big government controls every action. Like Rousseau, Hitler, and Muhammad, Wells wanted a world where those who do not fit in the community be killed. Wells' utopia had to rid itself of "persons with transmittable diseases, with mental disorders, with bodily deformations, the criminally insane, even the incurable alcoholic! All are to be put to death humanely – by first giving them opiates to spare them needless suffering!"[173] By "eliminating them; there is no escape from that, and conversely, the people of exceptional quality must be ascendant. The better sort of people, so far as they can be distinguished, must have the fullest freedom of public service, the fullest opportunity of parentage."[174]

Conservatives question if progressives have gone extreme, fighting for the underdog or the super dog? Or perhaps even the rabid dog? Hitler was a rabid leftist who believed in the *Übermensch*, where the world should be populated by only the supermen. Wells echoes the same evil repackaged under a different terminology. The end results are always the same – tyranny simply repackaged.

The purpose of Wells' book *The Shape of Things to Come* was to make English more lucid, more comprehensive and better able to function effectively as a "truly universal language."[175] It was an attempt to mirror the one world/one language of Shinar and all the daughters of Babylon wanting to unify the world under man's rule.

This echoes greatly all the other Shinarian Empires – Islam wanting Arabic and Hitler wanting German to become universal languages. Wells' world-utopia also contained a centralized think-tank and education system for the world: "As the individual brain quickens and becomes more skillful, there also appears a collective Brain, the Encyclopedia – the Fundamental Knowledge System which accumulates, sorts, keeps in order and renders available everything that is known. The Encyclopedia Organization, which centers on Barcelona, with its seventeen million active workers, is the Memory of Mankind. Its tentacles spread out in one direction to millions of investigators, checkers and correspondents, and in the others to keep the education a process in living touch with mental advance"[176]

Wells saw his new central encyclopedic organization "informing, suggesting, directing unifying" reaching into "every corner of the world".[177] It would "hold men's minds together in something like a common interpretation of reality."[178] Like Muhammad's Ummah –

which is "like one man: if his eye suffers, his whole body suffers" – and Hitler's Volk – Wells' utopia would be a world organ whose function would be to "pull the mind of the world together."[179] Wells observed that "a common ideology based on this Permanent World encyclopedia is a possible means, to some it seems the only means, of dissolving human conflict into unity."[180]

When progressive Franklin D. Roosevelt became President of the United States in March 1933, he expressly adopted a variety of measures to see which ones would work. He included several whose proponents felt their individual measures would be inconsistent with the measures of others. One of these programs was the National Recovery Administration (NRA), a scheme that saddled the American people with the worst era of monopolies they have ever experienced.

However monopoly is defined, its objective is to fix prices, to limit production or to stifle competition. Some critics of the NRA's codes and industry organizations saw a resemblance to an economic institution under Mussolini's corporatism.[181]

Journalist John T. Flynn, a former socialist, in his 1944 book *As We Go Marching*, surveyed the interwar policies of Fascist Italy and Nazi Germany, and pointed to what he called uncomfortably similar American policies. Flynn saw links between 'generic' fascism and a large number of policies of the United States. He said that "the New Dealers...began to flirt with the alluring pastime of reconstructing the capitalist system ... and in the process of this new career they began to fashion doctrines that turned out to be the principles of fascism."

William P. Hoar In his book *Architects of Conspiracy* wrote: "The economics of Fascist Italy were soon being imported into this country by President Franklin D. Roosevelt who's C.C.C., W.P.A., PWA and other Depression-era schemes proved so damaging."[182]

Roosevelt's National Recovery Act (NRA) attempted to cartelize the American economy just as Mussolini had cartelized Italy's. Under the NRA Roosevelt established industry-wide boards with the power to set and enforce prices, wages, and other terms of employment, production, and distribution for all companies in an industry. Through the Agricultural Adjustment Act the government exercised similar control over farmers. Interestingly, Mussolini viewed Roosevelt's New Deal as "boldly...interventionist in the field of economics."[183]

SECTION TWO

*T*YRANNIES ARE PSYCHOTIC

➤ Chapter 9 ◄

For God or For Psychopathic Vampires

Muhammad and his minions also conducted themselves in the voodoo-like act of blood drinking in which "Malik ibn Sinan drank his [Muhammad's] blood on the Day of Uhud and licked it up. The Prophet allowed him to do that and then said, 'The [Hell] fire will not touch you.'" and "Abdullah ibn az Zubayr drank his cupped blood. The Prophet said, 'Woe to you from the people and woe to the people from you.' But he did not object to what he had done."[1] Abu Saad Khodri who stated in a strong Hadith in *Sharh Hayat al-Sahaba*, regarding partaking in the blood of Muhammad: "When, at the battle of Uhud, the helmet-rings had been taken out of the Prophet's cheek, blood flowed from the radiant face of that Lord of the pure, and my father Malik Ibn Sinan sucked the wounds with his mouth, swallowing the blood. When they said to my father, 'Malik, is blood to be drunk?' my father replied, 'Yes, the blood of the Prophet of God I drink like a beverage.' At that time his Excellency, the Prophet, said, 'Whoever wishes to see one who has mixed my blood with his own, let him look at Malik Ibn Sinan: any one whose blood touches mine, him the fire of hell shall not desire.'"

Bizarre and psychotic narrations like this are too many to quote. They speak of drinking Muhammad's urine and eating his excrement. Christians would ask, "Would such abominations be chosen over the precious blood of the sinless Lamb of God?" No Bible believer drinks literal blood.

On top of drinking Muhammad's blood as a redemptive act they would also drink his urine. One woman consumed some of Muhammad's urine and he told her, "You will never complain of a stomach ache." He did not order any of them to wash their mouths out nor did he forbid them to do it again.[2]

This is no ancient practice. Today our youth are introduced to heavy metal music. Richard Valdemar, a former Los Angeles sheriff who has extensive experience with criminal gangs and the occult, wrote that many "Stoners" (later to evolve as MS-13) would ingest "blood and urine in occult ceremonies" and that one of these true metal music believers was Richard Ramirez, one of America's most notorious serial killers.[3]

Many gangs were influenced by the likes of Aleister Crowley, H.P. Lovecraft and Anton LaVey. These occult gangs also rejected the classic "oldies but goodies" in favor of AC/DC, Led Zeppelin, Black Sabbath, Ozzy Osborne, and Motley Crew. While on duty Valdemar and his OSS team conducted an investigation into the vandalization of a large Catholic cemetary. Valdemar and his team found that these gangs "played with several caskets and decomposed bodies and attempted to break into the tabernacle of the chapel altar. They also desecrated several religious statues. We soon discovered that the Home of Peace Jewish Cemetery across the street had also been vandalized. The Jewish flag and a mummified left hand of a male corpse had been stolen."[4]

While we are told that French Muslim riots resulted from social and class issues. In 2008, Muslim vandals in France desecrated 148 graves in the Muslim section of a military cemetery in northern France, hanging a pig's head on one of the headstones.[5]

What do such practices have to do with any social justice? In 2009, Muslims desecrated about 70 graves in two Palestinian Christian cemeteries. Gravestones had been smashed; metal and stone crosses were knocked off graves.[6]

While Muslims claim to believe in Biblical patriarchs, Palestinian Muslims desecrated the tombs of the Biblical Joshua, his father Nun, and Caleb ben Yefuneh in Israel. The gravesites, which Jewish pilgrims have visited for centuries, were reportedly smeared with animal and human feces and covered with garbage. The vandals also painted Nazi symbols and anti-Semitic slogans on the holy sites.[7]

During Nazi Germany, Nazis smeared excrement on church altars and church doors, desecrated shrines, and threw statues of saints into dung piles; when synagogues were not available to attack and loot, churches were targeted with Nazis yelling: "Down with Christians and Jews!"[8]

In Switzerland, Muslim teenagers soiled the altar with excrement and desecrated a church. They urinated into the baptism font, destroyed glassware on the donation table and destroyed vegetation.[9]

In Norway, the notorious black metal band, *Burzum*, was involved in many arsonist attacks on ancient Norwegian churches. The founder of this musical project was Varg Vikernes, a follower of Norse religion and a reactionary for Norway's pre-Christian past. Varg was found guilty of setting fire to three churches in the early 1990s.[10] When explaining his motivations for his terrorism he said, "They [the Christians] desecrated our graves, our burial mounds, so it's revenge."[11] He wrote that "for each devastated graveyard, one heathen grave is avenged, for each ten churches burnt to ashes, one heathen hof is avenged, for each ten priests or freemasons assassinated, one heathen is avenged."[12]

When asked about Islam in one interview, Varg responded that "Islam is an adversary to the Christian religions...we should join forces with them and fight Judaism and Christianity together with them. Besides, Islam is much closer to our philosophy of life than what Christianity is, after all they hail those who die in battle, they have a sense of honour and of course their view on women is far better than the Christian one. It is better with 'Allah hu akbar' in the morning seven days a week, than with church bells every Sunday."[13]

Worshiping Odin is really no different than worshiping Allah. They both lead to the hatred of Christianity and terrorism against the Cross. During the Viking Age (789-1085 A.D), the Norse pagans were nothing more than terrorists spreading their reign of horror across Christian Europe – attacking the monasteries, churches, the fortresses of Irish Lords, and farms.[14] The Vikings were no different than the Muslims who are terrorizing the world today. The Vikings pillaged through Christian Europe – kidnapping men, women, and children only to sell them as slaves to their Muslim neighbors in the east.

Just as the Muslims believe that the way to paradise is to die while fighting in battle, the Vikings fought in battle with viciousness, not fearing death for death would bring them to the Norse paradise – Valhalla – or the "Hall of the Slain."Valhalla, like the Islamic heaven, is filled with all kinds of debaucheries – orgies and endless alcohol. The Norse mythology is a faith that has much love from many leftists who usually pity the faith because Christianity replaced it.

Bible believers view Leftism and paganism as intertwined, hence its symphony with the devil; when it comes to Islam they consider it a moral equal. As the Qur'ân encourages its adherents to seek refuge in Allah from the evil of the retreating whisperer (jinn),[15] the Norse religion believes in elves that sit upon the dreamer's chest and whisper the bad dreams into the sleeper's ears.[16] Allah is the lord of jinn (demons). "I [Allah] have only created Jinns [demons] and men, that they may serve Me." (Qur'ân 51:56)

How can unholy demons serve a 'holy' Allah?

Like the Vikings, Joseph Smith also saw "a pillar of light" over his head; the light was "above the brightness of the sun."[17] Jinn as well are described as bright fire: "And the jinn, We created aforetime of essential fire." (Qur'ân 15:27) "And He created Jinns from fire free of smoke" (Qur'ân 55:15).

Paganism and spiritism are in reality a single entity that stems from Shinar – all lead to the rejection of the Bible.

→ Chapter 10 ←

Psychopaths Desecrate God's Image

Cannibalism is a common ritual within many pagan societies. The Aztecs are best known for their gruesome human sacrifices to various nourish gods such as Huitzilopoctli (The god of War) and Tlaloc (The god of Rain and Drought). Many of these regular sacrifices led to cannibalism of the captor's Calpulli members. Sacrifice and cannibalism seem to go hand in hand when it comes to Aztec society.[18]

The ancient Mexicans committed some of their most gruesome rituals in the Pyramid of the Moon, which was built about 2,000 years ago. Within the pyramid a newfound burial vault contained the remains of 12 people, all apparently sacrificed. Ten of them were decapitated. The victims had had their hands bound behind their backs. The decapitated bodies appear to have been tossed, rather than arranged, on one side of the burial.

Saburo Sugiyama, a professor at Aichi Prefectural University in Japan and at Arizona State University said that, "this foundation ritual must have been one of the most terrifying acts recorded archaeologically in Mesoamerica."[19]

Such acts of savagery are not only contained in the annals of ancient history. In Ramallah, two Israeli soldiers were kidnapped by Palestinian Muslims; they were subsequently tortured and beaten to death in the Palestinian Authority police station. Their lifeless bodies were thrown out of the station's second story window to a throng of men howling, "Allahu-Akbar" – god is great! They commenced to dismember and disembowel the soldiers' corpses, passing the entrails on a platter to a hysterical mob numbering in the thousands who rejoiced as they literally chewed and swallowed the remains of their hated Jews.[20]

One cannot enter the world of Islam without being accustomed to Nasheed, a rhythmic poetry that is sung without musical instruments which are totally prohibited in Islam. You would never hear musical instruments played in a mosque. Muhammad proclaimed musicians to be of the people dwelling in hell. Nasheed is much different than anything the Judeo-Christian world is accustomed to. To give a taste, perhaps I can share a part from a jihadist favorite titled *swarem* (sword):

We are those who built our forts
Out of the skulls
Which we brought from the land of the tyrant
By force and on top of the booty
Our Messenger is the one who made us
Noble builders of glory
Our Messenger is the sun of truth
Who lit the face of the world.

Does that sound like anything that is the norm in Church?

Building forts out of skulls is not a metaphor or hyperbole. Muslims literally built mounds (forts) out of human skulls. A wake-up call would be to study the *Memoirs of Baburnama* of the Mughal Empire. Tens of millions were killed during Islam's invasions of India and decapitated heads were piled as trophies.[21] During the late fifteenth century Babur, the founder of the Mughal Empire, who is revered as a paragon of Muslim tolerance by modern revisionist historians recorded several events in which infidel non-Muslims "were brought in alive [having surrendered] and ordered beheaded, after which a tower of skulls was erected in the camp."[22] It is in memory of such events that the jihadi nasheed song is sung today by jihadists worldwide.

While Islam's adventures in India are rarely discussed today, it is estimated that the number of those slain in the name of Islam is in the millions there. Dr. Younis Shaikh, in a *Study on Islam and Women* notes that millions of women were raped. Sexual violence occurred on a gory and unimaginable scale; it was standard practice for Islamic warlords like Ghori and Ghazni to unleash the mass rape and enslavement of hundreds of thousands of women after the slaughter of all males. The destruction of the Indian civilization began when Mohammad Bin Qasim conquered the Sindh kingdom in 712 CE. It took his Islamic army three days to slaughter the inhabitants of Debal, whose women and children were taken into slavery. When he tried to establish a just rule of law which enraged the very Islamic and murderous Governor Hajjaj bin Yousef, Qasim reverted to massacring between 6000 – 16,000 in Brahiminabad, selling the women and children in the Arab slave markets. During the 11th century Sultan Mahmud Ghaznavi utterly ruined India after invading it over 17 times, sending Hindu men and women to Islamic Afghani slave markets. Later, the new military instruments of the Muslim Turks and the Moguls followed. Delhi was decimated, its capture was assured and the whole of India became a slave camp as a result.

Since the advent of Saudi oil, petrodollars started to support the Islamic extremist movements worldwide, creating a thousand of its Islamic centers in the USA alone, brainwashing patrons with political propaganda. In Algeria, Thousands were raped and killed in 1993 alone. Over 80% of Egyptians practice Female Genital Mutilation and in Sudan during 1992 a religious decree (fatwa) was issued, giving justification to the military onslaught against the non-Muslims. Islamic barbarism and genocide continues in Darfur to this day. The Indonesian Islamic army mass murdered 200,000 East Timurian non-Muslims before East Timur got its independence. Pakistan's army invaded her province of East Pakistan in 1971, killing hundreds of thousands of Bengali Muslims and non-Muslims. Half a million women were raped in an attempt to create a half-breed loyal to Islam. Pakistan created the Taliban in Afghanistan.

No one should forget 1842 when the Afghani Muslims overtook the British garrison in Kabul and beheaded over 2,000 men, women, and children. The heads were placed on sticks around the city as decorations.[23] The practice continued during the 1980s, in Afghanistan, where an estimated 3,000 Soviet troops were beheaded by the Afghani Mujahideen, also common throughout the Iranian revolution: "In 1992, the mullahs sent a 'specialist' to cut off the head of Shapour Bakhtiar, the Shah's last prime minister, in a suburb of Paris. When the news broke, Hashemi Rafsanjani, then president of the Islamic Republic, and the example given by many Westerners as 'a moderate

Muslim,' publicly thanked Allah for having allowed 'the severing of the head of the snake.'"[24]

One Algerian "specialist" nicknamed *Momo lenain* (Muhammad the midget) was recruited by an Islamic group known as the GIA specifically for the purpose of chopping off heads: "In 1996 in Ben-Talha, a suburb of the capital Algiers, Momo cut off a record 86 heads in one night, including the heads of more than a dozen children. In recognition of his exemplary act of piety, the GIA sent him [on a free trip] to Mecca for pilgrimage. Last time we checked, Momo was still at large somewhere in Algeria."[25] In Pakistan, "Rival Sunni and Shi'ite groups have made a habit of sending chopped off heads of each other's activists by special delivery. According to one estimate, over 400 heads have been chopped off and mailed since 1990."[26] Beyond all of these very incriminating examples there are also the government-sanctioned beheadings that take place weekly in Saudi Arabia after Friday prayers just outside the mosques. Over the past two decades, the Saudis have decapitated at least 1,100 people for alleged crimes ranging from drug running to witchcraft and apostasy. In 2003: "The Saudi government beheaded 52 men and one woman …A condemned convict is brought into the courtyard; hands tied, and forced to bow before an executioner, who swings a huge sword amid cries from onlookers of 'Allahu Akbar!' Arabic for 'god is greater.'" [27]

What takes place during one of these beheadings is simply one of the most macabre things that you can imagine. With a very deliberate sawing and hacking motion, the head is severed. The "infidel" is heard screaming and gurgling until the knife passes through the throat in the exact same manner as a ritual animal sacrifice. In Islam, animal sacrifice is usually referred to as "Udhiyah or Dhabh." On Eid al-Adha (Day of Sacrifice), a Muslim holiday held during the Hajj (pilgrimage), an animal is often sacrificed. Before the animal is slaughtered, the knife wielder says Bismallah (In the Name of Allah) while others chant Yah Allah (Oh Allah)! Like the sacrificial goat or calf, the human sacrifice is often seen sitting bound before his captors, shivering with fear. It is not unlike any other such sacrificial ritual that may have occurred in various Middle Eastern pagan cults over four thousand years ago.

Among all of the world religions, only Islam has adherents that still practice overt human sacrifice. With regard to the recent spate of ritualized beheadings that have been broadcast by Islamic fundamentalist groups – the language, the manners, and the rituals are identical to Islamic traditional animal slaughter. Their cries of "Allahu Akbar" while performing such despicable acts only serve to bolster the arguments of those who make them.

So, who is this Allah and what does "Allahu Akbar" (Allah is greater) mean? Who is he greater than? What was so great about screaming this phrase while beheading Nicholas Berg, the Jewish-American contractor, Daniel Pearl (another Jew), and Kim-Sun-il, the Korean translator and evangelical Christian? All three of these men loved Muslims and even attempted to help them.

All of Muhammad's disciples beheaded in the name of their religion and hundreds of examples can be sited – Hadith, Muslim poetry (both ancient and modern), Muslim history, current events, and even graffiti that says, "We knock on the gates of heaven with the skulls of Jews," written on walls throughout Sharî'ah dominated cultures.

The favorite of Muslims, Khalid bin al-Walid, who earned the title, "The Unsheathed Sword of Allah" and fought under Muhammad's leadership as well as that of the first Caliph, Abu-Bakr, was dispatched to extend Islam's peace proposal to the people of Persia: "In the name of Allah, the Compassionate, the Merciful. From Khalid bin al-Walid to the governors of Persia. Embrace Islam so that you may be safe. If not, make a covenant with me and pay the Jizyah tax. Otherwise, I have brought you a people who love death just as you love drinking wine."[28]

When the Christians and Persians from Ullays turned down this peace offer, Khalid engaged them with an unfettered assault. The battle was so fierce that Khalid made a vow to Allah during the battle that if he defeated these resistors, he would make the canal that surrounded their village literally run with their blood. When the outcome was in Khalid's favor, it actually took a day and a half to behead all of the captives. The obstacle for Khalid was that the ravine of blood coagulated and Khalid's troops were eventually forced to eventually release water into the canal so that it would run red with the blood of the slain lest Khalid's vow be left unfulfilled.[29] Some of Khalid's men wanted to meticulously fulfill his wishes: "Even if you were to kill all the population of the earth, their blood would still not run... Therefore send water over it, so that you may fulfill your oath." Khalid had blocked the water from the canal. Now Khalid brought the water back, so that it flowed with spilled blood. Owing to this it has been called Blood Canal to this day."[30]

Even the prophet's grandchildren did not escape the blade. In an article that appeared in the New York Post on May 14, 2004 titled, *Chopping Heads*, Iranian-born journalist Amir Taheri outlines several other instances throughout Islam's history relative to the practice of beheading: "In 680, the Prophet's favorite grandson, Hussein bin Ali, had his head chopped off in Karbala, central Iraq, by the soldiers of the Caliph Yazid. The severed head was put on a silver platter and sent to Damascus, Yazid's capital, before being sent to Cairo for inspection by the Governor of Egypt. The Caliph's soldiers also cut off the heads of all of Hussein's 71 male companions, including the one-year-old baby boy Ali-Asghar."

Muslim historians and biographers were revisionists and portrayed Muslim tyrants as messiahs; Al-Dhaher Baybars (1260-1277) was depicted as a "worthy successor to Saladin." His image was built up as "the ideal Mujahid" and "the real hero of Islamic re-conquest of Frankish lands."[31]

When Baybars took Antioch from the Crusaders, he was annoyed to find that Count Bohemond VI had already left. He wrote to Bohemond, describing what his men did in Antioch: "You would have seen your knights prostrate beneath the horses' hooves, your houses stormed by pillagers and ransacked by looters, your wealth weighed by the quintal, your women sold four at a time and bought for a dinar of your own money!...You would have seen your Muslim enemy trampling on the place where you celebrate the Mass, cutting the throats of monks, priests and deacons upon the altars, bringing sudden death to the Patriarchs and slavery to the royal princes."[32]

Savagery in the world never ended until the advent of Christianity. Mexico would not have gotten to where it is today without the coming of Christianity by the Spanish Christians. Bernal Diaz Del Castillo, the 16th century adventurer and conquistador, wrote in his book *The Truthful History of the Conquest of New Spain* about how he witnessed the eating of "human meat, just like we take cows from the butcher's shops, and they have in all towns thick wooden jail-houses, like cages, and in them they put many Indian men, women and boys to fatten, and being fattened they sacrificed and ate them."[33] In his *History of Tlaxcala*, Diego Munoz Camargo writes: "Thus there were public butcher shops of human flesh, as if it were of cow or sheep"[34]

The Aztecs would have their victims laid on a sacrificial block, their chests were cut open, and each prisoner's heart was torn out while he was still alive. According to Richard Townsend, "Streams of blood [from the many sacrificed victims] poured down the stairways and sides of the monument [pyramid], forming huge pools on the white stucco pavement." The heads of the victims were commonly "strung up on the skull rack as public trophies, while the captor-warriors were presented with a severed arm or thigh." With great rejoicing, the severed body parts were taken home, where they were made into stew for special Aztec meals. The eating of human flesh was a ceremonial form of cannibalism[35] with no difference between these demonic rituals and Jeffery Dahmer or the gruesome murders that are happening in the Muslim world.

Commentating on Mel Gibson's *Apocalypto*, Craig Childs writes: "Indeed, parts of the archaeological record of the Americas read like a war-crimes indictment, with charred skeletons stacked like cordwood and innumerable human remains missing heads, legs and arms. In the American Southwest, which is my area of research, human tissue has been found cooked to the insides of kitchen jars and stained into a ceramic serving ladle. A grinding stone was found full of crushed human finger bones. A sample of human feces came up containing the remains of a cannibal's meal."

The conquistadors were hated for championing Christianity over the idols of the Mesoamericans. Hernando Cortes described these pagan rituals as "the most terrible and frightful thing [he and his men] have ever witnessed."[36] the Aztecs ate captured conquistadors with a sauce of peppers and tomatoes. They "sacrificed all our men in this way, eating their legs and arms, offering their hearts and blood to their idol".[37]

Witnessing these acts, Cortes, according to Castillo, made it his purpose to put "a stop to human sacrifices, injustices, and idolatrous worship."[38]

→ Chapter 11 ←

Moral Evolutionists or Psychopaths?

We need to make a choice – we either stand for Biblical morals or support moral evolutionists. We need to ask, ourselves if civilization in Europe arose from some moral zeitgeist. Who ended human sacrifices amongst pagan Prussians and Lithuanians during the fourteenth century?

According to the eighteenth century British writer Edward Ryan, the Prussians and the Lithuanians would have still done such rituals "to this day were it not for Christianity."[39]

If moral evolution contributed to moral advancement over time, does that mean the Prussians and Lithuanians were morally un-evolved compared to other European countries?

It is evident that morals are not the result of any era or time; they appear due to a change of worldviews. Parts of Africa that are pagan still see acts of cannibalism and tribal warfare while the African Christians have totally eschewed themselves from heathen culture. Progressives think that morality is not dependant on ideology but the standards of the time.

Take the well-known evolutionist Richard Dawkins who stated that Genghis Khan was more evil than Hitler because morals were of higher standards than in Genghis' time: "Hitler no doubt killed more people than Genghis, but he had twentieth century technology at his disposal. And did even Hitler gain his greatest pleasure, as Genghis avowedly did, from seeing his victims' 'near and dear bathed in tears'? We judge Hitler's degree of evil by the standard of today... Hitler seems especially evil only by the more benign standards of our time."[40]

Using such an argument, Osama Bin Laden has a stronger moral character than Genghis Khan did and Ahmadinejad is less evil than Hitler was! Thus lieth the illogical thinking of the leftist. Cain killed Abel with a rock; today people kill with scud missiles. Killing is still killing. Liberals apply kinder and gentler terms for murder. Killing of the sick and elderly is called euthanasia or "mercy killing". The only thing that has evolved is the terms we use for murder. Only leftists would make less of Hitler's evil.

My father once saw a restaurant sign that read 'Genghis Khan Buffet'. He commented: "You will never find a German naming a restaurant 'Hitler's Hoffbrau Schnitzel'" – I've never forgotten that. Asians raised with eastern philosophies have a different world-view. Germans are accustomed to Christian ethics but the holocaust was still committed by Germans. Again, Germany confessed its horrors, yet in Turkey it is illegal to speak of the Armenian genocide. Where are the cries of confession in the Muslim world?

So, how do progressives suggest we deal with tyrants? Richard Dawkins called the execution of Saddam Hussein "an Act of Vandalism", writing that it "will provoke violent strife between Sunni and Shi'a Muslims, and between Iraqis in general and the American occupation forces. This was an opportunity to set the world a good example of civilized behavior in dealing with a barbarically uncivilized man. In any case, revenge is an ignoble motive. The usual arguments against the death penalty in general apply. If Bush and Blair are eventually put on trial for war crimes, I shall not be among those pressing for them to be hanged. But I want to add another and less obvious reason why we should not have executed Saddam Hussein. His mind would have been a unique resource for historical, political and psychological research: a resource that is now forever unavailable to scholars. ...Imagine, in fancy, that some science fiction equivalent of Simon Wiesenthal built a time machine, traveled back to 1945 and returned to the present with a manacled Adolf Hitler. What should we do with him? Execute him? No, a thousand times no. Historians squabbling over exactly what happened in the Third Reich and the Second World War would never forgive us for destroying the central witness to all the inside stories, and one of the pivotal influences on twentieth century history. Psychologists, struggling to understand how an individual human being could be so evil and so devastatingly effective at persuading others to join him, would give their eyeteeth for such a rich research subject. Kill Hitler? You would have to be mad to do so." Of course most criminals would prefer to stay in a mental hospital being treated as a patient rather than being executed as a criminal. But that is the version of justice in the minds of the left, that is, if you want a country where psychological research is more valued than justice.

The French oceanographer Jacques-Yves Cousteau is internationally renowned as a marine explorer and defender of the oceans. He is also an evolutionary prophet who predicts of catastrophes to come. In a discussion with Senators Nunn and Lugar – April 28, 1997, Cousteau said: "It's terrible to have to say this. World population must be stabilized and to do this we must eliminate 350,000 people per day."[41] This would be 128 million per year. Would Cousteau himself become the first martyr of such a cause? No.

Richard Dawkins even seems to like some of the works of Nazi Germany: "I wonder whether, some 60 years after Hitler's death, we might at least venture to ask what the moral difference is between breeding for musical ability and forcing a child to take music lessons. Or why it is acceptable to train fast runners and high jumpers but not to breed them. I can think of some answers, and they are good ones, which would probably end up persuading me."[42]

Progressives always downgrade Spanish rule in the Americas and elevate the Aztecs who committed mass murder. Those who condone infanticide and assisted suicide calling for the lives of tyrants like Saddam Hussein and Hitler to be spared are just as destructive as Muslim fundamentalists. If such people are allowed to set up legislation the resulting conditions would be similar to Spain under Islamic rule, Nazi Germany and Communist Russia or a combination thereof. These are all colors of the same chameleon. If life is a dynamo that no one can fully explain, so is God. Evil also arises from a dynamo as a force we cannot fully fathom but can easily observe with the proper lens.

The whole purpose of academics like Dawkins, Hedges and Peter Singer is to create a revolution against the Bible. These, if they held office in this nation would no doubt close down every church and synagogue; morality would necessarily decay. It is doubtful that they will succeed. The Constitution with its decisive wording based on Biblical law would make it impossible for the left to have full control. The French revolution was established on the ideas of Jean-Jacques Rousseau whose ideologies led to France resembling Mesoamerican culture without regard for education – leftists take pride in Meso-americans' advancements in astronomy and mathematics. It is also worth noting that Jean Jacques Rousseau and Jules Verne used cannibals as fictional heroes in order to exalt what he termed as the "noble savage."

Leftists lament over the Europeans bringing Christianity to Mesoamerica. It was Franciscan friars who confronted what remained of the Aztec priesthood, demanding the end of human sacrifice. The Aztecs defended the practice. The Aztec High-priest responded to the friars with "life is because of the gods; with their sacrifice they gave us life…they produce our sustenance…which nourishes life."[43] One would think that the progressive elites would hate the gods. So, why does the left revile the Bible championing over the heathen religions? The answer might be a hard pill to swallow – they themselves, even though they do not recognize it, promote fascism and savagery even though they outwardly condemn it.

It was the priests, the so-called 'evil Catholics' who brought sanity and order to those lands just as the Protestants and the Catholics in Nazi Germany fought against Hitler's killing regime. Christianity civilized that land with the Biblical code of ethics and the Ten Commandments. If we took out one commandment – "thou shall not bear false witness" – it would ruin the entire American court system. Would the leftist rather live in a Christian Mexico or a pagan Mexico? Would the leftist rather live in a place where church bells tell people to attend service or one where flutes and drums play music indicating a new round of human sacrifice?

We have a choice between civilization and chaos, God or Tyranny, yet the left loves to romanticize the Mesoamericans and delegitimize the actions the European Christians took to civilize Latin America. They refuse to admit that it was the Cross and not paganism that initiated the advancement of the world. We must be intellectually honest – Mexico City and Santiago, Chile would have never existed without the introduction of the Bible to these lands.

The leftist might challenge the notion that Christianity is responsible for advancing the human condition, as exemplified by the success of the United States, by pointing to ancient Rome and Greece. Some will argue that these were advanced cultures while pointing to the example of the existence of Roman law.

Frederic Farrar has noted that "infanticide was infamously universal" among Greeks and Romans during the early years of Christianity.[44] Those born deformed or physically frail were especially prone to being willfully killed, often by drowning. Plutarch mentions the Carthaginians as offering "up their own children, and those who had no children would buy little ones from poor people and cut their throats as if they were so many lambs or young birds; meanwhile the mother stood by without a tear or moan."[45]

"But this was so long ago."

Is it? Today, in the Muslim world mothers and fathers have their own children commit suicide in order to attain Allah's forgiveness and it contains the same level of savagery. Mankind can still revive the evils of old.

Muslims argue that Islam banned *Wa'd Albanat* (female infanticide). If Islam values life, then why kill themselves and the 'infidel'?

Even the so-called educated philosophers of today echo sentiment similar to the philosophers of the ancient world and today's Partial Birth Abortion is no different from what the ancient Romans did. Seneca the Younger wrote that in Rome they "drown children who at birth are weakly and abnormal."[46] Are our laws really Roman or Biblically influenced? Roman philosopher Cicero justified infanticide, at least for the deformed, by citing the ancient Twelve Tables of Roman law: "deformed infants shall be killed."[47]

Perhaps we are returning to Roman laws as a result of a change in view due to the works of today's leftist thinkers. Today, pregnant women are asked to consider abortions of deformed children. The Christians in Nazi Germany were pretty much the only ones going against killing the deformed and handicapped. Only Christians fought such backward atrocious acts, which were not only committed by the Greco-Roman world but was common in India, Japan, the Brazilian jungle and even the Eskimos.[48]

It has been reported that the pagan Brazilians "eat human flesh when they can get it, and if a woman miscarries devour the abortive immediately. If she goes her time out, she herself cuts the navel-string with a shell, which she boils along with the secondine, and eats them both." (See E. Bowen, 1747: 532.)

James Dennis in his *Social Evils of the Non-Christian World* states that infanticide is still practiced in many parts of pagan Africa even today.[49]

British writer P. A. Talbot recorded in the 1920s on cannibalism in Nigeria among the Abadja tribe: "the whole body of anyone slain was ordinarily taken back to the village and there consumed, though it was taboo to eat women or children. A man only divided his 'kill' among his own family. The body was cut up and cooked in pots; the fingers, palms of the hands, and toes were considered the best eating. Sometimes, if a family had been satisfied, part of the body would be dried and put away for later. When an Nkanu warrior brought a head back, everyone who heard of the deed gave him a present, and much palm-wine was drunk. The trophy was boiled, and the flesh cut away. The skull was then taken out, accompanied with all the others in the village, and the flesh was then boiled and eaten. Much cruelty was practiced among certain of these tribes. For example, the Bafum-Bansaw, who frequently tortured their prisoners before putting them to death. Palm-oil was boiled in a big pot, and then by means of a gourd enema it was pumped into the bowels and stomachs of the prisoners. This practice was said to make the bodies much more succulent than they would otherwise have been. The bodies were left until the palm-oil had permeated them, and then cut up and devoured..."[50]

Infanticide was also "well known among the Indians of North and South America," that is before the European settlers, who reflected Christian values, outlawed it.[51]

Did native Indians advance to what America is today with their idolatrous living? In areas where Christianity is absent, savagery remains alive regardless of mathematical and astrological advancements. What would history say if progressives went to Mexico instead of Cortez? Would they have fought the pagan evils as hard as Cortez and his men did? They probably would have returned back to Spain and wrote an essay on how the Mesoamericans are suffering from poverty and disease and that the first world is at fault for not sending aid to Mexico.

Here lieth the leftist, the one who refuses to define evil. A leftist will never admit that it was the charging of the Holy Cross that civilized the world. Take Ireland, it's quite civilized and did not get that way as a result of paganism – something that the left states is a victim of being taken over by the Cross. If it were not for that Cross you wouldn't be able to travel to Ireland to go to a pub and listen to some bagpipes and tin whistlers play Danny Boy during St. Patrick's Day. Had the Cross never come to Ireland and you traveled there to experience cultural diversity by going to a solstice meeting, chances are you would probably get scalped.

Who was the culture warrior who contributed much in bringing the Cross to Ireland? St. Patrick, the man who is mostly affiliated with leprechauns and getting drunk with Guiness. Before St. Patrick introduced the Bible to Ireland, the Irish "sacrificed prisoners of war to war gods and newborns to the harvest gods."[52]

James Owen writing for the National Geographic (March 2009) writes: "Julius Caesar, who led the first Roman landing in 55 B.C., said the native Celts 'believe that the gods delight in the slaughter of prisoners and criminals, and when the supply of captives runs short, they sacrifice even the innocent.' First-century historian Pliny the Elder went further, suggesting the Celts practiced ritual cannibalism, eating their enemies' flesh as a source of spiritual and physical strength."

With progressive philosophy nothing will evolve or change – only the scale of horror mankind still does – bigger bombs combined with evil intent simply creates larger piles of corpses.

If Evolution is purely science, why do its advocates always advance into the metaphysical?

Why is morality and God's existence a major theme in Evolution? The Evolutionist cry of 'separation of church and state' is hypocrisy. *Evolution is in reality revolution – through evangelistic methods and aspirations to be a social engineer and to bring the evolutionary worldview into the public square in order to revolutionize politics, culture, economics, and every dimension of life.*[53] It has more to do with an ideology and its plight to destroy Christianity. The major academics espousing evolution bash the Bible, while championing abortion, stem cell research and other fascist systems.

Militant atheist and evolutionist Richard Dawkins is living out the inevitable consequences of the Darwinian worldview. Dawkins' hostility toward religion is *general* but attacks *Christianity* in particular. This has been evident from the earliest years of his writing career. He has written popular articles for secular humanist and atheist periodicals, and is bold to identify atheism as the only credible intellectual option in the modern era. He sees Christianity – and all forms of theistic belief – as intellectual viruses.[54]

If Karl Marx preached: "religion is the opium of the people" Dawkins affirms that religion is a "malignant infection." He explains: "[Religion] is the most inflammatory enemy-labeling device in history." Dawkins and his fellow atheists have no intention of respecting anything like the concept of religious liberty that has framed the American experiment: "Society, for no reason that I can discern, accepts that parents must have an automatic right to bring their children up with particular religious opinions and can withdraw them from say, biology classes that teach evolution."

In Dawkins' vision of a perfect world, undoubtedly he would be the authority to decide what children would and would not learn, and all would be atheists. In *A Devil's Chaplain*, Richard Dawkins helps us to understand the worldview and thinking behind the theory of evolution. As he applies to be the *devil's chaplain*, it appears that Richard Dawkins is superbly qualified for the job.[55] Evolutionists should set aside their extremist aspirations instead of accusing Christianity of being extreme. Evolution according to Dawkins "is the explanation for our existence … everything we know about life is explained by it." Creationists counter by asking, "Can evolution explain love and death or how were the oldest bacteria our common ancestors?"

How can Dawkins or Darwinism explain why Alister McGrath, an atheist-turned-Christian, also of Oxford and a professor of historical theology, become a student of molecular biophysics and possess the dual credibility in science and religion that Dawkins lacks, believe in God? McGrath argues that while Dawkins is a scientist writing about religion, he fails to study religion scientifically. And while Dawkins argues that God is improbable, even humanity's existence itself is overwhelmingly improbable. But of course we exist. "We may be highly improbable – *yet we are here*," writes McGrath. "The issue, then, is not whether God is probable but whether he is *actual*."[56]

Bible believers have asked for centuries, if the law of probability applies and indeed Dawkins wants to get scientific, how can Dawkins and his ilk explain the return of the state of Israel? "I shall plant them in their land and no longer shall they be pulled up" (Amos 9:15). If Christian Zionists, using circular reasoning, wanted the Bible to be fulfilled in order to prove the Bible, did they also cause the Holocaust in order to prove it as well? Without the Holocaust there would have never been a modern state of Israel. Or was it Nietzscheian eugenicists Nazi evolutionists that hated the Bible who ended-up inadvertently fulfilling the very elements in the Bible that they so much wanted to destroy? Either there is a God or the authors of the Bible were simply perfect guessers and the Bible was simply part of our evolutionary process that random selection chose the Jews just as the world seeks their destruction?

Dawkins next proposes that evolution shaped human brains to believe religious hypotheses; yet *all* of our thoughts, (including atheistic thoughts) are brain-dependent. McGrath cites as a witness atheist-Darwinist Stephen Jay Gould, who noted that half his Darwinist colleagues believed in God, and half did not. [57]

If Darwinism proves *Atheism*, how then are half of its followers *Theists*? How many Bible believers are atheists? Yet questioning Evolution can bring a swift accusation of being anti-science. Is this charge even valid? Bible believers have never had a problem with Newton, Einstein, Galileo and all of the other great minds of science. The grievance with evolution is on the basis of scientific evidence and ethics since Darwin himself doesn't only delve into how we evolved from primates, but how women are less evolved than men, how blacks are "anthropomorphous apes", and how we should eliminate the so-called "weak" individuals of society.

Do such claims have anything to do with science? It is pure ideology. The left accuses Christians of being fascist while they celebrate the birth of a racist fascist – Darwin. Today we have Darwin Day. What did Darwin do to deserve a holiday named after him? Bible believers assert that the reason is simple – Darwin bashed God. Why don't they have Newton day or Einstein day if they are so passionate about science?

The first writers on evolution were philosophical – it was Herbert Spencer who coined the phrase "survival of the fittest". In *The Principles of Biology*, Spencer depicted a constant struggle amongst species.[58] He wrote much on how a society should be based on the laws of evolution. 'Survival of the fittest' is not simply promoting 'fitness'. Perhaps reading Spencer's *The Man Versus The State* will elaborate his true view: "Thus by survival of the fittest, the militant type of society becomes characterized by profound faith in the governing power, joined with a loyalty causing submission to it in all matters whatever. And there must tend to be established among those who speculate about political affairs in a militant society, a theory giving form to the needful ideas and feelings; accompanied by assertions that the law-giver if not divine in nature is divinely directed, and that unlimited obedience to him is divinely ordered."[59]

Divinely directed? This becomes pure religion and ideology. The idea of survival of the fittest allows total militant control over the people who simply needed to 'submit'. This is also the view in Nazi Germany, North Korea, and Islamic Fundamentalism.

It is no wonder that Satanists uphold the survival of the fittest ideal. Anton LaVey, the founder of the Church of Satan desires a utopia without inferiors. Who are these inferiors? LaVey explains: "They have to be expected to come up to our standards rather than us lowering hurdles to suit them. If they can't, they should be told, probably for the first time in their lives, 'You know what? You're stupid! You're inferior!', instead of being protected from the effects of their incompetence. If a person is ethical, productive, sensitive, and knows how to conduct himself among human beings, fine; if he's an amoral parasite, he should be dealt with quickly and cruelly."[60] The inferior in LaVey's view are the non-Satanists. Cruelty is the method of treating non-believers, those who were never good or smart enough to be apart of the cause.

Islam, like Satanism, obviously contains the same treatment for non-Muslims, especially Christians and Jews. The Qur'ân also has methods of treating the inferior to them (i.e., non-Muslims): 'Fight those who reject Allah or the final judgment or do not forbid what Allah forbids, or follow Islam...' (Q 9:29)"

ISLAM AND EVOLUTION

Evolution is not a new discovery; Muslims worldwide claim that Allah revealed it in the Qur'ân. In promoting Theistic Evolution, Muslim academicians seek to gain merit with modern western thinkers that Islam has contributed so much in explaining the origin of the universe: "The universe, then, is a more complex and impressive creation than mankind himself. Modern scientific findings support the Big Bang Theory, which proposes that the universe took shape out of nothingness after a massive explosion, and that particles resulting from this blast came together to form planets, stars and entire galaxies. Similar reference is made in the Qur'ân: 'Do the Unbelievers not see that the heavens and the earth were joined together, before we clove them asunder?' (Qur'ân 21:30); and, "Then He turned to the heaven when it was smoke: He said to it and to the earth: 'Come together, willingly or unwillingly.' They said, 'We do come together, in willing obedience.' (Qur'ân 41:11)"

Qur'ân 21:30 and 41:11 is a major argument by so many Muslim scholars, academics and apologists fighting for Islam and science to satisfy modern audiences and argue for the miracle of the Qur'ân.

Even 'survival of the fittest' has become a common acceptance by Muslims. One Muslim professor explains: "In the [Muslim] students' bridge models, microevolution and the concept of 'the survival of the fittest' appeared on the accepted side of the equation. Students reasoned that it is impossible to deny the logic and empirical backing of these concepts. They also connected microevolution to theistic evolution, the idea that God has guided the adjustments in his creatures. Several students accepted the Big Bang and believed that the Qur'ân contains references to both the Big Bang and evolution theory."[61] Dr Khalid Anees, president of the Islamic Society of Britain confirms: "There is no contradiction between what is revealed in the Koran and natural selection and survival of the fittest."[62]

The big bang theory states that the universe originated from one piece of matter or a 'primeval atom.' Belgian priest, astronomer, and the father of the big bang theory, Georges Lemaître, described the primeval atom: "The radius of space began at zero; the first stages of the expansion consisted of a rapid expansion determined by the mass of the initial atom, almost equal to the present mass of the universe."[63]

Even if Muslims reject the idea of the earth being randomly formed they still accept the idea of the universe originating from a single piece of matter they believe was created by Allah. This echoes Lemaître, who believed that the big bang was created by God saying that it was "consonant with Isaiah speaking of the hidden God, hidden even in the beginning of the universe."[64] 'Survival Of The Fittest' advocates that which is contrary to the part of *The Declaration of Independence* that dogmatically bases all rights on the fact all men are created equal by God. If they were not created equal, they were certainly evolved unequal.[65]

A sane society is measured by the protection it has over its weakest citizens.

→ Chapter 12 ←

Psychopaths and Druggies

It is true that there is no difference between a Muslim who goes on a shooting spree and a non-Muslim lunatic who thinks the world wronged him and goes on a shooting frenzy. Both end up killing themselves in the end, since they know the authorities will kill them. While this is true, both murder – either for a personally self-developed ideology or a standard ideology – with the end goal of suicide. Eric Harris and Dylan Klebold who committed the Columbine High school massacre, then took their own lives, were social Darwinists – with no difference between that and the massacres Muslims commit during their suicidal acts. Once a society is infested with a non-Biblical ideology what we get isn't much different from the likes of Richard Ramirez, Jeffery Dahmer, Joseph Stalin, MS-13, and the Mexican mafia. All of these scorn its members from "picking up the Bible" or espousing any form of Christianity.[66]

Pagans, Satanists and Muslim Fundamentalists are all birds of a feather.

One could argue "What about the 'Christian' killer of Dr. Tiller?"

No official church condoned the act of killing a baby killer. On the contrary, churches universally condemned it, as did the wife of Tiller's killer – yet no evolutionist condemned any of Tiller's killings. Also, the label 'church' can be a case of stolen identity with no intent on following the Bible. Some entities that use 'church' can even be pro-Jihadists. One would never find Christian institutions supporting every institution that has the label 'church'. Christians do not support The Church of The Latter Day Saints.

A better example can be given when Benjamin Nathaniel Smith, a neo-Nazi and member of the World Church of the Creator whose motto is "Just as the Muslims have 'jihad', we have 'RAHOWA' (Racial Holy War)." In 1999 Smith hijacked a van and went on a three-day shooting spree targeting Jews, Blacks, and Asians, killing two and

115

injuring another eight. Smith later shot himself to death while police pursued him. His church considered him a martyr. There is no difference between what Smith did and the Trolley square shooting in which a Bosnian Muslim named Sulejman Talovic went on a shooting spree in a Salt Lake City Mall killing five and injuring four only to be killed by off-duty police officer thus becoming a Muslim martyr.

Talovic's motives were one hundred percent ideological just as Smiths' were, telling his girlfriend the night before the massacre "something is going to happen tomorrow that you'll never be able to forgive me about." His girlfriend also revealed a 'vision' that Talovic had while in Bosnia: "One evening, as the sun was falling, Talovic heard a horse outside of his family's home in Bare, where they lived after they left Talovici. He walked out and, standing before him was a white horse with two beautiful eyes, …And he said, 'Look,' and his aunt [who was also outside] couldn't see it there," at this moment his aunt considered him a "good-souled" person.[67] Talovic's killing spree came with the purpose of martyrdom, since a white horse is a sign in Islam for the prophet, martyrdom and paradise, just as the Columbine massacre and Benjamin Smith's killing spree came with the goal for martyrdom.

All these are filled with occult practices. In the 1980s, Cuban "Marielitos" brought Afro-Cuban cult beliefs into the Los Angeles drug and gang culture. Santeria, Voodoo, and Palo Mayombe followers became some of the most violent criminal gang members Los Angeles had ever seen. Across the city, small altars with caldrons or "gangas" of fruit, rum, and cocaine, as well as animal blood sacrifices, dotted the map. "Botanicas" (occult pharmacies) that sold the paraphernalia required for these rituals sprang up in every community.

Drug cartels from Mexico practiced their own rituals. "Brujeria" (Mesoamerican witchcraft) altars with figurines of the bandit saint "Jesus Malverde" or "Santisima Muerte" (holy death) were common in cartel drug houses. Cartel members wore amulets and placed figurines of occult symbols in their cars. Some even openly worshipped Satan.[68]

But these cultists take drugs, how dare one parallel them with Muslims who preach against drugs?

The largest drug dealers in the world are Muslim. Afghanistan is the world's largest opium provider, flooding the world with this deadly narcotic. The Biqa Valley in Lebanon as well produces tons of opium. Russian gangsters who smuggle drugs into Britain are buying cheap heroin from Afghanistan and paying for it with guns for Allah's holy Jihad. Smugglers told *The Independent* how Russian arms-dealers meet Taliban drug lords at a bazaar near the old Afghan-Soviet border, deep in Tajikistan's desert. The bazaar exists solely to trade Afghan drugs for Russian guns – and sometimes a bit of sex on the side. The drugs are destined for Britain's streets. The guns go straight to the Taliban front line. The weapons on sale include machine guns, sniper rifles and anti-aircraft weapons like the ones used in the attempt to assassinate the Afghan President Hamid Karzai. "We never sell the drugs for money," boasted one of the smugglers. "We exchange them for ammunition and Kalashnikovs."

NATO estimates the Taliban gets 40 to 60 percent of their income from drugs. The smugglers' claims suggest the real cost could be far higher. The smugglers described a bleak village with no homes, hidden in the desert near the border. Inside open-air courtyards up to 300 shopkeepers sit in small booths. They act as agents of the Russian mafia who supply the guns and spirit the drugs away. The Afghans are agents of corrupt officials in their government, said a mid-level lieutenant Daoud. Around them lurk Tajik prostitutes, selling themselves for a few scraps of surplus heroin. "They will do anything. They just want some heroin and we always have some spare," said another smuggler.[69]

In every community in the world where progressives abound so does esotericism, violence, prostitution and other perversities.

Scientology's founder, L. Ron Hubbard, was a drug addict and known occultist, being a huge follower of Aleister Crowley. Hubbard once wrote that in order to write up his religion he needed drugs. In a letter to his wife Mary Sue, Hubbard said that, in order to assist his research, he was drinking a great deal of rum, taking stimulants and depressants – saying that, "I'm drinking lots of rum and popping pinks and greys." His assistant at the time, Virginia Downsborough said that he "was existing almost totally on a diet of drugs." It is said that one of the origins of his Xenu story (more on that later) was drugs.[70]

Drugs do not lead to enlightenment – but to light beings.

Chapter 13

Fascists are Psychotics With a Superiority Complex

*M*y great-grandmother, Mrs. Parker, used to say, "Troubles begin when one thinks that the world owes them something." Criminals in her view seem to always say, "Life was unfair." She used to always say that she lost both of her parents to the flu pandemic of 1918 and had to live from one foster home to another. Yet she always knew that the world owed her nothing. I could learn more from her on morality than everything I ever learned in school or from any modern philosopher.

One of the main factors that killers have in common is they think the world has wronged them; they think everybody owes them something and someone must pay for all the ills they've suffered. This way of thinking mixed with elitism and superiority is an extremely dangerous concoction.

My great-grandmother would have been a better mentor to Barack Hussein Obama than Saul Alinsky – a Marxist with a chip on his shoulder, who believed that government should turn to Marxism because Capitalism and the establishment was backstabbing the poor. With his self-pity narcissism, Obama's mentor exalted Lucifer as the original rebel against the establishment in his book *Rules For Radicals*: "Lest we forget at least an over-the-shoulder acknowledgment to the very first radical: from all our legends, mythology, and history (and who is to know where mythology leaves off and history begins – or which is which), the first radical known to man who rebelled against the establishment and did it so effectively that he at least won his own kingdom – Lucifer."[71]

The methods and goals to achieve this revolution were clearly outlined: "The Revolutionary force today has two targets, moral as well as material. Its young protagonists are one moment reminiscent of the idealistic early Christians, yet they also urge violence and cry, 'Burn the system down!' They have no illusions about the system, but plenty of illusions about the way to change our world. It is to this point that I have written this book…" (Prologue) "A Marxist begins with his prime truth that all evils are caused by the exploitation of the proletariat by the capitalists. From this he logically proceeds to the revolution to end capitalism, then into the third stage of reorganization into a new social order of the dictatorship of the proletariat, and finally the last stage – the political paradise of communism…" (p. 10) "An organizer must stir up dissatisfaction and discontent… He must create a mechanism that can drain off the underlying guilt for having accepted the previous situation for so long a time. Out of this mechanism, a new community organization arises…" "The job then is getting the people to move, to act, to participate; in short, to develop and harness the necessary power to effectively conflict with the prevailing patterns and change them. When those prominent in the status quo turn and label you an 'agitator' they are completely correct, for that is, in one word, your function – to agitate to the point of conflict." (p. 117)

Obama is a chip off the old block when introducing 'change'. He intends to construct a civilian force under him: "We cannot continue to rely only on our military in order to achieve the national security objectives that we've set. We've got to have a civilian national security force that's just as powerful, just as strong, just as well-funded."[72] Obama plans to double the *Peace Corps'* budget by 2011, and expand *AmeriCorps, USA Freedom Corps, VISTA, YouthBuild Program*, and the *Senior Corps*. Plus, he proposes to form a *Classroom Corps, Health Corps, Clean Energy Corps, Veterans Corps, Homeland Security Corps, Global Energy Corps*, and a *Green Jobs Corps*.[73]

Obama has committed revolutionaries who have made it so high in his administration that several chief advisers have reached the level of "czar". Van Jones became a White House environmental advisor (czar) who co-founded an African American political advocacy group. In 1992, during the Rodney King riots in Los Angeles, Jones was arrested and jailed for his role in the protest. He said of his time in prison, "I met all these young radical people of color – I mean really radical: communists and anarchists. And it was, like, 'This is what I need to be a part of.' I spent the next ten years of my life working with a lot of those people I met in jail, trying to be a revolutionary..."

To Obama, the United States is not a model for the world. At Obama's *Dreams from My Father* book signing in New York, he stated: "The Basic Outline of the government we possess and our civic religion as a people is such that potentially at least, we could create a society that is a model for the world, it isn't right now."

Obama's Director of the Office of Science and Technology Policy czar, John Holdren penned a 1977 book that approved of and recommended compulsory sterilization and even abortion in some cases, as part of a government population control regime. Holdren writes in *Ecoscience*, co-authored by Malthus enthusiasts Paul and Anne Ehrlich, "Of course, a government might require only implantation of the contraceptive capsule, leaving its removal to the individual's discretion but requiring reimplantation after childbirth. Since having a child would require positive action (removal of the capsule), many more births would be prevented than in the reverse situation." Holdren and his co-authors also tackle the problem of illegitimacy, recognizing that it could be one consequence of a society which, in its effort to limit births, downgrades the value of intact nuclear families and encourages lifelong bachelorhood: "Responsible parenthood ought to be encouraged and illegitimate childbearing could be strongly discouraged. One way to carry out this disapproval might be to insist that all illegitimate babies be put up for adoption – especially those born to minors, who generally are not capable of caring properly for a child alone...It would even be possible to require pregnant single women to marry or have abortions, perhaps as an alternative to placement for adoption, depending on the society."

Cass Sunstein, regulatory "czar", proposed bans on hunting and eating meat while proposing that a dog be allowed to have an attorney in court. Sunstein has also written often in favor of animal rights. In a speech at Harvard University he said, "we ought to ban hunting." He also says that human "willingness to subject animals to unjustified suffering will be seen...as a form of unconscionable bar-

barity... morally akin to slavery and the mass extermination of human beings."

Carol M. Browner, US President Barack Obama's global warming czar-designate, was listed as one of 14 leaders of a socialist group's Commission for a Sustainable World Society, which calls for "global governance" and says rich countries must shrink their economies to address climate change.

Whether one believes in Saul Alinsky's Lucifer or a dynamo that evil stems from, evil is still linked to changing worldviews. *No terrorist or communist is made without converting him first into a cultist who believes that the others owe him something since his views are superior. Every cultist has a superior-centric philosophy in which he must out-muscle and surpass all who are not part of the cause. Outsiders are those who don't understand their supposed suffering, thus trying to become a dominant influencer in the world. This superiority complex is found in every communist, anarchist, Muslim fundamentalist activist and eco-terrorist who attacks fishing ships since they want to be the dominant movement so the world can see them and understand their power. In their minds they are victims that aren't understood in the world.*

They have a superiority complex. This whole Nietzschean philosophy of surpassing the common man is clearly seen in suicide bombings. The Muslim believes the world has been cruel to him and because he believes the world is corrupt he wishes to destroy himself to escape the world becoming his own Christ and his own god – he surpasses mankind, transforming "beyond human", as Nietzsche put it.

In Islam, strength is the way a Muslim transcends the rest of the world, or as the *Book of Jihad* reads: "Jihad is holy fighting in Allah's cause with full force of weaponry. It is given the utmost importance in Islam and is one of its Pillars. By jihad, Islam is established, Allah is made superior and he becomes the only god who may be worshiped. By jihad, Islam is propagated and made superior. By abandoning jihad, Islam is destroyed and Muslims fall into an inferior position. Their honor is lost, their lands are stolen, and Muslim rule and authority vanish. Jihad is an obligatory duty in Islam on every

Muslim. He who tries to escape this duty dies as a hypocrite." My father, upon his conversion to Christianity was considered inferior and had his land taken away.

Considering non-believers as inferior and believers as superior is not solely an Islamic tenet. Satanist Anton LaVey wrote that those who read the Satanic Bible and accept his doctrine "are those employed by the most self-realized and powerful humans on earth. In the secret thoughts of each man and woman, still motivated by sound and unclouded minds, resides the potential of the Satanist, as always has been."[74]

Non-believers are also regarded as less than human and as low as animals. Sheik Abu Hamza once said while lecturing to a group of Muslims, "If a kafir person (non-believer) goes in a Muslim country, he is like a cow."[75]

Crowley had a common idea for his utopia, writing that slaves must "accept the conditions of existence as they really are, and enjoy life with the quiet wisdom of cattle."[76]

Hamza has also said that if "a kafir is walking by and you catch him, he's booty – you can sell him in the market. Most of them are spies. And even if they don't do anything, if Muslims cannot take them and sell them in the market, you just kill them. It's O.K."[77] Non-believers become slaves in the Islamic utopia; similarly, Aleister Crowley wrote that "Christianity is the formula of the servile state" and that in his ideal state "[t]here will always be slaves, and the slave is defined as he who acquiesces in being a slave."[78]

Here is a look at what is considered to be the secular beliefs of Nietzscheism as described in *Thus Spoke Zarathustra*: "I teach you the overman. Man is something that shall be overcome. What have you done to overcome him? All beings so far have created something beyond themselves; and do you want to be the ebb of this great flood and even go back to the beasts rather than overcome man? What is the ape to man? A laughing stock or a painful embarrassment. And man shall be just that for the overman: a laughingstock or a painful embarrassment."[79]

Nietzsche believed that everything alive seeks to perfect and strengthen, thus mankind in their present state are just a mindless herd, more primitive than our ape ancestors and even the ancestors of the apes. Modern man is just a shapeless mass, a monster. The superman forges his own destiny; he is at his highest intellectual and creative ability. "Man is to ape as Superman shall be to man. Man is a polluted stream, which Christianity says must be rid of its pollutants – yet the end result will leave hardly anything left. The best remedy for this problem, however, is the Superman, who is such a large sea that he can accommodate polluted streams without worry or hurt."

L. Ron Hubbard was a typical cult leader – cruel and crooked. The world according Hubbard "is a rough universe. It is a terrible and deadly universe. Only the strong survive it, only the ruthless can own it."[80]

Scientology is Nietzschean with a goal to find an "aberrated state where one's energy is primarily absorbed attempting to straighten out personal problems, a person is unlikely to lift his gaze to the glories that could be his as a fully rehabilitated and able being, not just as homo sapiens."[81]

To Hubbard "Scientology is used to increase spiritual freedom, intelligence, ability, and to produce immortality."[82] Hubbard's philosophy echoes greatly with Nietzsche's writings, which stress greatly on becoming super human (over human). Nietzsche's idea of "the overman" (Übermensch) is one of the most significant concepts in his thinking.

According to Nietzsche an overman is an extraordinary person who is able to transcend the limits of traditional morality to live solely by his drive for power. This person is willing to risk all for the advancement of humanity, and can affect people's thinking through establishing their values. This means an overman will influence the lives of others, and this impact can last indefinitely.[83] Nietzsche offered grounds for the reprehensible Nazi ideology of a superior race exercising its will to power as it saw fit. Hitler was living out what Nietzsche had envisioned, trying to prove to himself as the Übermensch (overman) and the precursor to the Master race. He despised weakness as much as Nietzsche did and wanted to reevaluate the current social values, changing them into something that supported the aggressive instinct. He wanted to become, as Nietzsche called it a "lord of the earth."[84]

Nietzsche wrote in *The Genealogy of Morals*, "The sick are the great danger of man, not the evil, not the 'beasts of prey.' They who are from the outset botched, oppressed, broken those are they, the weakest are they, who most undermine the life beneath the feet of man, who instill the most dangerous venom and skepticism into our trust in life, in man, in ourselves...Here teem the worms of revenge and vindictiveness; here the air reeks of things secret and unmentionable; here is ever spun the net of the most malignant conspiracy – the conspiracy of the sufferers against the sound and the victorious; here is the sight of the victorious hated."[85]

The world of Nietzsche was not a world of humans but ravenous wolves. This 'overman' is a world in which the under dog has no chance. Despite his 'superior' strength, Nietzsche contemplated suicide after his rejection experience with the 'love of his life', Lou Salome, a promiscuous woman.

Today Richard Dawkins, also known as 'Darwin's Rottweiler,' laments on our modern ideas of eugenics: "In the 1920s and 1930s, scientists from both the political left and right would not have found the idea of designer babies particularly dangerous – though of course they would not have used that phrase. Today, I suspect that the idea is too dangerous for comfortable discussion, and my conjecture is that Adolf Hitler is responsible for the change." "Nobody wants to be caught agreeing with that monster, even in a single particular. The spectre of Hitler has led some scientists to stray from 'ought' to 'is' and deny that breeding for human qualities is even possible. But if you can breed cattle for milk yield, horses for running speed, and dogs for herding skill, why on Earth should it be impossible to breed humans for mathematical, musical or athletic ability? Objections such as 'these are not one-dimensional abilities' apply equally to cows, horses and dogs and never stopped anybody in practice." "I wonder whether, some 60 years after Hitler's death, we might at least venture to ask what the moral difference is between breeding for musical ability and forcing a child to take music lessons." In no way can Dawkins advance his ideology without the ultimate breeding of the superman.

Margret Sanger, a champion of Eugenics called for eliminating the unfit to create what she called 'clean race': "Birth control must lead ultimately to a cleaner race."[86]

So who was the race Sanger wanted to weed out? "We should hire three or four colored ministers, preferably with social-service backgrounds, and with engaging personalities. The most successful educational approach to the Negro is through a religious appeal. We don't want the word to go out that we want to exterminate the Negro population and the minister is the man who can straighten out that idea if it ever occurs to any of their more rebellious members."[87] "Eugenic sterilization is an urgent need...We must prevent multiplication of this bad stock."[88]

Eugenicists, like the typical snake oil salesman advocates that Eugenics is the solution for all political tensions, wars and strife. Singer writes, "Eugenics is...the most adequate and thorough avenue to the solution of racial, political and social problems."[89]

Eugenics was popular prior to WWII, and in the United States it led to the widespread practice of forcibly sterilizing 'undesirables'. Many in the US even lauded the Nazi government's public promotion of such principles as 'progressive'. The logical end of progressivism by 1945 was Europe in ruins, millions dead, families torn apart, an atom bomb detonated in Hirsohima and Nagasaki, millions missing in Stalin's Russia, and Mao massacring millions more.

ISLAM'S SUPERMEN

Like die-hard evolutionists, this hatred of the weak can also be found in Islam: "The strong believer is better and more loved by Allah than the weak one, but they are both good."[90] The typical Muslim fundamentalist believes "Physical toughness, strength, absence of luxurious living are virtues that should be present in the Muslim."[91] The Qur'ân says: "Against them [the unbelievers] make ready your strength to the utmost of your power, including steeds of war, to strike terror into [the hearts of] the enemies of God, and your enemies." (Qur'ân 8:60)

In 1981 on Muhammad the prophet's birthday, the Ayatollah Khomeni said in a speech that mercy "is against God."[92] Similarly in Aleister Crowley's *The Book of The Law* it reads: "We have nothing with the outcast and the unfit: let them die in their misery. For they feel not. Compassion is the vice of kings: stamp down the wretched and the weak: this is the law of the strong: this is our law and the joy of the world."[93]

Islam, like Nazism, is in essence an ideology of physical health, Muhammad being the one who said "your body also has a right over you."[94] The prolific Muslim scholar, Salih al-Fawzaan, commented on Muhammad's health-centric idea: "The believer who is strong in his belief, body, and actions is better than the weak believer, the one who has weak belief, or a weak body or weak actions. That is because the strong believer is productive and accomplishes things for the Muslims, and thus they benefit from his physical strength, actions, and strong beliefs. Islam is the Religion of strength, the Religion of honor, the Religion of prestige! So the strength that is sought from us in Islam is strength in belief and its tenets, as well as strength in our actions and bodies, because all of this brings forth good things for the Muslims. The believer who has strong belief is more likely to be fit and in shape. This is because he understands the importance of striving and staying in shape in preparation for it, while the weak believer may easily get fat and out of shape, from his overeating and laziness. Physical strength is a direct result of strength in belief."[95]

Even sexual strength is the pride of Muhammad the prophet of Islam. Islam records that the prophet's libido was equal to thirty men.[96] He would have intercourse with all his eleven wives in one night.[97]

Aleister Crowley, as well, saw physical strength as a priority for his utopia explaining that it must "have a sound physical stock to pick out rulers from."[98]

SECTION THREE

*I*SLAM AND
LEFTISM COMRADSHIP

Chapter 14

To Worship God or *The Earth Your God*

On the surface, Islam advocates the worship of the one true God but at its core idol worship is not far from it. Muslims, while they do not consciously accept that venerating the Black Stone, an asteroid, as a form of worship, yet they admit that it takes away their sins as they circumambulate it during the Haj for atonement by which it becomes a redeemer. The crux of this example is this; *Shinarians elevate planets and earth as God, even though they consciously deny it, as they cannot fathom what they do; since all such dogmas are filled with disclaimers.*

Islam is filled with disclaimers like "we do not worship except Allah" while they deify Muhammad giving him the titles: *Al-Maqam-Al-Mahmud* (The Glorious One), *Awal-Khalq-illah* (The first of Creation), *Muhammad* (The Praised One), *Al-Insan Al-Kamel* (The Perfect Man), *Rahmatan-lil-A'alameen* (Mercy to All Mankind), *Al-rasul Al-A'tham* (The Greatest of All sent by God), *Shafi* (Healer), *Munji* (Savior), *Mahdi* (The Guided One/Deliverer), *Al-Mustafa Al-Mukhtar* (The Chosen One), *Amir* (The Prince), *Khatimun-Nabiyeen* (The Seal of Prophets), *Al-Hadi* (The Guide), *Awal* (First), *Akher* (Last), *Sayyid Walad Adam* (The Leader of The Sons of Adam) and *Al-Siraj Al-Muneer* (The Luminous One, The Glowing Lamp).

Bible believers view any form of venerating earth and stones as heathenistic. The conservative and environmentalist views are diametrically opposed. The former advocates man over universe while the latter advocates universe over man.

Yet being created in God's likeness is elevating man over any other creation.

ISLAM AND ENVIRONMENTALISM

While Bible believers have no problem with protecting the environment they see mankind holding a position of dominion over the earth, that he was created in God's image, which is of far greater importance than the substance God created. Islam views this as blasphemous.

In the Qur'ân, humans are of lesser value than is creation: "the heavens and the earth is greater than the creation of man; but most people know not." (Q 40:57) Even the animal kingdom is on par with humans: "No creature is there on earth nor a bird flying with its wings but they are nations like you." (Q 6:38) Abdul Haseeb Ansari in *Islamic Law* explaining the significance of this verse warns against arrogance that the believers (Muslims) are "no better than other creatures." (p. 34) This denigration of humankind today even takes a scientific twist. Ingrid Newkirk, the president of People for the Ethical Treatment of Animals declared: "When it comes to feelings, a rat is a pig is a dog is a boy. There is no rational basis for saying that a human being has special rights."[1]

Islam also has many attributes comparable with environmentalism. Muhammad commanded his followers to care for the earth to the point that "Even when the Day of Judgment comes" that "if any one has a palm-shoot in hand, he should plant it."

Muhammad established *himas* (environmental laws) in Arabia. B.A. Masri writes that himas were established by Muhammad "some 14 centuries ago, and covers not only forests but also wildlife. According to these laws, certain areas, called *haram* or *hima*, are set aside and protected. This code of ecological conservation has its origins in the life and sayings of the Prophet Muhammad. One of the latter, reported by Bukhari and Muslim, the most reliable compilers of Muhammad's deeds, states that, 'Whoever plants a tree and looks after it with care, until it matures and becomes productive, will be rewarded in the Hereafter.'"

Yet Islam denigrates the *kafer* (unbelievers), even Jews who are said to have been transformed into detestable monkeys.

In fact, both environmentalism and Islam see the earth as a holy temple: "The earth has been created for me as a mosque and as a means of purification."[2] It is for this reason that Al Gore praises Islamic environmentalism: "The central concepts of Islam taught by the Qur'ân – *Tawheed* (unity), *khalifa* (trusteeship), *akharah* (accountability) – also serve as the pillars of the Islamic environmental ethic. The earth is the sacred creation of Allah."[3] It is also worthy to note that every one of Gore's translations of the Arabic terms is a misnomer; "tawheed" is not "unity" "khalifa" is not "trusteeship" and "akharah" is not accountability – tawheed is the Islamic Unitarianism that Allah is a single one that is set in contrast with the Christian Trinity; Khalifa in Islam is the vicar of Allah on earth and the supreme ruler of the Muslim Umma; Akharah is the judgment Day.

Gore swallowed his views on Islamic environmentalism hook, line, and sinker from Dr. Abdullah Omar Naseef, Secretary General of the Muslim World League during the *Muslim Declaration on Nature, 1986*: "So unity, trusteeship and accountability, that is tawhid, khalifah and akhirah, the three central concepts of Islam, are also the pillars of the environmental ethics of Islam. They constitute the basic values taught by the Qur'ân. It is these values which led Muhammad, (peace be upon him), the Prophet of Islam, to say: 'Whosoever plants a tree and diligently looks after it until it matures and bears fruit is rewarded,' ...Environmental consciousness is born when such values are adopted and become an intrinsic part of our mental and physical make-up."

Prince Sadruddin Aga Khan further explains: "Let us not forget that Muslims had formulated a bill of legal rights of animals as early as the thirteenth century and in Turkey Muslims had established environmental and cultural associations and initiated work on environmental issues long before the Ministry of Environment was established." According to Aga Khan and most Muslim scholars, Islam not only supports the environmental movement, but also was its founder. This environmental concern goes beyond the realm of being a care taker to communion: "we are witnessing a spiritual (in the widest sense of the word) re-birth and need to re-discover communion with nature." He even sees a unity with nature of all religions in this effort: "Ancient wisdom, Taoism, Zen Buddhism, Master Eckhart, St. Francis of Assisi, Ibn al A'rabi and mystics of all Faiths speak of the family of Man as a link in the chain of all beings on this Earth.

Indeed, mystics always tend to relate to each other in a spirit of true ecumenism, due to their common bond with Creation. And Creation is nature."

According to the Malaysia Wildlands Project: "...when we read the hadith, 'The whole earth has been made a mosque and pure for me', it can be deduced that every Muslim must keep the earth and its environment unpolluted and wholesome."[4]

Marjorie Hope and James Young in their work titled *The New Alliance: Faith and Ecology*, interview the distinguished Muslim philosopher Seyyed Hossein Nasr who "sees at the center of Islam a charge to protect the natural world – a world that reflects the higher reality of the transcendent God." He adds, "Well, in the West, it has certainly made some compelling statements. But one has to ask, 'What power does it have over the political domain?' The politicians may nod and even agree – but the developers go right ahead, cutting down woods, uprooting endangered species. That's a result of the Western dogma of separating science from the sacred and religion from the secular. In Islamic countries religion is a stronger force. In a *true* Islamic society, political leadership could act in accordance with the *Sharī'ah* as set out by doctors of the law. If they pronounced polluting industries and certain kinds of development in violation of Islamic principles, political leaders would have to take strong measures against transgressors. Remember, I am talking about what would happen in a true Islamic society. Unfortunately, today the West dominates the world economy, so Islam reacts to the West both economically and politically. The West sets the agenda."

As it is obvious from every statement we see, in Islam, one cannot divorce Sharī'ah from every aspect of life. Mr. Nasr seems to identify the problem as stemming from abandoning what he calls "true Islamic society". The interviewer then says: *"From reading your work, we've seen how destructive you feel the separation between religion and the secular domain to be."* He nodded. "That is rooted in Western modern science and its domination of our view of nature, a view that separates nature from the sacred. Renaissance humanism gave rise to a world centered on man instead of God. Human reason was no longer bounded by allegiance to anything beyond itself. Before, all civilizations looked beyond themselves to God – to revelation. I'm not hostile to Western science but to its claim to be the only valid science of the natural world. There are other ways of 'knowing.' Western science *has* become illegitimate because scientists and the rest of society fail to see the need for a higher knowledge into which it could be integrated. The spiritual value of nature is destroyed. We can't save the natural world except by rediscovering the sacred in nature."

To environmentalists, nature is elevated from serving man to being sacred. Islam in this view is the answer, but first, it must be part and parcel of the political structure that dictates legislation through Sharī'ah law for the preservation of nature.

Robert Muller, an environmentalist who worked for the U.N as Assistant Secretary General for 40 years and founder of the University of Peace echoes this Shinarian ideology of a dream he calls "Mt. Rasur", a Mecca for environmentalists and a place of pilgrimage: "I dream that the wonderful land of legendary Mount Rasur above the University for Peace will become some day an inspiring sacred place for the entire world."[5] And similar to Muhammad's earth being a mosque, Muller's holy-writ states: "Our natural Earth is a temple of God. No human temple will ever match it or replace it. It is time to organize human life in such a way that the Earth is preserved as God's temple."[6]

It is rare to find an environmentalist that does not hold to some form of god and an altar. Even the Stonehenge in the Georgia Guide has a ten commandments: 1. Maintain humanity under 500,000,000 in perpetual balance with nature. 2. Guide reproduction wisely – improving fitness and diversity. 3. Unite humanity with a living new language. 4. Rule passion – faith – tradition – and all things with tempered reason. 5. Protect people and nations with fair laws and just courts. 6. Let all nations rule internally resolving external disputes in a world court. 7. Avoid petty laws and useless officials. 8. Balance personal rights with social duties. 9. Prize truth – beauty – love – seeking harmony with the infinite. 10. Be not a cancer on the earth – Leave room for nature – Leave room for nature.

How can we fulfill the first commandment and maintain a population of 500,000,000? How can humanity keep mother earth happy if we do not sacrifice human lives for it? Why is the earth "infinite"? And if one thinks that this infinite is no deity and is just hyperbole, RC Christian the man who designed the stones explains: "The infinite here means the supreme being – whose will is manifest in the working of the cosmos – if we will seek for it." This way of thinking forms bio-terrorist groups such as *Earth First* whose motto states that there is no "compromise in defense of Mother Earth."

Bible believers view the elevation of animals as hypocritical since we all kill life and life can never be sustained without killing an innocent life – everyone on earth must participate in the act of this communion that life must die to preserve life. Perhaps this parallels the message of Christ. One seed dies for a kernel to grow – this is all around us. If we are a part of the environment and on equal par with the rest of the living, why then do they kill their equals? Why not advocate stopping killing at all levels, including all vegetation? In other words, all environmentalists kill to be sustained; they simply advocate the sacrifice of everyone but themselves to preserve the environment. It is this elevation of earth and cosmos over man that caused the ancient pagan cults to end up sacrificing the innocents on the altars of goddess earth regardless of their advances in science and astronomy.

Yet when we search deeper into such movements, they are indeed militaristic revolutions. *Earth First* was co-founded by Dave Foreman who proclaimed: "It's time for a warrior society to rise up out of the earth and throw itself against the human pox that's ravaging this precious, beautiful planet."[7] These are not peace activists but 'warriors'.

The environmentalists and Gaia gurus seek to cleanse the polluters of the planet – the spiritual dome. The fight does not only encompass issues of preserving the environment, but anyone who disagrees with their views. Islam upholds commandments to destroy those who are spiritually polluting the earth – the mosque and the spiritual dome of Allah: "fight them until there is no more Fitnah (mischief) and all submit to the religion of Allah." (Q 8:39) Using vehement rhetoric, Muhammad proclaims: "Do the bastards think that we are not their equal in fighting? We are men who think that there is no shame in killing."[8]

Even major environmentalist and population control fanatic, Harvard professor Peter Singer who champions infanticide and euthanasia in the name of saving the environment, romanticizes Islam as an environmental remedy: "Muslims clearly understand non-human animals to have souls."[9] Muhammad, according to Singer, was also a champion of environmentalism, a man who "compared the doing of good or bad deeds to other animals to similar acts done to humans."[10] On the Qur'ân, Singer writes that "Qur'ân 17:44 notes that nonhuman animals and the rest of nature are in continuous praise of Allah, although humans may not be able to understand this."[11]

To save this environment, Singer advocates that America should contribute more to world poverty: "America is taking far more than our fair share;"[12] and that population growth will ruin the environment. Singer, in all his writing, views the Bible as an enemy: "Christianity is our foe. If animal rights is to succeed, we must destroy the Judeo-Christian religious tradition."[13] In an article titled *Heavy Petting* Singer comments: "In the Judeo-Christian tradition – less so in the east – we have always seen ourselves as distinct from animals, and imagined that a wide, unbridgeable gulf separates us from them. Humans alone are made in the image of God. Only human beings have an immortal soul." In his work *A Companion to Ethics* it reads: "Christian ethics is intolerant and breeds intolerance."

MORAL EQUIVALENCY

So what do the progressives do with the likes of Osama bin Laden? Alan Wolfe in an op-ed in the *New York Times*, comments on Osama bin Laden's aspirations that "the whole world is split into two camps: belief and disbelief." Wolfe comments: "Osama bin Laden's words are chilling, not only because they threaten further terrorism, but also because they echo themes that have run through America's own religious history." Wolfe then goes on attacking Pat Robertson and Jerry Falwell as if they were equal to that of Hitler himself: "To be sure, religious fundamentalists have prominent political presence even now. Pat Robertson and Jerry Falwell, for example, are not averse to invoking a language of crusade in the political arena." Wolfe goes on writing that they "are, of course, American believers who evangelize, persuaded that those who do not believe as they do are destined for hell. Yet there are far more who believe that whatever their own path to God, other people will choose different paths that deserve respect."[14]

Equating Christians to Muslim terrorists is typical. HIV-positive homosexual journalist Andrew Sullivan writes in his book *The Conservative Soul*: "for Osama, as with the evangelical Christian right, there was a perfect Edenic past, a fallen present, and a perfect future promised."[15]

Pulitzer Prize winner and writer Chris Hedges of the Christian left, a conscientious objector, frequently expresses his discipleship with the cesspool of intellectual leftists: "the Christian right and radical Islamist, although locked in a holy war, increasingly mirror each other. They share the same obsessions. They do not tolerate other forms of belief or disbelief. They are at war with artistic and cultural expression. They seek to silence the media. They call for the subjugation of women. They promote severe sexual repression, and they seek to express themselves through violence."[16]

Bible believers fear that moral equivalency is spreading like a cancer even amongst the church elite. Rick Warren predicts fundamentalism will be "one of the big enemies of the 21st century"[17] but of what 'fundamentalists' does Warren speak? Liberal 'Christians', like Warren tend to disassociate themselves from mainstream Christianity which has become a stigma: "[I am] not a member of the religious right and I'm not a fundamentalist." Warren gets into moral equivalency: "Muslim fundamentalism, Christian fundamentalism, Jewish fundamentalism, secular fundamentalism – they're all motivated by fear. Fear of each other."[18]

DEFINING ENVIRONMENTALISM

So how do we define Environmentalism? The answer would be the whole crux of our writing. We define Environmentalism as having elements similar to what we see in Islam, Communism, Nazism and Darwinism. *Environmentalism, like every 'isim' is a system that advocates a process of serving goddess earth by ridding the world from the undesirables that consume her.* Christians see God having us defend ourselves, but never having to defend Him – God can defend Himself. Defending the faith from a Christian perspective is to have an open dialogue over religion. In Islam, it is promoting 'virtue' by defending the faith while protecting the earth from its 'mischievous' subjects through the application of force.

The Qur'ān's habit is always to introduce the fruit-punch – the love verses, "For this reason did We prescribe to the children of Israel that whoever slays a soul, unless it be for manslaughter or for mischief in the earth, it is as though he slew the whole of mankind; and whoever saves a life, it is as though he saved the whole of mankind." (Q 5:32) The cyanide is introduced in the next verse: "The punishment of those who wage war against Allah and His Messenger, and strive with might and main for mischief through the earth is: execution, or crucifixion, or the cutting off of hands and feet from opposite sides, or exile from the land: that is their disgrace in this world, and a heavy punishment is theirs in the Hereafter." (Q 5:33)

The god of Islam is similar to the god of the leftists who cannot survive without the adherents of the faith. They are all alike; they ascribe to a lord of mercy and compassion that initiates their holy writ with "in the name of Allah the most compassionate." Muhammad was compassionate with dogs, to even have promised heaven to someone that saved a thirsty dog. Megalomaniacs are not void of compassion. The Nazis, like Muhammad, were animal rights activists. Heinrich Himmler, who saw nothing evil in killing the multitudes of the innocent – created in God's image – seemed to have great compassion for the lost souls of the animals. Himmler once said regarding animals: "How can you find pleasure in shooting from behind cover at poor creatures browsing on the edge of a wood, innocent, defenseless, and unsuspecting?...It's really pure murder."

In August 1933, Hermann Goring barred the "unbearable torture and suffering in animal experiments," threatening to commit to concentration camps "those who still think they can treat animals as inanimate property."[19]

Even Mussolini: "As well as being an 'anti-globalizer', there were several other ways in which Mussolini would have appealed to modern-day greenies. He made Capri a bird sanctuary (Smith, 1967, p. 84) and in 1926 he issued a decree reducing the size of newspapers to save wood pulp to even mandate the use of gasohol – the mixing of industrial alcohol with petroleum products to make fuel for cars (Smith, 1967, p. 87). Mussolini also disliked the population drift from rural areas into the big cities and in 1930 passed a law to put a stop to it unless official permission was granted (Smith, 1967, p. 90). What Green/Left advocate could ask for more?"[20]

The song *Windsong* by the famous environmentalist singer John Denver deifies the wind:

The wind is the whisper of our mother the earth
The wind is the hand of our father the sky
The wind watches over our struggles and pleasures
The wind is the goddess who first learned to fly
The wind is the bearer of bad and good tidings
the weaver of darkness, the bringer of dawn

Allah, as the Qur'ân describes is the "lord of the dawn" and the one who created "the mischievous evil of Darkness, as it becomes intensely dark." (Q 113:1-3)

It is not accurate then to say that progressives have a negative view of religion. Progressives, in reality have a positive view of religion; so long as it is not the Bible. Why else would staunch leftists like Nietzsche, Hegel, Rousseau, Ward Churchill, George Galloway, Karen Armstrong, Lynne Stewart, Hitler, Norman Finkelstein along with liberal organizations like the ACLU and Code Pink, Women For Peace and countless others promote Islamist causes while at the same time hating

Biblical conservative values unless Islam and all other non-Biblical religions have more in common with the left?

Muslim apologists' assertion that Islam has much in common with the Bible – even superseding it – or that Islam adheres to conservative values is incongruous. Progressives have identified Islamic terrorism as "far-right" or "conservative" and on par with Judeo-Christian values while inserting the religion of Islam into the moderate camp.

Not all conservative values are made equal; the reality is that Islam attempts to wedge itself between the two monotheistic faiths, proclaiming it is one of the three great monotheistic religions while having little in common with Biblically conservative values and a great deal in common with the leftist progressive ideology. Why else would staunch leftists speak positively about Islam? Why do progressives support Islam? Is it possible that they share the same god? Could it be that all roads lead to their common god – the god of this world?

→ Chapter 15 ←

For God or For Rebellion

ISLAM – A PHILOSOPHY OF REVOLUTION

The more we view all the 'isims' the more we can make an iron clad argument – they have the spirit of rebellion. The Islamic Revolution has so much in common with leftist ideology. Iran's President Mahmoud Ahmadinejad predicted: "The wave of the Islamic revolution will soon reach the entire world." Sayyid Abul Ala Maududi, founder of Pakistani Jamaat-e-Islami political party, defined Islam as "a revolutionary ideology and program which seeks to alter the social order of the whole world and rebuild it in conformity with its own tenets and ideals...Islam wishes to destroy all States and Governments anywhere on the face of the earth which are opposed to the ideology and program of Islam regardless of the country or the Nation which rules it..."[21]

Maududi envisioned a unified Islamic state that would steadily expand throughout the subcontinent and beyond: "The Muslim Party will inevitably extend invitation to the citizens of other countries to embrace the faith which holds promise of true salvation and genuine welfare for them. Even otherwise also if the Muslim Party commands adequate resources it will eliminate un-Islamic Governments and establish the power of Islamic Government in their stead."

Maududi is true to Islam, Muhammad and the first caliphs: "It is the same policy which was executed by the Holy Prophet (peace of Allah be upon him) and his successor illustrious Caliphs (may Allah be pleased with them). Arabia, where the Muslim Party was founded, was the first country which was subjugated and brought under the rule of Islam."[22]

Ibn Khaldun, the famous 14th century Islamic historian and philosopher in his classic and most notable work *The-Muqaddimah*, says of jihad: "In the Muslim community, the holy war is a religious duty, because of the universalism of the (Muslim) mission and (the obligation to) convert everybody to Islam either by persuasion or by force. Therefore, the caliphate (spiritual), the royal (government and military) authority is united in Islam, so that the person in charge can devote the available strength to both of them at the same time."[23]

In his book, *Jurisprudence in Mohammed's Biography*, the renowned Egyptian scholar from Al-Azhar University, Dr. Muhammad Sa'id Ramadan al-Buti writes that offensive, not defensive, war is the "noblest Holy War" within Islam. "The Holy War (Islamic Jihad), as it is known in Islamic Jurisprudence, is basically an offensive war. This is the duty of Muslims in every age when the needed military power becomes available to them. This is the phase in which the meaning of Holy war has taken its final form. Thus the apostle of Allah said: 'I was commanded to fight the people until they believe in Allah and his messenger.' The concept of Holy War (Jihad) in Islam does not take into consideration whether defensive or an offensive war. Its goal is the exaltation of the word of Allah and the construction of Islamic society and the establishment of Allah's Kingdom on earth regardless of the means. The means would be offensive warfare. In this case, it is the apex, the noblest Holy War."[24]

Bible believers view Islam as an anti-Christ spirit that swapped *Calvary for Cavalry*, yet they are equated with them. Prominent liberals deride Bible believers as "the Taliban wing of the Republican Party", ignoring that Christians do not seek to die for God since His Son died for them. There are no fundamentalist Christian organizations that are pro-Taliban. The Christian message has nothing in common with Islam, which persuades its adherents that the Son of God never died for them at Calvary, yet Muslims must die for him in raids and military conquests.

So what motivates Muslims to fight and risk death? Simply, Christianity is a message of salvation – for one to die in the cause of Allah is an assurance of salvation and entry into paradise. Bible believers view this as a corruption of Christian dogma. The difference is that it's the *shaheed* (Martyr) who now atones for sin, even his own. Therefore, dying in Jihad is the ultimate way to transit one's soul instantly to paradise. Salvation as understood in the Christian perspective is only through the death of one perfect man, Jesus Christ. In Islam, the idea of Christ dying for all humanity is rejected. Islam considers this doctrine to be a corruption of the original faith, and views itself as the restoration of that faith.

Islam does retain a measure of Christianity's idea of salvation – that atonement is accomplished by death. However, the big difference is that in Islam, it's not the death of Christ that entitles you to heaven, but your own. So important is this concept, that a *shaheed* martyr in Islam can be an intercessor for 70 members of his/her family. Without this jihad-style death, you had better obtain enough merit to outweigh your sins in order to qualify for paradise. This is a dilemma that confounds all Muslims. The similarity in understanding this salvation is interesting. A suicide martyr is called "Fida'e," from the source word Fidyah (sacrificial lamb) as used in the Christian creed, and the best way for one to assure this salvation is to die in Jihad.

Bible believers deem this blasphemous and utter rebelliousness since it equates the Muslim work to what God offered through His Son Jesus Christ and by this the Muslim becomes like God. If one says that he can obtain salvation through his own death, he has proclaimed himself as possessing the attributes of God while mimicking the spirit of Antichrist, saying, "I will be like God". (Ezekiel 28, Isaiah 14)

This Islamic salvation occurs upon death and with the first drop of blood spilled, "A martyr has six bounties: He will be forgiven with the first drop of his blood that is spilt; He will see his place in Paradise (at the time of death); He will be saved from the 'Great Horror' (on the Day of Judgment); A Crown of Dignity will be placed on his head, which contains many conundrums, each one being more precious than this life and all that it contains; and He will have seventy-two women [virgins] of Paradise. Also, he will be allowed to intercede for seventy of his family members (who would have otherwise gone to hell)."[25]

The goal of Jihad is to gain salvation. The story of the Bedouin is given in schools throughout the Muslim world. It is intended to entice the youth to follow Jihad: "A Bedouin came to the Prophet, accepted Islam, and said: 'I wish to migrate (to Madeenah)'. So the Prophet asked some of his companions to take care of him. Then after a battle, the Muslims had gained some booty so the Prophet divided it and gave the Bedouin's share to some of his companions to look after, as the Bedouin was still at the rearguard. When the Bedouin returned, they gave him his share, so he asked them: 'What is this?' they replied: 'It is your share from the booty which the Prophet gave us to hold on to for you.' So the Bedouin took the booty and went to the Prophet and asked: 'What is this?' The Prophet said: 'Your share of the booty.' The Bedouin said: 'This is not why I believe in you and follow you; rather, I follow you so that I can get shot by an arrow right here, (and then he pointed to his throat) then die and enter Paradise.' The Prophet said: 'If you are sincere then Allah will grant you your wish.' After a short while, fighting resumed and the Bedouin's body was brought to the Prophet with an arrow in his throat at exactly the spot where he had pointed to the Prophet. Thereupon the Prophet said: 'He was sincere so Allah granted him his wish.' Then using his own garment, the Prophet shrouded the Bedouin, prayed the funeral prayer over him and was heard by his companions to say during the prayer: 'O Allah! This is your slave who migrated for Your sake and was killed as a martyr – and I testify to this'. Which testimony could ever be more honorable, sincere and truthful than this great one given by the Prophet?"[26]

CHANGE

So who is truly "the Taliban wing"? Leftists fail to point out that even the infamous 'Taliban' appears to parallel the Victorian progressive tradition. H.G Wells wrote that, "an order must have first arisen among a clash of social forces and political systems as a revolutionary organization. It must have set before itself the attainment of some such Utopian ideal as this modern Utopia does, in the key of mortal imperfection, realize. At first it may have directed itself to research and discussion, to the elaboration of its ideal, to the discussion of a plan of campaign, but at some stage it must have assumed a more militant organization, and have prevailed against and assimilated the pre-existing political organizations, and to all intents and purposes have become this present synthesized World State."[27]

Wells desired change. Islam also portrays itself as an ideology of change. Everywhere Islam goes it breaks a society down. It infiltrates and destroys from within. Like the ideologies of Robespierre, and other revolutionaries that changed established times and laws to set the calendar at the exact date their revolutions begin. The Islamic calendar begins in 622 A.D. when Muhammad started his military conquest in Medina. Like Muhammad's revolutionary take over, Hitler replaced the Christian calendar with the Nazi new year starting on January 30th – the day Hitler became chancellor of Germany or also known as the "seize of power." These parallel with the French Revolution. When Robespierre and his thugs took over the French monarchy they had with them a vision in which Christianity would cease to exist. They pursued this vision to the point that they got rid of France's traditional Gregorian calendar. The Jacobins set the first day of the first year as the 22nd of September 1792 (or the Year I), the day they seized control of France.

So many are the leftist educated elites who exalt Islam as a beautiful system of peace and justice, the same way they exalt the French, Iranian and Russian revolutions. In 2008, leftist author and academician Noah Feldman wrote that Sharī'ah law is better than the Christian based British law which "long denied married women any property rights or indeed legal personality apart from their husbands. When the British applied their law to Muslims in place of Sharī'ah, as they did in some colonies, the result was to strip married women of the property that Islamic law had always granted them – hardly progress toward equality of the sexes."[28]

Feldman wrote that without Sharī'ah there would be "no golden age of Muslim Spain".

Does Feldman think that Muslim Spain had hookah bars with liberals sipping lattes dialoguing the battle of the sexes?

Muslim Spain was a fascist government equal to that of Communist Russia. Islam didn't conquer Spain without the use of the likes of Noah Feldman. According to Evariste Levi-Provencal, one of the greatest historians on Muslim Spain, when Islam took over Spain "churches were converted into mosques. Although the conquest had been planned and conducted jointly with a faction of Iberian Christian dissidents, including a bishop, it proceeded as a classical jihad with massive pillages, enslavements, deportations and killings. Toledo, which had first submitted to the Arabs in 711 or 712, revolted in 713. The town was punished by pillage and all the notables had their throats cut. In 730, the Cerdagne (in Septimania, near Barcelona) was ravaged and a bishop burned alive. In the regions under stable Islamic control, Jews and Christians were tolerated as dhimmis – like elsewhere in other Islamic lands – and could not build new churches or synagogues nor restore the old ones. Segregated in special quarters, they had to wear discriminatory clothing. Subjected to heavy taxes, the Christian peasantry formed a servile class attached to the Arab domains; many abandoned their land and fled to the towns. Harsh reprisals with mutilations and crucifixions would sanction the Mozarab (Christian dhimmis) calls for help from the Christian kings. Moreover, if one dhimmi harmed a Muslim, the whole community would lose its status of protection, leaving it open to pillage, enslavement and arbitrary killing."[29]

In *The Myth of the Andalusian Paradise,* Darío Fernández-Morera writes that Abd al-Rahman III (912-961), "The Servant of the Merciful," declared himself Caliph of Cordoba. He took the city to heights of splendor not seen since the days of Harun-al-Rashid's Baghdad, financed largely through the taxation of Catholics and Jews and the booty and tribute obtained in military incursions against Catholic lands. He also punished Muslim rebellions mercilessly, thereby keeping the lid on the boiling cauldron that was multicultural al-Andalus. His rule presumably marks the zenith of Islamic tolerance. Al-Mansur (d. 1002), "The One Made Victorious by Allah," implemented in al-Andalus in 978 a ferocious military dictatorship backed by a huge army. In addition to building more palaces and subsidizing the arts and sciences in Cordoba, he burned heretical books and terrorized Catholics, sacking Zaragoza, Osma, Zamora, Leon, Astorga,

Coimbra, and Santiago de Compostela. In 985 he burned down Barcelona, enslaving all those he did not kill.

Bernard Lewis, one of the leading Historians on Near Eastern Studies in *The Pro-Islamic Jews* summed up the Golden Age as: "The Golden Age of equal rights was a myth, and belief in it was a result, more than a cause, of Jewish sympathy for Islam" (p. 401)

Overall, Feldman believes "Islamic law offered the most liberal and humane legal principles available anywhere in the world."[30]

Leftist academia's fascination with Islam has nothing to do with ignorance on history – but a hatred of their own history and its faith – they see common grounds with Islam's disenfranchisement with the world.

Islam and leftism are no different – they both seek the destruction of the Judeo-Christian civilization.

But do not think that these common allies are only among the elites. This type of self-destructive thinking has reached the Church of England where the archbishop of Canterbury Rowan Williams said that Muslims should be allowed to conduct Sharî'ah law for matters such as "marital law, the regulation of financial transactions and authorized structures of mediation and conflict resolution."[31]

While Spain was conquered by Islam with the help of liberal Christians – Muslims would use Great Britain's archbishop of Canterbury to slip in Sharî'ah in England.

Why would Rowan aid and abet Islam? Is he unaware of its goals or aspirations? No. Rowan is simply following the leftist creed of praising Islam. Rowan Williams is a die-hard evolutionist who believes "creationism is...a kind of category mistake, as if the Bible were a theory like other theories...if creationism is presented as a stark alternative theory alongside other theories I think there's just been a jarring of categories...My worry is creationism can end up reducing the doctrine of creation rather than enhancing it"[32]

The strange phenomenon is that Muslims are creationists. Why would leftists support creationists that are not Bible believers?

Leftists see themselves as having more in common with Islam than with Bible believing Christians. They have no trouble with trying to make peace with Holocaust deniers like Ahmadinejad of Iran or meeting up with the socialist dictator Hugo Chavez of Venezuela – they are all partners in a worldwide revolution. To leftist actor Sean Penn, Hugo Chavez is "much more positive for Venezuela than he is negative" and the Chavez-crafted constitution is "a very beautiful document."[33] President Barack Hussein Obama would proudly meet Hugo Chavez to supposedly improve America's "global image". While at the same time they always argue that fundamentalist Christians need not to be in politics.

Appearing on Larry King, former president Jimmy Carter claimed that Fundamentalist Christians have changed the faith by getting involved in politics. Yet Carter has the privilege of writing a book titled, *Palestine: Peace Not Apartheid.* Carter is not naïve on Middle East history; his views support Islam's revolutionary agenda. Carter is hypocritical; his goal is simply to persuade fundamentalist Christians that the true faith is politically motionless while Liberal Christians (like Carter) are exceptionally active in the political arena. This active nature is apparently demonstrated by requesting that president Obama remove Hamas from the list of terrorist groups. Leftists are equal to the Muslims in that they will try to pressure Christian activism while at the same time trying to enable the Muslims to spread their supposed peace proposals.

Leftists, under the guise of being Christian evangelicals, are even doing the terrorists' bidding. Reverend Jim Wallis the Social Justice advocate joined National Council of Churches chief Bob Edgar and the Islamic Society of North America Secretary General Sayyid M. Syeed to oppose any U.S. military action against Iran's nuclear weapons program. Instead, like Obama, they advocated "direct negotiations" with Iran. Wallis stated: "If America can resist its hammer habit with Iran, the world may be spared a nuclearized Iran and the disastrous consequences of another misguided military confrontation. The clear witness of America's religious community and our wisest military and foreign policy leaders may be essential to prevent those twin disasters."[34]

The so-called "America's pastor", Rick Warren, visited Syria and met with dictator Bashar al-Assad only to come back and hail "the religious coexistence, tolerance and stability that the Syrian society is enjoying due to the wise leadership of President al-Assad, asserting that he will convey the true image about Syria to the American people."[35]

In the 1930s George Bernard Shaw made a report that Stalin, Hitler, and Mussolini were the world's great "progressive" leaders since they "did things," unlike the leaders of those "putrefying corpses" called parliamentary democracies.[36]

Another elite leftist was Thomas Carlyle, the leading British disciple of Johann Wolfgang von Goethe and German Romanticism.[37] In his set of essays *Heroes and Hero Worship*, Carlyle describes Muhammad in his *"Hero as Prophet"* as a progressive and romantic icon: "Mahometanism among the Arabs. A great change; what a change and progress is indicated here, in the universal condition and thoughts of men!"[38] Carlyle also wrote against those who attacked the prophet saying that our "current hypothesis about Mahomet, that he was a scheming Imposter, a Falsehood incarnate, that his religion is a mere mass of quackery and fatuity, begins really to be now untenable to any one. The lies, which well-meaning zeal has heaped around this man, are disgraceful to ourselves only. When Pococke inquired of Grotius, where the proof was of that story of the pigeon, trained to pick peas from Mahomet's ear, and pass for an angel dictating to him? Grotius answered that there was no proof! It is really time to dismiss all that."[39]

Aleister Crowley, a favorite guru amongst many hippies (including John Lennon), who calls Satan "my lord", and a vicious hater of Christian beliefs, wrote in his work *The Book of The Law*: "With my Hawk's head I peck at the eyes of Jesus as he hangs upon the cross". He spoke greatly of Islam, writing that he "got a sheikh to teach me Arabic and the practices of ablution, prayer and so on, so that at some future time I might pass for a Moslem among themselves. I had it in my mind to repeat Burton's journey to Mecca sooner or later. I learnt a number of chapters of the Koran by heart. I never went to

Mecca, it seemed rather vieux jeu [old game], but my ability to fraternize fully with Mohammedans has proved of infinite use in many ways."[40] Crowley's "sheikh was profoundly versed in the mysticism and magic of Islam, and discovering that I was an initiate, had no hesitation in providing me with books and manuscripts on the Arabic Cabbala. These formed the basis of my comparative studies. I was able to fit them in with similar doctrines and other religions; the correlation is given in my 777. From this man I learnt also many of the secrets of the Sidi Aissawa; how to run a stiletto through one's cheek without drawing blood, lick red hot swords, eat live scorpions, etc. (Some of these feats are common conjurers' tricks, some depend on scientific curiosities, but some are genuine Magick; that is, the scientific explanation is not generally known."[41]

Crowley also wrote about his activity with Muslims, saying that when he saw Muslim men "cut themselves on the head (very rarely elsewhere) until the blood was streaming from their scalps on every side", he found it difficult to "refrain from dashing down my turban, leaping into the ring with a howl of 'Allahu akbar!' getting hold of an axe and joining in the general festivity. It literally took away one's breath. The only way I can express it is that one breathed with one's heart instead of with one's lungs. I had gotten into not dissimilar states while doing Pranayama, but those had been passive, and this was a – no, active is a pitifully inadequate word – I felt myself vibrating with the energy of the universe."[42]

If leftism is revolution so it is with Islam. Sayyid Qutb, whose writings became a primary foundational and philosophical literary source for the Muslim Brotherhood in Egypt, later became the primary catalyst for most Sunni Muslim terrorist organizations. Qutb was an accomplished Islamic philosopher who wrote on his distaste for Christianity, Jews and America. Even though some may think that his writings were rightwing or conservative – one will find them littered with leftist schemes quoting extensively the French Darwinist eugenicist, Alexis Carrel[43] who advocated the use of gas chambers to rid humanity of "inferior stock," prior to the Nazi implementation of such practices in Germany.

In the 1936 publication of Carrel's book, *L'Homme, cet inconnu* (Man, This Unknown) the publishers requested this introduction to the German translation of the book. He added the following praise of the Nazi regime, which did not appear in the editions in other languages: "the German government has taken energetic measures against the propagation of the defective, the mentally diseased, and the criminal. The ideal solution would be the suppression of each of these individuals as soon as he has proven himself to be dangerous." In doing so, he applauded the Nazi T-4 Euthanasia Program.[44] In Carrel's Nazi book *Man, This Unkown*, it reads: "We are unhappy. We degenerate morally and mentally. The groups and the nations in which industrial civilization has attained its highest development are precisely those which are becoming weaker, and whose return to barbarism is the most rapid."[45]

Similarly we find Qutb with the same contempt for the Muslim world that had western secular influence at his time writing that "we are in jaahiliyyah (barbarism), like that which was prevalent at the dawn of Islam, in fact more oppressive (i.e. severe). Everything around us is jaahiliyyah…"[46] Qutb followed Carrel's method and accepted his collectivist views on society. Carrel had his elite in a *scientific monastery* as Qutb's *avant garde*, and Carrel's *biological classes* are Qutb's *belief classes*. Whether *civilization* (Carrel) or *barbarism* (Qutb) – *neither are worthy of us*, because they contradict *our true nature* (Carrel) or Qutb's *good, healthy nature*.

Both are quite in agreement in their goal; Qutb follows Carrel in making "human nature" the condition and measure of all thought and action. Because "human nature" is simultaneously posited as god-given, both immunize "human nature" against criticism, because god answers queries as little as "nature" does objections. What Qutb calls "the Islamic method," the integration of education, ethics, economics and politics to a unified system of "divine uniqueness," matches Carrel's "unification of all capabilities and their coordination to a single belief."[47]

Some of Qutb's writings can hardly be distinguished from leftists who had a disdain for capitalism: "the exploitation of individuals and nations due to greed for wealth and imperialism under the capitalist systems are but a corollary of rebellion against God's authority...Look at this capitalism with its monopolies, its usury and whatever else is unjust in it; at this individual freedom, devoid of human sympathy and responsibility for relatives except under the force of law..."[48] Hatred for capitalism is a leftist tenet, and is common amongst mainstream Muslims. Yusuf al-Qaradawi, the world renown Muslim scholar who regularly gets a red carpet welcome from leftist European leaders, said that capitalism "is based on usury and securities rather than commodities in markets, [it] shows us that it is undergoing a crisis and that our integrated Islamic philosophy – if properly understood and applied – can replace the Western capitalism."[49]

Chapter 16

For God or For Marxist and Islamic Terrorism

Marxists, anarchists and Muslims mimic one another in many ways and at times even unite. While my father, Walid Shoebat, was speaking at Humbolt State University, a mob of anarchists, socialists, homosexuals and Muslim fundamentalists charged the stage with banners condemning America and Israel. Had it not been for Zackariah Izzat, an Egyptian convert from Islam to Christianity and a taekwondo black belt who was able to prevent the crowd from attacking the stage, the two police officers could not control the crowd; my father could have been seriously hurt. The crux of this story is to ask a question: If Islam is truly conservative, why would Muslims unite with anarchists, socialists, environmentalists and homosexuals?

The answer is simple: they share the same destructive worldview of mankind, all in the name of a superior worldview. The left has always held hands with terrorists, even before Islamic terrorism reared its head in this country. The Patriot Act that was enacted after the 9-11 attacks was never considered as a protection bill by the left but as an assault on civil liberties. Its critics liken themselves to the "Palmer Raids" crackdown on anarchist terrorists. Following the 1917 revolution in Russia, American anarchists launched a campaign of bombing and assassination against American officials, judges, and prominent citizens.

In 1918, almost 75 years before Osama bin Laden launched his jihad against the Western democracies, Bolshevik leader Vladimir I. Lenin issued what would be compared to a *fatwa* injunction against the same 'Great Satan' of Islam – the United States of America. In his *Letter to American Workers*, Lenin called on his acolytes to "play an exceptionally important role as uncompromising enemies of American imperialism" by joining the "civil war against the bourgeoisie." Most Americans ignored the rant, but within immigrant anarchist communities it resonated with significant force. In 1919 the first fruits of the Bolshevik incitement were witnessed, when a bomb was dismantled at the home of Seattle Mayor Ole Hanson. The next day, a Bolshevik bomb ripped the hands off of an employee of Georgia Senator Thomas Hardwick as he opened the deadly package; it also severely burned the senator's wife. A few days later 34 bombs were intercepted before reaching their intended targets which included such leading figures as Supreme Court Justice Oliver Wendell Holmes, North Carolina Senator Lee S. Overman, Utah Senator William H. King, Postmaster General Albert Berlson, and John D. Rockefeller.

Coordinated, violent, seditious riots were launched in several cities, most notably in Boston, and a bomb wrecked a municipal building in Brownsville, Pennsylvania. Eight American cities were bombed by anarchists who had already softened up the country a month earlier with a series of violent and coordinated riots. By 1920, anarchists detonated a bomb on Wall Street in the neighborhood of the future World Trade Center. The Wall Street bomb killed 40 innocent commuters and injured more than 400. The street was littered with dismembered corpses and puddles of blood.[50] The American government initiated a strong investigation into the attacks that revisionist historians label as the "Red Scare."

Modern historians portray the era as an exercise in government repression, a precursor of McCarthyism. Today, leftists see the prosecution of terrorists as racist or Islamophobic. Muslims, anarchists and Marxists are compatible allies. Each starts off as a lawless ideology that seeks to alter the law of the land. Leftists have been holding hands with the Islamists, not because there is an unholy alliance with a moral difference between the two, but because they both have an equal goal – the destruction of Western Civilization.

ISLAMIC SOCIALISM

While many Muslim scholars consider Russian Socialism to be atheistic, Islamic socialists argue that the principles of socialism, specifically that of land redistribution, are congruent with the laws of the Qur'ân, having roots in pre-soviet Russia. Pakistan, under the rule of Zulfiqar Ali Bhutto established a social government. Today, the PPP, under the guidance of Asif Ali Zaradi advocates a system based on Islamic socialism. Moammar Gadhafi of Libya established an Islamic socialist state in 1969. Even the Islamic Revolution of Iran is at times described as an example of Islamic Marxism.

But where does socialism separate from Islam? In *Al-Takaful Al-Ijtimai And Islamic Socialism* by Sami Hanna, he explains, "the common themes among the revolutionary regimes in Egypt, Syria and Iraq, may be traced back to the days of the Prophet Muhammad (PBUH) himself and his successors. This concept was expressed one way or another by the single call for social justice among the Muslims. But perhaps the most overt call came from Abu Dharr al-Ghifari who knew the Prophet and witnessed the remarkable social changes which took place in the new Muslim empire, especially during Uthman's reign when Abu Dharr issued his warning against the accumulation of wealth in the hands of the few whom the Caliph had appointed to rule the conquered regions."

Jamal al-Din al-Afghani, the Muslim theologian, philosopher and political leader, has examined Western socialism and suggested that Islamic socialism *ishtirakiyya* is far better.

Mustafa al-Sibai whose book *Ishtirakiyyat al-Islam* (Islamic Socialism) could be considered the most widely acclaimed by Egyptian authorities. He quotes from the Qur'ân: "The believers are brethren" (S. 49: IO), and continues: "To declare brotherhood among the individuals of any society necessitates *al-takaful* among them, not only in eating, drinking and bodily needs but also in every other necessity of life. The acknowledgment of brotherhood between two persons is an acknowledgment of *al-takaful* and *al-tadamun* (solidarity) between them in sentiments and feelings, in demands and needs, and in status and dignity. This is the truth of al-takaful al-ijtimai in Islamic socialism."

Despite having some differences, Marxism and Islamism have many similarities. Marxism is a universal utopia in which the poor 'have-nots' clean the coffers of the rich 'haves' – Islam's universal

Ummah has dissident wealthy Jewish communities and Christian nations taxed with Jizya by the Muslim-have-nots.

Both systems had a disdain for the Church. After the Bolsheviks took over Russia, Vladimir Lenin stole all of the land owned by the nobility and the church, and gave it to the have-nots. The land was stolen "for the benefit of the community" and was "to be distributed in equal shares." The private ownership of land was to be "abolished forever."[51]

Similarly, when the Muslims conquered Spain they took over Christian lands and destroyed their churches. Church property became under the control of the Ummah and thus Christians were forced to comply with the *Pact of Umar* that guaranteed the Islamic enforcement over Christian lands. In the document it reads: "We shall not build, in our cities or in their neighborhood, new monasteries, Churches, convents, or monks' cells, nor shall we repair, by day or by night, such of them as fall in ruins or are situated in the quarters of the Muslims."[52] The Ummah also demands that Jews and Christians pay Jizzya-poll-tax as income for the Muslims. The Muslim philosopher Al-Ghazali explains: "Jews, Christians, and Majians must pay the jizya [poll tax on non-Muslims]…on offering up the jizya, the dhimmi must hang his head while the official takes hold of his beard and hits [the dhimmi] on the protruberant bone beneath his ear [i.e., the mandible]… They are not permitted to ostentatiously display their wine or church bells…their houses may not be higher than the Muslim's, no matter how low that is. The dhimmi may not ride an elegant horse or mule; he may ride a donkey only if the saddle[-work] is of wood. He may not walk on the good part of the road. They [the dhimmis] have to wear [an identifying] patch [on their clothing], even women, and even in the [public] baths…[dhimmis] must hold their tongue…"[53]

Obadyah the Proselyte, in 1100 A.D, also wrote about the jizya tax: "When a Jew died, who had not paid up the poll-tax [jizya] to the full and was in debt for a small or large amount, the Gentiles did not permit burial until the poll-tax was paid. If the deceased left nothing of value, the Gentiles demanded that other Jews should, with their own money, meet the debt owed by the deceased in poll-tax; otherwise they [threatened] they would burn the body..."⁵⁴

Muslims have some Commandments that are equivalent to the Ten Commandments. The difference between commandments in the Bible and commandments in Islam is that while Islam is universal when it comes to enforcing its ideology – the laws of restraint only encompass the Muslim Ummah. It is for this reason that westerners are bewildered when they see Islamists break the basic Ten Commandment laws. So if Islam says 'thou should not murder', the injunction would really mean that a Muslim should not murder another Muslim. The punishment would be the death penalty. While if a Muslim kills a non-Muslim, he would only pay a fine since non-Muslims are subservient and are of a lesser value then Muslims.

Yet it doesn't matter – monotheistic Islam or atheistic Communism both still lead to the same result: the destruction of life, Gulag, end of both private ownership and individualism exalting the revolutionary founder to the level of godhood.

Another example of the life of non-Muslims under Islam are the writings of the pre-eminent historian of Mughal India, Sir Jadunath Sarkar who wrote the following in 1920 regarding the impact of centuries of jihad and dhimmitude on the indigenous Hindus of the Indian subcontinent: "A non-Muslim therefore cannot be a citizen of the State; he is a member of a depressed class; his status is a modified form of slavery. He lives under a contract (zimma, or 'dhimma') with the State: for the life and property grudgingly spared to him by the commander of the faithful he must undergo political and social disabilities, and pay commutation money. In short, his continued existence in the State after the conquest of his country by the Muslims is conditional upon his person and property made subservient to the cause of Islam. He must pay a tax for his land (kharaj), from which the early Muslims were exempt; he must pay other exactions for the maintenance of the army, in which he cannot enlist even if he offers to render personal service instead of paying the poll-tax; and he must show by humility of dress and behavior that he belongs to subject class. No non-Muslim can wear fine dresses, ride on horseback or carry arms; he must behave respectfully and submissively to every member of the dominant sect."[55]

The very same Qur'ān and Sunna that served as the rules of conduct in the seventh century remain the basis for Islamic law today. Although many Muslim countries have banned some of these laws as a result of Western influence, today the cry of the Muslim fundamentalist is to reinstate them, including slavery: "A slave is the property of his/her master. He/She is subject to the master's power, insomuch that if a master should kill his slave he is not liable to retaliation. With female slaves a master has the 'mulk-i-moot'at', or right of enjoyment, and his children by them, when acknowledged, have the same rights and privileges as his children by his wives. A slave is incompetent to anything that implies the exercise of authority over others. Hence a slave cannot be a witness, a judge, or an executor or guardian to any but his master and his children. A slave cannot inherit from anyone, and a bequest to him is a bequest to his master."[56]

Just as Marxism seeks the subjugation of the non-communist, Islamism has the subjugation of the non-Muslim. Antoine Fattal, in his 1958 *Le Statut Legal de Musulmans en Pays' d'Islam* remains the benchmark analysis of non-Muslims (especially Christians and Jews) living under the Sharī'ah (i.e., Muslim Law), observed: "If he [the dhimmi] is tolerated, it is for reasons of a spiritual nature, since there is always the hope that he might be converted; or of a material nature, since he bears almost the whole tax burden. He has his place in society, but he is constantly reminded of his inferiority...In no way is the dhimmi the equal of the Muslim.. He is marked out for social inequality and belongs to a despised caste; unequal in regard to individual rights; unequal in the Law Courts as his evidence is not admitted by any Muslim tribunal and for the same crime his punishment is greater than that imposed on Muslims...No social relationship, no fellowship is possible between Muslims and dhimmis..."[57]

Islamo-Fascism is a sister of Communist Russia or Nazi Germany. It did not stop in the Golden age of Islam, but is now reviving itself in our time. Even in the little town of Bethlehem, recently, Hassam El

– Masalmeh, who heads the Hamas contingent at the municipal council of Bethlehem, confirmed the organization's plan to reinstitute these Islamic laws on Christians. Part of this law also includes the prohibition of arms for the vanquished non – Muslims; the prohibition of church bells; and restrictions concerning the building and restoration of churches.[58]

France Presse reported an attack in Indonesia by the Islamic Anti-Apostate Movement, who stormed a church service in a Protestant church in the West Java town of Soreang. More than 30 churches have been forced to close in West Java and dozens more throughout the country in recent years due to Muslim violence, churches which were among the few spared during the outbreak of hostilities during 1997-1998, where hundreds of Christian churches were burned to the ground and never rebuilt.[59]

This Islamic attack on the church is equal to the attacks on the church by Russian Communists. Sharî'ah, in essence, is equal to the strict laws Stalin enforced on Christians. Interestingly, the communists were atheists and Darwinists and despite their ban on Sharî'ah in the Islamic Republics of Southern Russia, they established laws compatible with Sharî'ah.

For example, in October 1929 the seizure of all church bells was ordered because "the sound of bells disturbs the right to peace of the vast majority of atheists in the towns and the countryside." Anyone closely associated with the church was forced to pay heavy taxes. The taxes paid by religious leaders were ten fold from 1928 to 1930, and the leaders were stripped of their civil rights as many were arrested, exiled or deported. In many villages and towns, collectivization began with closure of the church and the removal of religious leaders. Nearly 14 percent of the riots and peasant uprisings in 1930 were sparked by the closure of a church or the removal of its bells. By March 1st 1930, 6715 churches were removed or destroyed. The communist authorities began to close churches down for reasons such as the "unsanitary condition of extreme age", "unpaid insurance", and nonpayment of taxes or other innumerable contributions imposed on the members of the religious community.[60]

In January 1930 the communist authorities launched a vast campaign to "evict all entrepreneurs." These small entrepreneurs whose average working capital did not exceed 1,000 rubles, 98 percent of whom did not have a single employee, were rapidly evicted by a tenfold increase in their taxes and the confiscation of their goods. They were stripped of their rights just like the "aristocrats" and "members of the possessing classes and of the apparatus of the old tsarist state."[61]

THE IRANIAN REVOLUTION AND ITS LEFTIST FRIEND

The far-left has always seen eye to eye with many revolutions. When the Iranian revolution was taking place, the philosopher Michael Foucault, who was influenced by the work of Frederick Nietzsche and Martin Heidegger and who, like Hegel and Rousseau, produced a philosophy which stated that society creates the beliefs of the individual through shifts in power and societal advances, went to Iran to praise the Mullahs.

Just as Heidegger interpreted National Socialism through the "rose colored glasses" of his own philosophy and Sartre would display a fascination with Communism and Third World dictators in the revolutionary 60's, the French postmodernist Michael Foucault had a thing for the 1978 Iranian revolution, or as David Frum put it: "Of all the absurd infatuations ever to sweep literary Paris, none has ever matched the absolute incongruity of Michel Foucault's enthusiasm for the Iranian Islamic revolution of 1979. Foucault, a man utterly devoid of religious feeling, a homosexual who reveled in the brutalities of San Francisco's sadomasochistic bar scene, decided in 1978 that the Khomeini revolution offered mankind's best hope for personal liberation."[62] When Foucault went to Tehran, he was France's dominant public intellectual, famous for a critique of modernity carried out through unsparing dissections of modern institutions that reversed the conventional wisdom about prisons, madness, and sexuality. In his most famous work, *Discipline and Punish*, Foucault argued that liberal democracy was in fact a "disciplinary society" that punished with less physical severity in order to punish with greater efficiency. More broadly, his counter narrative of the Enlightenment suggested that the modern institutions we imagined were freeing us were in fact enslaving us in insidious ways.

In the fall of 1978, an escalating series of street protests had placed the shah and the Iranian populace on a collision course. The uprising consisted of a broad coalition, including Communists, student leftists, secular nationalists, socialists, and Islamists. But by late 1978, the Islamists – directed by Khomeini from Paris, long a center for Iranian exiles – were the dominant faction. The shah was abdicated in January 1979, and Khomeini returned to rapturous rejoicing on Feb. 1, 1979.[63] Foucault was enthralled by the revolution, pronouncing Khomeini "a kind of mystic saint." The Frenchman welcomed "Islamic government" as a new form of "political spirituality" that could inspire Western radicals to combat capitalist 'hegemony.'[64]

Just as Hegel idolized the Islamic state and martyrdom, Foucault championed the Iranian revolution "as a form of 'political will.' It impressed me in its effort to politicize structures that are inseparably social and religious in response to current problems. It also impressed me in its attempt to open a spiritual dimension in politics" and exalted the martyrdom of the Iranian mujahadden Ali Shariati, who described martyrdom as a mystical experience, full of erotic charge, and beyond "science and logic."[65]

For God or For Tyranny

→ Chapter 17 ←

For Life or For Death

The North American Man/Boy Love Association *(NAMBLA)* would be proud of Islam's heaven. Not only is its heaven homoerotic but the sadomasochist Foucault exalts the Islamic tenet of self-destruction.

There is indeed, a correlation between his glorification of Islamic martyrdom and his philosophy. Michael Foucault, in an interview, was a proponent of suicide. He believed suicide to be a great personal victory. The taking of one's own life was an event, like a great play without an audience.[66] He wrote that we should "speak in favor of suicide... It appears that life is fragile and death is certain. Why must we make of this certainty a mere chance which in its sudden and inevitable character takes on the air of a punishment?"[67]

Foucault's romanticization of martyrdom echoes greatly Hitler's view of self-sacrifice. A favorite play of Hitler's was *Der Konig* (This King), written by the German playwright and Nazi Poet Laureate Hans Johst. The play centers on a heroic revolutionary who meets a tragic end because he's betrayed by reactionaries and the bourgeoisie. The protagonist takes his own life rather than abandon his revolutionary principles.

When Hitler met Johst (whom he later named poet laureate of the Third Reich) in 1923, he told him that he'd seen the play seventeen times and that he suspected his own life might end the same way.[68] A Muslim who fights for his own self-destruction is like the revolutionary in Der Konig, which is a major reason why Hitler exalted Islam and Himmler regarded it as an excellent faith which promised "that those who fall in battle will go to heaven"[69] and "two beautiful women to every courageous warrior who dies in battle."[70]

This exaltation of suicide was a common element within pagan societies way before Islam and is nothing modern. The Romans "regarded the power of self-destruction as an inestimable privilege."[71]

The Stoics largely believed that the moral permissibility of suicide did not hinge on the moral character of the individual pondering it. Rather, the Stoics held that whenever the means to living a naturally flourishing life are not available to us, suicide may be justified, regardless of the character or virtue of the individual in question. Our natures require certain "natural advantages" (e.g., physical health) in order for us to be happy, and a wise person who recognizes that such advantages may be lacking in his life sees that ending his life neither enhances nor diminishes his moral virtue.

The Roman philosopher Cicero wrote: "When a man's circumstances contain a preponderance of things in accordance with nature, it is appropriate for him to remain alive; when he possesses or sees in prospect a majority of the contrary things, it is appropriate for him to depart from life.... Even for the foolish, who are also miserable, it is appropriate for them to remain alive if they possess a predominance of those things which we pronounce to be in accordance with nature."[72]

Suicide has been dignified in many of the writings of philosophers such as Rousseau, Goethe and Flaubert, based on a romantic idealized 'script' for suicide, according to which suicide was the inevitable response of a misunderstood and anguished soul jilted by love or shunned by society.[73]

These were hardly void of a god and religion. They also espoused love of earth and universe. There was no meaning for life. There views were void of "for God so loved the world" or "offer your body as a living sacrifice" – everything they believed was contrary to the Bible.

The existential writer Jean-Paul Sartre was likewise struck by the possibility of suicide as an assertion of authentic human will in the face of absurdity. Suicide is, according to Sartre, an opportunity to stake out our understanding of our essence as individuals in a godless world. For the existentialists, suicide was not a choice shaped mainly by moral considerations but by concerns about the individual as the sole source of meaning in a meaningless universe.

To sociologists Durkheim and Laplace, suicide was increasingly viewed as a social ill reflecting widespread alienation, anomie, and other attitudinal byproducts of modernity.[74] Excusing suicide as a product of alienation and byproducts of modernity, a reminder of what the *Green Left*, a radical leftist newspaper in Australia, wrote on suicide bombing saying that it is a symptom of "poverty, desperation and hopelessness" and "rule by Western-backed elites".[75] In other words, suicide bombing is excusable as a way of liberating oneself from the ills of the universe by exalting the act as a form of self-liberation.

Evil simply cellophanes death and destruction with the pleasures of the afterlife; Muslims describe this suicide romantically as "the most supreme model of struggle and Resistance, the model of the Martyrs... these [Martyrs] are the climax of Jihad and the peak of Resistance. They are youth at the peak of their blooming, who at a certain moment, decide to turn their bodies into body parts and their blood into a flood of fire..."[76]

Islam romanticizes suicide in the likes of many of the Western world's well known thinkers like Foucault, who like the Nazis, saw Islam as a great revolutionary philosophy superior to Christianity. He often romanticized the Iranian revolution as a "peculiar destiny. At the dawn of history, Persia invented the state and conferred its models on Islam. [....] For the people who inhabit this land, what is the point of searching, even at the cost of their own lives, for this thing whose possibility we have forgotten since the Renaissance and the great crisis of Christianity, a political spirituality. I can already hear the French laughing, but I know that they are wrong."[77]

Foucault never considered the rights of women in Islam. This is demonstrated in his very last disillusioned missive, which appeared in *Le Monde* in May 1979. When an Iranian woman living in exile in Paris named "Atoussa H." wrote a letter to *Le Nouvel Observateur* in November 1978 castigating Foucault for his uncritical support of a solution that could prove to be worse than the problem, he airily dismissed her claims as anti-Muslim hate-mongering.[78]

So much for women's liberation!

The Islamic terrorists who kill themselves do it for bizarre erotic purposes, as the Koran says that in heaven there will be "dark-eyed houris (beautiful virgins)" (Q 44:51-55) and "boys (handsome) as pearls well-guarded." (Q 52:24)

What do Muslims complain about when accusing the West of being run by international Zionism, with its Hollywood and sexual licentiousness? All of the perversity that we have in the West also exists in abundance in the Muslim paradise where there are "angels and young boys (handsome) as pearls well guarded" (Q 52:24), "rivers of wine" (Q 47:15), served with "goblets filled at a gushing fountain white and delicious to those who drink it." "It will neither dull their senses nor befuddle them" (Q 37:40-48). "Rivers of milk of which the taste never changes; a joy to those who drink; and rivers of honey pure and clear" (Q 47:15). "Bosomed virgins for companions: a truly overflowing cup" (Q 78:31). These virgins are bashful and undefiled by man or demon.

Today sexual enticements play an integral element in recruiting Jihadists. The late author and journalist Muhammad Galal Al-Kushk wrote: "The men in Paradise have sexual relations not only with the women who come from this world and with 'the black-eyed,' but also with the serving boys." According to Kurum, Al-Kushk also stated, "In Paradise, a believer's penis is eternally erect."[79]

A Hamas youth leader in a Gaza refugee camp told Jack Kelley of USA Today that, "most boys can't stop thinking about the virgins."[80]

Sheikh Abd Al Fattah Jam'an speaking of Muslims in Palestine stated: "What is waiting for the suicide bomber in paradise is a harem of beautiful virgins who are delicate and pure, esthetic, passive, with no personality or self or ego, whose only role is to sexually satisfy the shahid and be ever ready to fulfill his desires."[81]

Some delights do not have to wait until Paradise: "Ibn Fahd asked Al-Hajjaj 'I have some slave girls who are better than my wives, but I do not desire that they should all become pregnant. Shall I do azl (withdrawal) with them?' Al-Hajjaj said 'They are your fields of culti-vation. If you wish to irrigate them do so, if not keep them dry.'"[82]

There are many references in the Qur'ân where certain sexual privileges are reserved only for Muhammad: "Forbidden to you also are married women, except those who are in your hand as slaves, this is the law of Allah for you" (Q 4:24). And in Qur'ân 33:50 we read: "O prophet; we allowed thee thy wives to whom thou hast paid their dowries, and the slaves whom thy right hand possess out of the booty which Allah hath granted thee, and the daughters of thy uncle, and of thy maternal aunt, who fled with thee to Medina, and any believing woman who hath given herself up to the prophet, if the prophet desired to wed her, a privilege to thee above the rest of the faithful."

One of Muhammad's wives was taken from his own adopted son, Zaid, as Allah declared that she was given to the prophet. Others were Jewish captives forced into slavery after Muhammad beheaded their husbands and/or families. The Qur'ân and Muhammad confirm this: "Thus [shall it be], and We will wed them with Houris [dark-eyed, celestial virgins], pure, beautiful ones."[83] "They shall recline on couches lined with thick brocade, and within reach will hang the fruits of both gardens. Therein are bashful virgins whom neither man nor jinnee will have touched [opening themselves] before them. Virgins as fair as corals and rubies."[84] "In each there shall be virgins chaste and fair. Dark eyed virgins sheltered in their tents whom neither man nor jinnee would have touched before. They shall recline on green cushions and fine carpets" (Q 55:70-77). "We created the Houris and made them virgins, loving companions for those of the right hand. That which is coming." (Q 56:36) "As for the righteous, they shall surely triumph. Theirs shall be gardens and vineyards, and high-bosomed virgins for companions, a truly overflowing cup" (Q 78:31-33).

→ Chapter 18 ←

To Covet or Not To Covet

COLLECTIVISM – HOW TO END PRIVATE PROPERTY

If the Ten Commandments mandate not to covet thy neighbor, his wife or his belongings, tyranny commands coveting everything. Stolen fruit tastes better than what you pay for in the market. Collectivism does not only infect obvious hosts in communist societies, for it exists in so-called Christian cults. If such cults are simply religions that provide a path to connect to the almighty as many claim, why then, do they seem to morph into ideologies, even systems of government to control commerce, finance, political outlook, constitutions and every aspect of government?

Joseph Smith envisioned a world under his ideology. He founded a philosophy called the "united order" where the Mormons' possessions are collective and the idea of private property no longer exists. In one of Mormonism's holy writ *Doctrine and Covenant* it reads that Mormons "are to be equal, or in other words, you are to have equal claims on the properties, for the benefit of managing the concerns of your stewardships, every man according to his wants and his needs, inasmuch as his wants are just – And all this for the benefit of the church of the living God, that every man may improve upon his talent, that every man may gain other talents, yea, even a hundred fold, to be cast into the Lord's storehouse, to become the common property of the whole church – Every man seeking the interest of his neighbor, and doing all things with an eye single to the glory of God. This order I have appointed to be an everlasting order unto you, and unto your successors, inasmuch as you sin not."[85]

The official program for the Nazi party mirrored the Mormon united order in that it wanted "the nationalization of all trusts", demanding "profit-sharing in large industries. We demand a generous increase in old-age pensions. We demand the creation and maintenance of a sound middle-class, the immediate communalization of

171

large stores, which will be rented cheaply to small trades people, and the strongest consideration must be given to ensure that small traders shall deliver the supplies needed by the State, the provinces and municipalities. We demand an agrarian reform in accordance with our national requirements, and the enactment of a law to expropriate the owners without compensation of any land needed for the common purpose."[86] Nazism's socialism is seen in H.G. Wells' writing: "the State should take away the land, and the railways, and shipping, and many great organized enterprises from their owners, who use them simply to squeeze the means for a wasteful private expenditure out of the common mass of men, and should administer all these things, generously and boldly, not for profit, but for service."[87]

Wells could care less about the property owners he wanted to rob, saying that to "abolish private property in these things would be to abolish all that swarm of parasites, whose greed for profit and dividend hampers and makes a thousand useful and delightful enterprises costly or hopeless. It would abolish them; but is that any objection whatever? And as for taking such property from the owners; why shouldn't we?"[88]

Coveting seemed to have infested many of the elites of that generation. It is no wonder that the progressive elites of today attack the Ten Commandments so relentlessly; they are coveting their neighbors' property as well as their children.

One of the first philosophical anarchists, William Godwin, summarized this when he wrote in his book *Political Justice* "that an individual, however great may be his imaginary elevation, should be obliged to yield his personal pretensions to the sense of the community at least bears the appearance of a practical confirmation of the great principle that all private considerations must yield to the general good."[89]

Coveting non-Muslim property was a fascination for Muhammad, the Muslim prophet, according to the stories of his conquests for land and booty. The Qur'ân says that "whatever ye take as spoils of war, lo! A fifth thereof is for Allah and for the messenger..." (Q 8:41)

If the Muslims were running low on Zakat there was always more treasure from infidels to plunder. That is how Muhammad always overcame being broke. Allah and Muhammad may have demanded one fifth but they always paid their mercenaries well. When one reads the many Muslim traditions about this subject, it is quite apparent that Muslims truly ascribe to the proverb: "stolen bread is sweeter." (Proverbs 9:17) As the story goes, "A horseman came [to Mohammed] and said: Apostle of Allah, I went before you and climbed a certain mountain where I saw the Hawazin tribe all together with their women, cattle, and sheep, having gathered at Hunayn... Mohammed smiled and said: That will be the booty of the Muslims tomorrow if Allah wills..."[90]

Upon studying Islam carefully, two sets of codes are discovered. One consists of abrogated Qur'ânic verses and commands for peace, used whenever objections against violence in Islam arise. The other is made up of commands exclusively for Muslims. Muslims are quick to share fantastic quotes from Islamic sources claiming that Jihad means self-defense: "Fight in the cause of Allah those who fight you, but do not transgress limits; for Allah loves not transgressors." (Q 2:190) Or the favorite, "Ten Commandments of Jihad" used by Muslim apologists who quote Caliph Abu Bakr upon commissioning Muslims for Jihad expansions: "Listen and obey the following ten commands and instructions: Do not betray any one (if you give a pledge). Do not ever steal from the war booties. Do not breach your pledge of allegiance. Do not mutilate the body of the killed enemy fighters or deceased. Do not kill a child or a minor. Do not kill an elderly man or woman. Do not kill a woman. Do not pull out a date palm tree (or any other trees) and do not burn it either. Do not cut or destroy a fruit tree. Do not slaughter a female sheep, a cow, or a camel except for your (required) food. You surely will pass by some people who isolate themselves and are secluded for worship of Allah as monks and else, thus leave them alone and do not disturb them ever. You will, surely, stop at some people on the road, who will bring forth for you all types of food dishes. Whenever you eat their food utter the name of Allah each time you eat. You will, surely, pass by a group of people who shaved the hair in the center of their heads, and left the surrounding hair long braids. Go ahead; kill these people, as they are the fighters and worriers who carry their swords against you, of the enemies. Go ahead, with the name of Allah."[91]

Isn't there a contradiction between "Jihad expansion" and all this talk of loving captive peoples? Why invade them in the first place? What transgression did Jerusalem do to Arabia to deserve Omar's invasion? Were the Muslims truly defending themselves when they invaded Spain?

Then you have the most amazing contradiction from Al-Ghazali: "One must go on jihad (i.e., warlike razzias or raids) at least once a year...one may use a catapult against them when they are in a fortress, even if among them are women and children. One may set fire to them and/or drown them...If a person of the Ahl al-Kitab [People of The Book – Jews and Christians, typically] is enslaved, his marriage is [automatically] revoked...One may cut down their trees...One must destroy their useless books. Jihadists may take as booty whatever they decide...they may steal as much food as they need."[92]

Muslim apologists love to quote Al Ghazali the famous theologian, philosopher, and paragon of mystical Sufism as a prime example of moderate Islam. Even Western scholars like the eminent W. M. Watt describes Al-Ghazali as "acclaimed in both the East and West as the greatest Muslim after Mohammed, and he is by no means unworthy of that dignity."

Had Westerners studied Al-Ghazali regarding Jihad and the treatment of the vanquished non-Muslim dhimmi peoples, perhaps they would not have been deceived by 'peace'.

Contemporary scholar Bassam Tibi sums it up this way: "At its core, Islam is a religious mission to all humanity. Muslims are religiously obliged to disseminate the Islamic faith throughout the world.[93] 'We have sent you forth to all mankind' (Q 34:28). If non-Muslims submit to conversion or subjugation, this call (da'wa) can be pursued peacefully. If they do not, Muslims are obliged to wage war against them."[94]

The Qur'ân even contains an entire chapter titled *Al-Anfal*, which translates as "the Booty" or "the Spoils of war." From the book *Al-Hidayah*, arguably the most widely read book of Islamic jurisprudence in the Muslim world, and used as a primary text in Islamic schools and seminaries mentions the motivating factor in the call to jihad: "After the Battle of Badr, the verse dealing with the booties was first revealed. The verse introduced the rule for the first time that the spoils of war would be the property of the soldiers who actually take part in the battle...That is one of the reasons why the soldiers of Islam fought tooth and nail. They would get Paradise in case of death in a Holy War, and booty in the case of conquest. Jihad is therefore the best source of all acquisitions."[95]

Muhammad attacked numerous tribes, villages and cities in order to raid their wealth to give to his new followers; this is also how the Mahdi is expected to imitate Muhammad. The Mahdi, during the seven years of peace proclaimed in Islam, will use the seized property and wealth of the nations that he defeats to distribute among his followers. One of the most popular traditions regarding the Mahdi is that "He will give away wealth profusely."[96] "In those years (the time of the Mahdi) my community will enjoy a time of happiness such as they have never experienced before. Heaven will send rain upon them in torrents, the earth will not withhold any of its plants, and wealth will be available to all. A man will stand and say, 'Give to me Mahdi!' and he will say, 'Take.'"[97]

SECTION FOUR

FOR GOD OR FOR PAGANISM

Chapter 19

To Love God or To Love All Other Gods

Paganism is the usual faith of the left. Likewise, Islam is occultism with a conservative shell.

We have mentioned how Muslims deny any pagan-astral connection or worship as they bow several times a day towards an asteroid – *The Black Stone* – that fell from the sky. While Muslims deny that this is worship and claim it to be symbolic, they also believe that paying homage to it is a redemptive act that takes away all sin. If indeed this image they venerate is simply an object, why then does it come to life and testify about all who touched it. The Black Stone – in Muslim view – will have eyes and ears and become alive.[1]

The writing in the Qur'ân would probably mingle well in today's bookstore shelves alongside Wicca and astrology. The Qur'ân is filled with astrological references and nature-based spirituality. One Wicca prayer reads: "By the power of moon and sun, By the power of Spirit, earth and sea, God and Goddess are part of One, As I Will, so mote it be!"[2] In the Qur'ân: "I swear by the sun and its brilliance, and the moon when it follows the sun" (Q 91:1-2)

Hitler himself wrote of a certain mystical power of the moon, writing that he often went "on bitter nights To Wotan's oak in the quiet glade With dark powers to weave a union – the runic letter the moon makes with its magic spell and all who are full of impudence during the day are made small by the magic formula."[3] *Wotan* was Hitler's *Ghar-Hira* where Muhammad's inspirations began with similar fascination: "by the Moon as a witness, and by the darkness of night as it wanes." (Q 74:32)

Joseph Smith's seclusions and visions are reflected on the old Mormon temple in Nauvoo, which is riddled with crescent moons, stars and sun carvings on limestone. Mormonism's *Doctrine and Covenant* reads: "Which truth shineth. This is the light of Christ. As also He is in the sun, and the light of the sun, and the power thereof by which it was made. Also He is in the moon, and is the light of the moon, and the power thereof by which it was made; As also the light of the stars, and the power thereof by which they were made…"4 Why would God be infused in the matter of the sun, moon and stars? Islam is riddled with parallels to Wicca, Nazism, Hinduism, and even ancient Babylonian and Mayan cults.

The left tries to have a progressive façade, claiming to be scientific advocates of change and the move forward. In Reality, the progressives are moving backward because while it's true they like change, Paganism is the change they seek.

Al Gore is not simply promoting a scientific global warming argument but an introduction to a paganistic, nature-based spirituality. In his *Earth In The Balance*, Gore introduces his god: "modern prayer of the Onondaga tribe in upstate New York offers another beautiful expression of our essential connection to the earth: 'O Great Spirit, whose breath gives life to the world and whose voice is heard in the soft breeze make us wise so that we may understand what you have taught us.'"5

If one thinks that Gore is simply making a reference – Gore even calls upon pagan gods for wisdom: "The richness and diversity of our religious tradition throughout history is a spiritual resource long ignored by people of faith, who are often afraid to open their minds to teachings first offered outside their own system of belief…But the emergence of a civilization in which knowledge moves freely and almost instantaneously throughout the world has spurred a renewed investigation of the wisdom distilled by all faiths…This pan religious perspective may prove especially important where our global civilization's responsibility for the earth is concerned."6

Then comes the thrust of Gore's message - to worship mother earth: "The spiritual sense of our place in nature predates Native American cultures; increasingly it can be traced to the origins of human civilization…A growing number of anthropologists and archeo-mythologists argue that the prevailing ideology of belief in prehistoric Europe and much of the world was based on the worship of a single earth goddess, who was assumed to be the fount of all life and who radiated harmony among all living things…Much of the evidence for the existence of this primitive religion comes from the many thousands of artifacts uncovered in ceremonial sites. These sites are so widespread that they seem to confirm the notion that a goddess religion was ubiquitous throughout much of the world until the antecedents of today's religions – most of which still have a distinctly masculine orientation – swept out of India and the Near East, almost obliterating belief in the goddess…"[7]

So who is the culprit behind the destruction of the earth-goddess? Gore gladly exposes it: "The last vestige of organized goddess worship was eliminated by Christianity."[8] Gore says we need to repent: "It seems obvious that a better understanding of a religious heritage preceding our own by so many thousands of years could offer new insights" (p. 261).

In a case of stolen identity, Gore repeats the Christian formula: "My own faith is rooted in the unshakable belief in God as creator and sustainer, a deeply personal interpretation of and relationship with Christ and an awareness of a constant and holy spiritual presence in all people, all life and all things" (p. 368).

Of course, without the secret pass, the disclaimer, this 'open-sesame', Gore will not be able to introduce his pagan views: "My understanding of how God is manifest in the world can be best conveyed through the metaphor of the hologram; I believe that the image of the Creator, which sometimes seems so faint in the tiny corner of creation each of us beholds, is nonetheless present in its entirety" (p. 265).

Neo-Pagans revere ancient goddesses such as Ishtar, a goddess in which Islam has roots. *Sahar* (Morning Star) has its links with Akkadian elletu (Ishtar) and Arabic *Hilal* (New Moon).[9] The term "new moon" is not simply some observance Muhammad had with the cosmos. It is quite embedded in Islamic spirituality. Stephen Langdon, in his work *The Mythology of All Races* confirms Islam's link: "Allat was a Babylonian, or earth and moon goddess. Her consort Allah was simply the god who impregnates the earth."[10]

No matter how Muslim apologists attempt to vindicate Islam's connection to such ancient deities by using disclaimers, one could find a litany of references in both the Qur'ān and the Hadith venerating the moon. Whenever Muhammad saw a new moon he said: "O Allah, let this crescent loom above us in safety, faith, peace and Islam. Make it a crescent of good and guidance. My Lord and your Lord is Allah."[11]

Allah was the Lord of the Moon. The worship of the moon is also attested to by proper names of people such as *Hilal*, a crescent; *Qamar.*[12] *Hilal* also means "the shining one" in ancient Aramaic Hebrew, Arabic and Ethiopian "Moon crescent." He is a Moon-god.[13] *Sahar* or *Shahar* is Hebrew for "dawn" or "morning star". It is noteworthy that the meaning of these two words *Hilal* and *Sahar* combined, make up the Islamic symbol of the crescent moon and star as described in chapter 13 of Isaiah of The Luminous One; *Heylel ben Sahar.*

→ Chapter 20 ←

For God or For The Dawn

The Night of Vision and the encounter Muhammad had with the angel of light are the bases of the Islamic claim. It describes the "rising of the dawn" for which Ramadan is commemorated and Muslims begin their fast as the crescent moon appears with Venus (morning star). Many Muslims wait until the late hours of the night gazing at the sky, waiting to see the sky open and the angelic host descend: "We have sent it to thee in the Night of Vision, what do you know of this Night of Vision. The Night of Vision is better then a thousand months. The angelic hosts descend [to earth] in it with the Spirit by command of their Lord. Peace shall it be until the rising of the Dawn (Morning star)" (Q 97).

The morning dawn (star) and the crescent moon are important symbols to Muslims everywhere. Even when terrorists from over 40 different organizations assembled in Tehran, they gave the name of the summit "Ten Days of Dawn."[14] The story in Isaiah 14 regarding 'The Luminous One' *Heylel ben Sahar* and his fallen angels seem to connect. The Qur'ân speaks of the angelic host descending to earth (dawn, the spirit, their lord).

The Qur'ân explains this dawn-god: "Say: 'I seek refuge in the lord of the Daybreak, from the evil of what he has created; and from the evil of the night when it comes on; and from the evil of the witches who blow upon knots, and from the evil of the envious when he envies'" (Qur'ân 113). The Qur'ân speaks of the dawn, when the angelic host came down from heaven.

If oceans can separate continents paganism seems to connect them even amongst peoples who never communicated in their era; it is astonishing to see how much in common these cults have. Quetzalcoatl, the Aztec serpentine bird who contrasts with Al-Buraq, the peacock-bird that Muhammad encountered was described similarly as "the Dawn god or the god of Light when day wants to come in...at daybreak. They say that it was created before the sun."[15] In the ancient book *Popol Vuh*, the ancient Mexican story of the creation of the world and the genealogy of the Quiche kingdom in Guatemala, contains a prayer to the gods, which parallels Qur'ânic prayers to Allah said by those believed to be some of the first peoples of the Quiche: "'Let it dawn; let the day come! Give us many good roads, flat roads! May the people have peace, much peace, and may they be happy; and give us good life and useful existence! ...grandmother of the sun, grandmother of the light, let there be dawn, and let the light come!' Thus they spoke while they saw and invoked the coming of the sun, the arrival of day; and at the same time that they saw the rising of the sun, they contemplated the Morning Star, the Great Star, which comes ahead of the sun, that lights up the arch of the sky and the surface of the earth, and illuminates the steps of the men who had been created and made."[16]

Thomas Stewart Denison, in his study of *Mexican (Mayan) Liguistics and Comparative Vocabulary* finds the gods Nanauatzin and Nanepaushat. The ancient Mexican moon-god[17] etymologically sounds like the god Nanaru, the Babylonian moon-god.

The crescent moon was also much revered in Aztec civilization in which they worshiped *Tecciztecatl* or 'Old moon god' who represents the male form on the planet. He is called "he who comes from the land of the sea-slug shell" because of the similar looks between the crescent moon and the slug.[18]

The worship of a dawn god can also go back, like the others, to ancient Hindu writings called the *Rigveda* in the tenth century B.C. which mentions *Ushas* or "the dawn": "The radiant Dawns have risen up for glory, in their white splendour like the waves of waters. She maketh paths all easy, fair to travel, and, rich, hath shown herself benign and friendly. We see that thou art good: far shines thy lustre; thy beams, thy splendours have flown up to heaven. Decking thyself, thou makest bare thy bosom, shining in majesty, thou Goddess Morning. ...O Goddess Dawn, much good thou bringest."[19]

Compare the Hindu prayer with Islam's oldest *nasheed* hymnal *Tala'a Al-Badru*: "O the White Moon rose over us from the Valley of Wada' and we owe it to show gratefulness where the call is to Allah."

→ Chapter 21 ←

For Honoring God or For Honoring The Sun and The Moon

In ancient Gaul they worshiped *Tarvos Trigaranus*, a bull god. *Tarvos* means 'bull'[20] and *Garanus* means 'crane' (the bird)[21] Tarvos Trigaranus is accompanied by three long-legged marsh birds.[22]

Tarvos Trigaranus stands for the "bull with three cranes (birds)", quite similar to Muhammad's annulled satanic verses when he exalted the three cranes: "Have ye seen "Lat and Uzzah, And another, the third goddess, Mannat these are the exalted cranes (intermediates) whose intercession is to be hoped for." Even when Muhammad corrected his satanically inspired verses remembered their position: "What! for you the males sex, and for Him, the females? Behold, such would be a division most unfair!" (Q 53:19-22).

Neo-pagans enjoy delving into the cesspool of heathen gods and goddesses, especially that of *"The Horned One"* a Celtic god of fertility, life, animals, wealth, and the underworld.[23] The Horned God, the most "male" (in the conventional sense), of the Goddess' projections, is the eternal Hunter, and also the animal which is hunted. He is the beast who is sacrificed that human life may go on, as well as the sacrificer, the one who sheds blood. He is also seen as the sun, eternally hunting the moon across the sky. The waxing and waning of the sun throughout the seasons is manifested in the cycle of birth and death, creation and dissolution, separation and return. The horns of the Horned God are believed to represent his domain over the woodlands, and his association with the bull and ram, the animal consorts of the Goddess. His horns also symbolize the crescent moon, the symbol of the Goddess, and represent the increase in all things, waxing fertility.

Neo-pagans believe that there is no association between the Horned God and the Luminous One mentioned in the Bible. They say Christians have erroneously tried to make such a connection.[24]

However, this horned one whose "horns symbolize the crescent moon" is the same god Allah of pre-Islamic Arabia and the same god the ancient Europeans committed human sacrifices to. Today, Allah has Muslims sacrifice themselves through martyrdom for his sake.

Islam is neo-Babylonian, connecting to the moon-god of ancient Mesopotamia originally called *Sin*, who was depicted as "a young bull (the strong bull of heaven) perfect in every part: his beard is said to be of lapis lazuli: his orb is a giant self-propagating fruit. The god's horns are taken to be a reference to the crescent moon, although they are also sometimes regarded as the boat in which he skims through the midst of the heavens."[25]

French historian Robert Briffault explains this resettlement: "[Sin's] supreme character passed in later times to his female counterpart, who finally replaced him. When the female aspect of the lunar deity came to displace the male, the wife of the moon-god became identified with the moon itself, while the goddess Ishtar maintained her association with the planet Venus. This identification is symbolically represented by the lunar crescent, enclosing the star within its horns, which is still the crest of Islam."[26] Caton Thompson's book, *The Tombs and Moon Temple of Hureidha*, discusses the uncovering of a temple of the moon god in southern Arabia. The symbols of the crescent moon and no less than twenty-one inscriptions with the name "Sin" were found in this temple. The Arabic word for 'god' is 'Ilah' and the moon god became synonymous with "al-Ilah," meaning "the god;" pagan Arabia believed that the moon god was the greatest of all the gods, hence the phrase "Allahu Akbar," meaning "Allah is greater." This is what led Muhammad to go one step further and proclaim in the Qur'ân that *la ilaha ila Allah* – there is no god but Allah.

Inscriptions of "al-Ilah" have been found on an idol with the crescent moon and star symbols. The pagan Arabs connected "Allah" to the names of their children. Muhammad's father was called AbdAllah, meaning "servant of Allah."

The least offensive name of the god in Mecca was Allah according to Muhammad's biographer, Ibn Hisham. He admits that the pagan Kinanah and Kouraish tribes called the supervising god of the Ka'aba *Ihlal*. They called the Ka'aba *Beit Allah* house of the god![27]

Muslims still practice the *Ihlal* during the pilgrimage reciting the same ancient formula called *labayk* used in the ritual when Muslims circumambulate (tawaf) roundabout the Black Stone. Such terms and even the Black Stone itself are nowhere to be found in the Qur'ân and have stemmed from Babel into pagan Arabia.

According to historian William St. Clair-Tisdall, *Ihalal* was used to address the deity of Allah in which the Haj ceremony was called *Ihalal* a metathesis of *Hilal*, meaning the crescent moon.[28] Even the killing of converts was not unusual in pre-Islamic practice in Arabia, just as it is not unusual today.

Even the punishment of abandoning the Arab faith seems to have been documented way before Muhammad. Josephus tells the story of Sylleus the Arab, who fell in love with Salome in Herod's kingdom, but he would not convert at her request for fear of being stoned by his people, the Arabs.[29]

Sir Leonard Woolley excavated a temple of the moon god in Ur (Babylon). His findings are displayed in the British Museum. In the 1950s, a major temple of the moon god was excavated at Hazer in "Palestine." Two idols of the moon god were found. Each was a statue of a man sitting upon a throne with a crescent moon carved on his chest, and the inscriptions confirm the items were idols. They also found several smaller statues bearing inscriptions identifying them as the "daughters" of the moon god.[30]

Today's Allah simply evolved through Islam from this horned god whose crescent symbol (the *Hilal*) is everywhere, including on the tips of minarets and in all the neo-pagan books. All pagan religions exalt the moon and sun, representing masculine and feminine deities.

Historically, *Allah* was a male fertility god married to his feminine form, *Allat* who was a Babylonian earth and moon goddess. Her consort Allah was simply the god who impregnates the earth (Allat).[31] The origin of Allah and Allat were as sun and moon deities just like Wicca where there is a huge stress on the god and the goddess in that they are the main tenets of the Wiccan faith, similarly, Allah and Allat translates to "the god and the goddess".

Wiccan writer Scott Cunningham writes that for "some Wiccans, watching the sun or moon rise and set each day is a ritual unto itself, for these are the heavenly symbols of the God and Goddess."[32] This parallels what Muslims believe, that the "Sun and the Moon are two of the Signs (ayat) of Allah: they do not darken for the death or birth of any person, but Allah strikes fear into His servants by means of them. So when you see them darken, remember and mention Allah, declare His Greatness, offer prayer, give in charity, and supplicate to Him and seek His forgiveness."[33]

Wiccans as well look to the eclipse as divine. In one Pagan wedding in the UK a couple decided to have their ceremony during an eclipse in which they believed that "there's sun god and a moon goddess inside everyone, and that an eclipse represents the man and the woman together," and during the celebration some wore masks of the Sun, others of the Moon, to symbolize the astronomical encounter. Druid Simon Michel said: "We all turned to look in the direction of the sun and we could see a V-shaped shadow of the moon moving across the moor."[34]

Cunningham writes that in the days of old "the God was the Sky Father, and the Goddess, the Earth Mother. The God of the sky…descended upon and united with the Goddess, spreading seed upon the land, celebrating her fertility."[35] Much like Allah was the phallus god who impregnated Allat, the earth goddess.

Similar beliefs can be found in Hinduism where the sky god Dyaus Pita, who is described as the "bull of earth"[36] is like Sin who became Allah depicted as a bull. This bull impregnates the earth goddess, Prithivi, with rain, causing crops to grow on her.[37]

Tonatiuh was the sun god worshiped by the Aztec people and whose name means "he who goes forth shining."[38] He too provided fertility to the earth, making crops grow[39] and similar to Allah, Tonatiuh was a warrior god who escorted the souls of men who died while fighting for his cause to paradise where they became an "eagle's companion."[40] Warriors for Tonatiuh would capture people in order to sacrifice them to him[41] this echoes greatly to how Muslims capture innocents and sacrifice them by decapitation to Allah.

The Greek goddess Aphrodite, who is popular for worship amongst neo-pagans, was worshiped by the Greeks, according to Aeschylus, as an earth goddess who is impregnated by the heavens: "The holy heaven yearns to wound the earth, and yearning layeth hold on the earth to join in wedlock; the rain, fallen from the amorous heaven, impregnates the earth, and it bringeth forth for mankind the food for flocks and herds and Demeter's gifts; and from that moist marriage-rite the woods put on their bloom. Of all these things I [Aphrodite] am the cause."[42] Aphrodite was Greek for "Venus" which is the same planet Muslims look up to every Ramadan when the crescent moon appears with Venus (morning star), which is the symbol of the Luminous One as referenced by Isaiah 14 *Hilal bin Sahar.*

Aphrodite also represents the black asteroid within the Ka'aba that Muslims go around seven times in Mecca that originated from a pagan vulva worship cult. The frame of the housing in which the black stone resides is in the shape of a vulva. Overall, the entire idol, asteroid and all, represents the goddess Aphrodite. Esther Harding states that: "On this black stone is a mark called the impression of Aphrodite ... An oval cleft signifying the 'yoni' or female genitals. It is the sign of Artimes the Goddess of untrammeled sexual love, and clearly indicates that the Black Stone at Mecca belonged originally to the Great Mother." According to Edward Rice: "Al'Uzza [Aphrodite] was especially worshipped at the Ka'aba where she was served by seven priestesses. Her worshippers circled the holy stone seven times - once for each of the ancient seven planets, and did so in total nudity."

John of Damascus said that the Black Stone had traces of the head "of the Semitic Venus (i.e. the Greek Aphrodite)."[43]

In the ninth century, Nicetas also spoke of the "idol of Xoubar" as representing Aphrodite.[44] John Tolan wrote that the eighth-century Byzantine writer, Georges the Monk, said that Muslims worshiped "god...the moon and Aphrodite."[45]

Constantine Porphyrogenitus' book, *The Administration of the Empire* stated: "Muslims pray also to the star of Aphrodite which they called Koubar, and in their supplication cry out 'Allah Oua Koubar', that is God and Aphrodite. They call God 'Alla'; and Oua they use for the conjunction and they call the star Koubar. And so they say Alla Oua Koubar."[46] Allah's wife, Allat, according to Herodotus, was worshiped as Aphrodite: "They believe in no other gods except Dionysus and the Heavenly Aphrodite; and they say that they wear their hair as Dionysus does his, cutting it round the head and shaving the temples. They call Dionysus, Orotalt; and Aphrodite, Alilat."[47] Today what we see when Arabs roam roundabout the Ka'aba in Arabia, shaved and half naked, is a throwback to pre-Islamic Arabia when Arabs walked around the Ka'aba naked and Allat was a goddess of sexuality. Ibn Ishaq writes: "An Arab woman was going around the house thus [nearly naked] said: Today, some or all of it [privates] can be seen, but what can be seen I do not make common property."[48] The original idea of kissing the black stone during the hajj was paganistic and sexual in origin. John of Damascus reported that: "rubbing and kissing [the Black Stone]…was extremely passionate." One of the primary reasons why the Muslims accepted the Black Stone was that they believed that "Abraham had sexual intercourse with Hagar on it."[49]

❖ Chapter 22 ❖

For God or For Zoroaster

According to historian W. St. Clair Tisdall: "the books of the Zoroastrians and Hindus... bear the most extraordinary likeness to what we find in the Koran and Hadith. Thus in Paradise we are told of 'houris having fine black eyes,' and again of 'houris with large black eyes, resembling pearls hidden in their shells.' ...The name houri too is derived from an Avesta or Pehlavi Source, as well as jinn for genii, and bihisht (Paradise), signifying in Avestic 'the better land.' We also have very similar tales in the old Hindu writings, of heavenly regions with their boys and girls resembling the houris and ghilman (young boys) of the Koran."[50]

The Qur'ân states that Allah "is the lord of Sirius" (Qur'ân 53:49) just as the Zoroastrian angel Tishtrya is the angel (Yazad) of the star Sirius, the brightest star in the night sky. The angel was worshiped as "the bright and glorious star [Sirius] who is the seed of the waters, powerful, tall, and strong, whose light goes afar; powerful and highly working, through whom the brightness and the seed of the waters come from the high Apam Napat."[51] And similar to Islam: "I swear by the heaven and the comer by night; and what will make you know what the comer by night is? The star of piercing brightness; there is not a soul but over it is a keeper" (Q 86:1-4).

Describing Allah, the lord of Sirius, the Qur'ân states that "the likeness of Allah's light is as a Lamp enclosed in Glass: the glass as it were a brilliant star: Lit from a blessed Tree, an Olive, neither of the east nor of the west, whose oil is well-nigh luminous, though fire scarce touched it: Light upon Light! Allah doth guide whom He will to His Light: Allah doth set forth Parables for men: and Allah doth know all things" (Q 24:35).

From 1994 to 1997, the Order of the Solar Temple members who also referred to their deity as the lord of Sirius became so paranoid they began a series of mass suicides, which led to roughly 74 deaths.

Farewell letters by members stated that they believed their deaths would be an escape from the "hypocricies and oppression of this world." Adding that they felt they were "moving on to Sirius."[52] It is no wonder why the Muslim *Mujahadeen* focus on being killed in battle. Every letter that is read prior to a suicide attack has expressions of desire to depart the earth's corruption to paradise in which lays the Ka'aba that holds the black stone star.

Just as Aphrodite is Allah's wife Allat, she was also Mithra,[53] a Zoroastrian deity identified with the dawn and as "shining like the sun."[54] Islam also compares greatly with Zoroastrianism. Both accounts have references of ascension to heaven and descent to hell. Muhammad had his Isra and Miraj (ascension) story where a creature called *al-buraq* and the angel *Taus Al-Malaeka* (Jibril) escorted Muhammad to hell and then to heaven. While in hell Muhammad "saw people whose heads were being shattered, then every time they would return to their original state and be shattered again without delay. He said: O Jibril, who are these people?' He replied: 'These are the people whose heads were too heavy (on their pillows) to get up and fulfill the prescribed prayers.' Then he saw a people who wore loincloths on the fronts and on their backs. They were roaming the way camels and sheep roam about. They were eating thistles and *zaqqum* – the fruit of a tree that grows in hell and whose fruit resembles the head of devils and white-hot coals and stones of Gehenna. He said: 'Who are these, O Jibril?' He replied: 'These are the ones who did not meet the obligation of paying sadaqa from what they possessed, whereas Allah never kept anything from them.'" He also "saw a man swimming in a river of blood and he was being struck in his mouth with rocks which he then swallowed. The Prophet asked: 'What is this, O Jibril?' He replied: 'This is what happens to those who eat usury.'"[55]

In Zoroastrianism, there is the story of Arda Viraf where the soul of a pious Dastur named Arda Viraf travels to heaven and to hell with the angel Adar and the divine messenger of Ahura Mazda Sraosha. During the trip, Arda saw "the souls of a man and a woman whose tongues were cut out. And I asked thus: 'What sin was committed by these bodies, whose souls suffer so severe a punishment?' Srosh the pious, and Adar the angel, said thus: 'This is the soul of that wicked man and woman who, amongst the living, spoke much falsehood and profanity [or untruth], and deceived their own souls.'" Viraf saw people "who swallowed and voided, and again swallowed and voided. And I asked thus: 'What souls are those of these?' Srosh the pious, and Adar the angel, said thus: 'These are the souls of those wicked who, in the world, believed not in the spirit, and they have been unthankful in the religion of the creator Ohrmazd. They have been doubtful of the happiness which is in heaven, and the torment which is in hell, and about the reality of the resurrection of the dead and the future body.'"[56]

Muhammad attained his vision through the communication with the luminous *Taus Al-Malaeka*, While Arda Viraf obtained his vision by remembering "the departed souls" and drinking "wine and narcotic."[57]

→ Chapter 23 ←

For God or For Zodiacs

Islam's link with Zoroastrian astrology can be detected from the Qur'ân itself. In *Al-Burj* "Zodiacal Signs" Allah declares: "[I swear] By the sky, (displaying) the Zodiacal Signs;" (Q 85:1) In *Al-hijr* "the stone-land" or "rock city" Allah declares: "And we have placed in the sky the signs of the zodiac, and have made them seemly to the beholders; and we have guarded them from every pelted devil; save from such as steal a hearing, and there follows him an obvious shooting-star."[58]

In Arabian Astrology, we find the Zodiac signs Libra *Meezan* (balance) *Al-Burj Zodiac*,[59] the Qur'ân declares: "Blessed be He who hath placed in the Heaven the sign of the Zodiac! who hath placed in it the Lamp of the Sun, and the light-giving Moon!" (Q 25:61). Such signs are even the names of the Qur'ânic chapters – The Balance, The Zodiac, The Star, The Sun, The Moon, The Dawn, The Morning Star, The Solace, The Day Break, The Jinn (Demons)…

In the Zoroastrian Pahlavi text it reads that the god "Aûharmazd produced illumination between the sky and the earth, the constellation stars and those also not of the constellations, then the moon, and afterwards the sun, as I shall relate. First he produced, the celestial sphere, and the constellation stars are assigned to it by him; especially these twelve whose names are *Varak* (the Lamb), *Tôrâ* (the Bull), *Dô-patkar* (the Two-figures or Gemini), *Kalakang* (the Crab), *Sêr* (the Lion), *Khûsak* (Virgo), *Tarâzûk* (the Balance), *Gazdûm* (the Scorpion), *Nîmâsp* (the Centaur or Sagittarius), *Vahîk* ı (Capricornus), *Dûl* (the Waterpot), and *Mâhîk* (the Fish);"[60] Babylonian mythology also preaches a story of a creation of astrology: "He (i.e., Marduk) made the stations for the great gods; The stars, their images, as the stars of the Zodiac, he fixed. He ordained the year and into sections he divided it; For the twelve months he fixed three stars. After he had…the days of the year…images, He founded the station of Nibir to determine their bounds; that none might err or go astray, He set the station of Bêl and Ea along with him. He opened great gates on both sides. He made strong the bolt on the left and on the right. In the midst thereof he fixed the zenith; The Moon-god he caused to shine forth, the night he entrusted to him…"[61]

⤞ Chapter 24 ⤝

For The Bible or For The Qur'ân

The Founding Fathers of the United States had deeply held views and decisively wrote the Constitution to protect us from a dangerous cycle that had been repeated throughout history by countries that abandoned Biblical law in favor of following man made principles. Muslim apologists counter that if Biblical law is used to form a nation, other religions (like Islam) should be incorporated as well. Aren't all religions equal? Why not incorporate Islamic laws? Muslim political activists argue that Islam is compatible with America and that Christianity has much in common with Islam.

Do they? Bible believers question the Qur'ân's revelation since in their view it does not compare with the Bible or if the Qur'ân can prove its source from a perfect creator? They argue that some of these Revelations were admitted to have been satanically inspired. The originator of the Bible, while constructing His instructions to man also instructed the ancient Hebrews to stone to death anyone committing such an error (Deut. 13:1-5). If Muslims indeed follow God why do they believe Muhammad whom Satan can inspire? Satan failed with Jesus and while Muhammad admitted a satanic connection, Jesus had nothing to confess – He after all is free of sin.

Muhammad claimed to have been inspired by a perfect god. How could the perfect god allow his document (the Qur'ân) to be tainted with something that later had to be annulled? Is one to believe that Satan tormented Job and tested Jesus but inspired Muhammad? While Islam rejects the Biblical Holy Trinity, Muhammad was induced into a state of mind by Satan introducing an unholy pagan trinity: "Have you seen Allat and Uzza and Manat the third?" Even their intersession was inspired through Lucifer: "These are the high flying cranes; verily their intercession is accepted with approval."

Are we to believe that Muslims who reject the intersession of Christ as "blasphemy" seem to accept that Muhammad can be inspired through Lucifer with a pagan trinity? Also, if Jesus cannot intercede for sin, how can the Muslim martyr do so?

Indeed, if cults like Mormonism and Islam connect to the Bible as they claim, why is it that Mormons pass out the *Book of Mormon* and not simply the Bible? The same goes for Muslims who pass out Qur'āns. Such books lack the prophetic elements and could not have been inspired by God but by imposters.

We will never find any prophet in the Bible that has ever been inspired through Lucifer. Joseph Smith admitted, "…some revelations are of God; some revelations are of man; and some revelations are of the devil."[62] Bible believers view Islam and Mormonism as cults since much cover-up takes place in order to protect the cult leaders. Neither do they see Allah as Yahweh or Muhammad as being equivalent to Jesus, who is sinless. They see Sharî'ah as the foundation for a man-made government created by Muhammad, a self-proclaimed lawgiver. How can Muhammad claim that Allah is the greatest when Allah ordained partnership for Muhammad over the earth: "the earth belongs to Allah and His Apostle"?[63]

The Islamic creed is a strange concept to Bible believers since no one finds any claim in the Bible that would equate God with man. Let's say that the earth belongs to Yahweh and Isaiah. This would put man on par with God. The earth belongs to God alone; He created it. It would be difficult then to put the Qur'ān on par with the Bible.

Bible believers see Islam as having indirectly elevated Muhammad to the level of God and if Jesus, in the Muslim view, is rejected as God, then one of the two is an imposter. Muhammad is a man who has elevated himself to a position worthy only of God. Bible believers see that no culture has ever totally eliminated a god – Nazis worshipped Hitler, Communists in Russia worshipped Stalin, Evolutionists of all sorts, past and present, have worshipped and continue to worship nature, and the "I am God" New Agers worship self. It never fails. Something or someone is always worshipped and in every experiment that eliminated Yahweh, the result has been tyranny.

The results can be shown through our research here, but no one can ever fully explain the intricate and complex workings of evil. Just as no one can ever explain Yahweh's intricate and complex workings, yet we can examine the results of following His laws in the Bible.

→ Chapter 25 ←

Just Who Are These Gods?

In the Qur'ân Allah desires Muslims to "seek refuge with [Allah] the Lord of the Dawn from the mischief of the evil he created...the mischievous evil of Darkness, as it becomes intensely dark"(Q 113:1-3). He is "the lord of men and jinn [demons]" (Q 69:43). "I only created jinn [demons] and man to worship me" (Q 51:56). The demons are even said to have been amazed with the Qur'ân, "We [the Demons] have heard a most amazing recitation" (Q 72).

As Bible believers read this, they see Lucifer in disguise. Isaiah describes Lucifer (The Luminous One) as the son of the dawn who brings all evil and destruction. In Islam, the demons can even be Muslim: "So, since we (jinn/demons) have listened to the guidance (of the Qur'ân), we have accepted (Islam): and any who believes in its lord (Allah) has no fear of loss, force, or oppression" (Q 72:13). The Qur'ân swears "by those (demons) who violently tear out (the souls), and drag them to destruction" (Q 79:1). The Biblical God is not the lord of demons!

Similarly, the Babylonian moon-god Sin is the Lord of darkness.[64]

Buddhism also honors demons. Nichiren Daishonin, a Buddhist monk and major teacher of Japanese Buddhism said that good demons "feed upon enemies of the Lotus Sutra, while evil demons feed upon the sutra's votaries."[65]

According to Buddhist writings, Buddha made a sermon and while he was preaching "monks, nuns...lay devotees,...great serpents, men, and beings not human, as well as governors of a region, rulers of armies and rulers of four continents, all of them with their followers, gaze on the Lord [Buddha] in astonishment, in amazement, in ecstasy."[66]

Demons in Buddhism, like the Qur'ân are depicted as being "struck with astonishment".[67] Buddha, like Allah, is referred to as "the lord of the world".[68] Similarly, Allah is referred to in the Qur'ân as *Malek-rab-Al-A'lameen* which means, "The Lord of the worlds" that is, this world, and the underworld: "O Allah, the Lord of the seven heavens and whatever it shadows. Lord of the two worlds and whatever it is carrying. Lord of the wind and wherever it goes. Lord of the devils and whoever is unguided. I ask you all the good blessings in this country and the best of its people and the best of whatever it has. I seek refuge from all the evils of this country, the worst of its people and the worst of what it has."[69]

When Bible believers see Muslim supplication to Allah, they are reminded of what has already been described in the Bible: "The *god of this world* who has blinded the minds of unbelievers, so that they cannot see the light of the gospel" (II Corinthians 4:4). "Now is the judgment of this world: now shall the *prince of this world* be cast out" (John 12:31). They view Muhammad as definitely connected to the Lord of the Air and the god of demons. In Ibn Ishaq's classic *Biography of Mohammed,* we find an account of Muhammad praying to his lord: "O Allah, Lord of the heavens and what they overshadow, and Lord of the Devils and what into error they throw, and Lord of the winds and what they winnow, we ask Thee for the booty of this town and its people. We take refuge in Thee."

To Bible believers, this would sound more like the Antichrist in the Bible who is addressed in the same way as Satan. Muhammad carries the same attributes as Allah: "Mohammed is the exemplar to both worlds, the guide of the descendants of Adam. He is the sun of creation, the moon of the celestial spheres, the all seeing eye; the torch of knowledge, the candle of prophecy, the lamp of the nation and the way of the people; the commander-in-chief on the parade-ground of the Law; the general of the army of mysteries and morals; The lord of the world and the glory of 'But for thee'; ruler of the earth and of the celestial spheres."[70]

Muhammad is never far from such attributes given to His Lord: "He, and only he, is without question the most excellent of mankind; he and only he, is the confidant of God. The seven heavens and the eight gardens of paradise were created for him. He is both the eye and the light in the light of our eyes. He was the key of guidance to the two worlds and the lamp that dispelled the darkness thereof."[71]

This Lord of the Worlds is well defined in *Al-Fatiha* (the opening) first chapter, and the most recited from the Qur'ân: "In the name of Allah, the Merciful, and Compassionate. Praise be to Allah, Lord of the two worlds; the Merciful the compassionate, King of the Day of Judgment, You we worship and You we call upon. Guide us along the straight path. The path of those to whom You have given grace, Not those deserving anger nor those who have gone astray" (Qur'ân, Al Fatiha). But even more amazing is that Allah is even claimed to be the Lord of the demons (Jinn in Arabic): "This is a Message sent down from the Lord of men and jinn (demons)" (Q 69:43); "I only created jinn (demons) and man to worship me" (Q 51:56).

How could Muslims follow a religion followed by demons? In Qur'ân 72:1-8 the Jinn describe their view of the Qur'ân: "Say (O Mohammed): It is revealed unto me that a company of the Jinn gave ear, and they said: Lo! It is a marvelous Qur'ân which guides unto righteousness, so we believe in it and we ascribe unto our Lord no partner. And (we believe) that He, exalted, be the glory of our Lord! Hath taken neither wife nor son, and that the foolish one among us used to speak concerning Allah an atrocious lie. And lo! We had supposed that humankind and jinn would not speak a lie concerning Allah; and indeed (O Mohammed) individuals of humankind used to invoke the protection of individuals of the jinn so that they increased them in revolt (against Allah); And indeed they supposed, even as ye suppose, that Allah would not raise anyone (from the dead), and (the Jinn who had listened to the Qur'ân said): We had sought the heaven but had found it filled with strong warders and meteors" (Qur'ân, Al-Jinn).

Why then does Hitler respect Buddhism and Islam? Bible followers are warned "[if] Satan casts out Satan, he is divided against himself; how then shall his kingdom stand?" (Mathew 12:25-26.).

WITCHCRAFT – SATAN'S UNIVERSAL LANGUAGE

Many cults mask themselves with Christian heritage. Mormonism and Islam contain many beliefs that are openly and obviously problematic. Joseph Smith delved into the demon Abraxas.[72]

The Basilidian sect of the Gnostics of the second century claimed Abraxas as their supreme god, and said that Jesus Christ was only a phantom sent to earth by him. Finally, Lucy mentions the "faculty of Abrac," which refers to the deity regarded by the second-century Basilidians as the "chief of the 365 genies ruling the days of the year."[73] Allah is also called the lord of genies.

In the Latter Day Saints movement, the use of seer stones and divination played a significant role in shaping the movement's history and theology. Seer stones and crystals *Urim and Thummim* are of a particular importance to Joseph Smith; it was these objects that helped discover the words of the *Book of Mormon*.[74] Using seer stones (sometimes called "peep" stones) is the act of "scrying" or "crystal gazing." Scrying has been used in many cultures as a means of seeing the past, present, or future; in this sense scrying constitutes a form of divination or fortunetelling.[75] Scrying can be traced as far back as 2,000 BC in Greece, as well as ancient Britain and its subsequent Celtic population, where they practiced many forms of scrying. The mediums often used were beryl, crystal, black glass, polished quartz, water, and other transparent or light-catching bodies.[76]

MUHAMMAD – THE POSSESSED POET

Bible believers also have problems when they read that Islam has its share of satanic connections. In one story Muhammad even asks one of his companions: "Which of you will follow me to a deputation of the jinn tonight?"[77]

Another incident in the annals of Islam involving the money keeper pertains to Lucifer infiltrating the money coffers at which point he "started stealing food." He was caught. The treasury keeper threatened to turn in Satan to Muhammad, Islam's apostle. Satan, in exchange for his release, began to teach the money keeper *Ayat Al-Kursi* (Qur'ân 2:255) which is the recitation Muslims use for protection from evil. When the story reached the prophet of Islam he said, "He who came to you at night told you the truth although he is a liar; and it was Satan."[78]

How could Satan teach the verses that protect Muslim followers from evil then be telling a lying truth? Christians would find this troubling. But the money keeper is a mere follower! Then we find Muhammad himself influenced to the point that "Magic was worked on Allah's apostle so that he used to think that he had sexual relations with his wives while he actually had not."[79] According to the Islamic scholar Alfred Guillaume, Muhammad's "inspiration and religious experiences are remarkably similar to those found in some form of spiritism. Shamanism, for example is notorious for fostering periods of mental disruption as well as spirit-possession. Significantly, Muhammad experienced Shaman-like encounters."[80]

During Muhammad's aspirations for prophethood, Islam records that he actually first considered himself a "Sahir." According to Alfred Guillaum a Sahir was a "man with a mysterious esoteric knowledge which was generally attributed to a familiar spirit called a jinn or shaytan [devil]."[81] Sahirs were considered wizards who "believed in the demon of poetry, and they thought that a great poet was directly inspired by demons."[82] Hasan ibn Thabit, a fellow poet and close friend of Muhammad, and one who praised him in his poetry, communicated with a female jinn who inspired his poetry: "[she] met him in one of the streets of Medina, leaped upon him and pressed him down." Jinns were considered "his brothers" who "weave for him artistic words...sent down to him from heaven in the night season."

To "send down" messages is even the same usage in Muhammad's account in which the Qur'ân was transmitted through the Luminous angel Islam called Jibril, and "as Hassan was thrown down by the female spirit and had verses pressed out of him."

So the first utterances of prophecy were pressed from Muhammad by the luminous angel. The resemblances even go further. The angel Gabriel is spoken of as the *qarin* 'companion' of Muhammad, just as though he were the Jinni accompanying a poet, and the same word, *nafatha,* 'blow upon', is used of an enchanter, of a Jinni inspiring a poet.[83]

Even Muhammad himself at first believed that he was demon-possessed and became distraught, even suicidal: "So I [Mohammed] read it, and he [Jibril] departed from me. And I awoke from my sleep, and it was as though these words were written on my heart...thought, 'Woe is me poet or possessed...I will go to the top of the mountain and throw myself down that I may kill myself and gain rest.' So I went forth to do so and then when I was midway on the mountain, I heard a voice from heaven saying, O Mohammed! Thou are the apostle of God and I am Gabriel."[84]

Muhammad wasn't the only possessed poet. The infamous anti-war activist, Alan Ginsberg, was a drug addict who boasted about his homosexuality and his attraction to young boys. In his most famous poem, *Howl,* Ginsberg writes about a chilling visitation from a 'god' who he describes as "Moloch" (possibly better described as "Baal Moloch").

In *Howl* Ginsberg writes: "angel-headed hipsters burning for the ancient heavenly connection to the starry dynamo in the machinery of night...and saw Mohammedan angels staggering on tenement roofs illuminated...Moloch who frightened me out of my natural ecstasy!...Wake up in Moloch! Light streaming out of the sky!"[85]

Another beat poet and friend of Ginsberg, Philip Lamantia, had a similar experience: "when reading the Koran on a couch one night, I was suddenly physically laid out by a powerful force beyond my volition, which rendered me almost comatose...I felt a radiance beyond even further within it and so, suddenly the outline of a benign bearded Face appeared to whom I addressed my desire to remain in this marveland who calmly replied: 'You can return, after you complete your work.'"[86] Aleister Crowley, the famous Satanist who, like Muhammad, communicated with an angel by the name of Aiwass who is described as "Horus the Child." Crowley, like Muhammad, described Aiwass as the "God or Demon", even linking him to Sumer.[87] Aiwass later abandoned Crowley, leading him into a state of depression.[88] Similarly, Muhammad's holy guardian angel abandoned him, which led to his attempted suicide. Ibin Abbas records Muhammad's account: "[the] Divine Inspiration was also paused for a while and the Prophet became so sad as we have heard that he intended several times to throw himself from the tops of high mountains".[89] Such suicide attempts are similar to what drug addicts suffer when going through withdrawals. Even from a young age Muhammad suffered from mania resembling that of a drug addict: "At the same time, he was probably, more or less, throughout his whole career, the victim of certain amount of self-deception. A cataleptic subject from his early youth, born – according to the traditions – of a highly nervous and excitable mother, he would be peculiarly liable to morbid and fantastic hallucinations, and alterations of excitement and depression, which would win for him, in the eyes of his ignorant countrymen, the credit of being inspired."[90] Muhammad's description of how al-Buraq ascended him to the heavens after the spirit cut him open provides an example: "I was taken by it [al-Buraq], and Gabriel set out with me till we reached the nearest heaven."[91]

Shaman priests go through similar trances and fall asleep for days then cut into pieces by the spirits. Mongols and the Manchu-Tungus, still initiate the shaman and introduce him to the supernatural beings, in whose presence he symbolically ascends the "tree-up-to-the-heavens."[92] Muhammad claims to have ascended to the heavens much like Shaman priests and the Zoroastrian Arda Viraf did after taking narcotics.

Joseph Smith in his first vision was "chosen" to receive certain secrets from an "angel of light." But before this episode took place, he was determined to know which of the many religions he should join. He questioned himself, "If any one of them be right which is it? And how shall I know it?"[93]

Like Muhammad who secluded himself in Ghar Hira, early one morning in the spring of 1820, Joseph attended secluded woods (Today named "The Sacred Grove") to ask God which church he should join. "A darkness gathered around him, and Smith believed that he would soon be totally destroyed…a light brighter than the sun descended towards him. With the arrival of the light. Then some power seized him and bind his tongue so that he could not speak."[94]

The tyrant of Iran, president Mahmoud Ahmadinejad, like Smith, claimed that he saw a "bright light surrounding him" while he was speaking at the the UN General Assembly on September 14, 2005. According to Ahmadinejad a U.N. member had told him that he saw a bright light surrounding him. Ahmadinejad stated in a video interview: "I felt it myself. I felt that the atmosphere suddenly changed, and for those 27 or 28 minutes, all the leaders of the world did not blink. When I say they didn't move an eyelid, I'm not exaggerating. They were looking as if a hand was holding them there, and had just opened their eyes to the message of the Islamic Republic."[95] While Joseph Smith was told by the angel of light to reject the churches, LDS First Presidency incorporated Islam: "Mohammed, Confucius, and the Reformers, as well as the philosophers including Socrates, Plato, and others, received a portion of God's light...to enlighten whole nations."[96]

SECTION FIVE

THE MYTH OF
NAZI CHRISTIANITY

➔ Chapter 26 ✦

When Did God Become Hitler?

RICHARD DAWKINS: Hitler by the way was a Roman Catholic.
BILL O'REILLY: He never was. He was raised in that home. He rejected it early on.
RICHARD DAWKINS: We can dispute that.

> *Hitler, history's leading tyrant at first was labeled as God. By the time everyone recognized that he was a tyrant – God was labeled as a Hitler.*

Dawkins would search for a label anywhere he could find one since Hitler officially was an altar boy during his childhood. But using partial fact is misleading since there is ample evidence of Hitler's new birth into what is termed Positive Christianity. When historians scratched beneath Hitler's *'Positive Christian'* label, his testimony went as follows: "I regard Christianity as the most fatal, seductive lie that has ever existed."[1]

Shouldn't Hitler's own testimony suffice?

Hitler sounded more like Richard Dawkins who sermonized his mantra with continual condemnations of God in the Bible as being a "malignant infection" and like Karl Marx's "religion is the opium of the people." Hitler was hardly like Catholic 'Bill O'Reilly' and aligned more with Dawkins; he "accepted evolution much as we today accept Einsteinian relativity."[2]

So why does the left accuse Hitler of being Catholic?

Leftists avoid the stigma caused by the Nazi leftist views by steering Nazism and its toxic waste off-course to the far right. That way, Catholics and Evangelicals can be transformed and driven into the 'extremist' camp. Jesus became the new Joseph Goebbels since He sends unrepentant sinners to a worse inferno than Auschwitz. The "new Nazis" would stand daily Nuremberg trials as a result. Yahweh would become the new Hitler who is, as Dawkins put it: "Jealous and proud of it; a petty, unjust, unforgiving control-freak; a vindictive, bloodthirsty ethnic cleanser; a misogynistic, homophobic, racist, infanticidal, genocidal, filicidal, pestilential, megalomaniacal, sadomasochistic, capriciously malevolent bully." Neronic progressives are true to their Neronian faith; with superb eloquence and skill, they transfer their sins to the very victims whom their ill devised plans destroy.

British political philosopher John Gray in his article *Don't Write Off Religion Just Yet* stated: "atheism was – according to the founders of the Soviet state, and in fact – always an integral part of the Communist project. Despite the vehement denials of Dawkins and Hitchens, terror in Communist Russia – and Mao's China – was also meant to bring about a utopian society in which religion would no longer exist."

If the left is correct, where are Hitler's enforcements of prayer and teaching the Bible in classrooms? What we find in Nazi text books contradicts what the revisionists claim, even breaking all Ten Commandments: "The teaching of mercy and love of one's neighbor is foreign to the German race and the Sermon on the Mount is according to Nordic sentiment an ethic for cowards and idiots."[3]

When it comes to the issue of Hitler's spiritual views, he was far more interested in eastern and Nordic religions. Hitler described Confucius, Buddha, and Muhammad as providers of "spiritual sustenance."[4]

Leftists are swift to point to Hitler's Catholic upbringing, insisting that it must have geared the young lad toward his tyrannical tendencies. Yet today few dare to question Barack Hussein Obama's Muslim upbringing for fear of the left's dreaded stigma of *Islamophobia*.

Neither can leftists change or reform an ideology like Islam; they would never label it as 'left-wing' since the subconscious of many progressives recognize the destructive end-results of this ideology. They would rather classify Islam as being towards the right when in reality it has more in common with their dogma.

Islam, Nazism and Leftism all hate The Cross. For the Muslim, the true Jesus is prophesied to descend "amongst you as a just ruler, he will break the Cross."[5] Hitler was not void of messianic aspiration; he was so messianic that in 1936, the Reich Church was founded. The Nazi church did not have the Christian Cross as its symbol but the swastika; the Bible was replaced by *Mein Kampf* which was laid on the altar next to a sword. Only invited Nazis were allowed to give sermons in a Reich Church.

The Nazis wished to replace Christianity with paganism. As the primary ideologue for Nazi philosophy, Alfred Rosenberg explains: "But today a new faith is awakening: the myth of the blood...Then in place of the Old Testament stories of cattle breeders and the exploitation of prostitutes, we shall have the Nordic sagas and fairy tales, at first simply recounted, later assuming the form of symbols."[6]

Rosenberg also wrote that in the Nazi church the altars must have "nothing but *Mein Kampf* (to the German nation and therefore to God the most sacred book) and to the left of the altar a sword."

Nazis were no crusaders, rather a crusade to replace Christianity: "the Christian Cross must be removed from all churches, cathedrals and chapels...and it must be superseded by the only unconquerable symbol, the swastika."[7] Rosenberg's statement echoes Islam's malignance for the church. The Mujahedeen Shura Council's mission is to "destroy the cross and to slash the throats of those who believe in the cross."[8] According to Arab historian al-Waqidi, the prophet Muhammad had such "a repugnance to the form of the cross that he broke everything brought into his house with that figure upon it."[9] It is prophesied that the Islamic messiah, the Mahdi, "will destroy the cross, kill the swine, revoke the capitation tax, and distribute goods in abundance. Property will be so vast that no one will accept it as charity."[10]

What about Hitler's other henchmen?

We shall discuss them throughout. Perhaps we can start with Martin Bormann, a leading Nazi official who was so close to Hitler that he named his eldest son "Adolf", who became the godson of Hitler. What Bormann said did not resemble Jerry Falwell but more closely echoed more to the lines of atheist Richard Dawkins. Bormann described the Christian churches as having "long been aware that exact scientific knowledge poses a threat to their existence.

Therefore, by means of such pseudo-sciences as theology, they take great pains to suppress or falsify scientific research...No one would know anything about Christianity if pastors had not crammed it down his throat in his childhood."[11]

Blaming Nazism on conservative Christians is inexcusable. Hitler was not even a capitalist: "We are socialists, we are enemies of today's capitalistic economic system for the exploitation of the economically weak, with its unfair salaries, with its unseemly evaluation of a human being according to wealth and property instead of responsibility and performance, and we are all determined to destroy this system under all conditions."[12] In a 1931 interview, Hitler told an influential editor of a pro-business newspaper: "I want everyone to keep what he has earned subject to the principle that the good of the community takes priority over that of the individual. But the State should retain control; every owner should feel himself to be an agent of the State... The Third Reich will always retain the right to control property owners." (Calic, Edouard, 1968). No leftist would denounce such quotes for it does profess the main theme of the leftist creed. Of course, not all what Hitler said was 'imperfect'. Yet it proves beyond doubt that Hitler was a die-hard leftist.

Progressives usually use the claim that when Hitler killed Communists, he did this in the name of conservatism. While his killing of communists is true, Hitler did not kill communists for their anti-Capitalism. Neither did he hate the tenets of communism. When Time Magazine made Hitler "Man of The Year", they explained Hitler's socialist policies: "Most cruel joke of all, however, has been played by Hitler & Co. on those German capitalists and small businessmen who once backed National Socialism as a means of saving Germany's bourgeois economic structure from radicalism. The Nazi credo that the individual belongs to the state also applies to business. Some businesses have been confiscated outright, on what amounts to a capital tax has been levied. Profits have been strictly controlled. Some idea of the increasing Governmental control and interference in business could be deduced from the fact that 80% of all building and 50% of all industrial orders in Germany originated last year with the Government. Hard-pressed for food stuffs as well as funds, the Nazi regime has taken over large estates and in many instances collectivized agriculture, a procedure fundamentally similar to Russian Communism."[13]

This is not all that dissimilar from what we see today - a war amongst terrorists with Hamas hating the P.L.O or Al-Qaeda hating Saudi religious leaders for not being puritanical enough. To Hitler, The Communist Party of Germany was not socialist enough. Hitler expounded: "Had communism really intended nothing more than a certain purification by eliminating isolated rotten elements from among the ranks of our so-called 'upper ten thousand' or our equally worthless Philistines, one could have sat back quietly and looked on for a while."[14]

Hitler actually looked to the French revolution as an inspiration: "The appearance of a new and great idea was the secret of success in the French Revolution. The Russian Revolution owes its triumph to an idea. And it was only the idea that enabled Fascism triumphantly to subject a whole nation to a process of complete renovation."[15]

Chapter 27

Nazism Hated Christianity

The decline of Christianity in Germany was what advanced Nazism; it could be said that when Germans abandoned God, Lucifer gave them one of his chaplains, Hitler. In his book, *The Dictators*, Richard Overy states that in the decades preceding the First World War Germany was becoming increasingly secular, and that after that war, from 1918 to 1931, 2.4 million Evangelical Christians formally renounced their faith as well as almost half a million Catholics. In Prussia, only 21% of the population took communion and in Hamburg only five percent of the population took communion.[16]

What about the Amazing Grace hymnal of Nazi Germany? Or who is this amazing one? And how was he the Messiah, the giver of all grace? The song of the Hitler Youth on a campfire trip would go something like this: "We are the happy Hitler Youth; We have no need for Christian virtue; for Adolf Hitler is our intercessor and our redeemer. No priest, no evil one can keep us from feeling like Hitler's children. No Christ do we follow, but Horst Wessel [Nazi martyr]! Away with incense and holy water pots. Singing we follow Hitler's banners; only then are we worthy of our ancestors. I am no Christian and no Catholic. I go with the SA through thick and thin. The church can be stolen from me for all I care. The swastika makes me happy here on earth. Him will I follow in marching step; Baldur von Schirach [Nazi youth leader] take me along."[17]

Before the Nazi youth was founded, a strong youth movement already existed in Germany. It began in the 1890s and was known as the *Wandervögel*, a male-only movement featuring a back-to-nature theme. Wandervögel members had an idealistic, romantic notion of the past, yearning for simpler days when people lived off the land. They rejected the modern, big city era and took a dim view of its predecessor, the industrial revolution, which had been started by their fathers and grandfathers.[18]

They found strict German schooling oppressive and rejected parental authority. They saw hypocrisy in politics and the social class system of Kaiser Wilhelm's Germany, which was based entirely on birth and accumulated wealth. Instead, they longed for a Jugend-kultur, a culture of youth led by youth, in which they would be truly valued.[19]

They wanted something greater to believe in instead of the Christian values of their parents. They delighted in rediscovering nature without any modern conveniences, traveling on hikes and sleeping out under the stars.[20]

They sang pagan folk songs around bonfires. The lyrics of the campfire songs would probably make John Denver sing along: "Through distant lands I wander, a simple troubadour, and praise in word and music Great Nature's majesty!"[21] The Wandervögel also developed a custom of greeting each other by saying "Heil." Regardless of what some might say, the Hitler youth was founded based on the Wandervögel. It was in the Wandervögel "that the word 'Fuehrer' originated, with its meaning of blind obedience and devotion…And I shall never forget how in those early days we pronounced the word Gemeinschaft ['community'] with a trembling throaty note of excitement, as though it hid a deep secret."[22]

The Wandervögel did not have to go far to find like-minded intellects to reassure their ideas; they were inspired by the works of anti-Christian thinkers Friedrich Nietzsche, Goethe, Hermann Hesse and Eduard Baltzer. These writers were no Chestertons or C.S. Lewises – they did not see Jesus as their role model but some of the most leftist writers in history.

Friedrich Nietzsche, whose writings influenced Hitler by writing that man has the ability of being an Übermensch or super-human, hailed Darwin's "calm annihilation of the fairy-tale fable of the creation of the World" and welcomed the support it supplied in his campaign for a "transvaluation of values" to overthrow the "morality of slaves." In *The Will to Power*, Nietzsche posited his love for eugenics writing that "society ought to prevent procreation: to this end, it may hold in readiness, without regard to descent, rank, or spirit, the most rigorous means of constraint, deprivation of freedom, in certain circumstances castration."[23]

But the Wandervögel's book club didn't stop at Nietzsche. They also read Goethe; a German poet, novelist, theorist, and homoerotic writer, who is said to be one of the giants of the literary world. He had a persistent dislike for the church, and characterized its history as a "hotchpotch of mistakes and violence." He wrote many melancholy and erotic books containing themes of homosexuality and suicide.

When Goethe was young he and his sister would recite a playwright dialogue between Satan and Adramelech with Goethe being Satan. While at a barbershop with their father, "Adramelech had to lay his iron hands on Satan: my sister seized me with violence, and recited, softly enough, but with increasing passion: Give me thine aide, I entreat thee: I'll worship thee if thou demandest."[24]

Goethe had an admiration for Islam. As a young man Goethe wanted to study oriental studies having always admired the first travelers to Arabia. He was fascinated by it and read everything they published about their trips. At the time of his *Divan* Johann Goethe trained himself with the professors of oriental studies – Paulus, Lorsbach and Kosegarten – in reading and writing Arabic. In his *Divan* Goethe wrote: "If from Eternity the Koran be of that inquire I not. ...That the Koran the Book of books must be, I hold as faith to duteous Moslems taught."[25] In another poem of the Divan Goethe writes: "If Islam mean submission to God's will, May we all live in Islam, and all die."[26]

He hated the Holy Trinity writing: "Jesus in silence His pure heart with thought of one sole God did fill; They who Himself to God convert Do outrage to His holy will. Mohammed also that which won His triumphs needs must seem as true – Through the idea of the One Alone did he the world subdue."[27] Following the model of Muhammad, Goethe scorned the Cross: "This wholly modern foolery, Stick crossed on stick, and must I sing this in its cold rigidity?"[28]

Another prophet for the Wandervögel was Herman Hesse, who at fifteen years old began to rail against adult authority and Christianity.[29] His character inconsistency drew him into several deep psychotic crises, such as repeated conflictual relations with his parents, a tentative escape from school, an early suicide attempt, as well as several internships in mental institutions, where he also learned Jungian psychoanalysis.[30] Hesse's self-destructive behavior was reflected in his novels, writing that in "each of us spirit has become form, in each of us the created being suffers, in each of us a redeemer is crucified."[31]

Such demented ideas are reminiscent of young idealistic Muslim victimcrats on a self-redeeming mission to die for Allah. Likewise, Anton LaVey commanded his followers to "[s]ay unto thine own heart, '*I am mine own redeemer.*'"[32]

In his *Siddhartha*, an Indian prince confused about life and its purpose wishes to attain Nirvana. It was such eastern philosophy that influenced Berkley and Haight-Ashbury – even Al Gore with his earth-centered spirituality. We must remember, there was much eastern philosophy that fueled the Nazi soul.

Hesse's anti-Church and family values is seen in his own works. *Narziss und Goldmund* (Death and the Lover) is a story regarding a young Goldmund who is brought to a monastery by his oppressive father, in order to gain instruction and to remove the sensual, artistic remembrance of an "indecent" mother from his memory. He is Left into the care of Narziss, a "fatherly" figure and one of the young masters of the convent. Goldmund ends up in a rebellion against the walls and their coercion. He leaves the monastery (a similar gesture to Hesse's own departure from the Theological Seminary in Maulbronn), becoming an artist and a lover.[33]

One of Hesse's most talked about novels is *Demian* in which the main character Emil Sinclair feels that his antisocial behavior is determined by some sort of metaphysical damnation. Max Demian helps him to act out the tormented energies of his soul, convincing him that he bears the "sign" of a demoniacal elite, whose roots can be traced back to Cain, a prominent dark figure of the Bible. Max

Demian teaches Sinclair that each person should "go beyond" and become a superior being, rejoicing in the exuberant integrity of his existence, which is a combination of luminous and dark forces.[34]

Emil Sinclair talks about the Greek god Abraxas, "whose symbolic task is the uniting of godly and devilish elements [in himself]".[35] This parallels the Buddhist Ying-Yang which represents the cosmic forces of good and evil complimenting each other. Demian explains that "Going beyond" means living off-limits, beyond good and evil (as Nietzsche also clamors), and experiencing liberty as a totalizing cosmic eruption, in which God and Devil come together. It is the fervor of creating a "new religion", embraced by strong, solitary persons who march on their way towards human and cosmic completeness that unites Demian and Sinclair. Although their social paths separate them for a while, they nevertheless share the belief that each person should find a spiritual "twin", who may help him to act out the repressed side of his personality.[36]

Another novel that played a great influence on the Wandervögel was *Steppenwolf* in which a man named Harry Haller unites himself with the "call of the wolf", which drives him to live as a social outcast, apart from human understanding and compassion.[37]

Haller hears "the wind of midnight howl. I cool with snow my burning jowl, and on the devil my wretched soul I bear."[38] Haller is a man tormented between his real self and his bourgeois mentality. Hesse explains the story writing that the bourgeois "is consequently by nature a creature of weak impulses, anxious, fearful of giving himself away and easy to rule. Therefore, he has substituted majority for power, law for force, and the polling booth for responsibility. It is clear that this weak and anxious being, in whatever numbers he exists, cannot maintain himself, and that qualities such as his can play no other role in the world than that of a herd of sheep among free roving wolves. …Nevertheless the bourgeois prospers. Why? The answer runs: Because of the Steppenwolves. …Despising the Bourgeois, and yet belonging to it, they add to its strength and glory; for in the last resort they have to share their beliefs in order to live."[39]

Steppenwolf carried a doctrine like Nietzsche and his Über-mensch, surpassing oneself and evolving into a superior being, that everybody "carries with him to the end traces of his birth, the slime and eggshells of a primordial world. Many a one never becomes a human being, but remains a frog, a lizard, or ant. Many a one is a human being above and a fish below. But each one is a gamble of nature, a hopeful attempt at forming a human being...we all come out of the same abyss; but each of us, a trial throw of the dice from the depths, strives toward his own goal."[40]

Steppenwolf not only served as one of the main "bibles" of the Wandervögel but also for the young hippie counterculture movement. Harry Haller, the social outcast protagonist of the novel, attracted the young rebels of the sixties precisely because of his split, half male, half female personality, which he transcends by means of love and magic. Numerous hippies of the sixties considered themselves "step-penwolves" in their urge for transgressing social order and discipline. They also loved Harry Haller because of his refusal to take up adult values and his desire to remain a paradoxically immature child of the universe.[41]

From Nietzsche, Goethe, and Hesse – all of these writers reflect the greater political mission of the Wandervögel. It is no wonder why they regarded family life "as repressive and insincere". The Wander-vögel believed that "parental religion was largely a sham, politics boastful and trivial, economics unscrupulous and deceitful, educa-tion stereotyped and lifeless". "Their goal," writes John Toland, "was to establish a youth culture for fighting the bourgeois trinity of school, home, and church."[42]

This is precisely what has happened with the Muslim youth – activism has become more important than education. *Islamism is in reality paganism sprinkled with a dash of Judaism, yet denying its core ethics – a wolf masquerading as a lamb but speaking as a dragon. It honors no father, be it the Father in heaven or the father on earth, for if the parents reject martyrdom they are forgotten, along with their loving hands that once rocked the child's cradle.*

→ Chapter 28 ←

For Carnivores or For Vegans –
The Third Reich and Vegetarianism

The Nazi Wandervögel's idea of 'going back to nature' is based on the belief that a purely organic diet goes a long way in determining how a society is formed. This is exactly why the Nazi party stressed the importance of health food, with Hitler and Himmler being vegetarians and crusaders against tobacco.

The Hitler youth was based on Der Wandervögel, which had a major philosophy of vegetarianism, thus the Hitler youth carried the same ideas. The Wandervögel's vegetarian ideas came from Eduard Baltzer, the founder of the *German Vegetarian Movement*. In 1866 Baltzer came to vegetarian nutrition through reading Theodore Hahns' *the practical handbook of the natural way of curing*. Baltzer wrote later on of how the book became a revelation to him: "Hahn's book contained so much historical material that I now saw gates and doors thrown open for me in this question (vegetarianism). I read while arranging the chaotically strewn notes for myself into a system. ...A new material and mental world appeared before my eyes in the manner of a revelation." For Baltzer, the animal was a fellow creature in need of protection: "Animal murder is not permitted for ethical reasons; the animal has its own right to life and requires protection by man."[43]

Vegetarianism, Hinduism and Buddhism were major influences for Nazism, the swastika being an eastern religious symbol. Heinrich Himmler was a strict vegetarian and was also an avid reader of the Hindu *Bhagavad Gita* and said that Hitler was ordained by "the Karma of the Germanic world".[44] Himmler believed himself to be the reincarnation of the tenth century German king, Henry the Fowler.

Vegetarianism is deeply rooted in Hinduism with one of the largest Hindu texts, the *Mahabharata*, which explains the nature of "self" and the aspects of karma, describing how those who kill, buy, and eat meat are committing *himsa* or sin: "The purchaser of flesh performs himsa by his wealth; he who eats flesh does so by enjoying its taste; the killer does himsa by actually tying and killing the animal. Thus, there are three forms of killing. He who brings flesh or sends for it, he who cuts off the limbs of an animal, and he who purchases, sells, or cooks flesh and eats it – all of these are to be considered meat-eaters."[45]

In one speech Himmler gave to his SS men, he sounded more like a pantheist than a minister: "A Volk [people] that has this belief in rebirth [reincarnation] and that honors its ancestors, and in so doing honors itself, always has children, and this Volk has eternal life."[46] Hitler was also a vegetarian and according to Joseph Goebbels, saw Christianity as having "no point of contact to the animal element, and thus, in the end, they will be destroyed. The Fuhrer is a convinced vegetarian, on principle. His arguments cannot be refuted on any serious basis. They are totally unanswerable."[47]

Nazi Germany was also one of the first countries to establish animal rights and environmental laws. In his book *The Nazi War on Cancer*, Stanford Professor Robert N. Proctor writes a great deal about the Nazis' antipathy for animal experimentation. In one example, the book features a Nazi cartoon depicting "the lab animals of Germany saluting Hermann Goring" for his protection of them.[48]

The Nazis passed laws regulating the slaughter of animals. Herman Goering announced an end to the "unbearable torture and suffering in animal experiments" and threatened to "commit to concentration camps those who still think they can continue to treat animals as inanimate property." Bans on vivisection were issued with horses, cats and apes being singled out for special protection.

A special law was passed regarding the correct way of dispatching lobsters and crabs and thus mitigating their terminal agonies. Crustaceans were to be thrown into rapidly boiling water. Bureaucrats at the Nazi Ministry of the Interior had produced learned research papers on the kindest method of killing. In the case of the Nazis, the moral inversion is particularly dramatic, since the Nazis' opposition to experimentation on animals was accompanied by their support for the grotesque and sadistic medical experiments on innocent Jews and others in Nazi concentration camps.[49] Vegetarianism, though often perceived as being healthy and supportive of animal rights, is well linked to a hatred for God.

The famous German romantic composer and influence to Hitler, Richard Wagner, officially became a member of the local Society for the Protection of Animals: "Until now I have respected the activities of such societies, but always regretted that their educational contact with the general public has rested chiefly upon a demonstration of the usefulness of animals, and the uselessness of persecuting them. Although it may be useful to speak to the unfeeling populace in this way, I nonetheless thought it opportune to go a stage further and appeal to their fellow feeling as a basis for ultimately ennobling Christianity. One must begin by drawing people's attention to animals and reminding them of the Brahman's great saying, Tattwam asi (That art thou), even though it will be difficult to make it acceptable to the modern world of Old Testament Judaization. However, a start must be made here, since the commandment to love thy neighbor is becoming more and more questionable and difficult to observe – particularly in the face of our vivisectionist friends..."[50]

Another popular figure in German leftist history was Arthur Schopenhaur, a vegetarian who is considered to be the chief interpreter of Buddhist ideas in his time. He described animals as "having no more consciousness of their own existence than mine."[51] He blamed Christianity and Judaism for animal cruelty writing that it "is pretended that the [so-called] beasts have no rights. They persuade themselves that our conduct in regard to them has nothing to do with morals, or, (to speak in the language of their morality) that we have no duties towards animals. A doctrine revolting, gross and barbarous, peculiar to the West, and which has its roots in Judaism."[52]

This whole idea of Christianity being a danger to animals is seen in today's philosophers as well. A great representation of this is Princeton University professor and animal rights pioneer, Peter Singer. Singer who is commended by Richard Dawkins and his ilk focuses much on the story of Creation writing that "Human beings are here seen as special because they alone of all living things were made in the image of God."[53] Singer writes that Jesus "appears never to have addressed the question of our relations with nonhuman animals" and that this is in contrast to "the teachings of Buddha."[54]

Singer sees Jesus as anti-animal rights because he cursed a fig tree in "a fit of anger at finding no figs" and also for doing an excorcism and casting the devils "into a herd of pigs."[55]

He scorns Biblical traditions as the reason why "western ethical thinking singled out human life" and therefore it is common western thinking that to "end a human life is to end the life of a being made in the image of God."[56] While applauding Darwin for his "disproof of the Hebrew myth of Creation"[57] and pushing our society to reject the idea of the sanctity of human life, Peter Singer, a modern day eugenicist, would have applauded the Nazis for their euthanasia, infanticide, and for their animal rights laws.

Singer supports the infanticide of children who are born ill or who have ill older siblings in need of the infant's body parts. An interviewer questioned him: "What about parents conceiving and giving birth to a child specifically to kill him, take his organs, and transplant them into their sick, older children?" Singer replied: "It's difficult to warm to parents, who can take such a detached view, [but] they're not doing something really wrong in itself."

When Singer was asked if there's "anything wrong with a society in which children are bred for spare parts on a massive scale?" Singer replied with "No."[58]

He also reaffirmed that it would be ethically O.K. to kill 1-year-olds with physical or mental disabilities, although ideally the question of infanticide would be "raised as soon as possible after birth."[59]

Ironically, Singer's mother suffered from Alzheimer's disease and he spent considerable sums on her care even though she wasn't human by his standards. When asked about this, Singer replied that he was not the only person involved in making decisions about his mother (he has a sister). He did say that if he were solely responsible, his "mother might not be alive today."[60] His mother died shortly after the interview.

Singer has a strong Jewish background but believes in a system that almost wiped it out. Bible believers view the likes of Singer as evil.

Would this be a harsh criticism of Singer?

Princeton professor Peter Singer does not only see a crime in killing animals but promotes bestiality as a normal way of life. In his article *Heavy Petting*, Singer explains: "Heard anyone chatting at parties lately about how good it is having sex with their dog? Probably not. ...The existence of sexual contact between humans and animals, and the potency of the taboo against it, displays the ambivalence of our relationship with animals."

Singer even encourages people to go back to antiquity: "There is a Greek vase from 520 BC showing a male figure having sex with a stag; a seventeenth-century Indian miniature of a deer mounting a woman; an eighteenth-century European engraving of an ecstatic nun coupling with a donkey, while other nuns look on, smiling; a nineteenth-century Persian painting of a soldier, also with a donkey; and, from the same period, a Japanese drawing of a woman enveloped by a giant octopus who appears to be sucking her [....], as well as caressing her body with its many limbs."

Is this is the writing of an intellectual? I think not. What is the difference between these statements and those of a madman?

Singer writes of our Christian culture's rejection of zoophilia as if it's a bad thing: "in the Judeo-Christian tradition – less so in the East – we have always seen ourselves as distinct from animals, and imagined that a wide, unbridgeable gulf separates us from them. Humans alone are made in the image of God. Only human beings have an immortal soul. In Genesis, God gives humans dominion over the animals. In the Renaissance idea of the Great Chain of Being, humans are halfway between the beasts and the angels. We are spiritual beings as well as physical beings. For Kant, humans have an inherent dignity that makes them ends in themselves, whereas animals are mere means to our ends. Today the language of human rights – rights that we attribute to all human beings but deny to all nonhuman animals – maintains this separation."

Such is the danger of rejecting that we are made in God's image. Muslims as well reject this Judeo-Christian belief. Michael Novak writes in his article *Another Islam* (Nov. 2002), that in "Islam, to conceive of an image of God is to fall very short of, even to falsify, His greatness. To speak of images of God is blasphemy. It marks one as an infidel – one who has not seen the point, and is in denial about the inconceivable greatness of God."

When a people reject the notion that they are made sacred and separate from the animals, they see themselves as being no different than the animals and moral decay becomes accepted through immoral behavior. As G.K. Chesterton put it: "*Man is an exception, whatever else he is. If he is not the image of God, then he is a disease of the dust. If it is not true that a divine being fell, then we can only say that one of the animals went entirely off its head.*"

WHAT IS BEHIND VEGETARIANISM?

"*Those who hate God love death.*"[61] The protection of animals over humans always breeds the death of the innocent.

The Bible actually warns us about those who are against eating meat, "*that in the latter times some shall depart from the faith, giving heed to seducing spirits, and doctrines of devils; Speaking lies in hypocrisy; having their conscience seared with a hot iron; Forbidding to marry, [and commanding] to abstain from meats, which God hath created to be received with thanksgiving of them which believe and know the truth.*"[62]

Vegetarianism does not stop right at the foot of the heathen but has infiltrated the church as well. Today we have new ideas such as "vegetarian Christendom" formed by the Christian Vegetarian Association founded by Nathan Braun who envisions a "vegetarian Christendom by 2150-2200."[63]

Braun drinks the usual kool-aid by describing Jesus, Socrates and Gandhi as great thinkers for vegetarianism.[64] Like Eduard Baltzer before him Braun's ideas are religious; one of the CVA's mission statements is to "share with non-vegetarian Christians how a vegetarian diet can be a powerful and faith-strengthening witness to Christ's love, compassion, and peace."[65]

The Bible views vegetarianism – the act of forbidding meats – as an abomination. God permitted the killing of animals since it represents Christ dying in order that we live. Likewise, the animal must die for us to eat and thus for us to survive. In the Christian view, God commanded the Jews in the Old Testament to sacrifice animals in order to provide temporary forgiveness of sins and to foreshadow the perfect and complete sacrifice of Jesus Christ.

Animal sacrifice is an important theme found throughout Scripture because "without the shedding of blood there is no forgiveness" (Hebrews 9:22). When Adam and Eve sinned, animals were killed by God to provide clothing for them (Genesis 3:21). After the flood receded, Noah sacrificed animals to God: "And Noah builded an altar unto the LORD; and took of every clean beast, and of every clean fowl, and offered burnt offerings on the altar. And the LORD smelled a sweet savour; and the LORD said in his heart, I will not again curse the ground any more for man's sake; for the imagination of man's heart [is] evil from his youth; neither will I again smite anymore every thing living, as I have done" (Genesis 8:20-21). God would have never forgiven mankind if Noah had not sacrificed animals.

Vegetarian Christians even cherry-pick verses to support their view: "The Bible relates that God accepted animal sacrifices. However, several later prophets objected to sacrifice, emphasizing that God prefers righteousness."[66]

God never condemned the sacrificial system but wanted righteousness to go with it.

To do good deeds for atonement is not a Christian belief but more of an Islamic tenet. The Qur'ân rejects the crucial role occupied by the death and resurrection of Jesus.[67] Conversion to Islam accompanied by good deeds in life, is the means of forgiveness in the Qur'ân: "O ye who believe! If ye keep your duty to Allah, He will give you discrimination (between right and wrong) and will rid you of your evil thoughts and deeds, and will forgive you. Allah is of infinite bounty" (Q 8:29).

John Deer, a so-called Catholic priest, is another vegetarian activist. He writes that Jesus "prefers the sacrifice of our own hearts and lives for the sake of justice and peace. He is far more radical than any of us can imagine. As Gandhi said, Jesus practices the revolution of nonviolence par excellence. He reveals that God is a god of nonviolence and wants us to enter that life of nonviolence."[68]

To say that Jesus preferred good deeds over sacrifice is considered heresy, for "our good deeds are like filthy rags". (Isaiah 64:5) No 'good deeds' can take away sin. Someone with no sin must be sacrificed for redemption. The killing of an innocent lamb is symbolic of Jesus Christ, for He was sinless.

The crux of the matter is this: to have faith in human works is to elevate man over God; Cain's vegetarian offering was rejected and Abel's animals were accepted.

One of my favorite songs is *O Successores Fortissimi Leonis* (You successors of the mightiest Lion) by Hildegard of Bingen in 11th century Germany, the heavenly song expresses the beauty and truth of Jesus' sacrifice (not human deeds) and how He is The Lamb of God, singing:

O followers of the bravest of lions
Between shrine and high altar governing through his ministry
As the angels sing praises and as they give aid to the people
You are one of those who do such things
Always having care in the service of the lamb...

O most victorious vanquishers
Who, hailing the foundation through your bloodshed
Of the church
Embraced the blood of the lamb
Eating of the fatted calf
O how great a recompense you have for you despaired of your
    Living bodies
Imitating the lamb of God
Enlarging his pain through which he brought you to the Renewal
    of your inheritance...

O stream of blood that sounded above
When all the elements entwined
In a lamentable voice with dread
Because the blood of their creator touched them
Cleanse us from our afflictions...

O force of immortality
Which regulated everything in your heart
By your word all things were made just as you desired
And your word itself took on flesh
In a form that led directly from Adam
And so his clothes from the most acute pain were cleansed

O how great is the benevolence of the savior
Who liberated all things by his incarnation
Which breathed holiness without a single link of sin
And so his clothes...
Glory be to the Father and Son and Holy Spirit.[69]

This beautiful peace of lyrical poetry describes Jesus Christ as "the lamb of God" since that is how the Bible describes Him.

God stopped Abraham from killing his son Isaac, saying "for now I know that thou fearest God, seeing thou hast not withheld thy son, thine only [son] from me." Notice the words "thine only [son] from me" (Genesis 22).

God would not stand for somebody sacrificing his or her son to die for sin – it had to be Jesus Christ who is pure and sinless. It could not be human works. God had to give "His only begotten Son, that whoever believes in Him should not perish but have everlasting life" (John 3:16).

Islam teaches the exact opposite of this. Muslim parents encourage their own children to sacrifice themselves to Allah for their salvation and for the salvation of 70 of their relatives.

But Vegetarians don't sacrifice their children as blood atonement!

This is true, but vegetarians do not eat animals therefore rejecting what Jesus Christ represents; an innocent dying for us to live – the bottom line is the sacrifice God offered.

Media was active when some archaeologists thought they found the body of Jesus.

Why?

Because such a discovery would obliterate Jesus Christ's resurrection, thus the Biblical claim would be destroyed.

While many Bible believers are distraught at such documentaries, I am strengthened – it never bothers me when they play so many documentaries on the media questioning even the existence of Christ with an array of questions: 'Are the Gospels reliable?' 'Did Jesus fall in love with Mary Magdalene?' 'Was Jesus gay?' 'Did Jesus steal ideas from Buddha?'...

I see the struggle and the focus on disqualifying only the Biblical accounts and no other. This is a confirmation that evil would not attack a lie. The History Channel and all other intellectually based media would never make a show questioning the reliability of the Qur'ân or Buddha. No one will find episodes like: 'Did Muhammad really split the moon in half?' 'Did Muhammad exist?' 'Muhammad's harem' 'The true history of Buddha'...

Truth is attacked all around while it counters on all directions.

This would remind me of Psalm 22:

Many bulls encompass me
Strong bulls of Bashan surround me
They open wide their mouths at me
Like a ravening and roaring lion

Had Biblical accounts been false, there would be no need to attack them; this is a confirmation for and not evidence against the Bible.

→ Chapter 29 ←

For Straights or For Gays and Dykes

Today homosexuals claim that their struggle is an issue of social discrimination. While this is the claim, their activism is a religious war and a spiritual struggle with Christianity.

In Lansing, Michigan a group of homosexuals and anarchists, dressed with masks resembling mujahadeen, attacked a church throwing condoms and having two lesbians kiss on the pulpit while homosexuals screamed "Jesus was a homo!" while queers began making out in front of the pastor.[70] A similar attack occurred at Hamilton Square Baptist Church in San Francisco in which homosexuals snatched Bibles from Christian hands and blocked entrances into the church.[71]

Yet Pat Boone, an American legend and famous singer was ridiculed in the media for his comment: "What troubles me so deeply, and should trouble all thinking Americans, is that there is a real, unbroken line between the jihadist savagery in Mumbai and the hedonistic, irresponsible, blindly selfish goals and tactics of our homegrown sexual jihadists. Hate is hate, no matter where it erupts. And by its very nature, if it's not held in check, it will escalate into acts vile, violent and destructive."[72]

While Boone's comments angered many on the left who then lashed out at him arguing that jihadists and homosexuals have nothing in common, it takes effort and research to explain Boone's comments.

Today's ardent Islamist warriors are not fighting for moral or conservative values. Neither do such behaviors exist in the closet; instead, manuals are written to ensure certain rules are followed. In the Taliban rule book or *Layeha*, examples of such rules can be found to aid the Mujahideen on how to conduct homosexuality: "Mujahideen are not allowed to take young boys with no facial hair onto the battlefield or into their private quarters."[73]

Islamic pederasty in the military is quite similar to Greco-Roman culture. The historian Florence Dupont writes that the Romans were so obsessed with pederasty that "beardless youths had to be prohibited from taking part in Saturnalia [a festival in honor of Saturn] in order to protect their virtue."[74]

John Racy, a psychiatrist with much experience in Arab societies, has noted that homosexuality is "extremely common" in many parts of the Arab world. Having sex with boys or effeminate men is actually a social norm. Males serve as available substitutes for unavailable women. The key is this: the male who penetrates is not considered to be homosexual or emasculated any more than if he were to have sex with his wife, while the male who is penetrated is emasculated. The boy is not considered to be emasculated since he is not yet considered to be a man. A man who has sex with boys is simply doing what many men do. As scholar Bruce Dunne has demonstrated, sex in Islamic-Arab societies is not about mutuality between partners, but about the adult male's achievement of pleasure through violent domination.[75]

Muslim apologists would argue that homosexuality has no part in Islam. Yet Islam's paradise is more fitting for members of the North American Man/Boy Love Association (NAMBLA). The Qur'ān describes the Islamic heaven as: "Round about them will serve, (devoted) to them, young boys (handsome), as pearls well-guarded."[76]

What the Muslims complain about when accusing the West of being run by international Zionism, with it's Hollywood and sexual licentiousness, all seems to exist in abundance in the Muslim paradise with its rivers of wine (Q 47:15) served with goblets filled at a gushing fountain, white and delicious to those who drink it. It will neither dull their senses nor befuddle them (Q 37:40-48). Even bosomed virgins for companions: a truly overflowing cup, (Q 78:31) these virgins are bashful, undefiled by man or demon. Sexual enticements play an integral element in recruiting jihadists. And if Muslims deny that the Qur'ān promotes homosexuality, that the "serving boys" are simply waiters, the late author and journalist Muhammad Jalal Al-Kushk wrote: "The men in paradise have sexual relations not only with the women [who come from this world] and with 'the black-eyed,' but also with the serving boys."

According to Kurum Al-Kushk, "In paradise, a believer's penis is eternally erect."[77]

The reference to "Ghilman'n Mukhaladun" can only refer to sex with young boys. Arabic poetry describes "Al-Ghilmaniyat." The Hanbalite jurist Ibn al-Jawzi (d. 1200) is one of the four schools (Madh'habs (rites)) of Fiqh or religious law within Sunni Islam (the other three being Hanafi, Maliki and Shafi`i). He is reputed to have said that "He who claims that he experiences no desire when looking at beautiful boys or youths is a liar, and if we could believe him he would be an animal, and not a human being."[78]

In the *Terminal Essay* of his translation of the *Arabian Nights*, Richard Francis Burton notes that, "The Afghans are commercial travelers on a large scale and each caravan is accompanied by a number of boys and lads almost in woman's attire with kohl'd eyes and rouged cheeks, long tresses and henna'd fingers and toes, riding luxuriously in Kajawas or camel-panniers: they are called *Kuch-i safari*, or traveling wives, and the husbands trudge patiently by their sides." Burton also reports a homoerotic proverb common in the area: *Women for breeding, boys for pleasure, but melons for sheer delight.*[79]

The Islamic paradise would probably please the mind of Roman emperor Commodus who kept a harem of 300 women and 300 boys.[80] The reason for the Greco-Roman culture's deceptions was its religion. Like Allah, the Greco-Roman gods did not set any moral standards, nor were they gods of repentance.

HITLER – NO FAN OF TRADITIONAL MARRIAGE

If George Bush was like Hitler as anarchists, Islamists and leftists claim, can we find Hitler defending Christian values making marriage to solely be between a man and a woman? True history can never be revised; Hitler actually hated marriage regarding it as "a thing against nature."[81]

But weren't Hitler's henchmen Christian? Ernst Roehm, the man most responsible for the rise of Nazism, indeed of Hitler himself[82] was the leader of a Nazi terrorist paramilitary organization called the SA Brownshirts, over two million strong, a cesspool of thugs and deviants who regularly met and were formed at the *Bratwurstglockl*, a gay bar in Munich, "to plan and strategize. These were the men who orchestrated the Nazi campaign of intimidation and terror. All of them were homosexual".[83]

These were no Sabbath observant or Sunday school regulars. One of the Brownshirts hymnals and a favorite was, "Storm Trooper Comrades, hang the Jews and put the priests against the wall."[84]

Historian H.R. Knickerbocker writes, "Roehm, as the head of 2,500,000 Storm Troops, had surrounded himself with a staff of perverts. His chiefs were almost without exception homosexuals. Indeed, unless a Storm Troop officer were homosexual, he had no chance of advancement."[85]

Many of the guards and administrators responsible for concentration camp horrors were themselves homosexuals. Famous Nazi hunter Elie Weisel was sent to Auschwitz, where he discovered that the head of his camp section "loved children," and observed that "there was a considerable traffic in young children among homosexuals there."[86] A Nazi administrator named Max Bielas had "a harem of little Jewish boys. He liked them young, no older than seventeen. He had a kind of parody of the shepherds of Arcadia, their role was to take care of the camp flock of geese. They were dressed like little princes... Bielas had a little barracks built for them that looked like a doll's house... Bielas sought in Treblinka only the satisfaction of his homosexual instincts."[87] This homosexual sadism was so severe that even if "the camp doctor happened to pass by after a mass whipping, and knew that a certain type of homosexual Scharfurhrer [Platoon Leader] and SS officer stood at a certain gate, he arranged a little special [whipping] entertainment for them, which he called a medical examination".[88]

Their SS scout leaders molested even Hitler youths. Himmler finally took a hard line against the molestation[89] not because the Nazis were anti-homosexuality and pedophilia, but in order to cover up the extent of sexual perversion in the party, and the extensive documentation about the rampant sexual deviance of numerous Nazi leaders.

The preeminence of homosexuals in the rise of German Nazism is no historical anomaly: "not ten percent of the men who, in 1933, took the fate of Germany into their hands, were sexually normal."[90] When the Nazis destroyed the Sex Research Institute, which was a major organization of the German homosexual movement, Ludwig Lenz, the assistant director of the Institute, stated that the Nazis destroyed the Institute because they "knew too much. It would be against medical principles to provide a list of the Nazi leaders and their perversions [but] Our knowledge of such intimate secrets regarding members of the Nazi Party and other documentary material – we possessed about forty thousand confessions and biographical letters – was the cause of the complete and utter destruction of the Institute".[91]

Most of Hitler's closest aides were homosexuals or sexual deviants. This circle included not only Roehm but the Hitler Youth leader, the Minister of Justice and the Minister of Economics, Hermann Goering, who is not officially known to have been homosexual but is known to have liked to dress in drag, paint his nails and put rouge on his cheeks.[92]

Nazis who loved war and homosexuality were no glitch, even when compared to all warlike nations in history. Historian Eva Cantarella stated: "the most warlike nations have been those who were most addicted to the love of male youths." Cantarella writes: "military homosexuality has been detected in the Azande of Africa and in the Amazon basin of South America." "Greek homosexuality had its origins in warrior life. The Thebans and Spartans were said to have taken their male lovers with them as comrades and sex partners."

In Japan, "the sons of Samurai families were urged to form homosexual alliances with warriors." Historian Max Gallow records how the Nazis clearly fell into a "homosexual warrior cult category." He describes how "S .A. leaders hired a homosexual pimp by the name of Peter Granninger, and paid him 200 marks a month to procure young attractive boys from the Hitler Youth to become participants in S.A. orgies."[93]

THE HITLER YOUTH – A REVIVAL OF OLD GREEK PEDERASTY

Delving into the "organic" in Nazism also involves delving into nature-centered paganism with the "effort to revive the Greek ideal of pedagogic pederasty in the movement of 'Wandering Youth' [Wandervögel]... Ultimately, Hitler used and transformed the movement... expanding and building upon its romanticism as a basis for the Nazi Party".[94] Wandervögel youths were indoctrinated with Greek paganism and taught to reject the Christian values of their parents (mostly Catholics and Lutherans).

The Wandervögel was affiliated with the popular magazine *Der Eigene*. Virulently anti-Semitic and nationalistic, the journal was dedicated to those who "thirst for a revival of Greek times and Hellenic standards of beauty after centuries of Christian barbarism."[95]

The Wandervögel was a boy's only group and envisioned a world of male purity free from Christianity. A known theorist of homoeroticism was Hans Bluher, who in his book *Der Wandervögel als erotisches phanomen* (The German Wandervögel movement as an erotic phenomenon) asserted that homosexuality was the bond that gave the movement cohesion and contributed to its success.

According to Bluher, the youth movement was secretly governed by erotic relations between the adolescents and the team leaders. Bluher made homosexuality a symbol of adolescent revolt against bourgeoisie family morals.[96]

Bluher favored a purification of German society under the guidance of elitist, all-male brotherhoods whose members would be bonded to one another by homoeroticism and charismatic leadership.[97] Hitler read Bluher's book *The Role of Eroticism* and "recognized that something of the kind [homo erotic male heroism] must exist."[98] Bluher wrote: "Hitler was very well acquainted with my books, of course, and he knew that this movement was a male movement founded on the same basic forces as the Wandervögel."[99]

Bible believers see this wanting of a purely male society as a satanic goal promoting hatred of women and procreation: "I will put enmity between you [Satan] and the women, and between thy seed and her seed [Jesus]" (Genesis 3:15). They view the feminist movement as actually anti-women always attempting to push the dark and self-destructive agenda that will lead women to nothing more than the sacrifice of their own children to Baal. The feminist movement has never mentioned the almost forgotten history of Nazi homosexual misogyny but at the same time has never ceased to arraign the Bible for racism, accusing Catholics and Protestants of a history of gender inequality. But what they accuse Christians of is what they are guilty of, hailing Margaret Sanger, a champion for abortion and an anti-Semite who collaborated with the Nazi party for the extermination of the unborn who were deemed inferior in her eyes.

We can see the future with the aid of history – university students immersing their minds into Nietzsche, Hesse, Goethe, and other writers whose ideas came from the pit of the abyss. The Wandervögel was just that – teenagers engaging their minds with the works of these writers, and with these young free thinkers, the Wandervögel evolved into the Hitler youth. Nazism was not a Christian crusade – it was a revolution against God.

Chapter 30

Christians – The Culture Warriors of The Third Reich

Regardless of elitist disagreements, systems like Nazi Germany had similarities with Communist Russia and even Islam's Andalusian era – all of which have much in common with leftist utopian aspirations. The only difference between these is that the Andalusian era was gold-plated by some western historians – as Bernard Lewis stated – as a result of sympathy by Jews towards Islam and not the reality of accurate history. The rest of it falls within the wisdom that History, as it has been said, is the propaganda of the victorious party.

Ever wonder why Islam has made no confessions for anything beginning from its advent through the subsequent empires of the Umayyads, Abbasids, the Fatimids, the Mughals, the Safavids, and Ottomans with a sinless record that virtually had no massacres, pillages, rape, plunder and extortion through Jizzieh and Dhimmi humiliation? It would be accurate to say that within all of mankind's history, Islam by far stands so unique that about it, the following could be said: "by peace he will destroy many" (Daniel 8:25). After all, we hear the repeated mantra from time immemorial – Islam is a peaceful religion.

What people endured under Nazism was similar to what Christians endured under Islam. Hitler banned religious charity and forced clergy to be put on government salary, placing clergy under government control. Regarding these laws, Hitler said that the church "will betray their God to us. They will betray anything for the sake of their miserable little jobs and incomes."[100]

Echoing atheists, Hitler said that it is "not opportune to hurl ourselves now into a struggle with the churches. The best thing is to let Christianity die a natural death... The dogma of Christianity gets worn away before the advances of science."[101]

Hitler saw the churches as nothing more then a political advantage, "a political power; he denied the reality of religion and faith...

On the other hand, political power for him won 'the luster of religious mastery.'" The religious sensibility of Hitler and his followers was channeled into political hopes; Germany's renewal became the National Socialist creed. In this way, political faith replaced religious faith, National Socialism became ever more a replacement for religion, and the party a substitute for the church."[102]

So under all of this deception and tyranny, a stand was taken against the Third Reich – not by atheists or pacifists but by Christians.

The true Christians of Germany had to rise up against the Nazi regime. They were not neutral nor did they attempt to build bridges, but they began a huge crusade against Hitler and his henchmen.

One of those crusaders was Clemens August von Galen, bishop of St Lambert's Church in Münster. In a sermon in Xanten Cathedral, preached in the spring of 1936, Bishop Clemens August accused the National Socialist regime of discriminating against Christians because of their faith, of throwing them into prison and even killing them. He described Germany as having "new graves which contain the ashes of those upon whom the German people look as martyrs." This sermon echoed far beyond the frontiers of Germany. Already at that time, Bishop Clemens August was prepared for the possibility that even he might be deprived of his liberty and hindered in the execution of his Episcopal office.[103]

There is much paranoia about Catholics; many evangelicals erroneously accuse the Catholic Church of being the Harlot of Babylon. Leftists accuse them of being sexists who prohibit condoms and birth control. Bishop Clemens August belonged to those bishops whom Pope Pius XI in January 1937 invited to Rome in order to discuss the situation in Germany and to prepare the encyclical letter *With Burning Anxiety*, which taxed and accused the National Socialist regime before the world public. Together with the other bishops, Bishop Clemens August, in several pastoral letters, stood up against the racial doctrine of the Nazis. In the Fulda conference of bishops he was one of those who demanded that a determined stand be made against National Socialism. Doing so in public was of utmost importance. In 1941, when the Third Reich had reached its height of power, the state authorities began to confiscate convents and monasteries and to expel the religious.[104]

Christians in the West seem to always be fighting evil wherever they are. In the West they fight against stem cell research, Planned Parenthood, and gun control which Hitler did unto Germany, passing the Nazi Weapons Act in 1938 which meant all German citizens "who wished to purchase firearms had to register with the Nazi officials and have a background check."[105]

Bishop Galen spoke on the Nazi persecution of Christians, mentioning the name "of a Protestant minister who served Germany in the first world war as a German officer and submarine commander, who later worked as a Protestant clergyman in Münster and for some years now has been deprived of his liberty, is well known to you, and we all have the greatest respect for this noble German's courage and steadfastness in professing his faith. From this example you will see, my Christians, that I am not talking about a matter of purely Catholic concern but about a matter of Christian concern, indeed of general human and national concern."[106]

While leftists like Wells, Shaw and Bertrand Russell were championing eugenics and birth control, Bishop Galen was taking a stance against the Nazi atrocities: "If it is once admitted that men have the right to kill 'unproductive' fellow-men even though it is at present applied only to poor and defenseless mentally ill patients then the way is open for the murder of all unproductive men and women: the incurably ill, the handicapped who are unable to work, those disabled in industry or war. The way is open, indeed, for the murder of all of us when we become old and infirm and therefore unproductive."[107]

Despite what atheists say, that 'morality doesn't come from the Bible but human goodness', Galen's passionate sermons against the Nazis were Biblically inspired, preaching "'Thou shalt not kill!' This commandment from God, who alone has power to decide on life or death, was written in the hearts of men from the beginning, long before God gave the children of Israel on Mount Sinai his moral code in those lapidary sentences inscribed on stone which are recorded for us in Holy Scripture and which as children we learned by heart in the catechism."[108]

It was Galen's sermons that encouraged the founding of the infamous non-violent resistance group *The White Rose*, by Hans and Sophie Scholl. Hans was inspired by one of Galen's sermons condemning Hitler's euthanasia program. Galen's protest encouraged Hans Scholl and Alexander Schmorell to publish their own anti-Nazi literature. The two wrote the first four leaflets of the White Rose. In May of 1942, Hans Scholl's sister, Sophie, discovered the secret activities of her brother, and confronted him about the serious risks he was taking. In spite of these dangers, she realized there was no turning back when she told Hans and his friends to "be performers of the word" and "not just listeners." She would now join them as an active co-conspirator.[109]

In their fourth leaflet, they express the Christian struggle throughout the ages. It expresses the essence and reality of evil's existence: "[Every] word that comes from Hitler's mouth is a lie. When he says peace, he means war, and when he blasphemously uses the name of the Almighty, he means the power of evil, the fallen angel, Satan. His mouth is the foul-smelling maw of Hell, and his might is at bottom accursed. True, we must consider the struggle against the National Socialist state with rational means; but whoever today still doubts the reality, the existence of demonic powers, has failed by a wide margin to understand the metaphysical background of this war. Behind the concrete, the visible events, behind all objective, logical considerations, we find the irrational element: the struggle against the demon, against the servants of the Antichrist. Everywhere and at all times demons have been lurking in the dark, waiting for the moment when man is weak; when of his own volition he leaves his place in the order of Creation as founded for him by God in freedom; when he yields to the force of evil, separates himself from the powers of a higher order; and, after voluntarily taking the first step, he is driven on to the next and the next at a furiously accelerating rate. Everywhere and at all times of greatest trial men have appeared, prophets and saints who cherished their freedom, who preached the One God and who with His help brought the people to a reversal of their downward course. Man is free, to be sure, but without the true God he is defenseless against the principle of evil. He is like a rudderless ship, at the mercy of the storm, an infant without his mother, a cloud dissolving into thin air. I ask you, you as a Christian wrestling for the preservation of your greatest treasure, whether you hesitate, whether you incline toward intrigue, calculation, or procrastination in the hope that someone else will raise his arm in your defense? Has God not given you the strength, the will to fight? We must attack evil where it is strongest, and it is strongest in the power of Hitler. So I returned, and considered all the oppressions that are done under the sun: and behold the tears of such as were oppressed, and they had no comforter; and on the side of their oppressors was power; but they had no comforter. Wherefore I praised the dead which are already dead more than the living which are yet alive."[110]

The White Rose was no Bertrand Russell, the atheist and pacifist who said: "from India to Spain, the brilliant civilization of Islam flourished. What was lost to Christendom at this time was not lost to civilization, but quite the contrary…"[111] and who wrote the book *Why I Am Not a Christian.*

What can we learn today from the White Rose? Today, it is not courageous to look into the past to write against and fight dead Nazis. Anyone could write against these and get away with it today, but what of writing against the living Nazis of our time – Islamic fundamentalists?

But what good are a couple of leaflets? As Zionist writer Pierre Van Paassen wrote just before his death: "A small flame can set an immense heap of wood on fire, and the most worthwhile things in life and in history have always come from exceedingly small minorities."[112]

My father, Walid Shoebat, usually says: *"One man can make all the difference, Noah in the end was right and everyone on earth died because they were wrong. One man can be right and the rest of mankind wrong."* Must people continue in error, only to find out when it's too late?

Sophie and Hans Scholl, along with others, became that small flame and they were willing to give their lives for it. Hans and Sophie

Scholl and other White Rose members were later captured by the Gestapo and beheaded under the Nazi "People's Court." Sophie's last words before her martyrdom were: "How can we expect righteousness to prevail when there is hardly anyone willing to give himself up individually to a righteous cause. Such a fine, sunny day, and I have to go, but what does my death matter, if through us thousands of people are awakened and stirred to action?"[113]

As my father also says, *"If you are willing to have the courage of John the Baptist, you have to expect to die like him. Being 'neutral,' 'in the middle,' 'balanced with the world,' avoiding being called an 'extremist phobic divisive bigot' are never the traits of noble causes."*

↯ Chapter 31 ↭

The Myth of Nazi Christianity

Progressive Revisionists have created the idea that Nazism was a Nationalist Christian movement when in reality it was a cesspool of a concoction of Hinduism mixed with Norse mythology and socialism.

Attempts like this avoid relevant literature, especially if they provide evidence contrary to their central thesis. Such were the writings of Richard Steigmann-Gall who argues in his study on the *Holy Reich* that the battles waged against Germany's enemies constituted a war in the name of Christianity. It is necessary to note the essential fact that National Socialism, above all, waged a war in the name of the 'Aryan-Germanic race', and preached a new and predominantly non-Christian faith, but not Christianity, the 'old faith'.[114]

Revisionists work from the premise that Nazis were Christians, avoiding the reality that the use of "Christian" is a classic case of stolen identity, in order to argue that the Holocaust was a church conspiracy.

In 1932 a movement called the "German Christians" emerged in order to replace the traditional Christian church and force it to submit under the control of Nazi policy. They wanted all churches to abandon the Old Testament and to accept "Positive Christianity" – a belief that Jesus Christ was an Aryan revolutionist socialist, who fought against the Jewish establishment to only later become a martyr on the cross.

This approach is nothing new. In the Palestinian institutions they promote a Palestinian Jesus fighting for social justice to only be crucified by Jews. He is depicted artistically as surrounded with barbed wire in Palestinian refuge camps; according to them, Jesus is a Palestinian revolutionist.

This can be found everywhere in Palestinian propaganda. Yasser Arafat, for example, even though a Muslim who denounced the Crucifixion as false, would find it fitting to tell crowds: "You are aware of the...disgust...all the Holy Sepulchre fathers feel for the descendants of the crucifiers of our Lord Jesus...crucifiers of your people...Jewish conquerors of the Holy Land of Palestine."[115]

Had Arafat denounced Islam and believed in the crucified Lord Jesus Christ? No, but he was entitled to do *Kitman* and *Taqyia* – Islam allows bending the truth including denial of Islamic edicts or even cursing the prophet of Islam in order to gain concessions: "After the conquest of the city of Khaybar by the Muslims, the Prophet was approached by Hajjaj Ibn `Aalat and told: 'O Prophet of Allah: I have in Mecca some excess wealth and some relatives, and I would like to have them back; am I excused if I bad-mouth you to escape persecution?' The Prophet excused him and said: 'Say whatever you have to say.'"[116]

Christian dogma insists that for one to be Christian one must believe in *The* Crucifixion, not *a* Crucifixion. Muslims believe that Judas Iscariot was crucified in place of Jesus – a revolutionist promoting a revolutionary social gospel – all void of the historic Jesus. Bible believers always argue that one cannot be a believer in a crucifixion as a figment of someone's imagination. Can a Muslim rob the title of a Jew or be an alcoholic who never drank a drop of liquor? Such is the mixing of fact with fiction and the production of oxymoronic labels. In the Muslim view, such absurdities exist – Abraham and Jesus after all were not Jews but Muslims. In Nazism, the same cyanide was applied – Jesus was a National Socialist.

It's a typical case of stolen identity; apply Jesus to any social or political revolution in which the promoter applies his thought to Jesus; he then himself becomes Jesus' mouthpiece. If Hanan Ashrawi of the P.L.O calls Jesus a 'Palestinian Revolutionist', in reality it is she who is the revolutionist and by extension, the mouthpiece of God.

If anything, The Nazi gospel was more of a mix of Paganism and Reverend Jeremiah Wright's social gospel. Hitler was a social gospel activist: "As Christ proclaimed 'love one another', so our call – 'peoples' community', 'public need before private need', 'communally-minded social consciousness' – rings out through the German

Fatherland! This call will echo throughout the world!"[117] Or as Goebbels put it: "We modern Germans are something like Christ Socialists."[118]

The way to eat the sheep is for the wolf to dress up with the skin of his last victim.

How else can Nazism penetrate the pasture? Christian Nazism, if indeed one can call it that, was based on an idea that Germans should sacrifice themselves for the cause, just as the "Aryan Jesus" did, when fighting against the Jewish establishment or the enemies of the Fuhrer. In other words, the Nazi now is Jesus, just as the Muslim martyr gives his life for Muhammad's cause. If only Jesus qualifies to give His life for sin, in both, Muslim and Nazi view, they themselves, and through their sacrifice can now redeem sin.

Such is Lucifer's proclamation "I am God".

Positive Christianity, today amongst Palestinians or in the past, always held the idea of self-sacrifice in battle with little difference from Islamic martyrdom.

Hitler youth boys at age 10 graduated into Young Folk where their oath was: "In the presence of this blood banner, which represents our Fuhrer, I swear to devote all my energies and my strength to the savior of our country, Adolf Hitler. I am willing and ready to give up my life for him, so help me God."[119] Another Hitler youth rite of passage was: "We affirm: The German people has been created by the will of God. All those who fight for the life of our people, and those who died, Carried out the will of God. Their deeds are to us holy obligation."[120]

Had Nazi Germany been a typical Christian culture during Nazism, one would find parades with nativity scenes and school children singing Church hymns of Silent Night and such. The Nazis changed the famous hymnals, the original "Silent night" became: "Silent Night! Holy Night! All is calm; all is bright, Only the Chancellor steadfast in fight, Watches o'er Germany by day and by night, Always caring for us."[121]

The Nazis no longer wanted Christmas to be seen as a Christian holiday but wanted it to be identified as having its roots in a pre-

Christian 'Nordic' celebration of the winter solstice. Although Christmas was celebrated all over the world, in Germany it came to be seen as a particularly German festival, full of survivals of a lost past – tree cults and solstice fires that modern Germans could reconnect with through 'Nordic' Christmas trees, and the flickering drama of pagan bonfires and torchlight parades.[122]

Irmgard Hunt describes his life in the shadow of Hitler's Alpine retreat on the Obersalzburg, recalling such efforts: "The word weihnacht (holy night) may have come from pagan times but had for ages stood for the blessing brought by the birth of Jesus. The Nazis, however, began to promote a different name for the holiday, calling it Julfest (Yuletide) or Rauhnacht (Rough Night) to emphasize a neopagan, Germanic concept that focused on the winter solstice, the harsh, dark times that required forbearance and strength, followed by the long-awaited return of the Sun."[123]

Then there were the great state-orchestrated celebrations that took place across the country, employing "fire and light to symbolize the revival of ancient 'Nordic' rituals and the 'national rebirth' of the German community", evocations of the pre-Christian past in which Hitler Youth brigades re-enacted 'solstice rituals', Storm Troopers gathered about blazing bonfires to swear 'oaths of fire' and torchlight parades through city streets were a common sight.[124]

They were encouraged to avoid kitschy Christmas decorations and to buy specially handcrafted objects of a more völkisch nature. One 1939 guide to creating the perfect Nazi home gushed over carved wooden Christmas tree stands and sounded more like a neopagan theme than a Bible verse: "Such a tree stand changes the festival, since it is a family heirloom that, however simple it may be, makes an impression. The wreaths symbolize the closed circle of our lives and of time, of the year and the months; the spokes symbolize the seasons."[125] Mothers and children were encouraged to make their own decorations shaped like Sun Wheels, runes or fertility symbols, linking the everyday sphere with the mythologized past of the eternal 'Nordic' nation.[126]

The Church resisted such tendencies as well as it could, and normal German people often realized that a conflict between two very different worldviews was being revealed in the struggle for Christmas. In December 1936, one young woman, Ursula Semlies, was traveling from her studies in Hanover to her home in Tilsit to spend the holidays with her family. When several SS men got on board, she found herself drawn into conversation about the meaning of Christmas. "Ach, wonderful," said one. "Now we're going home and finally Christmas, the 'Festival of the Family', and this Christian fuss no one believes in anymore." Ursula responded that for her Christmas was "still always a Christian Christmas". The SS men humored her, pointing out that the Bible was a "Jew book" and telling her she would one day see who was right on the subject. Ursula said that, while "in political terms" she was in complete agreement with Hitler, "in religious terms, I have my own views". The SS men told her that "The Führer wants the whole human being, and if there is any region in your heart that does not belong to the Führer, then you are not a convinced National Socialist and then the Führer cannot influence you." Ursula, despite her reservations about the Nazis' plans for Christmas, later joined the party.[127]

One of the notable organizers to try to replace Christianity in Germany was Jakob Wilhelm Hauer, founder of the German Faith Movement. Hauer wanted a new religion for Germany; mixed with Hinduism especially the ancient Bhagavad Gita as the language "eternal fate", "eternal law," "battle and tragedy" has its source in that text; and other elements such as "the Yogic tradition, pre-Christian Germanic beliefs, and German philosophical idealism."[128]

Like the postmodern spirituality of today, the German Faith Movement was not without meta-narrative, it was also based on myth, in this case a focus on Germanic and Icelandic sagas. Even though this was supposed to be a new religion for Germany, it was, in reality very old, for a new philosophy generally means the praise of some old vice in practice.[129]

But didn't Hauer use Christian elements in his ideas? Hauer after all used the example of Amos for a new prophet who will come to the world to deliver the people from hostile forces and give new hope to the future. But the truth is that Hauer was anti-Christian to the point that he wanted Germany to have "a new conception of God, not as one grasped by thought, but as the reality of inner experience."[130] In his German Faith Movement's journal *Sigrune*, it reads that "Jesus was a cowardly Jewish lout who had certain adventures during his years of indiscretion. He uprooted his disciples from blood and soil and, at the wedding at Cana, loutishly flared up at his own mother. At the very end he insulted the majesty of death in an obscene manner."[131] Hauer held Germany's first Pagan wedding. Hauer's sermon and call to worship was not "here in the sight of God" in "holy matrimony", but "Oh Mother Earth, from whom all love proceeds! And oh Father Heaven, who blesses with His light and weather! And all good Powers of the Air! May you rule over this man and this woman until their destinies are fulfilled!"[132]

When we have homosexual weddings in America, the real outcry is from the Catholics and Evangelicals. The same outcry was heard in Europe when pagan weddings were being held in Nazi Germany. In Vatican City, the Osservatore Romano, official news-organ of the Holy See, declared that the recent "blood purge" and "unheard of cruelties" perpetrated by Adolf Hitler were the direct result of Nazi pagan teaching. "It is incredible and shocking that final religious solace was denied to the men doomed," declared Osservatore. "A drop of liquor and a cigarette were not refused, yet Christ was denied to these unfortunate Germans. How sad their agony must have been. It is unheard of and terrifying to refuse to souls their supreme comfort: God's forgiveness. For the essence of Christianity is the quest of God's forgiveness."[133]

Meanwhile, German Protestants were gagged by Minister of Interior Dr. Wilhelm Frick and an effort was made to force all groups under a new German Protestant Constitution to be drawn up by Dr. Ludwig Müller, a onetime Army chaplain who was made *Reichsbischof* by Chancellor Hitler.[134] Dr. Frick decreed that "[there shall be] no discussion of church policies" in public assemblies of three or more persons or by printed or written words. Only the Reichsbischof did Dr. Frick exempt from this gag, and to him all other Protestants were supposed to listen in obedient silence.[135]

The Jewish attorney Julie Seltzer Mandel, a woman whose grandmother was a survivor of the Auschwitz concentration camp, gained access to 148 bound volumes of rare documents – some marked "Top Secret" – compiled by the Office of Strategic Services (or O.S.S., the WWII forerunner to the CIA). After scouring the papers, she published the first installment of them in 2002, a 120-page O.S.S. report entitled *The Nazi Master Plan: The Persecution of the Christian Churches*. Reporting on these O.S.S. findings in the *Philadelphia Inquirer*, Edward Colimore wrote: "The fragile, typewritten documents from the 1940s lay out the Nazi plan in grim detail: Take over the churches from within, using party sympathizers. Discredit, jail or kill Christian leaders. And re-indoctrinate the congregants. Give them a new faith – in Germany's Third Reich." He then quotes Mandel: "A lot of people will say, 'I didn't realize that they were trying to convert Christians to a Nazi philosophy.' ...They wanted to eliminate the Jews altogether, but they were also looking to eliminate Christianity."[136]

Tyrannies hate Christianity with a passion. The infamous journalist of the 1930s Dorothy Thompson, who was expelled from Nazi Germany for exposing Nazi fascism, wrote that most "of the leadership in the German Protestant revolt against the Nazifying of the church is German Nationalist, and the Nazi party has proceeded against these courageous Christians, arresting many of them, inflaming their congregations against them, insisting that they are traitors to the new Germany."[137]

Similar to the Islamic tyrannies of today, Nazi Germany had Christians "imprisoned for expressing religious beliefs."[138] Stanley High in his 1934 essay *The War On Religious Freedom* writes that the arrests of "Protestants and Catholics started in January and have continued at a daily pace. Prof. Karl Adam, distinguished Catholic theologian of Tubingen, was dismissed for stating that for Christians, Jewish history must always remain unique since it gave Jesus Christ to the world. Non-uniformed rowdies broke into the home of Gerhard Jakobi, second in command of the opposition pastors, and beat him up with brass knuckles. Goring commanded his inspector of secret police, Dr. Diehls, to gather data on the opposition pastors."[139]

Pagan weddings and forbidding Christians from speaking about the Bible in public is not right-wing conservatism but 'puritanical' leftism. If we are to protect our schools from the repetition of tyrannies, we need to stop the continual brainwashing administered to American children by progressive advocates who teach that the Nazis were right wing evangelicals; Hitler was a Roman Catholic; and the settlers that came to America were evil white Christians while the Native Americans were noble peace loving people who didn't want to do any harm to anyone, except for some head scalping here and there. Of course, that was in response to 'white Christian oppression'.

Not to be outdone by middle schools and high schools, most professors in the history field teach that the founding fathers were evil old white men who oppressed Native Americans, women, and blacks.

The American Civil Liberties Union has urged the Supreme Court to uphold a federal appeals court ruling that public schools are constitutionally barred from linking patriotism and piety by reciting the phrase "under God" as part of the Pledge of Allegiance. The ACLU claims "government should not be asking impressionable schoolchildren to affirm their allegiance to God at the same time that they are affirming their allegiance to the country."[140]

False history dooms us to only repeat true history.

SECTION SIX

YAHWEH VS ALL OTHERS

◆ Chapter 32 ◆

For God or For Lucifer

"These are the days when the Christian is expected to praise every creed except his own." – G.K. Chesterton

The Biblical God is described as Alpha (The Beginning), Omega (the end), Healer, Comforter, Protector, Almighty, Everlasting Father, The Son, The Holy Spirit, Truthful, Just, Righteous, Immutable (Unchangeable). He is also the Emmanuel – God With Us.

The main opposition to the God of the Bible (The Luminous One) is described in the Bible as "ruler of the demons" (Mathew 3:22), "unclean and hateful bird" (Revelation 18:2), "God of War" or the "God of Fortresses (War)" (Daniel 11:38), "Deceiver" (Revelation 12:9), "Liar" (John 8:44), "manslayer" "who caused death" (John 8:44; I John 3:8), (Romans 5:12), "ruler of the air" (Ephesians 2:2), "misleading the earth" (Revelation 12:9), "fallen from heaven" "morning star" (Isaiah 14:12-14), "beautiful angel" (Ezekiel 28:13-19), "lightening" (Luke 10:18), "deny father and son" (I John 2:22), "ruler of demons" (Luke 11:15), "ruler of the air" (Ephesians 2:1-2), "ruler of this world" (John 12:31-32), "power of darkness" (Colossians 1:13-14), "wicked one" (Ephesians 6:16), "the serpent" (Genesis 3:1), "afflicter" (Job 1:13-19, 2:7-8), "counterfeiter" (II Cor. 11:13-15, Revelation 2:9, 13) "deceives the nations" (Matthew 4:8-9, Ephesians 6:12), "Proud" (Ezekiel 28:12, I Timothy 3:6), "Wanting to be god" (Isaiah 14:12-14).

In the Bible, Lucifer is described as wanting to be God by creating his own religions: "By the multitude of thy merchandise they have filled the midst of thee with violence, and thou hast sinned" (Ezekiel 28:16).

The Biblical account attributes violence, rebellion and cults as the hallmark of The Luminous One and all his tyrannies. When it comes to any religion besides the Bible, we will find that their gods openly identify themselves with the same titles and names as those belonging to Lucifer as described in the Bible.

Take Allah of Islam as an example. Under all the disguises of being The Most Merciful and such He is also *Khayrul_makireen* (the greatest of all deceivers, schemer, conniver), *Al-Dharr* (the afflicter), *Al-Mumeet* (the causer of death) and *Al-Mutakabbir* (the most proud).

Allah is not the only god described as a deceiver. From the deserts of the Middle East – the Shinar cult reached the cold frosty forests of Scandinavia. Take Odin, the chief divinity of the ancient Scandinavian pantheon. Like Allah, Odin was called *Ginnarr* (Deceiver) and *Glapsvior* (Swift in Deceit).

Odin ruled over *Valhalla* (Hall of the Slain) and like the Islamic paradise with its carnal desires where *shaheed* warriors enjoy endless orgies with harems and endless wine,[1] Valhalla provides the heavenly harem or the *valkyria* to warriors slain while fighting the enemy.

And if Islam had its *mujahideen*, the Norse whom the Nazis exalted had the *berserkers*, warriors who terrorized much of Christian Europe. And just as the Muslim-Shi'a do *qama zani* (ritual self-mutilation) so did the berserkers, who did self-flagellation to whip themselves into a frenzy. They were ferocious fighters and just as the Muslim Dervishes, they were seemingly insensitive to pain. It was not uncommon for berserkers to even kill their own people in the heat of frenzy.[2]

Odin is not that much different from the Arabian war god Allah, with his frenzied Muslim followers. He is described as *Gapthrosnir* (One in a Gaping Frenzy), *Oðinn* (Frenzied One), *Oðr* (Frenzy, Fury), *Viðurr* (Killer), *Biflindi* (Spear/Shield Shaker), *Böðgæðir* (Battle Enhancer), *Herjafoðr* (Father of Battle), *Hildolf* (Battle Wolf), *Hjaldrgoð* (God of battle), and *Valtyr* (Slain God).

The Deceiver is not a title only in ancient times; *Thelema*, a religion created by the progressive thinker and occultist Aleister Crowley, wrote of this deceiver in his *Vision and The Voice*: "I am the greatest of the deceivers, for my purity and innocence shall seduce the pure and innocent, who but for me should come to the centre of the wheel...I am he of whom it is written: He shall deceive the very elect."[3]

In no way does the Biblical God Yahweh ascribe to Himself any such attributes. On the contrary, what should be surprising to all western progressives who are ashamed of their Judeo-Christian heritage and desire unity with all religions, is that the Bible attributes such titles not to Jehovah whom they so willingly reject but to Satan, the adversary who is described as he "who deceives the whole world" (Revelation 12:9). "When he [Satan] speaks a lie, he speaks from his own resources, for he is a liar and the father of it" (John 8:44). "He [Satan] was a murderer from the beginning, and abode not in the truth, because there is no truth in him" (John 8:44). "Forasmuch then as the children are partakers of flesh and blood, he also himself likewise took part of the same; that through death he might destroy him that had the power of death, that is, the devil" (Hebrews 2:14). Satan is also called Apollyon (destroyer) (Revelation 9:11).

And just as Lucifer is filled with pride (Ezekiel 28:12, I Timothy 3:6), Allah calls Himself *Al-Mutakabbir* (Pride filled, The most proud). Allah, in his own words, says: "Pride is My Wear, Supremacy is My Dress, I will break anyone who vies with Me for them and I do not care".[4] It is no wonder that the phrase yelled by Jihadists in every operation *Allahu Akbar* – means Allah is greater, most proud. Odin is no different, for he is *Hár* (High One, Proud) and *Jafnhár* (Just as High).

Allah in Islam is given the title of King. Yet his kingdom does not encompass the universe with its humanity and angelic host, but includes both mankind and demons, a concept rejected from a Judeo-Christian perspective since this attribute fits Lucifer.

The pride-filled god, the causer of death and affliction is none other than Lucifer who afflicted Job, caused the death of mankind in the Garden of Eden, and hailed himself as the Most Proud. Satan is described in Isaiah as son of the dawn who brings all evil and destruction. Yet in Islam, Allah is described as the bringer of evil: "Say: I seek refuge with [Allah] the Lord of the Dawn from the mischief of the evil He created…the mischievous evil of Darkness as it becomes intensely dark" (Qur'ân 113:1-3).

Contrary to the Biblical God Jehovah who was immune from creating anything evil, and similar to Islam's Allah, Odin contains the name *Bölverkr*, meaning "creator of evil and evil worker."

And if Satan in the Bible is the lord of the demons then so is Allah, being described as the "Lord of men and jinn [demons]" (Q 69:43). Allah created "jinn [demons] and man to worship Me [Allah]."5

The demons are so fascinated with Allah that they collectively refer to him as "our Lord" (Sura Al-Jinn). The demons love Allah and Muslims commune with them through chants, swearing "by the self-reproaching spirit, the accusing soul" (Q 75:1).

The Biblical Lord is not the Lord of demons, yet Allah specifically describes himself as "the Lord of men and jinn [demons]" (Q 69:43). Similarly, in the Norse religion, Odin is *Draugadrottin* (Lord of Ghosts).

Such titles are not restricted to Nordic and Arab deities. The god of the Hindus, Shiva, bears the name *Bhooteshwara* (Lord Of Ghosts And Evil Beings), *Bhutapala* (protector of the ghosts). Satan is described in the Bible as the "ruler of the demons" (Mathew 3:22).

In the Bible, demons are described as birds: "And he cried mightily with a strong voice, saying, Babylon the great is fallen, is fallen, and is become the habitation of devils, and the hold of every foul spirit, and a cage of every unclean and hateful bird" (Revelation 18:2). Similarly, Odin is the *Arnhofði* (Eagle Headed), *Hrafnass* (Raven God) and *Olgir* (hawk) And in Aleister Crowley's *The Book of The Law* it reads: "am the Hawk-Headed Lord of Silence & of Strength; my nemyss shrouds the night-blue sky."6 *The Book of The Law* also describes the god *Hadit* as the "winged snake of light". "Show thy star-splendour, O Nuit! Bid me within thine House to dwell, O winged snake of light, Hadit!"

This serpent of light even goes back to ancient Mexico where the Aztecs worshiped the solar deity *Quetzalcoatl* who was none other than the "feathered serpent".

Allah in the Qur'ân has "His throne upon the waters" (Q 11:7). Correspondingly, in an ancient Mexican poem, it praises a god who they believed to have "descended upon the water, into the beautiful glistening surface; he was as a lovely water cypress, as a beauteous green serpent; now I have left behind me my suffering."[7] The Bible describes Lucifer (The Assyrian) as a cedar tree setting himself upon the waters (Ezekiel 31:3-4).

Even Satan's rebellion in the Bible for which he claimed to have "ascended to heaven" (Isaiah 14:13) corresponds to Muhammad's ascension as he claimed in his *Isra* and *Miraj* account.

Muhammad is said to have mounted *Al-Buraq*, which is described as having colors of a peacock whose plumage was set with red rubies and corals, on which sat a white head of musk on a neck of amber. His ears and shoulders were of pure white pearls attached with golden chains, each chain decorated with glittering jewels.[8]

This '*Buraq*' has quite a resemblance to Lucifer in the Bible: "Thou hast been in Eden the garden of God; every precious stone [was] thy covering, the sardius, topaz, and the diamond, the beryl, the onyx, and the jasper, the sapphire, the emerald, and the carbuncle, and gold: the workmanship of thy tabrets and of thy pipes was prepared in thee in the day that thou wast created" (Ezekiel 28:13).

The angel that visited Muhammad was not the Biblical angel Gabriel as Muslims claim but *Tawus Al-Malaeka* or the peacock angel as defined in Muslim annals.

Tawus Al-Malaeka corresponds to the Babylonian cult of the *Yezidis* and its deity *Malek Taus* – the only difference is that Yezidis openly admit to their leader being of the archangels *Shaytan*, the exact name for The Luminous One (the Devil) even in the Qur'ân.

According to Historian Williams Jackson: "[T]he Yezidi religion shows distant survivals of the old Assryo-Babylonian worship of the sun, moon, and stars, for the faith retained the sun god Shamash under the form of Sheikh Shems, and the moon-god Sin as Sheikh Sinn, and emanation of God himself."[9] Yezidis are just being honest since most of them admit they worship Satan.

Mandaeans link to Malek Taus, predating the Yezidis by thousands of years. Mandaeism has historically been practiced primarily in Iraq. In Islam, the term "Sabians" (al-Ṣāi'ūn) is used as a blanket term for adherents to a number of religions, including that of the

Mandaeans. Islam even includes Sabians in the family of faiths: "Surely those who believe, and those who are Jews, and the Christians, and the Sabians, whoever believes in Allah and the Last day and does good, they shall have their reward from their Lord, and there is no fear for them, nor shall they grieve" (Qur'ân 2:62).

Malek Taus – Lucifer disguised as a peacock – is quite similar to the Hindu goddess *Durga* who carries the names *Mayoora Pichhavalaya* (Wearer Of Peacock-Feathered Bangles), *Shikhipichhadwaja Virajita* (Having Peacock-Feathered Flag) and the one who "shinest also with peacock-plumes standing erect on thy head, and thou hast sanctified the celestial regions by adopting the vow of perpetual maiden-hood. ...By them that call upon thee for the relief of their burdens, and by them also that bow to thee at daybreak on Earth [Muslims pray to Allah at daybreak], there is nothing that cannot be attained in respect either of offspring or wealth. And because thou rescuest people from difficulties whether when they are afflicted in the wilderness or sinking in the great ocean, it is for this that thou art called *Durga* by all."[10]

God in the Bible addresses Satan with: "You had the seal of perfection, full of wisdom and perfect in beauty" (Ezekiel 28:12). This description is identical to the angel Muhammad encountered and described in the Qur'ânic chapter of Al-Najm "the Star" as, "One Mighty in Power, the One endued with wisdom" (Q 56:5,6).

Are all these coincidence?

The Muslim Sufis identify the spirit that inspired the Qur'ân as the angel Jibril and refer to him as an angelic peacock: "God created the [Holy] Spirit in the form of a peacock."

The root word of Buraq (Muhammad's spirit guide) is "Brq" which means "lightning bolt" or "glowing light." The Bible describes Lucifer as "burning like a torch (or lamp)" (Revelation 8:10). This is exactly what the Qur'ân describes Allah as: "a lamp." Allah in the Qur'ân dedicates chapter Al-Noor (The Light) as the most significant description of Allah: "Allah is the light of the heavens and the earth; a likeness of His light is as a niche in which is a lamp, the lamp is in a glass, (and) the glass is as it were a brightly shining star, lit from a blessed olive-tree, neither Eastern nor Western, whose oil is nigh luminous though fire scarce touched it. Light upon light! Allah does guide whom He will to His light: Allah sets forth parables for men: and knows all things" (Q 24:35-36).

Light of the heavens, and brightly shining star or luminous, are satanic titles – "Lucifer" literally means the luminous one. Satan desires to be the bright shining star.

Even the Mahdi is identified by the prophet Muhammad as the "peacock of all angels and of the dwellers of the heavenly realm, he is dressed and adorned with the cloaks of light."[11] This "lightning bolt" described by Muhammad is described by Jesus: "I saw Satan fall like lightning from heaven" (Luke 10:18). The word 'Lucifer' also means "bearer of light," "luminous," or "the morning star." The Bible warns us regarding the manner in which Satan disguises himself "as an angel of light" (II Corinthians 11:14). John as well describes him: "I saw a star fallen from heaven to the earth. To him was given the key to the bottomless pit" (Revelation 9:1). This "star" is referred to as a "him," a person and not an actual star.

The Qur'ân even calls Allah "The Lord of Sirius" (Qur'ân, chapter of The Star, 53:49). Sirius is the brightest star in the night sky. The Zoroastrian angel Tishtrya is the angel of the star Sirius, being worshiped as "the bright and glorious star [Sirius] who is the seed of the waters, powerful, tall, and strong, whose light goes afar".

The same star is described in Revelation 8:10: "Then the third angel sounded: And a great star fell from heaven burning like a torch (or lamp), and it fell on the third of the rivers and on the springs of water." The "waters" is likely allegoric of "peoples, multitudes, nations, and different tongues" which Satan spiritually destroys (Revelation 17:15).

Why are we conditioned to believe that we all worship the same God? Especially since they have different names and each constructed a different religion? Could it be possible that these are all the same god under different names and religions? Could it be that these are simply an all-for-one – The Luminous One?

If we all worship the same God then their attributes should be equal with the Yahweh of the Bible – right?

Wrong.

Why do all gods besides Yahweh contain equal names to those of Lucifer and are described by these religions exactly as Lucifer is revealed in the Bible?

All man-made religions follow a similar theme of exalting man over God; regardless of claims, the final result always diverts away from the Biblical God Yahweh. Regardless of any supposed straight-path from Islam to Taoism, they all lead to a crooked destiny. If it's Islam's *AlSerata AlMustakeem* (Straight Path) to Taoism's *Tao* (The Way), they all deceive through supposed harmony and insist on a one world religion and One world Government – all attempt to reverse the initial rebellion in Shinar.

Both Islam and Yezidism demand five prayers a day at almost equal times. With Yezidism, they were ordained to pray at *Nivêja berîspêdê* (Dawn Prayer), *Nivêja rojhilatinê* (Sunrise Prayer), *Nivêja nîvro* (Noon Prayer), *Nivêja êvarî* (Afternoon Prayer), and *Nivêja rojavabûnê* (Sunset Prayer). The worshipers turn their face toward the sun, and for the noon prayer, they face toward Lalish (Yezidi holy site in Iraq) just like Muslims pray toward their holy site, Mecca.[12]

Similarly, in Islam prayer is obligatory and must be performed five times a day at *Fajr* (Dawn), *Dhuhr* (Noon Paryer), *Asr* (Mid-Afternoon Prayer), *Maghrib* (Sunset Prayer), and *Isha'* (Evening Prayer).

Quite similarly, the Zoroastrians pray five times a day – sunrise, noon, sunset, midnight and dawn. Ritual cleanliness and ablution are required before prayer, just as in Islam.

Concerning pilgrimages, Muslims must go to Mecca at least once in their lifetime while Yezidis take a six-day pilgrimage to Lalish once in their lifetime as well. Yezidis also must "baptize" themselves at the two springs of Lalish: the "white spring" (Kaaf-a Sipf), and the spring of "Zamzam",[13] the exact name of the Islamic pilgrimage site in Mecca – the *Well of Zamzam*. The water is considered health giving, and pilgrims (hajjis) collect it in bottles to bring back home to their own countries. One of the last things a hajji tries to do is to dip his or her future burial clothes in the Zamzam water.[14]

THE LORD OF LIGHT

In the Bible Satan is described as an "angel of light." (II Corinthians 11:14) An epithet that is common for false gods.

If the most popular hymn in America is Amazing Grace, in Islam it's *Tala'al Badr* (The Moon Has Risen) and is the cornerstone of all Muslim songs. The lyrics depict Muhammad's coming to Medina as the rising and glowing moon appears: "O the White Moon rose over us from the Valley of Wada' and we owe it to show gratefulness where the call is to Allah."

Allah is also described as this light, being "the Light of the heavens and the earth… The Parable of His Light is as if there were a Niche and within it a Lamp: the Lamp enclosed in Glass: the glass as it were a brilliant star…luminous…Light upon Light!" (Q 24:35).

The Norse god Odin is also described as "Lord of Light", as well as the Hindu god Shiva being called *Gopati* (Lord of Cattle and Lights), and *Vasu* (the Inner Light).[15]

The Hindu goddess Durga is also described as a "body bright as the newly-risen Sun, O thou efface beautiful as the full moon. …O thou that wearest bangles made of emeralds and sapphires, O thou that bearest excellent bracelets on thy upper arm. Thou shinest, thy face is beautiful. …O Goddess, thou shinest with a face that challengeth the moon in beauty."[16]

Even in modern times, heavy metal bands are reviving such deities. Iron Maiden in their song *Lord of Light* praise this lord of light:

Spiral path leads through the maze
   Down into the fiery underworld below
Fire breathing lead the way
   The Luminous One was just an angel led astray
Free your soul and let it fly
   Give your life to the Lord of Light

Anton LaVey describes Satan as: "the bearer of light, the spirit of the air, the personification of enlightenment. In Christian mythology he became synonymous with evil, which was only to have been expected from a religion whose very existence is perpetuated by clouded definitions and bogus values!"[17] LaVey's Satanic Bible posts the first of the "Enochian Keys" which describes the devil as the "Lord of the Earth, in power exalted *above* and *below*…[and] brighten your vestments with Infernal light."[18] Corresponding with Allah – *Malik-Rab-Al-Alameen* – He is the Lord of the worlds, that is 'this world and the underworld'.

The Roman goddess Selene is a goddess of light and much like the crescent moon is the symbol of Allah's religion, so a crescent is depicted over her head.[19]

Mormons as well worship the lord of light, despite claiming they worship Jesus, who according to Mormonism is the brother of Lucifer. Joseph Smith clarified in his vision that he saw "a pillar of light exactly over my head, above the brightness of the sun, which descended gradually until it fell upon me."[20] Mormons also believe that Jesus "is in the moon, and is the light of the moon, and the power thereof by which it was made; As also the light of the stars, and the power thereof by which they were made".[21]

THE LORD OF THE AIR

Anton LaVey describes Satan as the "spirit of the air", the same as the Aztec "feathered serpent" or *Quetzalcoatl*: "the god of the air."[22] In the Bible it is The Luminous One who is described as "prince of the air". (Eph 2:1-3). It all stems from the cult of Shinar in Babylon – Bel is the Semitic title for the ancient Sumerian god *Enlil* who was called "Lord of the Air"[23] to later transfer to Arabia through Nabonidus (555-539 B.C.), the last king of Babylon, who built Tayma in Arabia as the center of Moon-god worship.

As Segel, a historian of the ancient Middle East has stated, "South Arabia's stellar religion has always been dominated by the Moon-god in various variations."

THE LORD OF DAWN

So who is this Lord of the Dawn? Why does Allah command in the Qur'ân to 'swear by the dawn?'[24] The Roman poem *Metamorphosis* (by Ovid), concerning the history and the creation of the world, regards the dawn god as Lucifer:

Aurora, watchful in the reddening dawn
Threw wide her crimson doors and rose-filled halls
The Stars took flight
In marshaled order
Set by Lucifer
Who left his station last [25]

The Greek "dawn goddess" Eos is described in Homer's *Odyssey* as: "That brightest of stars appeared, Eosphoros [Morning Star], that most often heralds the light of early-rising Dawn (Eos Erigeneia)." Eos is also described as:

The first of all to wake
She tramples over transitory night
The mighty Goddess
Bringer of the light
Beholding every thing from Heaven's height
The ever youthful
All reviving Dawn
To every invocation She comes first [26]

Hail, gentle Dawn!
Mild blushing goddess
Hail! Rejoiced
I see thy purple mantle spread
O'er half the skies
Gems pave thy radiant way
And orient pearls from every shrub depend [27]

Ovid chronicles Eos with Lucifer (The Luminous One):

The vigilant Aurora opened forth
Her purple portals from the ruddy East

Disclosing halls replete with roses
  All The stars took flight whilst Lucifer
The last to quit his vigil
  Gathered that great host
And disappeared from his celestial watch [28]

From Greco-Roman mythology – the Shinar cult can be traced all the way to the humid city of Bangkok where lies the ancient *Wat Arun* or Temple of The Dawn. The temple has the looks and height of a ziggurat going up to seventy-nine meters tall with *Ravana*, a king of demons, guarding the temple.

The dawn god even reached all the way to Mexico where human sacrificing Mesoamericans worshiped *Quetzalcoatl*, the primordial god of creation. He was also known as the Lord of the East and was associated with the morning star. He was called *Tlahuizcalpantecuhtli* or the "lord of the star of the dawn."[29]

As the Mesoamericans made contact with Quetzalcoatl through rituals and chanting, the wizard Aleister Crowley made contact with the dawn god through open demonism: "O Thou dew-lit nymph of the Dawn, that swoonest in the satyr arms of the Sun! I adore Thee, I adore Thee, IAO!"[30]

The Hindu goddess Durga is described as the one who her worshipers "bow to…at daybreak [dawn] on Earth, there is nothing that cannot be attained in respect either of offspring or wealth. And because thou rescuest people from difficulties whether they are afflicted in the wilderness or sinking in the great ocean, it is for this that thou art called Durga by all."[31]

→ Chapter 33 ←

For God of For Chauvinists

"I will put enmity between you [Satan] and the women, and between thy seed and her seed [Jesus]" – Genesis 3:15

In the New Testament, Jesus had to come from the seed of a woman (Eve) birthed by the Virgin Mary, a woman to be called blessed throughout all generations. The verse is also telling us more – Satan harbors special hatred towards women, as they are the vessels to bring forth new life.

We can start off with one of the oldest known cults, the Yezidis of Mesopotamia who worship *Malek Taus* (Lucifer), the peacock angel.

Yezidis believe that in the beginning, Adam and Eve quarreled about which of them provided the creative element in the begetting of children. Each stored their seed in a jar, which was then sealed. When Eve's jar was opened it was full of insects and other unpleasant creatures, but inside Adam's jar was a beautiful boy child who grew up to marry a *houri* (heavenly woman) and became the ancestor of the Yezidis. Therefore, the Yezidi are regarded as descending from Adam alone.[32]

WOMEN IN NAZISM AND ISLAM

Within Islamic Fundamentalism and Nazism women are seen as nothing but producers of children for the cause. They were simply the vessel for man to procreate the *Übermensch* – the Arian superman. Islam sees women as "your fields, so go into your fields whichever way you like."[33] "Your wives are a tilth unto you; so go to your tilth when or how you will."[34]

While Muslim apologists make claims of the Qur'ân's pre-knowledge of biology and scientific advancement, there is no mention in Islam of the seed of the woman. Not a single reference to it.

Women producing children for the good of a military cause is found in Nazi philosophy. Heinrich Himmler explained that the "greatest gift for the widow of a man killed in battle is always the child of the man she has loved. SS men and mothers of these children…show that you are ready, through your faith in the Führer and for the sake of the life of our blood and people, to regenerate life for Germany, just as bravely as you know how to fight and die for Germany."[35] This wasn't an ideal for the triumph of conservative values but an agenda to place women as nothing more than breeders for the cause, exactly what's being taught in the Islamic world.

Famous Muslim poet Al-Khansa had four children who all died while fighting against the Persians. Before the battle she told her sons: "Tomorrow morning, rise from your bed hale and hearty and join the battle with fearless courage. Go into the midst of the thickest of the battle, encounter the boldest enemy and if necessary embrace martyrdom."[36]

After her four sons were slain by the Persians she rejoiced: "My sons I bore you with pain And brought you up with care; You have fallen today for the cause of Islam, Who says you are dead; You are very much alive, and alive with honor. I feel proud to be the mother of martyrs."[37]

A Muslim article titled *Raising Children to Jihad*, reads: "Let us press our children to our hearts and hoist our weapons onto our backs in preparation for the ultimate [stage]. We strive to fulfill our basic mission of sending the lions forth to the battlefields, like Al-Khansa, and they will vouch for us on the Day [of Judgment]."[38]

In a Lebanese TV interview, a group of women talked about life after their sons became martyrs. One mother explained that she was "willing for all my children to become martyrs. May my husband also become a martyr, and Allah willing, may I die as a martyr". Another mother said that compared to other mothers, the sacrifice of her son was "Nothing. It's true I sacrificed a son, but others have sacrificed two or three. I hope more of my sons will become martyrs."[39]

Similarly, in a Nazi Mother's Day card, intended for the wives and mothers of those who had died during the war, it contains an article titled *The Words of A German Mother: The Dead Live!* In the card the German mother whose son was slain in battle, explains how to live with the loss: "I wish to speak as a sister to all of these who are alone and sorrowing. I do not wish to speak of pain. Instead, I speak of the dead, who to me are not dead. After I first sank into dark sorrow, I now can see the sun and sky once again. […] We cannot and may not escape either to the future nor the past. Only from the past and the future, from faith and thankfulness, can we gather the strength to master the present, which is what the husbands and sons who fell for the fatherland expect of us, and the children to whom we pass on the torch of our lives will one day want to know that we fought and endured for their sakes."[40]

Muslim Fundamentalists and Nazis have the same view of martyrdom, life after death, and sacrifice for a universal utopia for the cause of supermen. These exemplify a reversal of Christian martyrdom, which is a result of persecution for *Calvary* rather then killing and dying during *cavalry*.

Cavalry was the pride of Umm Nidal, a Palestinian mother whose two sons became martyrs. She advised on how mothers should deal with grief when a son becomes a sacrifice to Allah: "I pray to Allah to strengthen them because the pain is hard and not easy to forget; but I say to all of them: 'Despite the pain and the battles and the blood that is shed, we must continue in the way of Jihad until victory or Shahada, until the entire homeland is liberated."[41]

Abortion doctors are considered saints in the eyes of the left. When the partial-birth abortion practitioner George Tiller was killed, the Pro-choice ministers called him a "martyr in the classical sense."[42]

Being Pro-Choice is also a destructive behavior: conceiving children, killing them, and then being seen as heroes for the cause of feminism.

Evil knows no boundaries; what evil knows is that once a mother sees her child an instant bond begins. When this happens, that strong bond would terminate not the child – but the act of killing.

Evil conjures up crafty ways to kill our senses, creating crafty labels. When it comes to abortion, a fetus is a leech; with Nazism, a young martyr for the Fuhrer; and with jihadists, their child is a sacrificial lamb, ready for the slaughter. Killing the instincts of people which allow them to recognize evil is the oldest tactic used by evil to get what it wants.

The hatred of women in an Islamic society is so immense that even if a woman is raped, she is stoned to death. In Somalia, a girl who was gang-raped by three men was stoned to death on charges of adultery.[43]

In Nigeria, a woman named Sufiyatu Huseini said she was raped, but the man she accused denied it, and instead Huseini was charged with adultery.[44]

In Iran, if a woman does not resist rape she will be stoned as an adulterer and if she *does* resist she will be hanged. A young Iranian girl named Nazanin was assaulted by three criminal men in the West of Tehran while strolling with her niece in a park in 2005. To defend herself she pulled out a knife and stabbed one of her assailants. The knife penetrated the ribs of her attacker who later died in the hospital. Despite the fact that she had been acting in self-defense, as shown by the evidence presented and the testimony of eyewitnesses, Nazanin was sentenced to death by hanging.[45]

Unlike Christianity, Feminism and Shi'a Islam do collaborate. Shi'a Islam permits *muttah* – a fixed-term temporary marriage which was originally permitted at the time of the Prophet Muhammad and is now being promoted in Iran by an alliance of Islamic clerics and feminists. The latter group is seeking to downplay the obsession with female virginity which is prevalent in both forms of Islam, pointing out that only one of the Prophet's thirteen wives was a virgin when he married them. Dr. Radhasyam Brahmachari explains: "*Muttah* marriage is temporary and remains valid only for a few weeks, days, or hours. It is, therefore, simply a kind of prostitution in the garb of marriage. The fabulously rich, mostly aged, Arabs from the Gulf countries come to India, get access to young girls of Hyderabad through *muttah* – of course, by paying fat cash to their parents as dowry (*mehr*). They use those young girls as a piece of toilet paper; and return home as the marriage automatically dissolves after the stipulated time. Below is one such case. In May 2004, an old man, named Muhammad Zafer

Yaqub Hassan al Jorani, came from Sharjah to Hyderabad – the capital of Andhra Pradesh – to undergo a cataract operation. On May 7, he married Haseena Begum – a 19 year old girl; and after two days, he divorced her. On May 24, he married another 16 year old girl Ruksana Begum. Haseena – ignoring threat to her life – went to a local police station to narrate her story and within an hour police arrested Jorani. Police also arrested someone called Shamsuddin who allegedly had played a mediator and received a cash amount of Rs 40,000 from Jorani paying Haseena's parents as *mehr (dowry)*. To be noted that Jorani had two wives and 11 children at Sharjah."

Hating women even when raping is a belief also shared by L. Ron Hubbard, the founder of Scientology, who said that it "doesn't give me displeasure to hear of a virgin being raped. The lot of women is to be fornicated."[46]

The source of such hatred for women comes from something so evil and intelligent that while it cannot be devised by man, it can only be carried out by him. How else can we explain such ancient hatred created by people who never focused on the Bible and who never knew about the original hatred between Lucifer and Eve?

DARWIN'S HATRED OF WOMEN

From the deserts of Arabia and Hitler's Germany to the intellectual elites in the universities of the 18th century who saw Darwinism as the most supreme of beliefs – Misogyny existed. What most Darwinists will not admit, while accusing the Bible of sexism, is that Darwin was an ardent misogynist.

Darwin wrote that a married man is a "poor slave, …worse than a Negro".[47] Many other anthropologists in Darwin's time agreed with this theory. Carl Vogt, a University of Geneva natural history professor who accepted many of "the conclusions of England's great modern naturalist, Charles Darwin," argued that "the child, the female, and the senile white" all had the intellect and nature of the "grown up Negro".[48]

Darwin also taught that women were less evolved than men and stated that women "are characteristic of the lower races, and therefore of a past and lower state of civilization… If two lists were made of the most pre-eminent men and women in poetry, painting, sculpture, music (inclusive of both composition and performance), history, science, and philosophy, with half-a-dozen names under each subject, the two lists would not bear comparison. We may also infer, from the law of the deviation from averages, so well illustrated by Mr. Galton, in his work on 'Hereditary Genius' that, the average of mental power in man must be above that of women."[49]

Even Stephen Gould, a very prominent and well-respected evolutionist, acknowledged that Darwin's view was quite popular amongst the elites in his time. Gould quotes Gustave Le Bon who was a pioneer in human behavior and an evolutionist: "Women… represent the most inferior forms of human evolution and… are closer to children and savages than to an adult, civilized man. They excel in fickleness, inconsistency, absence of thought and logic, and incapacity to reason. Without a doubt there exist some distinguished women, very superior to the average man but they are as exceptional as the birth of any monstrosity, as, for example, of a gorilla with two heads; consequently, we may neglect them entirely."[50]

Darwinian apologists would claim that Darwin and his ilk were behaving within the norms of their own culture and time in which women were second-class. Muslims use similar excuses for Muhammad. While they accuse Bible believers of being ardent fundamentalists, they in turn are stubborn, haughty, stiff-necked, closed minded, pride filled and their hearts are seared. They cannot see that Darwin in reality digressed from his time and the Christian tradition, for even during Darwin's time, women were held to a much higher moral standard than this. Yet this argument, that Darwin was simply being a 'machismo male centric bigot' is incongruent; the question is not a question of social standards but one about his so-called *Origin of Species* – an *alleged* science book.

ALEISTER CROWLEY AND WOMEN

Aleister Crowley, the world renowned Satanist, homosexual, and drug experimenter was also a zealous misogynist. The occultist actually accepted many Islamic beliefs and considered Muhammad to be one of the Gnostic Saints.[51]

Crowley maintained a vigorous sex life, which largely consisted of prostitutes and girls he picked up at local pubs and cigar shops, but eventually extended into homosexual activities in which he played the passive role.[52] He said that there "have been about four men in my life that I could say I have loved. ...Call me a bugger if you like, but I don't feel the same way about women. One can always replace a woman in a few days."[53]

He also wrote that gay sex "avoids contact with inferior planes [women and babies families]; that it is self-sufficient, that it involves no responsibilities, and that it leaves its masters not only stronger in themselves, but wholly free to fulfill their essential Nature."[54] This reminds me of when I was about thirteen-years old and I asked my far-left art teacher: "If the whole world turned gay then how would the population increase?" He replied with this: "Easy! Sperm insemination." So while the whole world is homosexual, the earth would need the female, not as partners but as factories. How is this Pro-feminist?

Evil will always hate women; this is real sexism and not the husband who mutually agrees with his wife to work while she stays home to rear children. Such are the arguments raised by the feminist movement.

Real sexism is homosexuality in which a man becomes so morally decrepit that he begins to reject the importance of the natural system of reproduction, and thus he begins to deem proliferation as useless and lusts after his own sex.

Crowley never accused Islam of abusing women but as a typical leftist would do, was always willing to accuse Christians of sexism, writing that a Christian girl's "virgin life is a sick ape's, her sexual life a drunken sow's, her mother life all bulging filmy eyes and sagging udders."[55]

WOMEN IN OTHER PAGAN LANDS

Some might argue that Christianity's advance in the treatment of women is not unique to Christianity, that "the Roman civilization is a perfect example. They were an advanced civilization that progressed women's rights."

New Age followers argue that unlike Christianity, the ancient religions elevated women through feminine deities. This argument has no merit. On the contrary, all non-Biblical religions demote women to a denigrated status.

As they were in Islam, under the Roman Empire women were deemed inferior and as Balsdon wrote in *Roman Women, Their History and Habits*: "[Without] the conversion of the Roman world to Christianity" there would be no "great change in women's status"[56] and as historian L. F Cervantes put it: "The birth of Jesus was the turning point in the history of women."[57]

Why then do feminists wish to push backward, un-advancing, pre-Christian religions that were significant in the ancient world such as in Greece, where melancholic poets were fond of equating women with evil?

Euripides has Hippolytus ask, "why has thou given a home beneath the sun, Zeus, unto women, specious curse to man?"[58] Aeschylus has a chorus declare: "Evil of mind are they [women], and guileful of purpose, with impure hearts".[59] Another Greek poet, Aristophanes, has the chorus in his play *Lysistrata* say, "For women are a shameless set, the vilest of creatures going".[60] Yet, my sixth grade history teacher taught us that the ancient Greeks were the pioneers for women's rights. When I told her that American feminists should stop screaming sexism since they already have rights in the US, she snapped at me by following the typical talking points, calling me a sexist.

So who really stopped the hatred of women? What ideals replaced Rome, Greece and the Middle East?

Who removed the Hindu practice of *suttee* in which Indian women were burned alive upon the death of their husbands? If women refused they were often forced to be burned, sometimes even by her own son(s). If a woman managed to avoid being scorched then she was shunned by her community as betraying Hinduism. A widow could only eat one meal a day and had to wear the dowdiest of clothes; she could no longer sleep on a bed; and her head was shaved monthly to look unattractive to men.[61] Hinduism is an anti-women religion but at the same time John Lennon, George Harrison and other leftists exalted it.

The left never acknowledges the respect given to women and widows by Christianity, since the British authorities in 1829, under the suasion of Governor-General William Bentinck, outlawed the practice of *suttee*. When the ban went into effect, many "cried that the foundations of Hindu society would be shaken if widows were not burnt alive."[62] Others argued that the ban violated Article 25 of India's constitution that gave the people freedom of religion.[63]

But of course India's "freedom of religion" is nothing like our first amendment right of religious freedom which would never adhere to the Hindu cliché: if a woman's "husband is happy, she should be happy; if he is sad, she should be sad, and if he is dead, she should also die."[64]

The British actually did more good for India than Gandhi, whom progressives elevate to sainthood. While Gandhi ended the British presence, he formed the Islamic nation of Pakistan that still terrorizes India, which is a beacon for terrorism and is responsible for the creation of the Taliban in Afghanistan. Today Pakistan has gone nuclear with 50-100 nuclear missiles.

India is not the only nation to blame. The practice of burning widows took place in pre-Christian Scandinavia, among the Chinese, the Finns, and the Maori in New Zealand, and by some American Indians before Columbus arrived.[65]

In China, they had the brutal system of foot binding in which very young girls, at about five years of age, had their feet bound causing the toes to stop growing and the feet to become stunted, a practice which existed for over a millennia. As one described it: "The Flesh often became putrescent during the binding and portions sloughed off from the sole; sometimes one or more toes dropped off."[66]

Despite what the leftists say – that Christianity is worthless – it was the act of missionaries calling for the cessation of foot binding which ended the sadistic act. Lin Yutang has shown that Christian missionaries led the crusade to abolish foot binding.[67]

Why do atheists wish to enforce laws to ban missionaries from Africa? Will atheism and Darwinism civilize that continent? On the contrary, most expeditions of the National Geographic type that one sees in documentaries on primitive peoples seem to focus on understanding their customs and habits. They always seem to protest the civilized world's intrusiveness into the primitive.

When reviewing history, leftists only cry "racism!" when Christian nations colonize lands run by savage rules, but nothing is said when Muslims pillaged Christian nations or when the Aztecs and Mayans chose to self-destruct.

Their broken record never ends – the Crusades, the British colonizing of India and Africa, the Spaniards coming to Mexico; they will blame the American government for stealing Native American land while failing to mention how the Aztecs took over other tribal areas; the Vikings attacking Christian lands, sacking their villages and destroying their churches, how the Sudanese Muslims have perpetrated a holocaust of over two million Christians, the fascist Hindu caste system, how Muhammad massacred and ethnically cleansed the Jews in Arabia, the Barbary pirate wars, etc. Shall I go on?

It was Christianity that played the predominant roll in removing all these savage rules; it began the practice of looking after "widows in their distress".[68] Jesus had compassion for the widow of Nai, whose son he raised from the dead (Luke 7:11-15) and chided the Pharisees for taking financial advantage of widows (Mark 12:40).

Jesus was also strongly against divorce, saying that anyone "who divorces his wife and marries another woman commits adultery against her" (Mark 10:11).

Hypocritically, the left still accuses Christianity of being anti-women while being in support of no-fault divorce, which in reality is one of the most destructive elements for ruining a family.

The Bible is the best advocate for women's rights.

Chapter 34

For Trinity or For Tyranny

The Christian belief in the Trinity is the most abhorred religious concept in Islam in which Jesus is "nothing more than a messenger of God, His word, directed to Mary, a spirit from Him. So believe in God and His messengers and do not speak of a 'Trinity' – stop, that is better for you – God is only one God, He is far above having a son, everything in the heavens and earth belongs to Him and He is the best one to trust" (Q 4:171). "Surely, disbelievers are those who said: 'Allah is the third of the three (in a Trinity)' (Q 5:73). "The true believers are only those, who believe in (the Oneness of) Allah and His Messenger (Muhammad)…" [3:85] "And whoever seeks a religion other than Islam, it will never be accepted of him, and in the Hereafter he will be one of the losers" (Q 24:62).

Christians see this as a red flag: "Who is the liar? It is the man who denies that Jesus is the Christ? Such a man is the antichrist; he denies the Father and the Son. No one who denies the Son has the Father; whoever acknowledges the Son has the Father also" (I John 2:22-23). Even the Old Testament affirms the Trinity: "Come near to Me, hear this; I have not spoken in secret, from the beginning; From the time that it was, I was there, And now the Lord God and His Spirit Have sent Me" (Isaiah 48:16). Amazingly, in one verse we see it: "From the time that it was (from the beginning was The Word), I was there, and now the Lord God (The Father) and His Spirit (The Holy Spirit) have sent Me (The Son)."

Yet the Qur'ân calls this blasphemy. What is staggering is that the context of Isaiah 48 is a confrontation between God and the Harlot of Babylon (Lady of Kingdoms). This Harlot is definitely anti-Trinity.

Christians further question the audacity of the Qur'ân's claim of 'holiness'; claiming membership in the family of great books like the Torah and the Gospels – when Biblically there is nothing holy about denying the Father, Son and Holy Spirit! Even the Jew does not deny

God being the Father and the Holy Spirit. And while Islam rejects the Biblical Holy Trinity, Muhammad can be induced into a state of mind by a luminous angel to introduce an unholy pagan trinity: "Have you seen Allat and Uzza and Manat the third? These are the high flying cranes; verily their intercession is accepted with approval." Even Goethe who was an inspiration behind Nazism hated the trinity, "Mohammed also that which won His triumphs needs must seem as true – Through the idea of the One Alone did he the world subdue."

All Muslims reject the intersession of Christ as "blasphemy," yet seem to accept that Muhammad can be inspired through the luminous angel with a pagan trinity?

To Bible believers, this would put Muhammad on par with Baphomet and the repugnant Satanic Bible: "Satanism represents the carnal instincts of man, or the opposite of spiritual nature, the pentagram is inverted to perfectly accommodate the head of the goat – its horns, representing duality, thrust upwards in defiance; the other three points inverted, or the trinity denied."[69]

The Apostle John also adds, "This is how you can recognize the Spirit of God: Every spirit that acknowledges that Jesus Christ has come in the flesh is from God, but every spirit that does not acknowledge Jesus is not from God. This is the spirit of the Antichrist, which you have heard is coming and even now is already in the world" (I John 4:2-3). "Many deceivers, who do not acknowledge Jesus Christ as coming in the flesh, have gone out into the world. Any such person is the deceiver and the Antichrist" (II John 1:7). From these verses, we learn that the antichrist is a spirit that is identified as a "liar" and a "deceiver" which specifically denies: 1. That Jesus is the Savior of Israel and the World. 2. The Trinity or that Jesus is The Son of God. 3. That Jesus is God who came in the flesh.

Both Muhammad and his proclaimed messiah the Mahdi perfectly embody this Antichrist spirit. Muhammad denied both "the Father and the Son." The Mahdi will come in Muhammad's spirit and do the same. That which is most holy to Christians is considered blasphemous in Islam, and what is holy in Islam is blasphemous to Christians. An understanding of Islam's contrarian ideology is crucial for everyone who wants to understand the attempt to contradict and undermine the basic teachings of the Bible. Islam makes it one of its highest priorities to deny all of the above points regarding Jesus and His relationship with the Father. Just ask any Muslim, "what are your main objections to Christians" and their immediate response will be "Jesus is not the Son of God. Neither is He God. Neither is God our Father. Neither did He die on the cross." Try it.

Beyond denying the Trinity, Islam also denies the Divine Incarnation of Jesus Christ as the Son of God, as well as his death, burial and resurrection.

But beyond all of this, Islam has memorialized its anti-Yahweh, anti-Christ theology specifically in a creedal formula. The *Shahadatan* is the Islamic creed or declaration of faith. In Arabic it reads as follows: *La ilaha il Allah, Muhammadan Rasul-Allah*. This means: "There is no God but Allah and Muhammad is The One sent by Allah [The Messenger of Allah]". The two elements of this creed are the following: Allah is the only One True Supreme God and Muhammad (The Praised One) is the seal and final messenger of Allah. These two components of the Shahadatan, in a very succinct manner, perhaps better than any creedal statement could, perfectly fulfill both dimensions of the definition of blasphemy. First, it attempts to claim that a god other than Yahweh is the Only True God. And secondly, the Shahadatan is blasphemous toward the God of the Bible because it attempts to place Muhammad in the position that only Jesus the Messiah can fill. We need to repeat this again – Muslims identify Muhammad as *Al-Maqam-Al-Mahmud* (The Glorious One), *Awal-Khalq-illah* (The first of Creation), *Muhammad* (The Praised One), *Al-Insan Al-Kamel* (The Perfect Man), *Rahmatan-lil-A'alameen* (Mercy to All Mankind), *Al-rasul Al-A'tham* (The Greatest of All sent by God), *Shafi* (Healer), *Munji* (Savior), *Mahdi* (The Guided One/Deliverer), *Al-Mustafa Al-Mukhtar* (The Chosen One), *Amir* (The Prince), *Khatimun-Nabiyeen* (The Seal of Prophets), *Al-Hadi* (The Guide), *Awal* (First), *Akher* (Last), *Sayyid Walad Adam* (The Leader of The Sons of Adam) and *Al-Siraj Al-Muneer* (The Luminous One, The Glowing Lamp). Such are the blasphemous names of Muhammad.

Yet despite the quintessentially blasphemous nature of the Sha-hadatan, it is recited into the ear of every Muslim child the moment after they are born. Even Barack Hussein Obama recited this formula in the call to prayer for the New York Times, in classical Arabic language. It is the verbally expressed, outward sign of conversion to Islam. According to Biblical theology, the Shahadatan could not be more perfectly blasphemous.

Scientology's founder, L. Ron Hubbard, denied Jesus' divinity saying that everybody has already died for their sins thus regarding Jesus' sacrifice worthless: "There was no Christ. But the man on the cross is shown as Everyman."[70]

The concept of the Trinity (Father, Son, Holy Spirit) and the one-ness of God to Christians is expressed thusly: "hear O Israel, the Lord your God the Lord in One" – is the main yardstick in identifying what is in the fold and what is considered cult. Christians are astounded when Muslims accuse them of worshipping three gods. This oneness of God is the thrust of the Christian creed. Had Islam's accusation been correct, Christians would have embraced Herbert Armstrong, the founder of the *World Wide Church of God* who denied the Trinity and made the Godhead into a family.[71] Armstrong said, "The doctrine of the Trinity is false," and "two Personages coexisted and nothing else did. No third Person is mentioned – no 'Ghost'".[72] Christians did not embrace Joseph Smith who preached "on the plurality of Gods. ...I wish to declare that I have always and in all congregations when I preached on the subject of the Deity, it has been the plurality of Gods."[73]

Joseph Smith ridiculed the Trinity: "Many men say there is one God; the Father, the Son and the Holy Ghost are only one God. I say that is a strange God anyhow – three in one, and one on three! It is a curious organization. ...All are to be crammed into one God, according to sectarianism. It would make the biggest God on all the world. He would be a wonderfully big God – he would be a giant or a monster."[74]

✦ Chapter 35 ✦

For God or For Devils

The main thrust of Christianity is the victory in the Resurrection of Jesus over sin and Satan. Christians view all other religions as those that exalt the loser. Every cult seems to have its founder communicate with the same beings. Although the names of such beings differ, their descriptions are the same. Muhammad and L. Ron Hubbard are two out of many great examples. If Muhammad communicated with the Jinn, Hubbard communicated with *thetans*. Scientology defines thetans as the source of life; it is recognized as the core of personality or essence of oneself, quite distinct and separate from the physical body or the brain.[75] Hubbard's thetans and Muhammad's jinn are the same. In Scientology there is the story of Xenu, king of the cosmos. The story even resembles the Biblical war in heaven; Hubbard describes the thetans who were cast out to earth, with one caveat; in Scientology, these fallen thetans are the good host and Xenu who seems to resemble Yahweh of the Bible was the evil one who feared being deposed from his throne by the thetans. Hubbard describes thetans as the "loyal officers" who were unfairly deposed and cast out of heaven.[76]

Hubbard's visions were similar to Muhammad's. Hubbard's "thetans" seem to match Muhammad's "jinn" who, according to Muhammad, once had access to heaven. Meteorites then were being "shot at them on every side so that they could find no place of safety."[77] The story resembles Hubbard's, when the thetans reached Teegeeack (Earth) the paralyzed thetans were unloaded and stacked around the bases of volcanoes across the planet. Hydrogen bombs were lowered into the volcanoes, and all were detonated simultaneously.[78] God in the Bible finally deals with the Lucifer: "Because thine heart is lifted up, and thou hast said, 'I am a God, I sit in the seat of God, in the midst of the seas" (Ezekiel 28:4). Satan wants to sit on God's throne. Hubbard's Lucifer seems to fit the true God and the true

God seems to fit Hubbard's Lucifer. To Hubbard, God's 'renegades' defeated the 'Loyal Officers [thetans]. Satan is trying to portray himself as the 'loyal officer.' As the thetans questioned forming "a question mark to the very idea of humanity", so did the jinn question, "searching for the unusual thing that had occurred on the earth".

Evil has its propaganda machine in high places with the same old ploy – reverse the story. We see this daily in the media – Palestinian refugees, Israeli occupation, and America's occupation of Iraq...

The historical fact remains that the biggest refugee problem in history is the Jewish refugee problem. These were refugees for two thousand years. It was Jordan that occupied Palestine illegally and Israel regained its home after two thousand years of exile. Everything is reversed. The United States also liberated Iraq from Saddam's tyranny. They are currently fixing up that country while the Muslim terrorists seek to destroy and kill in the name of liberty.

In both Islam and Scientology there is this belief that these fallen spirits can possess you. When Scientologists escalate themselves to the high level of OT3 (operating thetan three) they are told that they are possessed by thetans and can be cast out by talking to them telepathically.[79] Telepathy, Channeling and Telekinesis are still officially considered to be quackery science and is as ancient as Babylon. The difference is and as we see today – the best way evil can sneak in is to simply make it scientific. *If we link wizardry to science by creating new labels like telekinesis, telepathy, psychic detectives and channeling, then wizardry has found a loophole through pseudoscience and an excuse to be justified in a modern world.* Spritism and delving into occultism – from the Christian perspective – is to seek demonic possession.

If scientologists like L. Ron Hubbard sought possession so did Muhammad, the prophet of Islam: "Allah's Messenger said: 'Everyone has an attaché from amongst the jinn (devils)...' The Prophet's companions asked Allah's Messenger, is there one with you too.' He said: 'Yes, but Allah helps me so I am safe from his hand and he does not command me but for good.'"[80]

Reading some of Islam's *Sunnah* is like reading *The Exorcist.* Muhammad would be tortured by these demons, "shivering and shutting his eyes, there used to come over him what resembled a swoon, his face would foam, and he would roar like a young camel." Umar ibnu'l Khattab recorded that "inspiration descended on the Apostle of God, there used to be heard near his face as it were the buzzing of bees."[81]

During Muhammad's rivalry with the Quraysh tribe, the tribe chief Utba, made some proposals for Muhammad, trying to make peace with him, asking if Muhammad wanted "'sovereignty, we will make you king. And if this demonic spirit, which has possession of you, is such that you cannot get rid of him, we will find a physician for you, and exhaust our means trying to cure you. For often a demonic spirit gets possession of a man, but he can be rid of it.' The apostle listened patiently."[82] Islam's angels seem to even have resemblances to The Luminous One's minions. In the Qur'ân's Night of Vision (Muhammad's visitation) "The angelic hosts descend [to earth] in it with the spirit by command of their Lord. Peace shall it be until the rising of the Dawn (Morning star)" (Q 97). Who is this 'spirit' and how is Allah the lord of angels and spirits? According to Muslims this 'spirit' or 'the holy spirit' is the luminous Arch Angel whose minions descended on earth.

Even in the last days, with such minions descending, to a Muslim this is a holy moment much hoped for, but to a Christian this Islamic prophecy confirms what the Bible prophesied about – God casting the devil out of hell unto earth. In other words, the Qur'ân is the antithesis of the Bible: "And there was war in heaven. Michael and his angels fought against the dragon, and the dragon and his angels fought back. But he was not strong enough, and they lost their place in heaven. The great dragon was hurled down – that ancient serpent called the devil, or Satan, who leads the whole world astray. He was hurled to the earth, and his angels with him. Then I heard a loud voice in heaven say: "Now have come the salvation and the power and the kingdom of our God, and the authority of his Christ. For the accuser of our brothers, who accuses them before our God day and night, has been hurled down" (Revelation 12:17).

The cult Heaven's Gate founded by Marshall Applewhite and Bonnie Nettles, demanded worship of spirits, which fell from heaven.

Applewhite explains his six key points: "I and my partner are from the *Evolutionary Level Above Human* and we took over two human bodies in their forties, which had been tagged at birth as vehicles for our use. We brought a crew of students to Earth with us from the Kingdom of Heaven. Many of us arrived in staged crashes of spaceships and authorities confiscated some of our bodies. Others came before us to tag our bodies with special chips. Before our human incarnation, we were briefed by older beings with details about how to take over the human vehicle. The Kingdom of God is genderless, multiplying through metamorphosis, and its inhabitants have free will."[83]

Scientology and Heaven's Gate have much in common with Raëlism, the largest UFO cult in the world that advocates the worship of "the Elohim" – an extraterrestrial race or "those who came from the sky."[84]

Raëlism uses a Hebraic Biblical name for God, *Elohim*, and actually accepts Muhammad as a prophet while equating the *Elohim* to Allah.[85]

Just as Muslims believe in the Night of Vision, Raelians believe that in the day of judgment the *Elohim* will descend to earth: "Muhammed who said he would return from the seven heavens on al-Buraq, along with Moses, Buddha and all the other prophets, who are presently living with the *Elohim*, will return with them to the embassy [in Jerusalem] as foretold."[86]

This bizarre alien worship is seen as well in Mormonism where in an 1892 LDS publication under the heading *The Inhabitants of the Moon*, it reads that "the moon was inhabited by men and women the same as this earth, and that they lived to a greater age than we do that they live generally to near the age of 1000 years."[87] President Brigham Young not only taught the moon was inhabited, but the sun as well: "Who can tell us of the inhabitants of this little planet that shines of an evening, called the moon?…when you inquire about the inhabitants of that sphere you find that the most learned are as ignorant in regard to them as the ignorant of their fellows. So it is in regard to the inhabitants of the sun. Do you think it is inhabited? I rather think it is. Do you think there is any life there? No question of it; it was not made in vain."[88]

DEMONS TAKE THE IMAGE OF STARS

Non-Biblical religions are fascinated with stars and fallen asteroids. Aleister Crowley, the infamous occultist who was quite popular amongst 1960s hippies, wrote a passage quite related to star worship: "I am uplifted in thine heart; and the kisses of the stars rain hard upon thy body."[89]

Muslims also venerate a star, which fell from heaven called the Black Stone, an asteroid. When Muslims pray, they bow towards this Black Stone to worship Allah five times a day. The pilgrims who venerate the Black Stone have emptied their sins into it. This veneration of an asteroid would be blasphemous in Christian theology, especially since Jesus is the only one who takes upon Himself the sins of the world. In other words, the Black Stone is believed by Muslims to have come down from heaven, and takes upon itself the sins of mankind.

This Muslim Ka'aba is the ideal shrine to view when one wants to get the feel of how the ancient Semitic world worshiped Baal. Do not think that the Ka'aba is the only one of its kind, there are many that have been forgotten in ancient history.

The Book of Acts spoke of this very issue: "At last the mayor was able to quiet them down enough to speak. 'Citizens of Ephesus' he said. Everyone knows that Ephesus is the official guardian of the temple of the great Artemis, whose image fell down to us from heaven" (Acts 19:35). Artemis, in Ephesus (modern day Turkey), was often depicted with the crescent moon on her forehead and was sometimes identified with Selene (goddess of the moon) who the people in Ephesus worshipped.

There was an asteroid worshipping cult in the ancient world called Cybele (Qebele), the same word (*Qibla, Qibleh*) Muslims use for the Ka'aba that houses the Black Stone. Likewise, the worship of the Cybele was also associated with a Black Stone or meteorite that had fallen from the sky: "Varro states that the goddess was brought from a shrine called the Megalesion in the city of Pergamon while Ovid located the Mother's home on Mount Ida near the ancient city of Troy, which was under Pergamene control at that time. Livy seems to combine the two traditions in reporting that the Romans sought the help of the Pergamene King Attalos I in obtaining the goddess from Pessinous. Precisely what the Romans obtained is described in several sources: it was a small dark sacred stone not formed into any iconographic image that had fallen to the shrine of Pessinous from the sky."[90]

The stone associated with Cybele's worship was, originally, probably at Pessinus but perhaps at Pergamum or on Mount Ida. What is certain is that in 204 B.C. it was taken to Rome, where Cybele became 'Mother' to the Romans. The ecstatic rites of her worship were alien to the Roman temperament, but nevertheless animated the streets of their city during the annual procession of the goddess's statue. Alongside Isis, Cybele retained prominence in the heart of the Empire until the fifth century B.C. when the stone was lost. Her cult prospered throughout the Empire and it is said that every town or village remained true to the worship of Cybele.[91]

Fallen star worship became a significant religion in Rome when in the year 218, A Syrian named Elagabalus or Marcus Aurelius Antoninus became emperor of Rome and with his power established a Syrian god named Elagabalus or Baal (the emperor was named after this deity). Just as Muhammad wished to unite the Arabs under Allah, Antoninus "established Elagabalus as a god on the Palatine Hill close to the imperial palace; and he built him a temple…purposing that no god might be worshipped at Rome save only Elagabalus."[92]

Elagabalus was a worshipped black stone meteorite and according to Herodian, "was worshipped as though it were sent from heaven; on it there are some small projecting pieces and markings that are pointed out, which the people would like to believe are a rough picture of the sun, because this is how they see them."[93]

So what is the purpose of all these venerations? Cognate to Muhammad demanding all Christians and Jews to replace their crosses and temples with a crescent moon and to bow in the direction of the Black Stone, Antoninus declared "that the religions of the Jews and the Samaritans and the rites of the Christians must also be transferred to this place, in order that the priesthood of Elagabalus might include the mysteries of every form of worship."[94]

Without exception, all cults have one goal – to direct worship away from Yahweh to the rebellious Luminous One – Lucifer.

→ Chapter 36 ←

Allah's Jugend – At a University Near You

For years, America has had to endure watching many banners that say, "Zionism is Nazism", "American Imperialism" and an array of other oxymoronic phrases. These groups are no strange bedfellows. The reality is that Communists, Socialists, Anarchists and Islamists with their different colors are one and the same – Leftism, and its unity with similar causes has shoved its foot into the doorway using the university and the academic system.

The Muslim Student Association (MSA) which is set up on 150 university campuses across the U.S is a great example. In 2006, MSA-Brown organized a "Palestinian Solidarity Week" featuring displays depicting Palestinian suffering at the hands of Israeli "aggression" with displays of an "Apartheid Wall" on campuses to protest Israel's recent construction of a security fence. According to Al-Maryati, it was Israel that was behind 9/11.[95] Evil has a way of killing by accusing the victims of carrying out their own death, but in this case, the Nero syndrome never died out, since Nero is always innocent and a guinea pig is always found – Jews and Christians.

The MSA was actually founded by a Hitler-admiring Muslim named Hasan al-Banna, the godfather of the Muslim Brotherhood in Egypt in 1928.[96] It is no wonder that from its inception, MSA had close links with the Muslim World League, whose chapters' websites have featured not only Osama bin Laden's propaganda, but also publicity-recruiting campaigns for Wahhabi involvement with the Chechen insurgents in Russia.[97]

The MSA is notorious for its anti-Semitism and intimidation. And like the leftists in America, the purpose of the MSA is to destroy "Western civilization from within."[98]

This echoes what was happening during the Vietnam War era, where leftist college students would chant: "*Ho Ho Ho, Western Civilization has got to go!*"[99]

Today at our university campuses, Muslims bully conservatives and cry out "We will fight you until we are either martyred or we are victorious."[100] Islamic front groups have sponsored such events as "Anti-Zionist Week" and anti-Semitic rallies and held conferences where speakers praised Hamas as they chanted "Death to Israel" and "Death to the Jews."

At University of California-Irvine, the Muslim Student Union (MSU), another anti-Semitic and anti-American campus group, recently held programs openly supporting terrorist groups and calling for the destruction of Israel with such titles as "Hamas: the People's Choice" and "Israel: The 4th Reich."[101] These are the same type that were in the Nazi Student Organization in the twentieth century where young and idealistic students wanted to control the universities in which they would harass professors, speakers, and others who did not go with the Nazi flow. Classrooms were barricaded or occupied, threats were put in their mail, and denunciations were posted on campus bulletin boards and published in student newspapers. Lecturers were heckled and when administrators tried to block or punish these antics, the students mounted massive protests, often forcing the resignation of the administrator.[102]

The cries of Nazis are no different than the cries of Islamists. When Hamid Algar approached a group of students commemorating the Armenian Genocide at University of Berkeley he intimidated them with slurs: "It was not a Genocide, but I wish it was, you lying pigs...You are distorting the truth about history. You stupid Armenians, you deserve to be massacred!"[103] When do you ever hear such rhetoric from Christian groups?

No conservative event that is pro-America is left alone at any campus. At Tulane University, some 1500 people turned out to hear Ann Coulter give a speech connecting dots between Islam and the events of 9/11 and expressing the importance of continuing the War in Iraq. It took 15 police officers and personal security for Ms. Coulter to keep the crowd at bay.

If liberalism were pro-justice and pro-human rights as they claim, why would rowdy students at DePaul University in Chicago object to

Iranian dissident Amir Abbas Fakhravar speaking there? Fakhravar detailed the record of violence, murder and human rights mayhem by the Ahmadinijad regime. Robert Spencer, who accompanied Amir Abbas, responding to the angry question from the audience gave the prognosis: "Anyone who thinks that there has been a full and fair and open discussion of Islamo-fascism on our campuses and particularly in our Middle East Studies departments simply hasn't been paying attention."

Hearings by university professors are initiated at any inkling of any event exposing Islamic terrorism. At Texas State University, administrators interrogated Jessica Irwin, asking her to submit a written statement and to have her group's name removed from the David Horowitz Freedom Center. She received continuous calls and emails from anonymous persons asking her why she was hosting such an offensive event with demands not to continue the planning.[104]

Throughout American history we have been accustomed to filling out documents and answering all sorts of questions – Have you ever been involved in criminal activity, or were you ever a member of the Communist Party. Today, the motto is, are you now, or have you ever been, a conservative?

Today The American-Arab Anti-Discrimination Committee (ADC) and Muslim Public Affairs Council (MPAC) are very active in disrupting anti-Islamism and pro-Israel lectures. Patrick S. Poole notes that ADC President and former U.S. Representative Mary Rose Oakar sent a poison pen letter to every campus scheduled to host Islamo-Fascism Awareness Week. The arguments are typical and are repeated like clockwork. Such events are accused of seeking not to increase awareness, tolerance, and understanding, but instead to promote intolerance, fear, and bigotry.

To underscore the legal threat, the letter is co-signed by ADC Director of Legal Policy Kareem Shora, who recently opposed two measures banning illegal aliens from getting drivers licenses and allowing the government to track visa-holders from terror-friendly nations.

The ADC may oppose such educational measures as Islamo-Fascism Awareness Week because newly informed students may turn an eye in its direction. Founded by far-Left, one-term U.S Senator James Abourezk and once headed by James Zogby, the ADC has long acted as an apologist group for terrorist organizations.[105]

From the Islamic perspective, everything is reversed – America is terrorist and Hamas leaders are the finest of gentlemen. In 1994, then-ADC President Hamzi Moghrabi said, "I will not call [Hamas] a terrorist organization. I mean, I know many people in Hamas. They are very respectable…I don't believe Hamas, as an organization, is a violent organization." Two years later, his successor, Hala Maksoud, defended Hamas' partner in Mid-eastern terrorism, Hezbollah. "I find it shocking," Maksoud said, "that [one] would include Hezbollah in…[an] inventory of Middle East 'terrorist' groups." MPAC was actually angered by Israel's 'attempted assassination' of Hamas' second in command, Abdel-Azziz al-Rantissi, and its subsequent 'assassination' of Hamas' founder and commander, Sheikh Ahmed Yassin and also published a eulogy for Arafat describing him as "the revolutionary and statesman who championed the cause of the Palestinian people for over four decades".[106] Calling somebody a revolutionary sounds more like left-wing rhetoric than a conservative lecture. Anyone who exposes terrorism is now a racist, Islamophobic, bigoted, divisive, xenophobic and guilty of hate crimes. To MPAC, evangelist Pat Robertson is a terrorist. During their supposed anti-terror conference, they compared Robertson with Osama bin Laden, a comparison the left uses.

Anarchists, communists, and Muslims in America are united in their hatred of western civilization and Christianity. Americans must be vigilant. All it takes is to change the minds of a single generation, and the rest becomes history. Liberal evangelists are complying. Take Rick Warren, pastor of Saddle Back Church who spoke for the terrorist supporting MPAC alongside lesbian gay-rights singer Melissa Etheridge, speaking the standard new-age pastor talking-points: "I love Muslims…gays…Al-Qaeda no more represents Islam than the Klu Klux Klan represents Christianity." The 'love' expression these days excludes mentioning anything about Jews massacred by Palestinian terrorists or Armenians massacred by Turks. Christian fundamentalists view Warren as lukewarm, that Christianity is not neutrality and neither is it "center right". Warren, like Jimmy Carter, denounces fundamentalist Christians as extreme.

✧ Chapter 37 ✧

For Going Forward or For Going Backward – To Antiquity

Many on the left, especially in the feminist movement, are becoming fascinated with pre-Christian paganism – wizards, warlocks and magical spells. This is not the first time westerners attempted to abandon their Christian heritage. Adolf Hitler saw Germany's pre-Christian religion as a victim of the Cross: "Christianity was not content with erecting an altar of its own. It had first to destroy the pagan altar."[107] Hitler lamented that "Each one of us today may regret the fact that the advent of Christianity was the first occasion when spiritual terror was introduced into the much freer ancient world."[108]

SYMPATHY FOR THE DEVIL

The Nazis lamented Christianity's triumph over paganism despite Christianity's victory over the tribal savagery that brought civilization to Germany.

Typical of today's criticism of the *Salem Witch Hunt*, The SS chief, Heinrich Himmler saw Christianity as a force which ruined witchery all over the world: "The witch-hunting cost the German people hundreds of thousands of mothers and women, cruelly tortured and executed."[109] He dedicated considerable resources for the SS to investigate the witch-hunts and prove that they were attempts to crush Aryan civilization and the true German faith. The SS put together what amounted to their own X-Files unit – dubbed Special Unit H (for Hexen or "witches") – to expose supposedly thirty-three thousand cases of witch burning, in countries as far away as India and Mexico.[110]

Feminists today, as did the Nazis in the past, also exalt the pagan world for being defeated by Christianity. The out-of-commission Playboy bunny and feminist activist Gloria Steinem is rhapsodic about "pre-Christian" and "matriarchal" paganism. In *Revolution From*

Within she laments in all earnestness the "killing of nine million women healers and other pagan or nonconforming women during the centuries of changeover to Christianity."[111]

Again, the best way evil can connect mankind to paganism is to simply make it scientific. If we link earth worship to science by creating new labels like 'environmentalism' then paganism just found a loophole and an excuse to be justified in a modern scientific world.

While Al Gore portrays his mission as the messianic protector of the climate and that science found evidence that the earth is heating – his real agenda is to bring back the romanticism of pre-Christian times: "The ancient civilizations that disappeared during significant natural climate changes in the past could tell us a great deal that we seem not to want to hear. What if our children, because of our actions, face not just a year without a winter but a decade without a winter? Will that be our most significant legacy? The answer may well depend on whether we can learn from the ancient cultures that disappeared..."[112] Gore reflects Hindu religion: "The sacredness of water receives perhaps the greatest emphasis in Hinduism. According to its teachings, the 'waters of life' are believed to bring to humankind the life force itself. One modern Hindu environmentalist, Dr. Karan Singh, regularly cites the ancient Hindu dictum: 'The Earth is our Mother, and we are all her children.' And in the *Atharvaveda*, the prayer for peace emphasizes the links between humankind and all creation: 'Supreme Lord, let there be peace in the sky and in the atmosphere, peace in the plant world and in the forest; let the cosmic powers be peaceful; let the Brahma be peaceful; let there be undiluted and fulfilling peace everywhere.'"[113] Gore would rather glorify Brahma and Allah instead of Jehovah of the Bible: "Islam, for example, offers familiar themes. The prophet Muhammad said, 'The world is green and beautiful and God has appointed you His stewards over it.' The central concepts of Islam taught by the Qur'ân – *Tawheed* (unity), *khalifa* (trusteeship), *akharah* (accountability) – also serve as the pillars of the Islamic environmental ethic. The earth is the sacred creation of Allah...The Qur'ân declares that 'we have created everything from water.' In the Lotus 'Sutra,' Buddha is presented metaphorically as a 'rain cloud,' covering, permeating, fertilizing, and enriching 'all parched living beings, to free them from their misery to attain the joy of peace, joy of the present world and joy of Nirvana...'"[114]

The pagan mantra is typical. One food company *Gaiam* holds a similar reactionary philosophy based on the pre-Christian religion of ancient Greece: "Gaia, mother Earth, was honored on the Isle of Crete in ancient Greece 4,000 years ago by the Minoan civilization. This civilization valued education, art, science, recreation and the environment and believed that the Earth was directly connected to their existence and daily life. The concept of Gaia stems from this ancient philosophy that the Earth is a living entity."[115]

Wicca, another popular cult amongst the left, also is a reactionary ideology "based upon the reconstruction of pre-Christian traditions"[116] and at the same time looks to Christianity as the ultimate enemy for it was Christianity which triumphed over the pre-Christian faiths of the Christian nations of today.

Wiccan writer Scott Cunningham writes that the pre-Christian gods "didn't die when the ancient pagan religions fell to Christianity in Europe. Most of the rites vanished, but they weren't the only effective ones. Wicca is alive and well and the deities respond to our calls and invocations."[117]

In other words, Wicca is an ideology, which is angry with Christianity for championing over the West's heathen gods, and envisions the West returning to its pre-Christian past.

Often times in a neo-Pagan book one finds some demonic complaint against Christianity for replacing the backward Pagan religions. This reminds me of the documentary I had to watch in world history class in the eleventh grade, which went on and on about how the evil Catholic Spaniards burned the "holy books" of the Aztec saints. I didn't get it. What is so special about books that encouraged the massacre of thousands of people for the sake of the gods? I began to ask, "Who cares?!" Lucky for me I had a conservative history teacher at the time and he himself cared less about some backward holy texts – thank God. He was better than my ninth grade teacher who everyday would make us write a mountain of notes to prepare for a future test.

One day I didn't see the purpose of copying the notes because all I saw on the board was rhetoric about how Columbus and his men raped, pillaged and killed. I asked her if she was going to mention how Columbus discovered many of the peppers in Mexico – "oh yeah, yeah, of course, the peppers, yeah ok" she responded, but of course she never talked about the peppers because to her it wasn't about history but a war against Western civilization. I cannot leave out the fact that it was this same teacher who told us that we should experiment with different sexual fetishes and that Terry Schiavo deserved death.

There is this romanticism today going back to the ancients, even to the violent gods of the terrorist Vikings. Occult writer Ed Fitch writes that Norse religion "left us with ideals of strength, individuality and honor, stressing the value of family, friends, and folk." He then bewails that the Eddas were altered "by Christian writers."[118] Scandinavia did not advance under the Eddas, Vikings or tribal warfare. The music of Vivaldi and Mozart came under Christianity, not Odin and Freya. Fitch also wrote that the purpose of his writing was to "help us return to our ancient roots."[119]

Pagan reactionaryism is also amongst so called secular elites such as Paul Ehrlich, a fanatic of population control who petitioned government to control fertility rates. Ehrlich wrote that in order to dramatically decrease the population in America it needs to replace its Judeo-Christian roots with Animism – a religion which only exists predominantly in third world nations: "Somehow we've got to change from a growth-oriented, exploitative system to one focused on stability and conservation. Our entire system of orienting to nature must undergo a revolution. And that revolution is going to be extremely difficult to pull off, since the attitudes of Western culture toward nature are deeply rooted in Judeo-Christian tradition. Unlike people in many other cultures, we see man's basic role as that of dominating nature, rather than as living in harmony with it. Professor Lynn White, Jr., has elegantly discussed this entire problem in Science magazine. He points out, for instance, that before the Christian era trees, springs, hills, streams, and other objects of nature had guardian spirits. These spirits had to be approached and placated before one could safely invade their territory. As White says, 'By destroying pagan animism, Christianity made it possible to exploit nature in a mood of indifference to the feelings of natural objects... Both our present science and our present technology are so tinctured with orthodox Christian arrogance toward nature that no solution for our ecological crisis can be expected from them alone. Since the roots of our trouble are so largely religious, the remedy must also be essentially religious, whether we call it that or not.'"[120]

To call for the end of Christian tradition in the West is to call for the death of Western Civilization itself. History tells us that Christianity civilized Europe and to think otherwise is cultural suicide.

HINDUISM – NOTHING CLOSE TO CHRISTIANITY

Srila Prabhupada established the International Society for Krishna in order "to promote the well being of society by teaching the science of Krishna consciousness according to Bhagavad-Gita and other ancient scriptures."[121] This promotion of the well being of society established the Hindu caste system in which all men are created unequal. The ranks in Hindu society come from a legend in which the main groupings, or varnas, emerge from a primordial being. From the mouth come the Brahmans – the priests and teachers. From the arms come the Kshatriyas – the rulers and soldiers. From the thighs come the Vaisyas – merchants and traders. From the feet come the Sudras – laborers. Each varna in turn contains hundreds of hereditary castes and sub-castes with their own pecking orders. They are then the people who are *Achuta*, or untouchable. The primordial being does not claim them. Untouchables are outcasts – people considered too impure, too polluted and with bad karma, to rank as worthy beings. Prejudice defines their lives, particularly in the rural areas, where nearly three-quarters of India's people live. Untouchables are shunned, insulted, banned from temples and higher caste homes, made to eat and drink from separate utensils in public places, and, in not uncommon cases, are raped, burned, lynched, and gunned down.[122]

According to 2005 statistics there are 110,000 of these violent crimes committed against the Achuta each year.

Girdharilal Maurya, an untouchable, bought a piece of land and built himself a farm. When men from the Rajput caste began to cause him trouble, he sought help from the police. To punish him for this, eight men from the Rajput caste attacked his farm while he was gone. They broke his fences, stole his tractor, beat his wife and daughter, and burned down his house. The message was clear: Stay at the bottom where you belong.[123]

This is Hinduism. It's no wonder Himmler read the Bhagavad-Gita that encourages the caste system, writing that it was created "according to the differentiation of Guna and Karma."[124] Many leftists that looked up to the fascist and totalitarian religion of Hinduism as a wonderful worldview also supported eugenics, fascism, abortion and euthanasia.

THE LEFT'S VISION OF 'DANCING WITH WOLVES'

Probably one of the biggest of the reactionary ideas among the left is this romanticism of Native Americans and how European Christians imperialized them. Iranian President Ahmadinejad exalted the Indian Natives: "Who lived on the land of America 250 or 300 years ago? Don't the rulers of America today rule because of the massacre of the Native Americans? If we accept the principle that anybody whose forefathers ever lived on any land 2,000 or 3,000 years ago should rule today, then America should be ruled by the native Americans who are there today. There is proof that they existed. There are films, photos, documents, maps, and their descendants."[125]

Romanticizing the Native Indians is one of the largest weapons Leftists use in the culture-war against Christian civilization. Leftist Christian and former president of the Union Seminary in New York, Donald Shriver, writes in his book *Honest Patriots* apologized for slavery and treatment of tribal peoples. More provocatively, he suggests apologies for displaced Tories during the American Revolution, to Mexicans for the Mexican War, to Filipinos for the Spanish American War, to Germans and Japanese for aerial bombing during World War II, to Koreans and Vietnamese and of course to Iraqis.

Shriver wondered why Americans could not as readily commemorate and admit their so-called crimes as Germans have for Nazism: "Germans have a keen interest in American history especially the history of Native Americans." ... "They are prompt to call it a genocide, and they wonder why the real history of native Americans gets buried in cowboy-and-Indians movies. I tell them that we are doing better these days in the history books and in the movies, but we have a long way to go. Is there, for example, any memorial in Charlottesville to the Indians who used to live here?"[126]

Shriver's sympathy for the Germans being bombed in WWII is the same reason why he laments the plight of Native Indians – he champions savage civilizations and boils when he sees Christian culture prevail over evil.

There was no genocide against Native Americans by the Europeans. After the arrival of European settlers the death toll amongst the Natives did not rise dramatically because of "systematic killing" but because of infectious disease, which was responsible for between seventy-five and ninety-five percent of their deaths.[127]

What is ignored in much of the leftist propaganda is the true savagery of the Native Indians' inter-tribal warfare. In 1860, an article on the *Missouri Republican* was written about the brutality of the Natives: "[W]e gather some news in regard to the upper country, and the up-trip of the fleet. Forts Clark and Kip on the Missouri and Fort Sarpy on the Yellow Stone have been abandoned by the Fur Company. The various tribes of Indians along the upper river are reported to be engaged in a war of extermination. Every-day almost, war parties were seen on the bank of the river. Bleeding scalps were seen dangling from sticks at the door of the lodges of the chiefs and big men. Murmuring out complaints were the burden of the speeches at every council held. They complain of the government of the Indian Agents and of one another. The probabilities are that they will allow no peace to each other till a strong military post is established at some point in their country, as the Agents feel that until this is done their influence has but little force in controlling the turbulent spirit of the young and ambitious warriors."[128]

LEFTISM – A PAGAN SAVAGERY

Why is there such sympathy from the left for Islam, abortion, the savages of Mesoamerica, the French revolution, the Russian revolution, the Mexican revolution, the Iranian revolution, assisted suicide, euthanasia and the other degenerate systems and historical moments? How quickly such revolutions are forgotten and, worse still, considered respectable.[129]

The ones who love savage societies and hate Christian civilization are the savages of our time. Just as the pagans in the French, Russian, Mexican, and Iranian revolutions wished to obliterate Christianity in their nations, the leftists in America wish to demolish any trace of western civilization. They push for changing the Constitution and history and by degrading the image of our Western heroes such as Washington, Jefferson, Adams, Newton, and many others – making them look like godless heathens.

Every bit of the history of advanced civilization brought by Christianity is to be degraded by leftist historians. When the Muslims conquered Jerusalem and forced Christians and Jews under their fascist yoke it was 'the evil white Christian crusades that came to Jerusalem and ruined the beautiful Muslim land in the name of God and Cross', yet when Muslims conquered Spain, for 800 years burning churches, massacring Christians and Jews and placing them under heavy taxes, it was 'Muslim Spain that treated Christians and Jews greatly. While Christians were in the dark ages, Muslims were sitting around in a hookah bar, discovering great advances in science and algebra.'

According to the revisionists Christianity brought nothing while Islam, godless philosophers, and the theory of evolution brought everything.

What did Nietzsche bring? He brought books about how to become superior to others, pro-Islam and anti-Christian writings, and writings that support eugenics.

How about Rousseau? He brought socialism, the massacre of thousands of Christians, and the near destruction of France.

How about Darwin? He brought eugenics, euthanasia, a primordial soup myth that somehow got transferred into pseudoscience, a fraudulent scientific excuse for the massacre of countless unborn children, and the degrading of the human race which brought delight to the eyes of Stalin and other dictators.

What about Sarte? He brought revolution against the church and the support of communism to the point that he denied the facts of Stalin's massacres. What else is new with such people?

What about Hegel? He was a pro-Islam lunatic who wished for socialism and total government control over society.

What about Heidegger? He was a fascist philosopher who saw his philosophy coming to pass when the Nazis seized power over Germany.

What about Muhammad? He brought the massacre of millions, the near conquering of all of Europe, the Barbary pirate wars, the destruction of Christianity in much of the east, September 11th, and all of the major terrorist attacks around the world including the loss of our freedom of expression through fear of Islamophobia labels.

What about Hinduism? It gave us suttee, the caste system and an exchange program between rats and humans in which the rats got the grain and the humans got their disease – all for the dream that the rat could be someone's dead uncle. The cow could roam roundabout while Indians starved by the millions.

And what about the Crusades – the leftists' quick draw against everyone who brings up Islam? There is no equivalence between the initial mission of the crusades and the initial Islamic mission.

Richard Dawkins writes in *The God Delusion* that Ann Coulter, "American religious leaders and faith-based politicians chillingly recall the narrow bigotry, heartless cruelty and sheer nastiness of the Afghan Taliban, the Ayatollah Khomeini and the Wahhabi authorities of Saudi Arabia" (P. 288). He also writes that "the Koran or Qur'ân, adding a powerful ideology of military conquest to spread the faith. Christianity, too, was spread by the sword, wielded first by Roman hands after the Emperor Constantine raised it from eccentric cult to official religion, then by the Crusaders, and later by the *conquistadors* and other European invaders and colonists, with missionary accompaniment. For most of my purposes, all three Abrahamic religions can be treated as indistinguishable."

Historians and Christian critics have written much on Constantine's political genius of combining Romanism with Christian dogma in order to expand his empire. While Dawkins can never recite anything from Christian instruction that would approve Constantine's incorporation of the cross into his battles, he would conveniently use the acts of warriors as an argument to attack Christian humility and virtue.

The left uses the Crusaders as evidence for their idea equating Christian fundamentalism with Islamic fundamentalism.

Is this a valid argument?

History tells us 'no.'

"The Crusade," notes historian Bernard Lewis, "was a delayed response to the jihad, the holy war for Islam, and its purpose was to recover by war what had been lost by war – to free the holy places of Christendom and open them once again, without impediment, to Christian pilgrimage."[130] No serious historian can deny that Muslims invaded Sicily in 827 and than conquered it in 902. In 846 the Muslims entered the city of Rome where they plundered the churches of St. Peter and St. Paul. There were also attacks against Christians in Spain during the 10th and 11th centuries. In the Levant, the Battle of Manzikert occurred in 1071 with the Muslims defeating the Byzantine Christians. In 1091 Muslims drove the Christian priests out of Jerusalem. The Muslims also tried and failed to capture Constantinople, the citadel of Eastern Christianity, between 668 and 798.[131] Nearly four hundred years after the Muslim conquests in Palestine, they destroyed the Church of the Holy Sepulcher in Jerusalem in 1009 under Caliph el Hakim.[132] All of these attacks against Christians were perpetrated well before the Crusades were ever initiated in 1095.[133] These numerous attacks on Christian sites, which went on for a period of over five-hundred years, provided more than enough justification for the Crusades to begin a defensive attack against the Muslim pagans.

Emperor Alexius in the East asked Pope Urban II in the West to help him recruit soldiers for the Byzantine army. The objective of the Crusaders was to roll back the Turkish Muslim conquest of Asia Minor, as well as to keep Christianity from being completely destroyed in the East[134] and to also protect Turkish and European Christian pilgrims.[135] The Crusades were not an act of imperialism nor a pre-emptive strike but an act of self-defense.

What would leftist historians write had the Christians conquered Mecca and Ottoman Turks charged there to stop the Crusades from conquering the lands of Islam? The left would be praising the Muslims as great fighters for freedom while referring to the Crusades as fascists. But the fact remains that it was the Muslims who were the invaders.

Islam conquered Spain for 800 years; Portugal for 600, Greece, 500; Bulgaria, 500; Rumania, 400; Serbia, 400; Sicily, 300; and Hungary for 150 years.[136] If the left is all about fairness and fighting imperialism where are their writings on how Tariq ibn Ziyad terrorized Spanish Christians when conquering Spain ordering Christian prisoners to be "cut to pieces and their flesh boiled in cauldrons"?[137]

What about liberal Christians like Rick Warren who apologizes for the Crusades? Would Rick Warren write anything near that magnitude to Hans Scholl or Bishop Galen as they fought Hitler? Warren is busy "building bridges" with Islam and Bashar al-Assad of Syria. He promotes passing out free condoms and "clean needles to intravenous drug users"[138] in Africa and India. What will Warren tell Jesus in His second coming? "Lord, I gave condoms in your name! I gave clean needles in your name. I built bridges with homosexuals, Islam, Hinduism, and Buddhism in your name!"

Perhaps the Warrens of Christendom could heed the words of our Lord: "depart from me. I never knew you, all you workers of iniquity" (Luke 13:27). Christ was not crucified for Warren to make a peace treaty with the terror supporting organization Muslim Public Affairs

Council. Christ died for the Sophies and the Galens and what they did for Him and for humanity.

I admire the words of G.K. Chesterton when he said after being awarded an honorary Holy Cross Crusader by Worcester College on May 1st, 1931: "I have to thank you for this very great honor and I do so with all my heart. I can only say that I am not much of a crusader but at least I am not a Mohammedan."

Chapter 38

For God The Eternal or For Tyranny That Will End

O'Reilly: "Jesus was a real guy, I could see him. You know I know what he did and so I am not positive that Jesus is God but I'm throwing in with Jesus rather than throwing in with you guys because you guys can't tell me how it all got here. You guys don't know."

Dawkins: "We're working on it, physicists are..."

Even the ones that claim they worship nothing still end up believing in something that supposedly came out of something else and could have never come out of nothing. They could even claim that life came from matter. And when it is argued that God is beyond matter, they question who created Him. Yet they never question the source of matter and argue that we need to wait for the fulfillment of their predictions and that perhaps those future advancements will find an answer entering into the realm of predictive atheistic prophecy.

But yet, despite the overwhelming evidence that is counter to the idea of life coming from non-life, we still have people, especially in academia, who accept that God did not create the universe but that the universe was caused into existence. But this is flawed since time, space and matter were once non-existent. How could they bring themselves into existence?

Another crucial point is that everything in the universe is a *caused cause*. A tree is planted because somebody planted a seed into the soil – that seed exists because a tree expelled that seed out into the earth...we have trillions of caused causes in the universe.

One crucial question is then proposed: since everything is a *caused cause* then what was the cause that started it all? There had to be an 'uncaused' cause since we cannot say that there is an eternal amount of *caused causes*. This would make the universe eternal with neither a beginning nor an end.

Even the big bang theory states that before time and space came into existence, a "primeval atom" exploded and in a slow process the universe randomly formed. If space is the measurement between objects and even according to the big bang theory, did not exist before the atom exploded, then why wasn't this primeval atom omnipresent? And how could this atom exist without space for it to be present in?

Also, time is the measurement used to sequence events, so if time did not exist before the great explosion then how did the primeval atom progress itself from the moment of its standing to the moment of its destruction? How could it form and explode without the existence of time to sequence these events?

One might ask – what if time has always existed?

If this is true, how did we get to this very point in time?

How did you get yourself to the point that you are now reading this very sentence without time?

If time has always existed, then you cannot call it "time" for it always has a beginning and if it didn't, nothing would exist.

If you believe in the big bang then you must believe that matter always existed and it is thus eternal because the theory states that matter was there before time and space came to be. But this is surely unscientific since matter could not have existed without time and space. Furthermore, the laws of thermodynamics say that matter can never be created nor destroyed.

How then did matter create itself?

We then are forced into a corner – something outside of matter, time, and space must have put matter time, and space into existence.

It is obvious that whatever placed matter, time and space must be matter-less, timeless (eternal), and space-less (omnipresent).

This would perfectly fit the description of God.

Well, then you might ask: "if you believe that God always existed then why can't I believe that matter always existed?"

Now we get to the crux of this whole issue. You can believe that. The only problem is – you cannot call it science.

We are then back to square one – faith.

But faith in God has more merit. "For faith is the substance of things hoped for – the evidence of things unseen." (Hebrews 11:1)

I admit that I have faith that God created the universe but my faith makes a lot more sense since we know by evidence that there was a beginning to matter, time and space – these cannot create themselves. And if you believe that the universe formed itself then that takes a great deal more faith than the faith defined in the Bible. All of us are fundamentalists.

Today and unfortunately, history is repeating itself; the very old arguments are circulating our media and education. The trends seem to focus on Christianity as the 'source of all evil.' God has become the focus of many arguments that we need to eliminate Him from all facets of life, seeking to abolish Christianity as an archaic ideology that focuses on a war between God and Satan.

While many who consider themselves progressives would agree that we do have a struggle between good and evil, they also view as primitive, anyone who believes in the existence of God or the Devil. In the view that progressives hold, good is in the eye of the beholder. It can evolve and progress by the creation of our own hands and that mankind has an intrinsic skill to refine himself through and by himself.

Throughout Christian history, as well as with the case being made here, *anyone that desired to abolish God has simply advanced government to become God.* (G.K. Chesterton)

We have seen this over and over – the French Revolution, Nazi Germany and Communism – all attempted to abolish Christianity and the end result was tyranny.

In the Christian view, tyrannies are born when mankind follows his own will, ignoring that a creator has already ordained the best roadmap to serve both God and the needs of humanity.

Other Christian nations ended up under tyrannical control since they had external influences – Islam invaded and Islamized Syria, Turkey and Egypt in order to abolish Christianity and spread its tyranny for decades to come – even until now. Every Christian nation that was taken over by Islam fell under tyranny, and the ones that are left are still on the radar for Islamists who argue that their prophet declared that Islam will first conquer Constantinople and then Rome [the West].[139]

If vigilance is the cost of freedom, Christians in the West need to be on guard. Political Jihad is active and while westerners focus on the daily explosive acts of suicide bombers, they ignore that it's the political act that we need to focus on. Islamists work closely with liberals on all levels, even infiltrating churches that turned liberal, the White House, the media and even establishing their own set of laws in Britain, splitting its constitution in order to adapt Sharī'ah Law for Muslims.

Through Islamic invasions or internal struggles, Christians need to be on watch. Today, liberals and even president Barack Hussein Obama, a supposed convert from Islam, have infiltrated our culture while our guard was down to openly declare that America is not a Christian Nation. By this, they are doing Islam's bidding, thereby chipping away at our foundation as our laws are being rewritten to undermine the Constitution which was etched in stone by our forefathers – arguing that our Founding Fathers did not extract our laws from God in the Bible, but from mere men (philosophers).

On the other hand, Christians in the United States defend the constitution as being based on the absolute laws of God, stemming from the Bible. For if we say that our Declaration of Independence and our Constitution are based on what man wrote, then by this, man's work is subject to change through and by man. But if our values came from God, then who can change them but the unchangeable God? After all, our Declaration of Independence refers to God as "the Supreme Judge of the World," and that all men are "endowed by their Creator with certain unalienable Rights, that among these are Life, Liberty and the pursuit of Happiness."

THE END OF SHINAR AND THE DESTRUCTION OF BABYLON

Bible believers contend that in the Bible, God does not only concentrate on His creation account. They do not only find God through the observation of His cosmos or by the wonder of His works or by presenting history but by keeping His prophetic word. Bible believers tend to feel the rejection by progressives who accuse them of doomsday mania. The accusations go both ways since Bible believers also accuse progressives of pushing a doomsday scenario with respect to their showing dire concern over *Global Warming* and *Population Explosion*, which in their view is being propagated by the prophets of doom who have introduced policies in support of abortion and industrial control.

We all have to make choices. No matter what, a label must be applied to the forehead of everyone; we either believe the prophets of the progressive atheists who promote doomsday through use of quackery pseudoscience, belief in Mayan priests, astrology, Islamic prophecy, or we trust the Bible. Everyone believes in some sort of predictions. Even when we invest, we predict a better time ahead.

THE BIBLE'S PREDICTION REGARDING THE FUTURE OF BABYLON

The Biblical God is not done with Shinar. He stands against Babel and Bel. How could some believe that Babylon's creation account is parallel to the Biblical story, especially when they collide? God stands against Babylon. In a dual-pronged prediction, the Bible combines both ancient Babylon and Arabia, by summarizing the culmination of Babylonian spirituality in a prophetic proclamation: "Babylon is taken, Bel is confounded, Merodach [Marduk] is broken in pieces; her idols are confounded, her images are broken in pieces" (Jeremiah 50:2).

This destruction is not exclusive to ancient Babylon which is simply a type, but the future center of Arabia with the sound of its destruction heard at the Red Sea: "The earth is moved at the noise of their fall, at the cry the noise thereof was heard in the Red sea" (Jeremiah 49:21). The Red Sea is a geographic indicator as to where the Last-Days Babylon will be located. Mecca and Dammam sit near the Red Sea. Some may object, saying that Jeremiah 49 is speaking about Edom, which was primarily located in modern day Jordan. Yet in Ezekiel 25 "Edom" stretches from Teman (Yemen) to Dedan (Saudi Arabia)" (v. 13). Greater Edom included all of the west coast of the Arabian Peninsula.

Her destruction is described by Jeremiah: "'As Sodom and Gomorrah were overthrown, along with their neighboring towns,' says the LORD, 'so no one will live there; no man will dwell in it,'" (Jeremiah 49:18).

How was Sodom and Gomorrah destroyed? According to the Bible it was fire that rained down from heaven.

Jeremiah 49 is ultimately speaking of the Last-Day's judgment of Mystery Babylon that is associated with ancient Babylon. Throughout the Bible, only Mystery Babylon is described as being completely and utterly destroyed in this same way. Beyond this, the passage specifies that the region we are dealing with contains the cities of Teman and Dedan which are nowhere near Iraq, or ancient Babylon. Also, the Red Sea borders Arabia, not Iraq.

In Isaiah 21:9, Isaiah levels a prophetic oracle against Babylon: "Babylon is fallen, is fallen," is the same announcement used in Revelation 18:1-2. Yet this prediction is not ultimately about ancient Babylon (Iraq), but the Mystery Babylon of Revelation. Ancient Babylon was simply a *type* of the Last-Days Babylon. The names in this prophecy are all areas in Arabia:

"The burden against Dumah" (v. 11)

"The burden against Arabia" (v. 13)

"All the glory of Kedar will fail" (v. 16)

Dumah and Kedar are in Arabia as the text shows: "All the glory of Kedar will fail" (v16). All of the locations mentioned in Isaiah 21 are in the desert of Arabia, the region of Revelation 17 which is surrounded by many waters (seas). Arabia in fact, is referred to by Arabs as *Al-Jazeera Al-Arabia*, literally the *Arab Island* or the *Arab Peninsula* or the "Desert of the Sea." (v. 1). National Geographic[140] and Bernard Lewis[141] recognize it as such.

Some might argue that the context of Isaiah 21 is only historical. But it is difficult to ignore the multiple references to Kedar, Tema, Dedan and Dumah throughout the Book of Isaiah. Dumah is in Saudi Arabia near Yathrib (Medina), and today is known as "Dumat el-Jandal." Dumah, one of the sons of Ishmael, is also associated with Edom and Seir in Isaiah 21:11. Historians generally identify Dumah with the Addyrian Adummatu people.[142] By these and other references, we can conclude that Dumah stands for Arabia.

We will also examine the crucial text of Isaiah 34 with the destruction of Edom, including its oil. It would be impossible to allude to Isaiah 34 as an historic reference because the purpose of the destruction against Edom relates to the final Battle of Jerusalem, in which the Lord Himself will be present and fighting. In Habakkuk 3 this takes place in "Median" which is in Arabia. The Psalms even give us a literal reference to Edom being the daughter of Babylon (born of Babylon): "Remember, O Lord, against the sons of *Edom* the day of Jerusalem, who said, 'Raze it, raze it, to its very foundation! O *daughter of Babylon*, who are to be destroyed,'" (Psalm 137:7-8).

Arabia being the daughter of Babylon was made so by Nabonidus, who extended Babylon to Yathrib (Medina) and introduced the worship of the Moon-god. These Old Testament predictions concerning the utter destruction of Babylon cannot be referring exclusively to the ancient city of Babylon because it was inhabited for roughly five hundred years after these prophecies were given until around 141 B.C. when the Parthian Empire took over the region and the city was emptied of inhabitants. After this, the city slowly decayed. But it never suffered a fate anywhere near the utter destruction that was suffered by Sodom and Gomorrah – with fire raining down from heaven as many of these prophecies describe.

Isaiah 21 also agrees with several passages in Jeremiah and Revelation that refer to Babylon. Contenders to this interpretation would have a difficult time refuting the very direct Biblical references. The names used in these passages make it clear that the reference is not to Babylon on the Euphrates river. Not once do they speak of Nineveh, Ur, Babel, Erech, Accad, Sumer, Assur, Calneh, Mari, Karana, Ellpi, Eridu, Kish, or Tikrit. All of the literal names referenced are locations in Arabia, which was also part of the ancient Babylonian Empire.

LITERAL OIL – ISAIAH 34

In nearly identical language to what we have already read concerning Mystery Babylon in Revelation 17 and 18, we read: "For it is the day of Jehovah's vengeance, and the year of recompenses for the controversy of Zion. Its *streams* shall be turned into *pitch* and its dust into brimstone; its land shall become burning pitch. It shall not be quenched night or day; *its smoke shall ascend forever*" (Isaiah 34:8-10).

Incredibly, almost three millennia before the discovery of fuel oil, Isaiah predicted the burning of the very thing that was used in Babel to build a name for the rebellious ones – the pitch. Pitch is bitumen and tar, which technically is simply crude oil. The Bible even speaks of an end-times tyrant identified as "Nimrod" in Micah 5 whose spiritual roots go back to Babel and that God will raise seven leaders (allies) that will destroy him.

Notice that the land shall not be "like" burning pitch but shall actually *become* burning pitch – there is no simile here. This prediction could only be fulfilled in an oil rich land. The word for "streams" (*nachal*) is not water streams but "torrent", "torrent-valley", "wadi /valley", "mine", or "tunnels" and thus need to not be understood strictly as streams of water.

Obviously water would never burn like pitch as the verse mandates. The picture painted is literally of a land that turns into a river of burning wells (tunnels) of petroleum.

Again, this judgment against "Edom" extends from Teman to Dedan: "Therefore thus Says the Lord GOD; 'I will also stretch out mine hand upon Edom, and will cut off man and beast from it; and I will make it desolate *from Teman; and they of Dedan* shall fall by the sword,'" (Ezekiel 25:12-13).

Teman is a place name meaning "right side" that is "southern." The Edomites were a clan descended from Esau (Genesis 36:11, Genesis 36:15; I Chronicles 1:36). Teman was a city that was associated with the Edomites (Jeremiah 49:7, Jeremiah 49:20; Ezekiel 25:13; Amos 1:12, Obadiah 1:9, Habakkuk 3:3). Teman has often been identified with Tawilan, fifty miles south of the Dead Sea, just east of Petra, though archaeological evidence does not confirm the site as the principal city of southern Edom. Others understand Teman to designate southern Edom in general. To others still, the link with Dedan (Jeremiah 49:7; Ezekiel 25:13) suggests Teman is on the Arabian Peninsula.[143]

Because the Bible chose to identify Teman with Dedan, we need to accept that Teman is in South Central Arabia in Yemen. Dedan is well defined and was an ancient city in central Saudi Arabia that is now known as Al-Ula.[144]

THE EXTENT OF ARABIA'S DESTRUCTION

This destruction of Arabia is complete and fits the description made by several Biblical writers whose predictions correlate with Isaiah 34: "Therefore *in one day* her plagues will overtake her: death, mourning, and famine. She will be consumed by fire, for mighty is the Lord God who judges her. When the kings of the earth who committed adultery with her and shared her luxury *see the smoke of her burning*, they will weep and mourn over her. Terrified at her torment, they will stand far off and cry: 'Woe! Woe, O great city, O Babylon, city of power! *In one hour* your doom has come!' … *Every sea captain, and all who travel by ship, the sailors, and all who earn their living from the sea*, will stand far off. *When they see the smoke of her burning*, they will exclaim, 'Was there ever a city like this great city?'" (Revelation 18:8-10, 17-18).

Ships on the Red Sea can easily see Arabia's destruction. This Babylon will be destroyed violently and swiftly "and in one day," "with such violence," she will be "consumed with fire." The judgment on the Harlot is permanent. There will never be heard in this city the sound of music or musicians. Workers will never rebuild the city. The sound of tradesmen will never be heard or seen in her again. All agriculture will cease. There will be no weddings. All signs of human habitation will be permanently eliminated. Apart from Sodom and Gomorrah, this type of utter destruction has never been seen in any other city, including Hiroshima and Nagasaki. "After her destruction, Babylon will merely be a home for demons, evil spirits, and scavenging desert creatures" (Revelation 18:1-2).

This is in line with the ancient eastern perception that desolate desert wastelands were the dwelling place of demons and unclean spirits. The point being emphasized is that after Babylon is destroyed, there will be absolutely no human life ever found there again. Jeremiah agrees; he describes this: "So desert creatures and hyenas will live there, and there the owl will dwell. It will never again be inhabited or lived in from generation to generation" (Jeremiah 50:39).

Isaiah confirms a similar fate: "It shall be a habitation of jackals" (Isaiah 34:14). And again later, the destruction of Babylon is described as being absolute. Isaiah speaks of this event: "For I will rise up against them, says the Lord of hosts, and cut off from Babylon its name and remnant, and offspring and posterity, says the Lord...I will sweep it with the *broom of destruction*" (Isaiah 12:15).

The broom of destruction? Anyone who has seen footage of a nuclear explosion has seen the fury and the power of the ominous cloud that sweeps up everything in its path. Could this verse be describing a nuclear explosion? "And I will show wonders in the heavens and in the earth; Blood and fire and pillars of smoke" (Joel 2:30). Could the pillars of smoke be the scene of mushroom clouds from a nuclear explosion?

Amazingly, the destruction of Arabia is not a prediction that is only declared in the Bible. Islamic prophecy also predicts the destruction of its bride Mecca by Muslim nations: "The final battle will be waged by Muslim faithful coming on the backs of horses...carrying black banners. They will stand on the east side of the Jordan River and will wage war that the earth has never seen before. The true Messiah who is the Islamic Mehdi...will defeat Europe...*will lead this army of Seljuks*, He will preside over the world from Jerusalem because *Mecca would have been destroyed...*"[145]

Medina is not immune from this destruction: "The flourishing state of Jerusalem will be when *Yathrib* (Medina) is in ruins, the ruined state of Yathrib will be when the Great War comes, and the outbreak of the Great War will be at the conquest of Constantinople and the conquest of Constantinople when the Dajjal (Antichrist) comes forth. He (the Prophet) struck his thigh or his shoulder with his hand and said: This is as true as you are here or as you are sitting."[146]

Yathrib is another name for Medina, the city of the Prophet Muhammad, the second holiest city to Islam. Constantinople is Istanbul in Turkey. Many radical Muslims believe that Istanbul has been under the control of secular hypocritical Muslims until its recent restoration to the Islamists. So according to this prophesy, after the fall of Istanbul to the true Muslims (through recent elections in 2007, this has just occurred), Medina will be destroyed.

Why would Islam predict the destruction of its own holy place?

Well, its author, the Luminous one knows the Bible.

How could Islam be the 'truth' if in the end its central headquarters is destroyed?

SELF FULFILLED PROPHECY?

While many progressives accuse Bible believers of ushering in self-fulfilled prophecies, a common counter argument by Bible believers is that the Bible predicted the return and establishment of Israel. Regardless of political affiliation, no one on earth today can argue that Israel does not exist. Progressives would argue that the Christian west ushered all of this in order to prove the Bible. Yet here lays the flaw with such objection; Israel would have never existed without the Holocaust that finally forced the establishment of the state of Israel. The Holocaust in Germany was not orchestrated by Bible believers since Hitler had no interest in proving Bible predictions but was bent on destroying God's chosen people – the Jews. Since the Holocaust was the reason Israel was created, how then can anyone argue that Bible believers orchestrated the Holocaust in order to prove the Bible? Or was it that the very ones who wanted to destroy the Biblical proclamations ended up inadvertently fulfilling the very elements they so much wanted to stop! It was the enemies of the Bible that helped fulfill it.

Bible believers contend that they are not interested in Armageddon. Evangelicals especially believe they will be raptured or taken away before it happens – they would rather escape Armageddon or at least prolong its advent.

In the end, the good news is God's victory over tyranny. The choice is yours. Are you for God or for tyranny?

Choose wisely!

For God or For Tyranny

This book is a case for the war between God and The Luminous One. After reading this I hope that you have reflected on the points that I have made. Now it is your responsibility to equip your mind with the tools to scan evil and to judge every idea that comes forth from man's mouth, thinking critically to determine if it is God's ethics or Satan's. Ideas should be judged regardless of who they come from be it Christian or non-believer, conservative or liberal. If it is from the mind of man you cannot trust it; evil is so deceptive that it can even cloak itself with the label of 'Christian' or 'conservative' – only to do the Devil's bidding.

You must use even more knowledge to articulate judgment of ideas if they come from those who appear as sheep, for behind that soft wool may be the teeth of a wolf that knows the easiest way to infiltrate the flock is to camouflage himself as part of it.

The one who recognizes this false sheep can no longer be a sheep but a shepherd who must guide the herd around the wolf in sheep's clothing, equipping as many as possible with truth on how to identify the wolf.

When driving a car, doing so defensively is the best way to prevent being involved in an accident. When it comes to the most important decision faced by all of us – the salvation of our souls – shouldn't we try to prevent a spiritual accident by choosing the wrong road?

Do not think for a second that once you are a shepherd the wolves will stop attacking you. Conversely, they will hate you even more and will organize packs against you. It only takes one wolf to destroy a herd but many more to kill a shepherd skilled with the sword of truth. And that is the sword that Christianity offers you – the sword of knowledge against the Devil and his soldiers that I hope you will un-sheathe.

→ References ←

INTRODUCTION & PART ONE

1 Dinesh D'Souza, The Enemy At Home: The Cultural Left and Its Responsibility for 9/11

2 Christianity Today, by Michelle Vu, Christian Post Correspondent Wednesday, 11 July 2007

3 Richard G. Hovannisian, editor. The Armenian Genocide in Perspective. Oxford, U.K.: Transaction Books, 1987. pp. 123-124

4 The Key Elements in the Turkish Denial of the Armenian Genocide: A Case Study of Distortion and Falsification by Vahakn N. Dadrian, Director, Genocide Research Project Zoryan Institute September 1999

5 Ibid

6 After the death of Abel for example, Adam composed an elegy (rithâ') in which he cried for his son; Wahb Ibn Munabbih, Kitâb al-Tîjân fî mulûk Himyar, Sanaa, Edition Markaz al-dirâsât wa al-abhâth al- yamaniyya, s.d, pp. 24-25

7 AbsoluteAstronomy.com, Genesis

8 James B. Pritchard, ed., Ancient Near Eastern Texts Relating to the Old Testament (Princeton, N.J.: Princeton University Press, 1950), 60-72. Taken from Redeeming science, A God Gentered Approach by Vern S. Poythress, pp. 71

9 Redeeming science, A God Gentered Approach by Vern S. Poythress, pp. 71

10 Ibid, See W. G. Lambert and A. R. Millard, Atra-hasis: The Babylonian Story of the Flood (Oxford: Oxford University Press, 1969). In my summary I have smoothed over some of the obscurities.

11 Ibid, pp. 71-72

12   Wenham, Genesis, 9. But Collins, Genesis 1–4, chapter 9, and Umberto Cassuto, A Commentary on the Book of Genesis (Jerusalem: Magnes, n.d.), 1:7, rightly point out that the polemical effect is indirect. Genesis 1 is first of all a positive account of God's acts of creation. From Redeeming science, A God Gentered Approach by Vern S. Poythress, pp. 72

13   Ibid, pp. 73

14   The Babylonian Legends of the Creation and the Fight Between Bel and the Dragon Told by Assyrian Tablets From Nineveh, Discovery of the Tablets, Project Gutenberg's The Babylonian Legends of the Creation, by British Museum Produced by the PG Distributed Proofreaders

15   Inscription of Nebuchadnezzar, Library collection: "World's Greatest Literature", Published work: "Babylonian and Assyrian Literature", Translator: Rv. J. M. Rodwell, M.A. Publisher: P. F. Collier & Son, New York, Copyright: Colonial Press, 1901

16   Encyclopedia Britannica

17   Dictionary Of Ancient Deities, pp. 309, Marduk

18   Allah, His Heritage In Paganism, Bergson, Snorri G., Goddesses and Wicca Worship, 'Neo-paganism at its most deceptive form, Islam and Goddess Worship Chpt. IV, pg. 15, 1998-2000

19   Allah, His Heritage In Paganism, Langdon, Stephen H, The Mythology of All Races, Vol V, Archeological Institute of America, Boston, 1931, pg. 5-19

20   Narrated by ibn Abbas also by Tirmidhi: "The messenger of Allah concerning the stone said: 'Allah will bring it forth on the day of resurrection, and it will have two eyes with which it will see and a tongue with which it will speak, and it will testify in favor of those who touched it sincerity."

21   The Encyclopedia Of Religion, Reference Islam George Braswell Jr

22   The Myth of Europa and Minos," by P. B. S. Andrews. Greece & Rome, Vol. 16, No. 1 (Apr., 1969), pp. 60-66

23   Index of Moon Gods and Moon Goddesses, by N.S Gill, About.com

24   Euphorion, fr. (FHG III 72); Etymologicum Magnum 771, 56; cf. Etymologicum Gudianum, Sturz 537, 26 Gyges and Homer, by Livio C. Stecchin

25   The Hatstings Encyclopedia of Religion and Ethics, Vol I, pp. 326

26   Arthur Jeffrey, ed., Islam: Muhammad and His religion (1958), pp. 85.

27   Ibid

28   Ibid

29   The Social Contract, By Jean-Jacques Rousseau, Book I, Chapter 6 The Social Compact

30   Ibid, Chapter 9 Real Property

31   Sahih Muslim

32   Qur'ân 49:13

33   Website On Ideologies Of War, Genocide And Terror, The Psychoanalytic Interpretation Of Reality: Theory And Method, By Richard Koenigsberg

34   Liberal Fascism, By Jonah Goldberg, Adolf Hitler: Man of The Left, pp. 69, Schouenbaum, Hitler's Social Revolution, pp. 62

35   Liberal Fascism, Liberal Fascist Economics, pp. 298, By Jonah Goldberg

36   Islam One World, www.Islamoneworld.net

37   Jihad in Islam by Sayyeed Abul A'la Almaududi, Islamic Publications (Pvt.) Ltd, page 8

38   Open Letter to the Pope, the Archbishop of Izmir (Smyrna), Turkey, Reverend Guiseppe Germano Barnardini, speaking in a recent gathering of Christians and Muslims as documented by Abdullah Al-Arabi, The Islamization of America, (The Pen vs the Sword), Los Angeles, CA, 2003), page 8

39   Book IV, 8. Civil Religion

40   Ibid, Book IV, 8. Civil Religion

41   Eugenics, History, See Chapter 3 in Donald A. MacKenzie, Statistics in Britain, 1865-1930: The social construction of scientific knowledge (Edinburgh: Edinburgh University Press, 1981)

42   Francis Galton, "Eugenics: Its definition, scope, and aims," The American Journal of Sociology 10:1 (July 1904)

43   Kantsaywhere by Francis Galton, pp. 414

44   Darwin 1882, pp. 134.

45   The Negro Project, Margaret Sanger's Eugenic plan for Black Americans, By Tanya L. Green, Malthusian Eugenics."

46   American Death Camps, The Holocaust, Meet Margaret Sanger Founder of Planned Parenthood

47   Environmentalists help Uranium's price, By James Finch

48   Charles Darwin, from his autobiography, 1876

49   Quoted from Professor Frey (1970) in his introduction to the Penguin Classics edition of Malthus' "An Essay On The Principle Of Population"

50   Rebirth of Reason, Multiculturalism: A Tool of Collectivism, By Edward W. Younkins.

51   Stephen Moore Washington Times on October 13, 1999

52   Birth Control For Others by Nicholas Kristof, The New York Times, March 23, 2008

53   Ibid

54   Population Explosion, Is Man Really Doomed by Otto Friedrich, September 13, 1971

55   "Eco-Catastrophe!". Ramparts. Sept 1969. pages 24–28.

56   "When Paul's Said and Done: Paul Ehrlich, famed ecologist, answers readers' questions". Grist Magazine. August 13, 2004

57   The Population Bomb Revisited, Paul R. Ehrlich and Anne H. Ehrlich, page 67

58   Yale Environment 360, The Population Bomb, Has it been diffused, August 11, 2008

59   Ibid

60   Population Explosion: Is Man Really Doomed? By Otto Friedrich, Monday, September 13th, 1971 HP-TIME.COM

61   Demographic Winter, Exposing the Century's Overlooked Crisis by Don Feder, March 27th, 2008.

62   What Happened on the Way to the Roaring 2000's? by Harry S. Dent April 17, 2003

63   From Malthus To The Club Of Rome by Paul Neurath, 1994, pp. 6

64   Ibid

65   Ibid

66   "Population: Delusion and Reality" by AMARTYA SEN (New York Review of Books September 22, 1994)

67   Ibid

68   Stephen Moore Washington Times on October 13, 1999

69   How to Take the Chill Out of Demographic Winter. A speech by Don Feder to the New Generation Church, Riga, Latvia, November Nov. 15, 200

70   Joy Resmovitz, Horowitz Assails Academic Climate, 10, 26, 2007

71   The Social Contract, Book IV, Chapter VIII Civil Religion

72   Albert Speer, 1905-1981

73   The American Thinker, The Nazis and Christianity, By Bruce Walker

74   The New American, Hitler and Christianity, Written by Selwyn Duke Sunday, 08 June 2008 18:15, Hitler: A Study in Tyranny, By Allan Bullock, Bullock derived this quotation from the book Hitler's Table Talk

75   Jean Jacques Rousseau, The Social Contract, trans. Book 4, chap 8, pp 204-223

76   Ibid

77   Dachau Scrapbook, The 25 Points of Hitler's Nazi Party.

78   Ibid

79   Hitler Was a Leftist, Hitler's Persecution of the Christian Churches, Adolf Hitler, Quoted by Albert Speer, pp. 96, Inside the Third Reich

80   Qurayza Massacre, and PBS By: Andrew G. Bostom FrontPageMagazine.com, Friday, December 20, 2002

81   Italics mine. Republicanism And Religion, Philadelphia Society, Williamsburg, Virginia, October 4 2003, Ellis Sandoz, Alexis de Tocqueville, The Old Regime and the French Revolution [4th ed., 1858], trans. Stuart Gilbert, Anchor Books, 1955, pp. 13f

82   Ibid

83   American Daily, Nazism, Marxism, and Islam, By Bruce Walker, Guns or Butter? By R.H. Lockhart, 1938

84   The History Guide, Robespierre's Republic of Virtue, Richard W. Lyman and Lewis W. Spitz, eds., Major Crises in Western Civilization, vol. 2 (New York: Harcourt, Brace & World, 1965), pp.. 71-72

85   Qur'ân 8:12

86   Telegraph.co.uk, Vendée French call for revolution massacre to be termed 'genocide', By Henry Samuel in Paris

87   Ibid

88   Ibid

89   Ibid

90   FrontPage Magazine, Turkey's Dark Past, By Gamaliel Isaac, Monday Nov. 22 2004, The Sword and The Prophet, By Serge Trifkovic

91   Ibid, The Smyrna Affair, By Marjorie Housepian

92   Why Robespierre Chose Terror, By John Kekes, City Journal, Wednesday April 19 2006

93   New University, Students Remember the Armenian Genocide, by Florin Yousefian Volume 37, Issue 25 | Apr 26 2004

94   Witnesess To The Armenian Genocide, Excerpted from her memoir, taped recorded in June 1972

95   Why Robespierre Chose Terror, By John Kekes, City Journal, Wednesday April 19th, 2006

96   Why Robespierre Chose Terror, By John Kekes, City Journal, Wednesday April 19 2006

97   Ibid

98   Vásquez, Kazstelia. "Cristeros Became Mexican Martyrs 1926-1929." Borderlands 21 (2002-2003): 14. Borderlands. EPCC Libraries, http://www.epcc.edu/nwlibrary/borderlands

99   New Advent, Catholic Encyclopedia, French Revolution

100   Life, Liberty, Fraternity, Religion: The Cult Of The Supreme Being, La Convention nationale, réimpression faite textuellement sur le moniteur original, vol. 21 (Paris, 1842), 683–84 (from the Gazette nationale, no. 262, 22 Prairial, an II [10 June 1794])

101   Why Robespierre Chose Terror, By John Kekes, City Journal Wednesday, April 19, 2006, Norman Hampson

102   Surah al-Anfal 73

103   Qur'an 5:33

104   Prophet of Doom, Craig Winn, Chapter 21 – Blood and Booty, quoted from Tabari

105   For The Soul of The People, By Victoria Barnett, The Omens, Nationalism, Nazism, and The Churches: The Early Periods, pp. 30

106   From The Fidelity Archives - Published From 1982-96, Operation Parricide: Sade, Robespierre & The French Revolution, By Erik von Kuehnelt-Leddihn, History of Jacobinism by Abbe Barruel

107   Public Interest, no. 145 (Fall 200)

108   Latreille, A. FRENCH REVOLUTION, New Catholic Encyclopedia v. 5, pp. 972-973 (Second Ed. 2002 Thompson/Gale) ISBN 0-7876-4004-2, SPIELVOGEL, JacksonWestern Civilization: Combined Volume pp. 549, 2005 Thomson Wadsworth, Tallet, Frank Religion, Society and Politics in France Since 1789 pp. 1, 1991 Continuum International Publishing

109   Islamic Faith and the Problem with Pluralism, by Majid Nurcholish, Oxford Islamic Studies Online

110   The White House, Office Of The Press Secretary, June 2nd, 2009

111   Turkey's Dark Past, By Gamaliel Isaac, Monday Nov. 22 2004, 'The Rape of northern Cyprus', 5.6.1976

112   Cristero Rebellion: part 1 - toward the abyss by Jim Tuck, 1: Toward the abyss

113   ACLU, ACLU Asks U.S. Supreme Court to Review Iowa's Sex Offender Residency Restriction (9/29/2005)

114   Human Nature and the French Revolution: From the Enlightenment to the Napoleonic Code, 13 August 1793, Archives parlemantaires, 1/72/126/1

115   18th floreal Year II, Archives parlementaires, 1/82/138/2. From Human Nature and the French Revolution: From the Enlightenment to the Napoleonic Code, 13 August 1793, pp. 107

116   Ibid, 13 August 1793, Archives parlementaires, 1/72/126/2

117   Ibid, 22nd frimaire Year II, 12 December 1793: Moniteur no. 84, 24th frimaire, 14 December, 339/2

118   Ibid, To the convention, 18 December 1792: J. Guillaume, Proces-verbaux ducomite d'instruction publiqu, Paris, vol.. 1, 196

119   Hitler Said It Best, By Linda Schrock Taylor

120   Standing For Liberty: Marriage, Virtue, and the Political State, By Allen Carlson Ph.D, Koonz, Mothers in the Fatherland, pp. 408.

121   Into The Den of Infidels, How I came to Know God, pp. 79-80, By Paul

122   Ibid, Friedrich Engels, The Origin of the Family, Private Property and the State (Chicago: Charles H. Kerr & Co., 1902 [1884])

123   Ibid, Alexandra Kollontai, "Communism and the Family," Komunistka (No. 2, 1920)

124   Ibid, Kollontai, "Communism and the Family," pp. 9.

125   Ibid, Kollontai, "Communism and the Family." pp. 8, 10

126   Liberal Fascism, By Jonah Goldberg, Woodrow Wilson and the Birth of Liberal Fascism, page 88, Michael McGerr, A Fierce Discontent: The Rise and Fall of the Progressive Movement in America, 1870-1920 (New York: Free Press, 2003), pp. 66, 59

127   The Philosophy Of History, By Charles Hegel, Chapter II, Mohamadism

128   Ibid

129   The Philosophy of History By Hegel, 1956 Dover edition of Hegel's The Philosophy of History, part 4, section 2, chapter 3: "The Eclairissement and Revolution". Hegel on the state, 258

130   Sahih Muslim, Book 31:, Book 031, Number 5940

131   The Islamic Foundation in UK, Towards Understanding the Qur'ân . Also see Tafheem.net, Islamicstudies.info, Zawaj.com, Editorials, Brotherhood - The Basis of Islamic Society, By M. Adil Salahy, The Muslim December-January 1975/6

132   BBC News, 'Jihad' magazine for women on web, By Sebastian Usher, Al-Khansa

133   From The Philosophy of Right (addition to s. 258), by Hegel 1821

134   Jihad Watch, April 19, 2005, Sina: Is Political Islam Fascism? Iran Zamin News Agency

135   Ibid

136   Ibid

137   Sayyid Qutb's Milestones, Elmer Swenson Last Updated: 6-27-2005, FromPage 26-7

138   abc NEWS, Domestic Spying Lawsuits Face Uphill Battle, By JOHN COCHRAN, Jan. 17, 2006

139   Ibid

140   Inspired from G.K. Chesterton, ILN 9/11/09

141   See Liberal Fascism by Jonah Goldberg

142   Liberal Fascism, By Jonah Goldberg, Woodrow Wilson and the Birth of Liberal

       Fascism, pp. 86

143   Ibid

144   Liberal Fascism, By Jonah Goldberg, Woodrow Wilson and the Birth of Liberal Fascism, pp. 88, John G. West, Darwin's Conservatives: The Misguided Quest (Seattle: Discovery Institute, 2006), pp. 61

145   Ibid

146   Woodrow Wilson, The Constitutional Government of the United States (New York: Columbia University Press, [1908] 1961), pp. 56-57

147   RenewAmerica, Slouching towards a "living Constitution", By David N. Bass, November 22, 2003

148   Ibid

149   Ibid, Quoted from John Dewey, The Public and its Problems, 1927, pg 34

150   Ibid

151   The Enquirer, The Constitution: A living document? Looking
        beyond the text a matter for debate By Ray Cooklis Enquirer staff
        writer, Sunday, September 12, 2004

152   Liberal Fascism, By Jonah Goldberg, Woodrow Wilson and the
        Birth of Liberal Fascism, Woodrow Wilson, Leaders of Men, ed. T.H.
        Vail Motter (Princeton, N.J.: Princeton University Press, 1952),
        pp. 20, 25-26

153   The Antichrist, By Friedrich Nietzsche, pp. 59-60

154   A Modern Utopia, By H.G. Wells, Chapter 9 The Samurai, Section 1

155   Wells, ref. 21, pp. 163

156   Maxims For Revolutionists, By G.B. Shaw, Property

157   The American Journal of Sociology, Volume X; July, 1904; Number 1

158   From John Lennon's Mind Games Album

159   Secret Germnay: Stefan George and His Cricle, By Robert Edward
        Norton, Quoted From Steiner

160   Secret Germany: Stefan George and his circle By Robert Edward
        Norton, The Jung Cult: Origins of a Charismatic Movement, By
        Richard Noll,p. 166-172.; Germany at the fin de siècle: culture,
        politics, and ideas, By Suzanne L. Marchand, David F. Lindenfeld,
        The Myth of Matriarchal Prehistory, Cynthia Eller, esp. pp. 33-34

161   The Aquarian Age, By Elsa M. Glover, X. Universal Friendship,
        Heindel, Max. The Rosicrucian Cosmo-Conception Oceanside,
        California: The Rosicrucian Fellowship, 1973

162   The Constitution of Islamic Republic of Iran. Iranchamber.com

163   Syed Akbar Kamal: Interview With Adnan Oktar Wednesday, 10
        June 2009, 12:13 pm Opinion: Syed Akbar Kamal*

164   Why the Turkish-Islamic Union Is Necessary, By Harun Yahya

165   Ibn Kathir, The Signs Before the Day of Judgement (London, Dar
        Al-Taqwa, 1991), pp. 18

166   Holiest wars By Timothy R. Furnish. pp. 87

167   Kabbani, The Approach to Armageddon, an Islamic Perspective.
        pp. 228

168   Ibn Maja, Kitab al-Fitan #4084 as quoted by Kabbani, pp. 231

169   Sunan Abu Dawud, Narrated by Umm Salamah, Ummul Mu'minin

170   Daily life during the Holocaust By Eve Nussbaum Soumerai, Carol D. Schulz

171   Gardner, ref. 19, pp. x

172   Gardner, ref. 19, pp. x

173   Journal of the American Society for Information Science 50 (May 15, 1999): 557-579, H.G. Wells's Idea of a World Brain: A Critical Re-Assessment, By W. Boyd Rayward, School of Information, Library and Archive Studies, University of New South Wales, A Modern Utopia (Wells 1905)

174   Wells, 1905, pp. 36

175   Ibid, Shape of Things to Come, By H.G. Wells, pp. 419

176   Wells, 1933, pp. 419-20

177   Ibid, pp. 71

178   Ibid, pp. 35

179   Ibid, pp. 85

180   Ibid, pp. 62

181   Herbert Hoover. The NRA. Reply to Press Inquiry, Palo Alto. May 15, 1935

182   Architects of Conspiracy by William P. Hoar, pp. 127

183   Sheldon Richman, Fascism, From The Concise Encyclopedia of Economics. 1993, 2002

PART TWO

1   Islam Watch, Ash Shifa, pp. 36 Chapter 6 Islamic Black Magic (Voodoo), By Abul Kasem, Ash Shifa, pp. 36

2   Ibid

3   Criminal Gangs and the Occult, By Richard Valdemar

4   Ibid*

5   Muslim graves desecrated in French WW1 cemetery, From Reuters

6   Telegraph.co.uk, Christian graves desecrated in the West Bank, Published: 1:15AM BST 25 May 2009

7   Arutz Sheva, Shut Down Orient House By Michael Freund, from the February 20 Jerusalem Post

8   November 17, 2007, The American Thinker, The Nazis and Christianity, By Bruce Walker

9   Dhimmi Watch, Church desecrated in Switzerland, November 18, 2006

10   aftenposten.no, Police nab 'The Count' after he fled jail, By Berglund*

11   Michael Moynihan, Lords of Chaos, pp. 88; quoted in: M. Gardell, Gods of the Blood, pp. 306

12   quoted after M. Gardell, Gods of the Blood, pp. 306, 307. Translation by M. Gardell

13   BURZUM, Interview carried out and written up by Rainer, http://www.mourningtheancient.com/burzum.htm

14   An overview made by Pierre BarthŽlemy (Les Vikings, Paris, 1988) of attacks made by the Vikings in the period 795 - 1098*

15   Qur'ân 114: 1-5

16   Prose Edda/Gylfaginning (The Fooling Of Gylfe) by Sturluson, Snorri, 13th century Edda, in English. Accessed Apr. 16, 2007 Gylfaginning in Old Norse Accessed Apr. 16, 2007. Marshall Jones Company (1930). Mythology of All Races Series, Volume 2 Eddic, Great Britain: Marshall Jones Company, 1930, pp. 220-221

17   Joseph Smith's First Vision, The First Vision, JSH 1:15-20

18   Pacific Lutheran University, Aztec Cannibalism by Whitney Arnold

19   LiveScience, Grisly Sacrifices Found in Pyramid of the Moon, By LiveScience Staff, posted: 02 December 2004 04:40 pm ET

20   A New Dreyfus Affair By: Joanna Chandler, FrontPageMagazine.com | Wednesday, August 29, 2007

21   The Baburnam—Memoirs of Babur, Prince and Emperor, translated and edited by Wheeler M. Thacktson, Oxford University Press, 1996, pp. 173, 174, 246, 266, 393, 394, 407

22   Ibid

23   Chopping Heads by Emir Taheri, New York Post, May 14th, 2004

24   Ibid

25   Ibid

26   Ibid

27   CBS News, Saudi Arabia's Beheading Culture, June 27th, 2004

28   At-Tabari, Vol XI, The Challenge to the Empires, In Series: The History of at-Tabari, (Ta'rikh al-rasul wa'l-muluk), Translated by K.Y. Blankenship, SUNY series in Near Eastern Studies, Bibliotheca Persica, State University of New York Press, Albany New York, 1993, pp. 44-45

29   op. ci t., al-Tabari, XI, pp. 24.

30   Ibid

31   The Crusaders by Carol Hillendbrand. pp. 237. From Holt, The Age of the Crusades. pp. 97

32   Thomas Madden, The New Concise History of the Crusades, Rowman & Littlefield, 2005. pp. 181-182.

33   Díaz del Castillo [c.1568] (1992, pp. 579). In the original Spanish: "[...] comer carne humana, así como nosotros traemos vaca de las carnicerías, y tenían

34   Excerpt translated from Muñoz Camargo [c.1585] (1947, pp. 153). In the original Spanish: "Ansí había carnicerías públicas de carne humana, como si

35   How Christianity Changed The World, By Alvin I. Schmidt, The Sanctification of Human Life, pp. 66, Richard Townsend, The Aztecs (London: Hudson and Hudson, 1992), 100

36   Hernando Cortes, Letters from Mexico, trans. and ed. Anthony Pagden (New Haven: Yale University, 1986), 35

37   Bernal Diaz del Catillo, The Conquest of New Spain, trans.. J.M. Cohen (New York: Penguin Books, 1963), 387

38   Bernal Diaz del Catillo, The True History of the Conquest of Mexico, trans. Maurice Keating (New York: National Travel Club, 1938), 87

39   Edward Ryan, The History of the Effects of Religion on Mankind: In Countries Ancient and Modern, Barbarous and Civilized (Dublin: T.M. Bates, 1802), 267

40   The God Delusion, By Richard Dawkins, pp. 268-269

41   UNESCO Courier, Nov, 1991 by Bahgat Elnadi, Adel Rifaat. See also False Dawn by Lee Penn. P. 240.

42   Sunday Herals, August 10th, 2009

43   Human Sacrifice in Aztec Culture Bloody Rituals Played a Key Role in Mesoamerican Religion, Terry Long, Nicholson, Henry B. (1971). (in) Handbook of Middle American Indians. University of Texas Press. pp. 402.

44   Frederic Farrar, The Early Days of Christianity (New York: A.L. Burt Publishers, 1882), 71

45   How Christianity Changed The World, By Alvin I. Schmidt, The Sanctification of Human Life, pp. 48, From Moralia 2.171 D

46   De Ira 1.15

47   How Christianity Changed The World, By Alvin I. Schmidt, The Sanctification of Human Life, pp. 49, From De Legibus 3.8

48   Jack Lindsay, The Ancient World (New York: G.P Putnam's Sons, 1968), 168

49   James S. Dennis, Social Evils of the Non-Christian World (New York: Flemming H. Revell, 1898), 69-70

50   P. A. Talbot, Southern Nigeria, Clarendon Press, 1926 (3 vols.)

51   James S. Dennis, Social Evils of the Non-Christian World (New York: Flemming H. Revell, 1898), pp. 135

52   Thomas Cahill, "Ending Human Sacrifice," Christian History 60 (1998): 16

53   The Devil's Chaplain: Richard Dawkins on Christianity by Albert Mohler, Author, Speaker, President of the Southern Baptist Theological Seminary

54   Ibid

55   Ibid

56   Deconstructing Dawkins, Alister McGrath's Challenge of Famous Atheist Is Bracing But Does Not Go Far Enough By: Logan Paul Gage, Christianity Today, February 1, 2008

57   Ibid

58 Herbert Spencer: Social Darwinism in Education, Foundations of Education, Ornstein & Levine, Educational Philosophy, Edward J. Power, Educational Ideologies, William F. O'Neill, Herbert Spencer on Education, Andreas M. Kazamias, Prepared by Julie Ann Keb

59 The Man Versus The State, Postscript, By Herbert Spencer, 1884

60 The Secret Life of a Satanist, pg 214

61 Islam And Evolution. From Al-Bab, An Open Door To The Muslim World. Quote from Farida Faouzia Charfi, a science professor at the University of Tunis

62 Creationism: Science and Faith in Schools, Wednesday 7 January 2004, guardian.co.uk

63 From Georges Lemaitre, 'La formation des nebuleuses dans l'univers en expansion', Comptes Rendus (1933), 196, 903-4. Trans. Helge Kragh, Cosmology and Controversy: The Historical Development of Two Theories of the Universe (1996), 52

64 'The Primeval atom Hypothesis and the Problem of Clusters of Galaxies', in R. Stoops (ed.), La Structure et l'Evolution de l'Univers (1958), 1-32. Trans. Helge Kragh, Cosmology and Controversy: The Historical Development of Two Theories of the Universe (1996), 60

65 From G.K. Chesterton, Chapter 19, What I Saw In America, 1922

66 Criminal Gangs and the Occult, By Richard Valdemar

67 Militant Islam Monitor, Sulejman Talovic's Salt Lake City Murder Spree Was An Act Of Jihad

68 Criminal Gangs and the Occult, By Richard Valdemar

69 Drugs for guns: how the Afghan heroin trade is fuelling the Taliban insurgency, By Jerome Starkey in Kunduz, Tuesday, 29 April 2008

70 Corydon, pp58-59, 332-333; letter filed as evidence in Church of Scientology v. Gerald Armstrong, 1984, Los Angeles Superior Court, Case No. C420153., Atack, part 4, ch. 1, "Scientology at Sea."

71 Rules for Radicals by Saul Alinskey, opening page

72   Obama's Civilian National Security Force ("Senator Obama was nearly 17 minutes into his July 2 speech... in Colorado Springs, Colorado when he deviated from his pre-released script" and made this statement without the teleprompter.")

73   Ibid

74   The Satanic Bible, pg 104-105

75   Bio-chem suits found in London mosque, Posted: January 26, 2003, 3:21 pm Eastern, © 2009 WorldNetDaily.com

76   The Law is for All, pg 131

77   From Obsession, by Waynne Coping

78   The Confessions of Aleister Crowley, Penguin, pg 539

79   Nietzsche's Superman, By Anna Knowles, Towards the Ubermensch, also Course Reading: Overman

80   L Ron Hubbard and Jesus Christ, L. Ron Hubbard, Scientology: A History of Man, pp. 38

81   Scientology, Auditing, The State of Operating Thetan.

82   Horrible Truths for Scientologists: Body Thetans, By Roland Rashleigh-Berry, Body Thetans

83   Nietzsche's idea of an overman and life from his point of view, The Cambridge Companion to Nietzsche, ed. B.Magnus and K.M. Higgins, Cambridge University Press, 1990, Nietzsche, Life As Literature, Alexander Nehamas, Havard University Press, 1994, Nietzsche for Beginners, M.Sautet, Writers and readers, 1990, Nietzsche:A Critical Reader, Philosophy II lecture handouts.

84   Court Tv, Crime Library, Criminal Minds and Methods, Nietzsche and Hitler

85   Friedrich Nietzsche's Influence on Hitler's Mein Kampf, By Michael Kalish, June 2004, The Genealogy of Morals (III 14) By Friedrick Nietzsche.

86   Margaret Sanger. Woman, Morality, and Birth Control. New York: New York Publishing Company, 1922. pp. 12.

87   Margaret Sanger's December 19, 1939 letter to Dr. Clarence Gamble, 255 Adams Street, Milton, Massachusetts. Original source: Sophia Smith Collection, Smith College, North Hampton, Massachusetts. Also described in Linda Gordon's Woman's Body, Woman's Right: A Social History of Birth Control in America. New York: Grossman Publishers, 1976.

88   Margaret Sanger, April 1933 Birth Control Review.

89   Margaret Sanger. "The Eugenic Value of Birth Control Propaganda." Birth Control Review, October 1921, page 5

90   Introduction to Islam, Some of The Human Qualities Allah Almighty Loves, Strength, Muslim narrated

91   Islam's Green, Travels, thoughts, talks of Abdur-Raheem Green, The toughness of Shamyl

92   Khomeini's speech on the day of celebration of the birth of Muhammad: 1981

93   The Book of The Law, Liber AL vel Legis, sub figura CCXX, as delivered by XCIII = 418 to DCLXVI, Chapter II, line 21

94   Recreation and Fitness in Islam, By Justin Ducote.

95   Recreation and Fitness in Islam, By Justin Ducote

96   Bukhari, Volume 1, Book 5, Number 268: "Prophet was given the strength (sexual) of thirty men"

97   Volume 1, Book 5, Number 268: "The Prophet used to visit all his wives in a round, during the day and night and they were eleven in number. Prophet was given the strength of thirty (men)."

98   Do What Thou Wilt by L. Sutin, pg 393

PART THREE

1   Charles Oliver, "Don't Put Animal Rights Above Humans," USA Today, June 11, 1990, pp. 10A

2   Al-Bukhari I: 331

3   Al gore, Earth In The Balance, pp. 260

4   Malaysia Wildlands Project, Islamic Guidance For Environment Protection, Cleanliness and Beaufication

5   Mt. Rasur, The Legend and The Dreams, By Robert Muller, The Bench Of Dreams, Idea 447

6   Paradise Earth, By Robert Muller, Edited By Douglas Gillies

7   Earth Day Got You Down? By Mark Hartwig

8   Ishaq: 489

9   In defense of animals, By Peter Singer, pp. 74

10   Ibid

11   Ibid.

12   Reporter Online, Peter Singer: A More Sustainable World, by Maximiliano Herrera

13   Dictionary of ethics, theology, and society, By Paul A. B. Clarke, Andrew Linzey, Ecological Theology, pp. 263, Singer 1987: 7 Also, "Match the Quotes," Resource Roundup, March 2002, page 8. Also, "Christian Pulpits Invaded," Insider's Report, 1998, page 4. Hardcopy: Copy of the "Christian Pulpits Invaded" article.

14   Fundamentalist Islam, Christianity and tolerance, Posted: October 16, 2001 1:00 am Eastern, By David Limbaugh, © 2009 Creators Syndicate, Inc.*

15   Religion of Peace? By Robert Spencer, Wars of Religion, pp. 16

16   Ibid, American Fascists: The Christian Right and the War On America, By Chris Hedges, pp. 24

17   RICK WARREN - FUNDAMENTALIST OR FINAGLER? By Paul Proctor, By Paul Proctor March 15, 2006, NewsWithViews.com, Quoted From The Philadelphia Enquirer

18   Ibid

19   Liberal Fascism, The New Age: We're All Fascists Now, pp. 386

20   MODERN LEFTISM AS RECYCLED FASCISM By: John J. Ray, M.A.; Ph.D.

21   Syed Abul Ala Maududi, "Jihad in Islam," Address at the Town Hall, Lahore, April 13, 1939. Reprinted at http://host06.ipowerweb.com/~ymofmdc/books/jihadinislam

22   Ibid

23   The Muqqadimah, In Introduction to History, by Ibin Khaldun. pp. 183, Translated and Introduced by Franz Rosenthal. Princeton University Press

24   Jurisprudence in Muhammad's Biography, Dr. Muhammad Sa'id Ramadan Al-Buti. pp. 134, 7th edition)"

25   Narrated by Al-Miqaddam Ibn Ma'di Karib, Tirmidhi and Ibin Maajah

26   Narrated by Shaddaad Ibn Al-Haad

27   A Modern Utopia, By H.G. Wells, Chapter 9 The Samurai Section 1

28   The New York Times, Why Sharia? By Noah Feldman

29   Evariste Levi—Provencal, Histoire de l'Espagne Musulmane, Paris, 1950, Vol. 1; and Dufourcq, Europe Medievale sous Domination Arabe, see especially chapter 1, 'Les Jours de Razzia et d'Invasion'

30   The New York Times, Why Sharia? By Noah Feldman

31   Archbishop's Lecture - Civil and Religious Law in England: a Religious Perspective Thursday 07 February 2008

32   Close. "Transcript: Rowan Williams interview | World news | guardian.co.uk, Tuesday 21 March 2006 09.13 GMT

33   NewsBusters, Sean Penn: Hugo Chavez Is 'Much More Positive' for Venezuela Than Negative, By Lynn Davidson

34   The Mullahs' Religious Left Allies, By Mark D. Tooley FrontPageMagazine.com Wednesday, July 19, 2006

35   Rick Warren denies making statements to Syria news, By Spero News*

36   Liberal Fascism, Franklin Roosevelt's Fascist New Deal, pp. 134, By Jonah Goldberg

37   The History of Economic Thought Website, Utopians and Socialists, Thomas Carlyle

38   Our Fathers' Godsaga, By Victor Rydberg, ON HEROES, HERO-WORSHIP, AND THE HEROIC IN HISTORY, LECTURE II. THE HERO AS PROPHET. MAHOMET: ISLAM. [May 8, 1840.], By Thomas Carlyle

39   Thomas Carlyle, On Heroes, Hero-Worship, & The Heroic In History, 1993, University Of California Press, pp. 38

40   The Confessions of Aleister Crowley, 48, {388}

41   Ibid

42   The Confessions of Aleister Crowley, 61, {522), The whole
       statement was "With these weapons the men cut themselves on the
       head (very rarely elsewhere) until the blood was streaming from
       their scalps on every side. They were, of course, quite unconscious
       of any pain, and those of them who were actually blinded by the
       blood were yet able to see...But I was hard put to it to refrain from
       dashing down my turban, leaping into the ring with a howl of
       "Allahu akbar!" getting hold of an axe and joining in the general
       festivity. It literally took away one's breath. The only way I can
       express it is that one breathed with one's heart instead of with
       one's lungs. I had gotten into not dissimilar states while doing
       Pranayama, but those had been passive, and this was a — no,
       active is a pitifully inadequate word — I felt myself vibrating with
       the energy of the universe. It was as if I had become conscious of
       atomic energy or of the force of gravitation, understood positively
       and not merely as the inhibition to rising from the ground. I do not
       know how long I stood there holding myself in, but judging from
       subsequent calculations it must have been over an hour: the sense
       of time had entirely disappeared. But I became suddenly aware of
       a terrific reaction; I felt that I had missed my chance by not letting
       myself go and perhaps been killed for my pains. At the same time I
       was seized with a sudden sense of alarm. I felt myself to be outside
       the spiritual circle. I was sure that someone would discover me
       and a swift shudder passed through me as I apprehended my
       danger. Fortunately, I had sufficient presence of mind to resume
       my mantra and melt away from the multitude as silently as I had
       descended upon it."

43   Existential Space, Thursday, October 20, 2005, Alexis Carrel and
       Sayyid Qutb, From 2003 article published by Die Zeit by Frankfurt
       historian, Rudolph Walther, entitled "The Strange Teachings of
       Doctor Carrel: How a French Catholic doctor became a spiritual
       forefather of the radical Islamists"

44   Quoted in Reggiani, pp. 339

45   Man, the Unknown, By Alexis Carrel, pp. 27 and 28

46   Milestones, By Sayyed Qutb, pp. 21

47   Existential Space, Thursday, October 20, 2005, Alexis Carrel and Sayyid Qutb, From 2003 article published by Die Zeit by Frankfurt historian, Rudolph Walther, entitled "The Strange Teachings of Doctor Carrel: How a French Catholic doctor became a spiritual forefather of the radical Islamists."

48   Sayyid Qutb's Milestones, Elmer Swenson, Last Updated: 6-27-2005, From pp. 11 and 139

49   CNS News, Islamic Finance System 'Can Replace Capitalism' Monday October 13, 2008, By Patrick Goodenough, International Editor, Quoted from Qatar's Gulf Times Qaradawi's words would have made Che Guevara fire his gun in the air. Why wouldn't he? Guevara was a terrorist like Zarqawi and Shamil Basayev, they hated capitalism and America calling it "the enemy of humanity." On The Media, From NPR, Guerilla Marketing, November 02, 2007, [MUSIC UP AND UNDER] *

50   Yesterday's Jihadists By: Chuck Morse FrontPageMagazine.com Wednesday, September 07, 2005

51   THE FUNDAMENTAL LAW OF LAND SOCIALIZATION, Decree of the Central Executive Committee, February 19, 1918

52   Islam: Truth or Myth? Pact of Umar, (probably drafted during the time of Umar b. Abd al Aziz who ruled 717- 720 AD) from Al-Turtushi, Siraj al-Muluk, pp. 229-23

53   Al-Ghazali (d. 1111). Kitab al-Wagiz fi fiqh madhab al-imam al-Safi'i, Beirut, 1979, pp. 186, 190-91; 199-200; 202-203. [English translation by Dr. Michael Schub.]

54   Scheiber, A. "The Origins of Obadyah, the Norman Proselyte" Journal of Jewish Studies (Oxford), Vol. 5, 1954, pp. 37. Obadyah the Proselyte was born in Oppido (Lucano, southern Italy). He became a priest, and later converted to Judaism around 1102 A.D., living in Constantinople, Baghdad, Aleppo, and Egypt *

55   Jadunath Sarkar, History of Aurangzib, Vol. III- Northern India, 1658-1681, Chapter XXXIV, "The Islamic State Church in India", excerpts from pp. 283-297

56   Digest of Islamic Law by N. Baillie. pp. 367. Premier Book House, Pakistan.

57   Antoine Fattal, Let Statut Legal de Musulmans en Pays' d'Islam, Beirut, 1958; pp. 369, 372

58   American Thinker, December 30, 2005, 'Democrats' For Jihad and Jizya, By Andrew G. Bostom

59   Islam's Global War against Christianity, By Patrick Poole*

60   The black book of communism, By Stéphane Courtois, Mark Kramer, Jonathan Murphy, Published by Harvard University Press, 1999*

61   Ibid Their rights were stripped away just like the Christians in Spain.

62   Againts The Grain, Saturday, September 01, 2007, Revolutionary Intellectuals, Quoted from David Frum's Diary, Saturday, August 25, 2007, David's Bookshelf 39

63   The Boston Globe, The philosopher and the ayatollah, By Wesley Yang | June 12, 2005

64   The western roots of Islamism, Guest Writer (Terra, Sol) Middle East & Islamic*

65   Foucault and the Iranian Revolution: gender and the seductions of Islamism, By Janet Afary, Kevin Anderson, Michel Foucault, Published by University of Chicago Press, 2005, Shariati 1970, 154

66   Michel Foucault, Theorist Web Project, CCJ 5606 Fall 2000, Scott McGaha, Maier-Katkin, 2000

67   Michel Foucault (1996) The simplest of pleasures' in Foucault Live (Interviews, 1961-1984), New York: Semiotext(e), pp. 295-6. Translation modified. French original 1979

68   Liberal Fascism, By Jonah Goldberg, Chapter 2 Adolf Hitler: Man of the Left, pp. 59-60, From Lukacs, The Hitler of History (New York: Vintage, 1997), pp. 84

69   MilitantIslamMonitor.org, Heinrich Himmler's Remarkable Admiration For Islam: "It Promises Beautiful Women In Heaven" May 26, 2009 Heinrich Himmler's Remarkable Admiration For Islam: "It Promises Beautiful Women In Heaven", By EMERSON VERMAAT, Quoted by Peter Longerich who recently published a 1035-page study on Himmler quoting, inter alia, from documents in the German Federal Archives in Berlin ("Bundesarchiv Berlin")

70   Ibid: "Mohammed knew that most people are terribly cowardly and stupid. That is why he promised two beautiful women to every courageous warrior who dies in battle. This is the kind of language a soldier understands. When he believes that he will be welcomed in this manner in the afterlife, he will be willing to give his life, he will be enthusiastic about going to battle and not fear death. You may call this primitive and you may laugh about it, but it is based on deeper wisdom. A religion must speak a man's language."

71   J.B. Bury, A History of the Later Roman Empire (New York: American Book Company [1889] 1958), 575

72   Stanford Encyclopedia of Philosophy, Suicide, First published Tue May 18, 2004; substantive revision Tue Jul 29, 2008, 2.1 Ancient and Classical Views of Suicide, Cicero, III, 60—61

73   Stanford Encyclopedia of Philosophy, Suicide, First published Tue May 18, 2004; substantive revision Tue Jul 29, 2008, 2.3 The Enlightenment and Modern Developments, Lieberman 2003

74   Ibid

75   Green Left Online, Jakarta bombing: symptom of poverty, war and desperation, 17 November 1993, By Max Lane

76   MEMRI, Debating the Religious, Political, and Moral Legitimacy of Suicide Bombings: Part IV Debating the Religious, Political, and Moral Legitimacy of Suicide Bombings: Part IV By By Yotam Feldner, From Editorial of Al-Risala

77   An excerpt from Foucault and the Iranian Revolution Gender and the Seductions of Islamism, By Janet Afary and Kevin B. Anderson, What Are the Iranians Dreaming About? By Michel Foucault

78   The Boston Globe, The philosopher and the ayatollah, By Wesley Yang June 12, 2005

79   From an review of the Egyptian press in the London daily Al-Quds
      Al-Arabi, the veteran Egyptian journalist Hasanain Kurum
      explained that Sheikh Tantawi*

80   USA Today, June 26th, 2001

81   Jerusalem Post, 9, 6, 2001

82   Malik 362:1221

83   The Evidence Smoke, 44:54 Shakir, M.H., "The Qur'ân ". Tahrike
      Tarsile Qur'an, Inc, Elmhurst N.Y, 1993

84   The Beneficent, 55:54-58 Dawood, N.J., "The Koran", Penguin,
      London, England, 1995

85   D&C, Section 82: 17-19

86   Dachau Scrapbook, The 25 Points of Hitler's Nazi Party

87   The Misery of Boots, By H.G. Wells, pp. 35

88   Ibid, pp. 38-89

89   William Godwin, Political Justice, Book III Principles of
      Government, Chapter IV Of Political Authority

90   Book 14, Number 2495: Narrated Sahl ibn al-Hanzaliyyah

91   Sahih Muslim, 1731

92   From the Wagjiz, 1101 A.D, quoted by Andrew Bostom, Islamic
      Holy War and the Fate of non-Muslims. See also FrontPage
      Magazine, Jamie Glazov, Friday 13, 2004

93   Bassam Tibi, War and Peace in Islam, in Terry Nardin, ed., The
      Ethics of War and Peace: Religious and Secular Perspectives,
      Princeton, NJ: Princeton University Press, 1996, pp. 130

94   Ibid

95   Al-Hidayah, Mishkat II. pp. 406

96   Sahih Hakim Mustadrak, related by Abu Sa'id al_Khudri (4:557
      and 558), as quoted by Kabbani pp. 233. Paving The Way For The
      Coming Mahdi

97   AlTabarani, Related by Abu Hurayra, as quoted by Izzat and Arif.
      pp. 9

PART FOUR

1   Narrated by ibn Abbas also by Tirmidhi: "The messenger of Allah concerning the stone said: 'Allah will bring it forth on the day of resurrection, and it will have two eyes with which it will see and a tongue with which it will speak, and it will testify in favor of those who touched it sincerity."

2   The Inner Sanctum, Pagan Spells and Rituals, Eclectic Circle Ceremony for Solitaries

3   Diverse Druids, By Robert Baird, Published by The Invisible College Press, LLC, 2003, pp. 36

4   D&C, Section 88: 7,8,9

5   Al Gore, Earth in the Balance. Ecology and the Human Spirit (New York: Houghton Mifflin Company, 1992), 265

6   Ibid. pp. 258-259

7   Ibid. pp. 261

8   Ibid

9   Expositor's Bible Commentary, Isaiah 14, General Editor Frank Gaebelein, Zondervan

10   Allah, His Heritage In Paganism, Langdon, Stephen H, The Mythology of All Races, Vol V, Archeological Institute of America, Boston, 1931, pg. 5-19

11   On the authority of Talhah ibn `Ubaydullah, [Narrated by Tirmidhi, who said it is a good (hasan) hadith

12   Ibn Warraq. Why I am not a Muslim

13   Finn Rasmussen, The Ugaritic Text, Early Letter Names

14   Ten Days of Dawn, The Terrorism Research Center, February 1, 1979, Khomeini Returns From Exile Called the Beginning of the Ten Days of Dawn, commemorating the ten days of unrest which ended with Khomeini taking power on February 11 (the Day of Victory)

15   The Myth of Quetzalcoatl, By Enrique Florescano, Raúl Velázquez, Lysa Hochroth, Codex Vaticano Latino, 3738

16   Popul Vuh, Part 3, Chapter 3, Meta Religion

17   The Primitive Aryans of America, by Thomas Stewart Denison, pp. 162, 116* Mexican Linguistics including Nauatl or Mexican in Aryan Phonolog, A Mexican Aryan Comparative Vocabulary. pp. 85. Also, see NATICK DICTIONARY By James Hammond Trumbull, Bureau of American Ethnology. pp. 76.

18   Encyclopedia Mythica, Tecciztecatl, by Micha F. Lindemans

19   Rig Veda, tr. by Ralph T.H. Griffith, [1896], at sacred-texts.com, HYMN LXV. Dawn., "The radiant Dawns have risen up for glory, in their white splendour like the waves of waters.. She maketh paths all easy, fair to travel, and, rich, hath shown herself benign and friendly. We see that thou art good: far shines thy lustre; thy beams, thy splendours have flown up to heaven. Decking thyself, thou makest bare thy bosom, shining in majesty, thou Goddess Morning. Red are the kine and luminous that bear her the Blessed One who spreadeth through the distance. The foes she chaseth like a valiant archer, like a swift warrior she repelleth darkness. Thy ways are easy on the hills: thou passest Invincible! Self-luminous! through waters. So lofty Goddess with thine ample pathway, Daughter of Heaven, bring wealth to give us comfort. Dawn, bring me wealth: untroubled, with thine oxen thou bearest riches at thy will and pleasure; Thou who, a Goddess, Child of Heaven, hast shown thee lovely through bounty when we called thee early. As the birds fly forth from their restingplaces, so men with store of food rise at thy dawning. Yea, to the liberal mortal who remaineth at home, O Goddess Dawn, much good thou bringest."

20   Delmarre 2003 pp. 291-292

21   Delmarre 2003 pp. 175

22   Oxford University Press, Celtic Mythology, Tarvos Trigaranus

23   Encyclopedia Mythica, Cernunnos, By Dr. Anthony E. Smart

24   The Horned god, Guiley, Rosemary Ellen. The Encyclopedia of Witches and Witchcraft. New York: Facts On File, 1989 [ISBN 0-8160-2268-2] 163-164, Starhawk. The Spiral Dance: A Rebirth of the Ancient Religion of the Great Goddess. [Special 20th Anniversary Edition] New York, Harper SanFrancisco, 1999 [ISBN 0-06-250814-8], DeJonge, Alex. The Life and Times of Grigorii Rasputin. New York, Coward, McCann and Geoghegan, 1982

25 Contenau 248, 292

26 Briffault v3 78

27 Van Netton, Allah Divine or Demonic, pg.... 94

28 St. Clair-Tisdall, Sources Ch.2

29 Josephus, 226, 1987 ed., p 440

30 Yadin Yigal, Hazor, (New York: Random House, 1975), (London: Oxford, 1972), (Jerusalem: Magnes, 1958)

31 Langdon, Stephen H, The Mythology of All Races, Vol V, Archeological Institute of America, Boston, 1931, pg. 5-19 also see Zwemmer, (Ed) The Daughters of Allah, By Winnett, F V, MWJ, Vol. XXX, 1940, pg.. 120-125)

32 Wicca: a guide for the solitary practitioner, By Scott Cunningham, Published by Llewellyn Worldwide, 1989, pp. 10

33 Salat-al -Kusuf: The Prayer of the Eclipse, Usama Abu Zayd, Islam and the solar eclipse, Bukhari.

34 BBC News, Tuesday, 24 August, 1999, 11:53 GMT 12:53 UK, Pagan weddings eclipse hearts

35 Ibid, pp. 13

36 Indo-European poetry and myth, By Martin Litchfield West, RV 6.44.21

37 Encyclopedia Brittanica, Dyaus, in Hinduism (religion): Cosmogony and cosmology

38 Echoes of the Ancient Skies, By Edwin C. Krupp, pp. 65

39 The Aztecs: new perspectives, By Dirk R. Van Tuerenhout Edition: illustrated Published by ABC-CLIO, 2005

40 Dictionary of Ancient Deities By Patricia Turner, Charles Russell Coulter Published by Oxford University Press US, 2001, pp. 427*

41 The Aztecs: new perspectives By Dirk R. Van Tuerenhout Edition: illustrated Published by ABC-CLIO, 2005, P 183

42 The Great Mother ~ sovereignty and wholeness, By Alicia Sherwood M.A., From Aeschylus Fragment 25 in Suhr 1969: 39

43 Heresy, pp. 88, 137

44 Ibid, Meyendorff. Byzantine, pp. 95

45   Tolan. Saracens, pp. 44, fn. 19, pp. 296: "Alain Ducellier. Chretiens d'Orient et Islam au Moyen Age. Armand Colin, Paris, 1996, pp. 161-164; Migne, JP (editor), Patrologiae Graecae Cursus Completes (162 vols.), Paris, 1857-1886, vol. 110:873

46   Meyendorff. Byzantine, pp. 95

47   Histories III:38

48   Ibin Ishaq. Sirat, pp. 88

49   Ibid, Sahas. Heresy, pp. 88-89

50   Sources of the Qur'ān : Zoroastrian and Hindu Beliefs, By W. St. Clair Tisdall, Chapter 5

51   Tishtar Yasht, I, Translated by James Darmesteter, From Sacred Books of the East, American Edition, 1898

52   Wikipedia, Cult Suicide, Solar Temple

53   Herodutus and Mithras: Histories I.. 131, By: M. J. Edwards Corpus Christi College, Oxford 1990, Herodotus 1.131

54   Videvdat 1.28-29

55   COMMEMORATING THE PROPHET'S RAPTURE AND ASCENSION TO HIS LORD, III. The Collated Hadith of Isra' and Mi`raj

56   The Book of Arda Viraf, Transcribed and kindly contributed by Chris Weimer, Translated by Prof. Martin Haug, of the University of Munich, revised from the MS. of a Parsi priest Hoshangji. From The Sacred Books and Early Literature of the East, Volume VII: Ancient Persia, ed. Charles F. Horne, Ph.D., copyright 1917

57   Ibid

58   See Qur'ān 15: 14-18

59   Islam and Astrology

60   Pahlavi Texts, Part I, Chapter I (SBE05), E.W. West, tr. [1880], at sacred-texts.com

61   The Seven Tablets of Creation, by Leonard William King, 1902, The Fifth Tablet

62   Mormon Quotes, David Whitmer, Address To All Believers In Christ, Chapter: 18, pp.: 30-31, Paragraph: 1

63   The Qur'ân and Ahadith on the Concept of Protection and Friendship, By Sam Shamoun, Narrated Abu Huraira, Sahih al-Bukhari, Volume 4, Book 53, Number 392

64   The Seven Evil Spirits, R.C. Thompson, translator, The Devils and Evil Spirits of Babylonia, London 1903: "and night he was dark (i.e., Sin), in the dwelling of his dominion he sat not down, The evil gods, the messengers of Anu, the King, are they, Raising their evil heads, in the night shaking themselves, are they, Evil searching out, are they, From the heaven, like a wind, over the land rush they...the gleaming Sin has been sadly darkened in heaven..."

65   WND, 912

66   The Lotus of the true law homage to all the buddhas and bodhisattvas, Chapter I, Introduction

67   Ibid

68   The Buddha-karita of Asvaghosha - Book XVI, pp. 182, Line 69

69   Remembering Allah the way the Prophet Did, Examples of Thikr by Amr Khaled. Also see The life and religion of Mohammed By Muḥammad Bāqir ibn Muḥammad Taqī Majlisī, James Lyman Merrick.

70   In Praise of the Prophet, Shaikh Farid Ad-Din Attar, Book of God. pp. 424.

71   Ibid

72   LaMar Petersen's book, The Creation of the Book of Mormon: "Lucy [Joseph Smith's mother] provided an even more revealing glimpse into the Smith family's involvement in magical abracadabra and other aspects of folk magic: 'Let not the reader suppose that because I shall pursue another topic for a season that we stopt our labor and went at trying to win the faculty of Abrac [Abraxas], drawing magic circles or soothsaying [sic] to the neglect of all kinds of business. [We] never during our lives suffered one important interest to swallow up every other obligation but whilst we worked with our hands we endeavored to remember [sic] the service of and the welfare of our souls.'" Salt Lake City Messenger, April 1999, #95, Was Joseph Smith a Magician?, LaMar Petersen's new book The Creation of the Book of Mormon. A, Abraxas, overman666.tripod.com/Diction.html*

72 LaMar Petersen's book, The Creation of the Book of Mormon: "Lucy [Joseph Smith's mother] provided an even more revealing glimpse into the Smith family's involvement in magical abracadabra and other aspects of folk magic: 'Let not the reader suppose that because I shall pursue another topic for a season that we stopt our labor and went at trying to win the faculty of Abrac [Abraxas], drawing magic circles or soothsaying [sic] to the neglect of all kinds of business. [We] never during our lives suffered one important interest to swallow up every other obligation but whilst we worked with our hands we endeavored to remember [sic] the service of and the welfare of our souls.'" Salt Lake City Messenger, April 1999, #95, Was Joseph Smith a Magician?, LaMar Petersen's new book The Creation of the Book of Mormon. A, Abraxas, overman666.tripod.com/Diction.html

73 One Nation Under Gods, By Richard Abanes

74 Wikipedia, Seer Stones and The Latter-Day Saints: "For behold, the language which ye shall write I have confounded; wherefore I will cause in my own due time that these stones shall magnify to the eyes of men these things which ye shall write." also see LDS.org, The Scriptures, Ether 3: 24

75 Wikipedia, Scrying, A Symbolic Representation of the Universe: Derived by Doctor John Dee Through the Scrying of Sir Edward Kelly Aleister Crowley, Adrian Axwirthy, Crystal Gazing: Study in the History, Distribution, Theory and Practice of Scrying Theodore Besterman, Scrying for Beginners: Tapping into the Supersensory Powers of Your Subconscious ~Donald Tyson, Crystal Gazing: Its History and Practice with a Discussion on the Evidence for Telepathic Scrying ~Northcote W. Thomas, Andrew Lang, Crystal visions, savage and civilised, The Making of Religion, Chapter V, Longmans, Green, and C°, London, New York and Bombay, 1900, pp. 83-104., Shepard, Leslie A. Encyclopedia of Occultism and Parapsychology. Gale Research, Inc., 16

76 Ibid

77 Allah, His Heritage In Paganism, Zwemmer, Influence of Animism on Islam, pg. 59

78 Bukhari: Verse 6, Book 61, N530

79   Bukhari:V7B71N660: The Hadith continues, "That is the hardest kind of magic as it has such an effect.. One day he said, 'O Aisha, do you know that Allah has instructed me concerning the matter I asked Him about? Two men came to me and one of them sat near my head and the other near my feet. The one asked, 'What is wrong with this man?' 'He is under the effect of magic.' 'Who cast the magic spell on him?' 'Labid, an Arab ally of the Jews and a hypocrite.' 'What material did he use to cast the spell?' 'A comb with hair stuck to it.' 'Where is that comb and hair?' 'In a skin of pollen of a male palm tree kept under a stone in the well of Dharwan.' So the Prophet went to that well and took out those things, saying, 'That was the well shown to me in the dream. Its water looked red and its palms looked like the heads of devils. My companions removed those things.' I said, 'Why didn't you just treat yourself?' He said, 'Allah has cured me, and I don't want to spread evil among my people.'"

80   Allah, His Heritage In Paganism, Alfred Guillaume, Islam, New York: Penguin Books, 1977, pp. 24-25, 37, 56, passim; cf. Michael Harner, The Way of the Shaman, New York: Bantam, 1980

81   Allah, His Heritage In Paganism, Guillaum, Alfred, Islam, New York, Peguin, 1977, pp. 28

82   Ibid, Tabari Vol. 9, page 167, note 1151

83   The Religious Attitude 'and Life in Islam By Duncan Black MacDonald, pg. 56-57

84   Ibin Ishaq:106.

85   Howl, By Allen Ginsberg

86   Howl by Allen Ginsberg TEILITE edition prepared by: Gregory Veen Jack Kerouac had given anecdote of Philip Lamantia's celestial adventure to author in early 1950s. Poet Lamantia in note written for author May 25, 1986, New Orleans, provides this accurate account

87   Crowley 1974, ch. 7

88   Mahendranath, Shri Gurudev (1990), The Scrolls of Mahendranath. Seattle: International Nath Order

89   Muhammad's Suicide Attempts, By Silas, Ibn 'Abbas said regarding the meaning of: 'He it is that Cleaves the daybreak (from the darkness)' (6.96) that Al-Asbah. means the light of the sun

90   Allah, His Heritage in Paganism, Rodwell, J.M., The Koran, New York, 1977, pp. 14

91   Ibid, Volume 5, Book 58, Number 227: Narrated Abbas bin Malik

92   Shamanism. (2009). In Encyclopædia Britannica.. Retrieved June 14, 2009, from Encyclopædia Britannica Online

93   Wikipedia, Joseph Smith

94   Encyclopedia of Mormonism, Vol. 1, First Vision, Backman, Milton V., Jr. Joseph Smith's First Vision. Salt Lake City, 1980. Smith, Joseph. The Personal Writings of Joseph Smith, comp. and ed. Dean C. Jessee. Salt Lake City, 1984

95   Inside Iran: Signs of the Apocalypse July 7, 2006 By George Thomas CBN News Sr. Reporter

96   Daniel K. Judd, "The Spirit of Christ: A Light amid Darkness," Liahona, May 2001, 18, Statement of the First Presidency, 15 February 1978

PART FIVE

1   Adolf Hitler, quoted in Larry Azar, Twentieth Century in Crisis (1990), pp. 155

2   Larry Azar, Twentieth Century in Crisis (1990), pp. 180

3   Hans Hauptmann, Bolshevism in the Bible (Nazi textbook), 1937, quoted pp. 28, The War Against God, edited by Carl Carmer

4   Islam and Eastern Religions, Jean Michel Angebert, The Occult and the Third Reich. Macmillan Publishing 1974, pp. 246

5   Hadith vol. 3:656

6   Alfred Rosenberg, Myth of the Twentieth Century, 1932, quoted pp. 6, The War Against God, edited by Carl Carmer

7   The Rise and Fall of the Third Reich, by William L. Shirer, pp. 240 in some editions, pp. 332 in others. Chapter headed "Triumph and Consolidation", subsection "The Persecution of the Christian Churches"

8   Iraq's al-Qaida threatens to 'destroy the cross', By AP AND JPOST
     STAFF

9   From al-Waqidi, "Dictionary of Islam" page 63

10   Reported in Bukhari, Tirmidhi, and Musnad

11   From Kirchliches Jahrbuch fur die evangelische Kirche in
     Deutschland, 1933-1944, pp. 470-472, quoted pp. 245-247, George L.
     Mosse, Nazi Culture: A Documentary History

12   Speech of May 1, 1927. Quoted by Toland, 1976, pp. 306

13   Time Magazine; January 2, 1939, San José State University -
     Department of Economics

14   Schouenbaum, Hitler's Social Revolution: Class and Status in Nazi
     Germany, 1933-1939(New York: Norton, 1980), pp. 19; Michael
     Burleigh, The Third Reich: A New History(New York: Hill and
     Wang, 2000), pp. 245.

15   Adolf Hitler, Mein Kampf, trans. Ralph Manheim (repr., Boston:
     Houghton Mifflin, 1999), pp. 533.*

16   American Thinker, The Nazis and Christianity, By Bruce Walker,
     November 17th 2007

17   Gene Edward Vieth Jr., Modern Fascism: The Threat to the Judeo-
     Christian Worldview [St. Louis: Conccordia, 1993], P.37

18   Kennedy, Gordon; Ryan, Kody (2003), Hippie Roots & The
     Perennial Subculture*

19   The History Place, Hitler Youth, Beginnings*

20   Ibid

21   Daisyfield Guitar Music About "Mit Sing und Sang", German lyrics,
     by Ludolf Waldmann, English translation by Tom Potter

22   Hartshorne: 12

23   Eugenics apostle — What champions of evolutionist Darwin won't
     mention, By Peter Quinn 3/8/2007 Commonweal Magazine: A
     Review of Religion, Politics and Culture*

24   Autobiography By Johann Wolfgang von Goethe*

25   Goethe, West-Eastern Divan, TRANSLATED BY EDWARD DOWDEN

26   Ibid

27   Ibid

28   Ibid

29   Hermann Hesse, Background, Childhood, and Youth, J.Sobel and HHP 5/2/97

30   Hermann Hesse's Spiritual Formula, By Stefan BORBÉLY, pp. 13

31   Demian, By Hermann Hesse, Translated by Stanley Appelbaum, pp. 1

32   The Satanic Bible, pg 33

33   Hermann Hesse's Spiritual Formula, By Stefan Borbely, pp. 17

34   Ibid, pp. 19

35   Ibid, pp. 80

36   Ibid, pp. 19-20

37   Ibid, pp. 20

38   Ibid, Hesse 76

39   Ibid, Hesse, 60

40   Demian, By Hermann Hesse, Translated by Stanley Appelbaum, pp. 2

41   Hermann Hesse's Spiritual Formula, By Stefan Borbely, pp. 17

42   John Toland, Adolf Hitler: The Definitive Biography (New York: Anchor Books, 1992), pp. 75

43   IVU, Eduard Baltzer (1814 - 1887)

44   Heinrich Himmler, By Roger Manvell, Heinrich Fraenkel, Chapter VI, The Miraculous Hands, pp. 182

45   Vegetarianism: Non-violence as Daily Practice, From Jennifer Polan, for About.com, "Mahabharata," 115:40

46   The Times Online, From The Sunday Times July 20, 2003 Quest of the Nazis, Quoted from Padfield

47   The Nazi War On Cancer, By By Robert N. Proctor, Chaper 5, pp. 136

48   Jewish World Review, Cruelty to Animals Leads to Cruelty; Kindness to Animals Doesn't Lead to Kindness, By Dennis Prager, Quoted From "The Nazi War on Cancer," By Stanford Professor Robert N. Proctor, Princeton University Press, 1999

49 Ibid

50 Monsalvat - the Parsifal pages, Vegetarianism and Antivivisection, Richard Wagner to Ernst von Weber, author of The Torture-Chambers of Science, 14 August 1879

51 International Vegetarian Union, The Ethics of Diet - A Catena, by Howard Williams M.A., 1883, SCHOPENHAUER, 1788-1860 (text from the 1st edition, 1883).

52 Ibid

53 Rethinking Life and Death, By Peter Singer, pp. 166

54 Ibid

55 Ibid

56 Ibid, pp. 168

57 Ibid, pp. 171

58 World Magazine, Blue-State Philosopher, By Marvin Olasky

59 Ibid

60 The Pursuit of Happiness, Peter Singer interviewed by Ronald Bailey December 2000

61 Proverbs 8:36

62 1 Timothy 4:1-4

63 canadianchristianity.com, Toward a vegetarian Christendom, By Aren Roukema

64 Ibid

65 The Christian Vegetarain Association, Our Mission

66 The Christian Vegetarain Association, FAQ's

67 See Surah 4:157-158; 3:55

68 Christianity and Vegetarianism, By Fr. John Dear, S.J.

69 HILDEGARD VON BINGEN: Celestial Harmonies — Naxos 8.557983 Responsories and Antiphons (Oxford Camerata), [2]

70 Lesbians, condoms go wild in attack on Christian church, Lesbians, condoms go wild in attack on Christian church

71 The Traditional Values Coalition, The War On Christians Begin

72 Hate is hate, in India or America, World Net Daily, 2009

73   Die Weltwoche, From the highest leader of the Islamic Emirates of Afghanistan

74   Florence Dupont, Daily Life in Ancient Rome, trans. Christopher Woodall (Cambridge: Blackwell Publishing, 198), 206

75   FrontPage Magazine, Boys of The Taliban, By James Glazov, Monday Jan. 1 2007, David Pryce-Jones, The Closed Circle: An Interpretation of the Arabs (Chicago: Irvin R. Dee, 2002), pp. 131, Bruce Dunne, "Power and Sexuality in the Middle East," Middle East Report, Spring 1998. For a further discussion on the widespread homosexuality among men in Muslim societies in North Africa and South Asia, and how married men having sex with boys and other men is considered a social norm, and not "homosexual," see Arno Schmitt and Jehoeda Sofer (eds.), Sexuality and Eroticism Among Males in Muslim Societies (New York: Harrington Park Press, 1992)

76   Muslim access, At Tūr, Surah 52, the mount

77   Muhammad, Terrorist or Prophet?, Jihad (Holy War) & Islamic Martyrs, Hadith: Al hadiths, Vol. 4, pp. 172, No.34: Hozrot Ali (r..a) narrated

78   James T. Monroe, in Homoeroticism in Classical Arabic Literature, pp. 117

79   Sir Richard Burton, Kama Sutra: the Hindu art of lovemaking, intro. Pathan proverb, also reported in similar forms from the Arab countries, Iran and North Africa

80   ROME IMPROVEMENT, Neon Magazine (2/99)

81   Hitler's Table Talk, pp. 353

82   The Gay Conspiracy!, Reductio Ad Hitlerum: Christians, Nazis, and Gays, By Michael Wagner, The Pink Swastika: Homosexuality in the Nazi Party, pp. 39, By Scott Lively and Kevin Abrams, Founders Publishing Corp., 1995

83   The Gay Conspiracy!, Reductio Ad Hitlerum: Christians, Nazis, and Gays, By Michael Wagner, The Pink Swastika: Homosexuality in the Nazi Party, pp. 42-43, By Scott Lively and Kevin Abrams, Founders Publishing Corp., 1995. The quote included "Roehm and associates — Edmund Heines, Karl Ernst, Ernst's partner Captain Rohrbein, Captain Petersdorf, Count Ernst Helldorf and the rest — would meet to plan and strategize"

84   The truth about homosexuality and the Nazi Party, By Bryan Fischer, The Pink Swastika: Homosexuality in the Nazi Party, by Scott Lively, Founders Publishing Foundation, 1995

85   From H. R. Knickerbocker, Is Tomorrow Hitler's? 200 Questions on the Battle of Mankind, pp. 34

86   The truth about homosexuality and the Nazi Party, By Bryan Fischer, The Pink Swastika: Homosexuality in the Nazi Party, by Scott Lively, Founders Publishing Foundation, 1995

87   International Committee For Holocaust Truth: 1996 Report #3, Steiner, Treblinka, pp. 117f

88   International Committee For Holocaust Truth: 1996 Report #3, Poller, Medical Block Buchenwald, pp. 103

89   International Committee For Holocaust Truth: 1996 Report #3, Remple, Hitler's Children: Hitler Youth and the SS, pp. 51f

90   The Gay Conspiracy!, Reductio Ad Hitlerum: Christians, Nazis, and Gays, By Michael Wagner, The Pink Swastika: Homosexuality in the Nazi Party, pp. 101, By Scott Lively and Kevin Abrams, Founders Publishing Corp., 1995

91   Ibid

92   The truth about homosexuality and the Nazi Party, By Fischer, The Pink Swastika: Homosexuality in the Nazi Party, by Scott Lively, Founders Publishing Foundation, 1995

93   The Other Side Of The Pink Triangle, By Kevin E. Abrams, Cantarella, Eva, Bisexuality in the Ancient World, Yale University Press, New Haven & London, 1992, pp. 71, Herdt, Gilbert, The Sambia. McGraw Hill Incorp., 1981, pp. 202., Gallo, Max, The Night of the Long Knives, New York: Harper & Row 1972:60

94   Homosexuality and the Nazi Party, by Scott Lively, Rossman: 103

95   Liberal Fascism, By Jonah Goldberg, Chapter 10 The New Age: We're All Fascists Now, pp. 379

96   A history of homosexuality in Europe, By Florence Tamagne, pp. 254

97   H. Bluher, Die Rolle der Erotik in der manlichen Gesellschaft. Eine Theorie der menschlichen Staatsbildung nach Wesen und Wert (Jena, 1917)

98   The Hidden Hitler By Lothar Machtan, Die Rolle der Erotik in der manlichen Gesellschaft. Eine Theorie der menschlichen Staatsbildung nach Wesen und Wert, (Stuttgart, 1962), 28

99   Ibid, Hans Bluher, Werke und Tage. Geschichte eines Denkers (Munich, 1953), 256

100   Herman Rauschning, The Voice Of Destruction (New York: Putnam, 1940), pp. 50

101   Hitler's Table Talk, pp. 59

102   For The Soul of The People, Omens, Nationalism, Nazism, and the Churches: The Early Period, Quoted From Historian Bernd Hey

103   Kirchensite.de, Four Sermons in Defiance of The Nazis,Clemens August, Count von Galen

104   Ibid

105   Nazi Weapons Act of 1938 (Translated to English). The New York Times commented on Hitler's gun control laws writing that after Hitler conquered France Nazi law forbade "the French to do things which the German people have not been allowed to do since Hitler came to power. To own radio senders or to listen to foreign broadcasts, to organize public meetings and distribute pamphlets, to disseminate anti-German news in any form, to retain possession of firearms all these things are prohibited for the subjugated people of France"—from the New York Times, July 2, 1940, 20

106   St. -Paulus-Dom, Munster, Sermon by Bishop Clemens August von Galen. Münster, 13th. July, 1941

107   Dr. Paul Byrne on Brain Death, Sermon by the Bishop of Munster, Clemens August Count von Galen, on Sunday 3rd August 1941 in St. Lambert's Church, Munster, Appendix: If the principle that men is entitled to kill his unproductive fellow-man is established and applied, then woe betide all of us when we become aged and infirm! If it is legitimate to kill unproductive members of the community, woe betide the disabled who have sacrificed their health or their limbs in the productive process! If unproductive men and women can be disposed of by violent means, woe betide our brave soldiers who return home with major disabilities as cripples, as invalids! If it is once admitted that men have the right to kill "unproductive" fellow-men" even though it is at present applied only to poor and defenceless mentally ill patients" then the way is open for the murder of all unproductive men and women: the incurably ill, the handicapped who are unable to work, those disabled in industry or war. The way is open, indeed, for the murder of all of us when we become old and infirm and therefore unproductive. Then it will require only a secret order to be issued that the procedure which has been tried and tested with the mentally ill should be extended to other "unproductive" persons, that it should also be applied to those suffering from incurable tuberculosis, the aged and infirm, persons disabled in industry, soldiers with disabling injuries!

108   Ibid

109   STUDY GUIDE FOR SOPHIE SCHOLL: THE FINAL DAYS, Produced by Vicky Knickerbocker Outreach Coordinator at the Center for Holocaust and Genocide Studies UNIVERSITY OF MINNESOTA, TWIN CITIES CAMPUS, Dumbach and Newborn, pp. 60

110   In 1942, members of the student resistance organization THE WHITE ROSE SOCIETY released these anti-Nazi leaflets, The Fourth Leaflet

111   History of Western Philosophy, London, 1948, pp. 419

112   Pierre Van Paassen, A Minority of One, An obituary by Morris Alexander published in The National Jewish Monthly, Pierre-van-Paassen.com

113 Spartacus Education, Quote: Else Gebel shared Sophie Scholl's cell and recorded her last words before being taken away to be executed: "It is such a splendid sunny day, and I have to go. But how many have to die on the battlefield in these days, how many young, promising lives. What does my death matter if by our acts thousands are warned and alerted? Among the student body there will certainly be a revolt."

114 See article by Manfred Gailus, A Strange Obsession with Nazi Christianity: A Critical Comment on Richard Steigmann-Gall's The Holy Reich, Technical University of Berlin published in The Journal of Contemporary History. Vol. 42, No. 1, 35-46 (2007)

115 Arafat's Jesus, By Gerald A. Honigman February 5, 2003, Originally published in Jewish Xpress Magazhine

116 Al-Sirah al-Halabiyyah, v3, p61

117 The Holy Reich, By Richard Steigmann-Gall, ifZ ED 60/7 (n.d., n.p.). This passage in Wagener's memoirs is left out of the volume edited by Turner, including the lengthier German edition, Hitler aus nachster

Nahe: Aufzeichmungen eines Vertrauen 1929-1932 (Frankfurt a.M., 1978)

118 Ibid, Goebbels, Michael, 66

119 Hitler's Rise from Felon to Fuhrer, Institute of International Studies

120 Calvin, German Propaganda, Youth Ceremonies, Rites Of Passage For The Youth

121 Burleigh, op. cit., p260

122 Fortean Times, How The Nazis Stole Christmas, By David Sutton, December 2007, Frederic Spotts points to Hitler's fascination with fire, "which made figures, banners and flags shimmer in an eerie glow. Fire was an element in the scenography of the commemorative ceremonies that gave him such pleasure. Torches, bonfires, Bengal lights, fireworks, flares, pyres, flames rising out of enormous braziers all produced a wondrous spell." Spotts, op. cit., p58

123 Irmgard Hunt, On Hitler's Mountain: Overcoming the Legacy of a Nazi Childhood, Atlantic Books, 2005, p45

124   See Joe Perry, "Nazifying Christmas: Political Culture and Popular celebration in the Third Reich", in Central European History, Vol. 38, no. 4, 2005, pp588—592 and Burleigh, op. cit., pp223—228.. Perry, p575

125   Ibid, Wolfgang Schultz, "Auch an seinem Heim erkennt man den Nationalsozialisten!" Die Hoheitsträger 3 (August 1939), pp16—18

126   Ibid

127   Ibid, See Alison Owings, Frauen: German Women Recall the Third Reich, Penguin, 1995, p59

128   New Religions and the Nazis, By Karla Poewe, Routledge , New York and London , 2006., pp. 34

129   G.K. Chesterton

130   Patrick Henry College, New Religions and the Nazis by Karla Poewe, Routledge , New York and London , 2006. Review by Rev Dr Ross Clifford Principal, Morling Theological College Sydney President, Baptist Union of Australia, pages 34 and 76-77

131   The German opposition to Hitler, By Michael C. Thomsett, pp. 56, Salzburger Chronik, April 30, 1937

132   TIME Magazine, Pagans and Gags, 1934

133   Ibid

134   TIME, July 10, 1933

135   Ibid

136   The New American, Hitler and Christianity, Written by Selwyn Duke Sunday, 08 June 2008 18:15

137   Nazism: An Assault On Civilization, Part One, The Record Of Persecution, By Dorothy Thompson, pp. 14

138   Ibid, pp. 5

139   Ibid, The War On Religious Freedom, By Stanley High, pp. 37

140   ACLU, ACLU Asks U.S. Supreme Court to Review Iowa's Sex Offender Residency Restriction (9/29/2005)

PART SIX

1   MEMRI TV, 1/3/2005, Clip No. 463, Palestinian-Kuwaiti Sheik Ahmad Qattan on Allah's Rewards to a Martyr

2   Encyclopedia Mythica, Berserks, By Micha F. Lindemans

3   Aleister Crowley, The 20th Aethyr, The Vision and The Voice

4   Hadith, narrated by Abu Hurraira, Abi Sayeed Al-Choudury, see rudood.com, attributing deception to Allah, Scholar Abilrahim Sharif, August 9, 2006

5   Qur'ân , Adh-Dhariyat, 56

6   The Book of the Law, By Aleister Crowley, Chapter III, verse 51)

7   XV. Hymn to a Night-God, SACRED SONGS OF THE ANCIENT MEXICANS, WITH A GLOSS IN NAHUATL. BY DANIEL G. BRINTON [1890]

8   The Prophet's Night Journey and Ascension, The Buraq (Heavenly Beast)

9   An Encyclopedia of Religions, By Maurice Arthur Canney, See William Jackson

10   The Mahabharata, Book 4: Virata Parva, Section VI

11   "Thus says the great prophet (Allah's prayers and supplications be upon him) Mahdi is the peacock of all angels and of the dwellers of the heavenly realm, he is dressed and adorned with the cloaks of light."

12   Encyclopedia of the Orient. LexicOrient. Retrieved on 2007-08-17

13   Encyclopedia Iranica, Yazidis, By Christine Allison

14   Encyclopedia of the orient, Zamzam, By Tore Kjeilen

15   Names of Shiva, From the Rig Veda

16   The Mahabharata, Book 4: Virata Parva, Section VI

17   The Satanic bible, By Anton Levay, The Book of The Luminous One, The Enlightenment

18   Italics mine, The Satanic bible, By Anton Levay, The Enochian Language and the Enochian Keys.

19   Homeric Hymn to Selene, Homer writes on Selene: "Muses, sweet-speaking daughters of Zeus Kronides and mistresses of song, sing next of long-winged Moon! From her immortal head a heaven-sent glow envelops the earth and great beauty arises under its radiance. From her golden crown the dim air is made to glitter as her rays turn night to noon, whenever bright Selene, having bathed her beautiful skin in the Ocean, put on her shining rainment and harnessed her proud-necked and glittering steeds, swiftly drives them on as their manes play with the evening, dividing the months. Her great orbit is full and as she waxes a most brilliant light appears in the sky. Thus to mortals she is a sign and a token"

20   The Church of Jesus Christ of Latter-day Saints, Joseph Smith's First Vision

21   D&C, Section 88: 7,8,9

22   The history of ancient Mexico, By Thomas Francis Gordon, pp. 183

23   Allen Ross , Th.D., Ph.D

24   Q89: 1

25   Metamorphosis, By Ovid

26   Apollodorus, Biblioteca 1.4.4

27   Somerville Oswalt, Concise Encyc. Greek & Rom. Myth

28   Ovid, Met. II.114ff, tr. Brookes More

29   Aztec Calander, Gods and Deities, Quetzalcoatl, Codex Borbonicus

30   The Confessions of Aleister Crowley, 544

31   The Mahabharata, Book 4: Virata Parva, Section VI

32   Wikipedia, Yazidi, Myths

33   Plowing fields and marrying little girls in the Qur'ân , By James M. Arlandson, MAS Abdel Haleem, The Qur'an, Oxford UP, 2004

34   Q2:223 A

35   Standing For Liberty: Marriage, Virtue, and the Political State, By Allen Carlson Ph.D, Koonz, Mothers in the Fatherland, pp. 14, 393

36   Women Of Distinction, By Ma'n Abul Husn. Full quote as follows: I
      have borne you with pain and brought you up with great care. I
      have brought no dishonor to your family and no slur to your tribe. I
      have wrought no indignity to your father's prestige, and there can
      be no doubt about the sanctity of the character of your mother.
      Now, therefore, listen to me. Remember the great merit of fighting
      for defending your faith; remember the Qur'ān ic injunction of
      adopting patience in the midst of distress. Tomorrow morning, rise
      from your bed hale and hearty and join the battle with fearless
      courage. Go into the midst of the thickest of the battle, encounter
      the boldest enemy and if necessary embrace martyrdom."

37   Ibid

38   From Sada Al-Jihad, vol. 14, Rabi' Al-Awl 1428 (March-April 2007

39   MEMRI, Special Dispatch - No. 819 November 25, 2004, MEMRI TV
      Project: Mothers of Hizbullah Martyrs: We are Very Happy and
      Want to Sacrifice More Children, Al-Manar TV (Lebanon),
      November 11, 2004

40   prepared by the Hauptkulturamt of the Reichspropagandaleitung,
      1944. Full quote as follows: "I wish to speak as a sister to all of
      these who are alone and sorrowing. I do not wish to speak of pain.
      Instead, I speak of the dead, who to me are not dead. After I first
      sank into dark sorrow, I now can see the sun and sky once again.
      [...] We cannot and may not escape either to the future nor the
      past. Only from the past and the future, from faith and
      thankfulness, can we gather the strength to master the present,
      which is what the husbands and sons who fell for the fatherland
      expect of us, and the children to whom we pass on the torch of
      our lives will one day want to know that we fought and endured
      for their sakes."

41   MEMRI, Special Dispatch - No. 673 March 4, 2004 No. 673, Umm
      Nidal: 'The Mother of The Shahids', The Al-Jazeera television
      program Opposite Direction, on June 29, 2002

42   The Canonization of George Tiller, By Cathy Ruse and Austin Ruse

43   Sky News, Gang-Raped Girl Stoned By Mob

44   Rape in Islam: Blaming the Victim By: Robert Spencer
      FrontPageMagazine.com | Thursday, January 23, 2003

45   FaithFreedom.org, Iran: A 17 year old girl is sentenced to death by hanging

46   L. Ron Hubbard, Affirmations

47   Darwin 1958:234

48   Institute For Creation Research, Darwin's Teaching Of Women's Inferiority, By Jerry Bergman, Ph.D., 1863:192

49   Darwin, 1896:563,564

50   Gould, 1981:104,105

51   Thelemapedia, Islamic god forms, See Liber Aleph and The Heart of the Master

52   Magical World of AC, Francis King, page 5

53   Letter to Montgomery Evans, January 17, 1929, O.T.O. archives, quoted Sutin pp. 334

54   Magick in Theory and Practice cap IV, fn. p 27

55   The Old and New Commentaries to Liber AL, By Aleister Crowley

56   J.V.P.D. Balsdon, Roman Women: Their History and Habits (New York: John Day, 1963), 283

57   L.F. Cervantes, "Women," New Catholic Encyclopedia (New York: Mcraw-Hill, 1967), 14:991

58   How Christianity Changed The World, By Alvin J. Schmidt, Women Receive Freedom and Dignity, pp. 99, Hippolytus 616-17

59   Suppliant Maidens 748-49

60   Lysistrata 368-69

61   How Christianity Changed The World, By Alvin J. Schmidt, Cited in Bready, Lord Shaftesbury, 13

62   Ibid, Rawlinson, India: A Short Cultural History, 279

63   Ibid, Stanley Wolpert, A New History of India (New York: Oxford University Press, 2000) 233

64   Narasimhan, Sati, 27

65   How Christianity Changed The World, By Alvin J. Schmidt, Women Receive Freedom and Dignity, Dorothy K. Stein, "Women to Burn: Suttee as a Normative Institution," Signs: Journal of Women Culture and Society (Winter 1978), 253

66   Howard S. Levy, Chinese Foot Binding: The History of a Curious Erotic Custom (New York: W. Rauls, 1966), 26

67   How Christianity Changed The World, By Alvin J. Schmidt, Lin Yutang, My Country and My People (New York: Halcyone House, 1953), 168

68   James 1:27

69   The Satanic bible, By Anton Levay, Symbol of Baphomet

70   The Hubbard Quotes Collection, Class VIII course lecture #10 on the ship Apollo, October 3, 1968. "Everyman is then shown to have been crucified so don't think that it's an accident that this crucifixion, they found out that this applied. Somebody somewhere on this planet, back about 600 BC, found some pieces of R6, and I don't know how they found it, either by watching madmen or something, but since that time they have used it and it became what is known as Christianity. The man on the Cross. There was no Christ. But the man on the cross is shown as Everyman."

71   Worldwide Church of God Christian or Cult?, The Good News, February, 1979, pp. 1

72   Ibid, Mystery of the Ages, pp. 37

73   Concerned Christians, The Polytheistic Trinity of Mormonism, Joseph F. Smith, Teachings of the Prophet Joseph Smith, pp. 370

74   Joseph F. Smith, Teachings of the Prophet Joseph Smith, pp. 370, 372, insert added, (Concerned Christians, The Polytheistic Trinity of Mormonism, Joseph F. Smith, Teachings of the Prophet Joseph Smith, pp. 370)

75   What Scientology wont tell you, an information pack, The Beliefs and Teachings of Scientology, Dianetics: The Modern Science of Mental Health, Science of Survival, A History of Man, Scientology 0-8, The Scientology Handbook

76   Jon Atack, A Piece Of Blue Sky (Kensington Publishing Corporation, New York, 1990; ISBN 0-8184-0499-X): "Xenu was about to be deposed from power, so he devised a plot to eliminate the excess population from his dominions. With the assistance of 'renegades,' he defeated the populace and the 'Loyal Officers,' a force for good that was opposed to Xenu. Then, with the assistance of psychiatrists, he summoned billions of people to paralyze them with injections of alcohol and glycol under the pretense they were being called for 'income tax inspections.' The kidnapped populace was loaded into space planes for transport to the site of extermination, the planet of Teegeeack (Earth)." The hundreds of billions of captured thetans were taken to a type of cinema, where they were forced to watch a "three-D, super colossal motion picture" for 36 days. This implanted what Hubbard termed "various misleading data" (collectively termed the R6 implant) into the memories of the hapless thetans, "which has to do with God, the devil, space opera, et cetera."

77   The Jinn, Maududi's Qur'an commentary: "The jinn used to be able to eavesdrop on heaven but suddenly they found that angels had been set as guards and meteorites were being shot on every side so that they could find no place of safety to hear the secret news. They had set about searching for the unusual thing that had occurred on the earth to explain why the security measures had been tightened up. Many companies of jinn were moving about in search when one of them, after having heard the Qur'ân from the Prophet, formed the opinion that it was the very thing which had caused all the gates of the heavens to be shut against them."

78   Jon Atack, A Piece Of Blue Sky (Kensington Publishing
      Corporation, New York, 1990; ISBN 0-8184-0499-X): "Simultaneously,
      the planted charges erupted. Atomic blasts ballooned from the
      craters of Loa, Vesuvius, Shasta, Washington, Fujiyama, Etna, and
      many, many others. Arching higher and higher, up and outwards,
      towering clouds mushroomed, shot through with flashes of flame,
      waste and fission. Great winds raced tumultuously across the face
      of Earth, spreading tales of destruction. Debris-studded and sickly
      yellow, the atomic clouds followed close on the heels of the winds.
      Their bow-shaped fronts encroached inexorably upon forest, city
      and mankind, they delivered their gifts of death and radiation. A
      skyscraper, tall and arrow-straight, bent over to form a question
      mark to the very idea of humanity before crumbling into the
      screaming city below..."

79   Horrible Truths for Scientologists: Body Thetans, By Roland
      Rashleigh-Berry, Body Thetans

80   Muslim: B039N6757* Muhammad even admitted being attacked
      by demons* Bukhari:V6B60N332

81   Allah, His Heritage In Paganism, "Mizanu'l Haqq" by C.G. Pfander
      D.D., pp. 345-356

82   Prophet of Doom, By Craig Winn, Satan's Bargain, From Ishaq:132-
      3

83   Court TV, Crime Library, Criminal Minds and Methods, The Real
      End

84   Who are the Raelians? By David Chazon

85   Rael.org

86   New York Times, Word for Word/The Raëlian Agenda; And You
      Figured Cloning a Human Would Be Their Biggest Challenge, By
      NOAM COHEN

87   The Young Woman's Journal, published by the Young Ladies'
      Mutual Improvement Associations of Zion, 1892, vol. 3, pp. 263-64

88   Journal of Discourses, vol. 13, pp. 271

89   Rewards for the Scribe, The Rapture of Hadit in Hiding, "In the Daylight I see not Thy Body of Stars, O Beloved. The little light of the Sun veils the Great Light of the Stars, for to-day Thou seemest distant. The Sun burns like a great Torch, and Earth seems as one of His little Spheres, filled with life. I am but a tiny spermatozoon, but within me is the fiery and concentrated essence of Life. Draw me up into Thyself, O Sun! Project me into the Body of Our Lady Nuit! Thus shall a new Star be born, and I shall see Thee even in the Daylight, O Beloved."

90   In Search of God the Mother, Roller, pp. 265

91   Maarten J. Vermaseren, Cybele and Attis, trans. A.M.H. Lemmers, Thames and Hudson, 1977 cited in Baring and Cashford, op. cit.

92   Historia Augusta, The Life of Elagabalus, Part 1

93   Herodian V, 3,5, Loeb trans

94   Ibid

95   FrontPage Magazine, The Muslim Students Association at Brown, Friday April 4th 2008

96   The Muslim Students Association and the Jihad Network By: FrontPage Magazine, FrontPageMagazine.com |Thursday, May 08, 2008

97   Ibid

98   Ibid

99   By: In Mortal Danger, Jamie Glazov, FrontPageMagazine.com | Thursday, August 03, 2006

100   Abdul Malik Ali, the imam of Masjid Al-Islam, Oakland, California. From Militant Islam Monitor.org, April 12, 2009

101   FrontPage Magazine, June 5th, 2008

102   Liberal Fascism, By Jonah Goldberg, Chapter 5: The 1960s: Fascism Takes to the Streets, pp. 168

103   Campus Watch, Middle East studies in the News, You Stupid Armenians, You Deserve to be Massacred, by Shaké Hovsepian Usanogh: Periodical of Armenian Students, April 24, 1999

104   The American Thinker, December 15, 2004, With friends like these, By Rachel Neuwirth

105   Ibid

106   The American Thinker, December 15, 2004, With friends like these, By Rachel Neuwirth

107   Alfred Rosenberg, The Myth of the Twentieth Century

108   Mein Kampf, By Adolf Hitler, Volume Two — The National Socialist Movement, Chapter V: Philosophy and Organization

109   Adam LeBor and Roger Boyes, Seduced by Hitler (Naperville, Ill.: Sourcebooks, 2001), pp. 119

110   Liberal Fascism, By Jonah Goldberg, Chapter Ten The New Age: We're All Fascists Now, P.370

111   Gloria Steinem, Revolutionary from Within: A Book of Self-Esteem (Boston: Little, Brown, 1993), pp. 13; see also David Rieff, "Designer Gods," transition, no. 59 (1993), pp. 20-31

112   Earth In The Balance, By Albert Gore, Climate and Civilization: A Short History, pp. 79

113   Earth In The Bounds by Al-Gore pp. 261

114   Ibid

115   Gaiam Somebody! The ethos and 'ethnicity' of Fresh Fields, By Jonah Goldberg

116   The Celtic Connection, What Is Wicca?

117   Wicca, By Scott Cunningham, Section I, Theory, Chapter 1, Wicca and Shamanism, pp. 10

118   The Rites of Odin, By Ed Fitch, An Introduction to Odinism: An Old Religion in a New Age, xxii

119   Magical rites from the Crystal well, By Ed Fitch, Introduction, ix

120   Paul R. Ehrlich.. The Population Bomb: Revised & Expanded Edition (1968, 1971). SBN 345-24489-3-150, pp. 155

121   Isckon.com, About ISKCON

122   National Geographic, Untouchable, By Tom O'Neill

123   Ibid

124   From the Bhagavad-Gita 4:13

125   Iranian President Ahmadinejad asks: are Jews human beings?, Aug 3, 2006 MEMRI, Iranian..ws

126   Dishonest Non-Patriot By: Mark D. Tooley FrontPageMagazine.com
       Thursday, December 18, 2008

127   The 10 Big Lies about America, By Michael Medved, Big Lie#1:
       America Was Founded On Genocide Againts Native Americans,
       pp. 15

128   From the Tri-Weckly Missouri Republican. St. Louis. July 12. 1860

129   G.K. Chesterton, From The Listener. 3-6-35

130   Bernard Lewis, The Arabs in History, Oxford University Press, 1993,
       pp. 163-4

131   The Great Divide, By Alvin J. Schmidt, Chapter 6, pp. 143-144, For
       further discussion, see Paul Fregosi, Jihad in the West: Muslim
       Conquests from the 7th to the 21st Centuries (Amherst, NY:
       Prometheus Books, 1998)

132   Ibid, Guenter B. Risse, Mending Bodies, Saving Souls (New York:
       Oxford University Press, 1999), 139

133   Ibid

134   Ibid, Raymond H. Schmandt, The Crusades: Origin of an
       Ecumenical Problem (Houston: University of Saint Thomas Press,
       1967), 16

135   Ibid

136   Ibid, JW, 23-24

137   Mark Williams, The Story of Spain (Malaga, Spain: Santana, 2000),
       52

138   HIV/AIDS Caring Connection, How to S.T.O.P. AIDS

139   Narrated by Ibn Abu Shaibah, al-Darimi, al-Hakim and Ahmad
       from Abdullah Ibn Amr Ibn al-A'as who said: 'while we were sitting
       with Allah's Messenger (SAW) and we were engaged in writing,
       Allah's Messenger (SAW) was asked: 'Which city will be
       conquered first, Rome or Constantinople?' Allah's Messenger
       (SAW) said: "The city of Heraclius will be conquered first"

140   Forger, Archibald, Arabia, the Desert of the Sea. National
       Geographic (December 1909), 1039-1062.

141   Bernard Lewis, The Arabs in History, page 15, B.L.London 1947

142   The Twelve Tribes of Ismael, Nabatea.net

143   Holman Bible Dictionary

144   Encyclopedia Britanica, The Online Encyclopedia, Al-Ula

145   Yawm Al-Ghadab, Safar Alhwaly

146   Narrated by Mu'adh ibn Jabal: Translation of Sunan Abu-Dawud, Battles (Kitab Al-Malahim), Book 37, Number 4281